MYSELF

BETTER LEFT UNSAID

By DAISY PRINCESS OF PLESS

Edited with an Introduction and Notes by

MAJOR DESMOND CHAPMAN-HUSTON

WITH THIRTY-ONE ILLUSTRATIONS

NEW YORK
E. P. DUTTON & CO., INC.

976

First Printing, - - - *July 1931*
Second Printing, - - - *July 1931*
Third Printing, - - - *July 1931*
Fourth Printing, - - - *July 1931*

DEDICATED

TO THE MEMORY OF

SIR JOHN MURRAY, K.C.V.O.,

who, in almost the last, and best, letter he ever wrote, expressed the most generous appreciation of my first book, and thereby paid me the greatest compliment I have ever received, cheered me in a dark hour, and gave me courage to send out another little paper ship on the great seas of literature.

D. OF P.

LA NAPOULE, A.M.,
   1931 : *In the Spring.*

EDITOR'S INTRODUCTION

IN her earlier volume of selections from her diaries[1]
the Princess of Pless was mainly concerned to
present a picture of social and political life in the
highest European circles in pre-war Europe, and to
give an inside account of life in Germany throughout
the Great War : the remarkable success of her unique
and vivid volume resulted in a very wide demand for
a successor in which the authoress might reveal something more of a personality that seems to have proved
almost as winning and attractive in the pages of a book,
as it is in life. Scores of reviewers, and hundreds of
letter-writers, have begged the Princess to publish
another book that would tell them " something more
about herself " : the present volume is the result. In
it the authoress is predominantly personal. Her
station, and the circles in which she moved in England
and on the Continent make inevitable the appearance
in her diary of many prominent people and events ;
nevertheless, what we have here is essentially a self-
portrait of the writer. Those who love human nature
will eagerly read every line ; those who cherish the
odd belief that any revelation of the human soul, heart,
and body is always indecent will read the volume
shudderingly, and will condemn, or they will not read
it—and will condemn it even more emphatically on
hearsay.

[1] *Daisy Princess of Pless*, by Herself. Murray, London ; Dutton,
New York ; Reissner, Dresden ; Gyldend alske Boghandel, Copenhagen.

Let it straightway be admitted that the selecting and editing of the extracts from the six hundred thousand words of the diary of the Princess has been no easy task. In every private diary there must be a great deal that sounds egotistical, much that, apparently important at the time, ultimately proves trivial, and innumerable passages which, in the eyes of some people, are bound to appear indiscreet. If, as Dr. Johnson said, no man is on oath in an obituary notice, then no woman is on oath in her private diary. She writes down from day to day what she does, feels, thinks : she has not one eye on her contemporaries and the other on posterity. That is why private diaries, written without any thought of publication, have an appeal, an interest, a value and a vitality which, for most of us, no other form of literature can provide. In this comparatively rare class of book the things which Autolycus would call unconsidered trifles are, to the reader, precious beyond the most deeply considered utterances of the sages. We feel that, far from communing with prophets, priests and kings we are enjoying the perhaps rarer and more precious privilege of consorting intimately with human beings. We elbow them in crowds, watch (too often with cold shivers down our backs) their odd behaviour when self-consciously preening themselves in the limelight, overhear the shuffle of their slippered feet, catch glimpses of them in their gardens, their homes, on their journeys, peep at them when they eat, drink, gossip, boast, squander time, sleep, flirt—overhear them even when they make love ; we watch their tears, see them chew the bitter cud of failure, taste the golden apple of success ; in fact we see them do all the queer things which we humans do and totality of which, for some obscure egotistical reason, we insist on identifying as Life—with a capital letter.

Now in no work of fiction are all these things done exactly as they are in everyday life, and the nearest we can get in literature to the actual savour of living is when we are permitted the privilege of reading a diary artlessly kept, frank, spontaneous and, above all, unpremeditated, or, if you like, illogical, and inconsequent, as most of man's life is unpremeditated, illogical and inconsequent.

Princess Daisy has, and always has had, a keen eye for unconsidered trifles. In addition to the big things of life she sees its little wayward revealing moments, and she records them : the pathos and futility of it all seem at moments to overcome her as they do everyone, yet, the salt sanity of laughter being never far away, she very seldom succumbs either to self-pity or vain regret.

If one might hazard a reason why the Princess was never able to obey King Edward's wise injunction that she should become a good German it would be to say that Germans, at any rate the type of pre-war Germans by whom she was largely surrounded, insisted on taking themselves and life too seriously. Placing, as she always did, personality, character, capacity, achievement before all arbitrary standards, the Princess never greatly cared where she marched in the procession of life so long as she felt that she had a place there by right of her womanhood and not because of her beauty, birth or rank. Many of the regretful moments in her diaries are expressions of discontent because circumstances divorced her from realities and kept her wasting nearly all her time and talents on a purely decorative and ceremonial existence. In the queer cross-section of pre-war German society in which she lived this rebelliousness was considered deplorable, if not indeed subversive. All those little Highnesses and Serene Highnesses, who were far from being Royal—

with all the weight, authority and responsibility attached to Royalty—and who yet considered themselves greatly elevated above the mere nobility, had to make up in pretentiousness what they lacked in genuineness. One is reminded of the Englishman who, upon being created a Baronet, complained that he had ceased to be a gentleman and had not become a Peer, when one thinks of these innumerable Princelings, mediatized and otherwise, who deliberately spent their existence precariously balanced above the axis of a see-saw. They could not understand, much less sympathize with one of their order who cared not whether the see-saw was up or down, so long as she was enjoying the thrill of being seated on the tip, and revelling in all the fun of the fair. The Princess was always her authentic self ; most of those close to her could never admire anything that did not, at least in appearance, conform to a type. There is in the German character much to admire, much which we might advantageously emulate, but it has an extraordinary and apparently incurable passion for squeezing individuals into categories. This is one of the root causes of the great difficulty of attaining a close understanding between Germans and Anglo-Saxons. The German mentality, with its strong instinct for order and design, preferably imposed upon it from above, almost venerates labels ; whereas, to the Anglo-Saxon, a label is a mere travelling convenience, to be altered, torn off, or replaced when it has fulfilled its purpose of conveniently enabling the user to reach a certain desired, perhaps merely temporary, destination. This worship of externals is often carried by Germans to absurd lengths ; whereas the Briton's innate indifference as to whether our words, actions and policies match, or do not match, too often seems to the German and the Frenchman the rankest hypocrisy.

The only serious criticism of the Princess's previous book that I personally encountered was the charge that it lacked literary perfection. The critic, apparently, utterly failed to see that a diary exhibiting literary perfection might be anything in the world you liked —but it would not be a diary. The Princess wrote her diary on steamers, in trains, in the garden, between the courses of a meal, when she was well, when she was ill—anytime and anywhere. Much of it was written late at night after long and strenuous days. She wrote—often through sheer physical weariness—briefly and hurriedly. But for the most part, she wrote before the events of which she spoke were crystallized on the scroll of time, and her chronicle has therefore a vividness and reality which no calculated piece of beautiful prose could ever achieve. Little or no attempt has been made to " improve " the diarist's style. Where anything has been altered it was merely to remove an obscurity ; essential explanations, reduced to the minimum, have been put in footnotes in order to avoid the risk of misrepresenting the writer.

II

Readers of *Daisy Princess of Pless* must have been struck by the writer's unusual, indeed remarkable perception of the trend, and probable outcome, of political policies and events ; as this perceptivity was not that of a mind unusually gifted in the political sense, or of any profound study or application, some other explanation must be searched for. Moving in the European circles in which she did it was of course comparatively a simple matter for the Princess to acquire and retain that facile knowledge of current affairs which comes easily and familiarly to all who are born in, or move in, an atmosphere of high international politics : even so, this does not fully explain the Princess's vision and

wisdom concerning the political necessities of pre-war
Europe. Those who favour the idea of a spiritual
direction in human affairs, transcending worldly wisdom, may find interest in searching for some psychic
explanation of the unusual political intuition with
which the Princess was blessed (or cursed), and of
which we have many examples in her diary ; it will be
sufficient to note here three of major importance.

As early as 1896, when the Princess began to
organize a Diamond Jubilee presentation from
German women to Queen Victoria, she came up unexpectedly and in very concrete form against the fact that,
even then, there was no love lost between Germans
and English ; inevitably this impression was strength-
ened by almost everything that took place in Germany
and England between that year and 1902, the period
covering the South African War.

From that time until August, 1914, the Princess had
to face almost daily the, to her hateful, fact that the
chasm between the land of her birth and that of her
adoption was slowly but surely widening and deepening.
Her intense preoccupation with the horrors she foresaw (and its tragic effects on her personal life) are now
in some degree matters of history. Fear gives us eyes
behind, and it may be explained that the dread of a
conflict between Germany and Great Britain made the
Princess acutely aware of what, in spite of all attempts
to avert it, was really going to happen. However, as
has been suggested, such an explanation will not
account for all the facts.

At the end of 1911 and beginning of 1912, through
Baron Stumm—of the Berlin Foreign Office—the
Princess tried to interest the Emperor William II. in
an influentially sponsored attempt of an independent
and privately inspired nature to bring together into
one European Council all those politicians, publicists,

scientists, artists and humanists who believed in the possibility of Europe voluntarily organizing itself as one law-abiding, peace-keeping, progressive entity, with ideals other than greed and mere material success. The venture, apparently, came too early : yet, the logic of events being inexorable, something like this very scheme is now, at last, being seriously advocated by Monsieur Briand and other eminent European statesmen.

Early in 1914 the Princess actively associated herself with some of the few far-sighted men and women with a lofty outlook who then proposed an Association of Peoples on lines similar to that which, after the war, came into existence as the League of Nations—too late to avert the greatest and most-uncalled-for catastrophe in history.

In November, 1918, before the ink on the signatures to the Armistice was dry—and while politicians, presumably responsible, were declaring their intention of " hanging the Kaiser " and enslaving the German peoples—the Princess wrote in her diary that the day must come, and would come, when Germany and England would be friends, working together without treaties or legal obligations, in a spirit of brotherhood, in the common cause of civilization and justice. That belief is, we hope, being slowly but surely fulfilled. The youthful outlook of the younger generations unobscured by the bloodshot memories of war, the bitter prospect of common economic disaster, and sober, ordinary common sense have combined to bring about the consummation which the Princess foresaw and, to her everlasting credit, welcomed and prayed for in that grim November of 1918 when, under varying disguises, hymns of hate were being wantonly chanted, not only in effete, war-worn old Europe, but in strong new lands beyond the seas.

III

The Princess's diary reveals an inner spiritual incompatibility between the writer and her environment that made it impossible for her ever really to take root in Germany. Here we have the day-to-day struggle by which she strove to adapt herself to conditions fundamentally uncongenial, with its spasmodic successes, frequent failures, occasional despairs. Whilst she appeared to the onlooker to have everything in the way of beauty, charm, position and wealth that life can offer, there was ever present the gnawing inner sense of failure which follows like their shadow all those who fail to come to terms with an uncongenial background from which they cannot escape. We are often annoyed at the spectacle of so much splendid energy frustrated ; but we are never dismayed or hopeless, because the Princess herself is never either one or the other. Through everything she is stayed (as, later on, she was throughout the Great War) by an inner sense of wide spiritual freedoms ; a belief in immutable, ultimately beneficent, design ; a passion for the exhaustless refreshment of the beauty of nature ; a profound faith in the impregnable sanctity of human experience and human destiny.

Over-impulsive by nature, and never seriously disciplined mentally, the diarist utters judgments that are sometimes too sweeping and over-emphatic, yet are never mean or ignoble ; never spiteful, and never deliberately unfair. Those most outspokenly criticized in her pages may complain that she misunderstood them ; they can never feel that she is either bitter or malicious. Moreover, they will (if there be any need) forgive her, because she never spares even herself. Naturally her instinct is to be studiously fair to herself, but she is far too shrewd and frank for serious self-deception. Surrounded by flattery, she is always probing to discover how much of it is sincere ; and few things are more self-revealing, more essentially modest—in the true sense of the word—than the merciless analysis of her own good looks by this world-famous beauty. In front of her private mirror she amuses, without embarrassing, us by her naive attitude towards her personal appearance ; in the pages of her diary she is equally honest and outspoken about the secrets of her heart.

When writing of historic characters she may seem at times too lenient for the facts, but this was seldom really so : the facts are nearly always fully given in the diary, but in many instances the time for publishing the full truth—if it ever comes—has not yet arrived. One great difficulty has been to quote sufficient to show that the critic's vision was true, and yet avoid seriously hurting anyone's feelings by prematurely publishing too much.

If readers of the Princess's first book realized that they had met a charming acquaintance, readers of this one will feel that they have met a true fellow-wayfarer and a sincere friend. There is in the writer's heart a great love for all mankind, and for the whole of nature ; her every thought and action exhibits an understanding and sympathetic vision embracing the entire circumference of life : these things, between reader and writer, are a powerful bond.

D. C.-H.

Madrid.

21st *February*, 1931.

CONTENTS

CONTENTS

PAGE

CHAPTER EIGHT

Queen Alexandra and Princess Victoria as jolly Chatsworth guests—Opening a London Club for Young Men—Dream love and real life—German men bad dancers—A nasty German relative—My two sons—Silver wedding of Emperor and Empress and Marriage of Prince Eitel Fritz—My husband has an accident—His illness in Vienna—Our enormous expenditure—Count Larisch lends me his hacks —Ball at the British Embassy—Rude Archdukes—Fascinating Buda Pest—Vienna Society—A Children's Party at Buckingham Palace—An enduring Friendship—A Court at Buckingham Palace—Dinner Party at Marlborough House —Sir Henry Campbell Bannerman—King Edward on Count Metternich—He chaffs me as usual—My party for the Imperial Manœuvres—Merry Royal ' Grass ' Widows —The Duchess of Sparta (Queen Sophie of Greece)—A bad professional and a good amateur singer—Silesian ' County ' Society—In a Berlin Sanatorium—A greedy Count—Tea with the Crown Princess Cecile—Her delightful baby—Berlin scandal—A happy Christmas at Fürstenstein.

CHAPTER NINE

Which is the ideal Religion ?—Life hereafter—The Riviera again—Prince Arthur of Connaught—My attractive sister-in-law—Adèle Countess of Essex—The Duke of Marlborough makes hay of the dinner table—Happy moments at Beaulieu—Paris—A disgusting French entertainer— Princess Murat's Party—Christening my Diary—Beautiful Dresden—Illness of my Father-in-law—Celebrating my birthday—A holiday on the Baltic—An ill-mannered young Prince—The Grand Duchess Anastasia—The Crown Prince and Princess—I fall in love with tennis—My solitary success on the Turf—Death of my beloved Father-in-law—Confusing Royalties at Castle Schwerin—*Ma Fantaisie*—Changes—Financial responsibilities—Stag Shooting —Changes at Promnitz—The *Oberförsters* and *Försters*— German mourning—My loss of ambition—Charming visit to Prince Salm-Salm and the Archduchess Christa—Visit to Marmor Palace, Potsdam—The Emperor's annoying New Year Levee—The friendliness of the Crown Prince— The Babelsberg Palace—Its drab Interior—Private apartments of Emperor William II and the Empress at Potsdam —Love is blind they say—My husband gives me sables— Christmas presents.

LIST OF ILLUSTRATIONS

CHAPTER ONE

The truth of things is a perfect food for fine intelligences ; but it is not for wandering wits.

LEONARDO DA VINCI.

I HAVE dared to call this book *Better Left Unsaid*,[1] a title prophetically chosen for me by a Victorian relative, long since deceased. He, because he was undoubtedly male, and in the very best Victorian tradition, believed absolutely in females being seen and not heard. Not that he liked overmuch of us to be seen. Even before we were born we were provided with a large trunkful of clothes delicately referred to in whispers as a layette ; from our birth onward until we " came out " at the age of seventeen or eighteen we were secluded in a nursery and, when we did happen to meet anyone from the outside world, were admonished to keep our (as yet unopened) eyes demurely fixed on the ground. At our marriage to a man with whose christian name we had just been permitted to become vaguely acquainted, but of whom we knew practically nothing else, we were modestly swathed in a massive sheath of white shiny satin, and our face, dyed a deep maidenly crimson, because of the fact that for the first time in our virginal lives we were actually touching the elbow of a man and, also—of course for the first time—listening to words about love and marriage, was carefully covered by yards of ancestral Brussels lace. Our nice bringing-up, unaided, had made it quite impossible for us even to have heard,

[1] The English edition (John Murray, London) appears under the title *From My Private Diary*.

much less understood, the outspoken, not to say coarse manner in which the Anglican Prayer Book in good round English lays down the " first cause for which matrimony was ordained." Had we not, while listening to many dreary sermons, already taken the precaution of becoming acquainted with these hectic passages, then one's maidenly blushes might indeed have been a reality and not a convention. This ordeal over, we " went away," buttressed in several yards of good stout " serviceable " English cloth, and when, after many embarrassing experiences, we reached at last the nuptial chamber I hesitate to mention the sort of garment we put on lest none of my younger friends should believe me ; it is sufficient to say that it was fearfully and horribly made. It was lucky for us if our bridegroom had never been " fast " and therefore, presumably, never seen the skimpy and fascinating garments then worn only by " ladies who were not ladies " and now flaunted by the oldest, plainest and most virtuous.

This, then, was the convention into which I was most inconsiderately tumbled, and into which I never perhaps quite succeeded in fitting myself. It will all sound to young ears as if I were born a hundred years ago—the Victorian tradition, to us so near, is to them so unbelievably far away.

Although, to my surprise and delight, my first book sold so largely in Europe and the United States, I must not be so conceited as to think that everyone in the world has read it. Therefore the recording here of a few facts about my family may perhaps be permitted.

My maternal grandmother, Lady Olivia FitzPatrick,[1] lived with us a great deal ; we all adored her, and she

---

[1] Lady Olivia Taylour, m. 1853 the Reverend Frederick Fitz-Patrick (1815–1895) of Cloone Grange, Co. Leitrim and Warren Hall, Cheshire.

had a deep and lasting influence on all our lives. Her
father, Thomas, second Marquess of Headfort, was
born as long ago as 1787 ; she herself was born in
1824 and died in 1916. Their joint lives therefore
covered a period of nearly a hundred and fifty years.
Consequently, we were, so to speak, always under the
direct shadow of the late Georgian and early Victorian
tradition, and a very wonderful tradition it was in
many ways. We may laugh now at its mock modesties,
its heavy clothes and food, its evasions, its denials and
acceptances, but, when all is said, it stood firmly for
something fine and imperishable. Great-grandfather
Headfort was Lord Chamberlain to Queen Victoria (the
highest office in the English Royal Household) ;
Granny Olivia, her brother Thomas [1] who afterwards
became the third Marquess, and her sisters, Virginia [2]
who married Joseph Sandars, and Mary [3] who died
unmarried, were, therefore, brought up under the
immediate influence of Queen Victoria's austere, but
friendly and happy Court, and such influences, whatever we may say, abide. The friendship of the British
Royal Family for ours was almost an inheritance, and
we all have cause to be gratefully proud of it. In spite
of the cramping traditions and conventions in which
she must have grown up, Grannie Olivia had about her
something extraordinarily human, vivid, free and independent. True, she was always a great lady ; but she
was better than that, she was a real, outspoken, great-
hearted gentlewoman.

She had only two surviving daughters ; my mother,
whom we always called Patsy, and my aunt Min, who
married a Brooke [4] of Summerton, by whom she had
two sons, Geoffrey and Walter, and a daughter Madge,

[1] 1822–94. [2] Lady Virginia Sandars, 1828–1922.
[3] Lady Mary Juliana Taylour, 1825–1907.
[4] John Monk Brooke of Castleknock, brother of Sir George Brooke
of Summerton, 1st Bt.

now Lady Fowler ; and secondly, Colonel Guy Wyndham, younger brother of the fascinating George Wyndham, and a member of the remarkably interesting family of which Lord Leconfield is the head. My mother somehow seems to have escaped entirely the benumbing and inhibiting influence of the less admirable side of Victorianism. To extraordinary beauty, wit, brains, charm and fortitude she united an audacity and freedom which, in the society into which she was born, aroused gossip and even criticism. She did not care. When in 1872 she married my father, Colonel Cornwallis-West,[1] she became her own mistress at the age of seventeen, and from that day until the day of her death in 1920, her own mistress she remained. Looking back, I marvel at her matchless courage and her abiding resolve to live her own life. How I wish, now that it is too late, that I had been sufficiently brave to follow her example. I admire modern youth enormously, and nothing appeals to me more than their determination to live their own lives in their own way, making their own mistakes perhaps, yet unhesitatingly accepting responsibility for their own failures.

When in doubt about anything I am accustomed to look to nature for help and guidance and nearly always receive it. The trees and flowers have their roots in the ground ; of course if they would survive they must have them firmly there, but it is by their own inherent strength that they flourish, and not by continual reference to their ancestry. Directly they peep above the soil they turn instinctively to the sun for light and life, and it is not the past sunshine which warmed the life of their ancestry that nourishes them,

[1] Colonel William Cornwallis-West (1835–1917) of Ruthin Castle, Denbighshire, and Newlands Manor, Hampshire, Lord-Lieutenant of Denbighshire 1870–1916 ; M.P. for Western Division of Denbighshire 1885–92.

but the sunshine of the day and hour in which they live. My mother and I were alike in that we respected the past and all that was good in its achievements, but we lived in and for the present, and eagerly welcomed strange and varied experiences. Indeed, to us both, these things were a vital necessity and this often gave our actions an appearance of fickleness and instability not entirely justified by the facts. Even now, while sometimes looking regretfully towards the past, I like to propel the little craft of my existence eagerly forward into the unknown. Instinctively I dislike what some of my American friends call the " band wagon " ; all the same, I should hate more than anything to be amongst the " also rans " in the enthralling steeple-chase called life.

All my life movement has been to me a vital necessity. I have craved it as men crave wine. I love to travel on foot, on horseback, by motor, by aeroplane or air-ship or, most joyously of all, by sea. Strange scenes, strange peoples, strange experiences—I have always longed for without ever having had the full courage and determination to make them mine. Like many others I have found for this urge some assuagement in books, and in the wildest scenes of nature. Nothing brings me closer to the heart of life's content than a great storm at sea. I have also found great happiness in contact with my fellow human beings. Circum-stances having now made travel and active social inter-course a trial rather than a pleasure, I must find happi-ness where I can. There is always the sea, my garden, my old friends, and now, thanks to the delightful encouragement of many people unknown to me per-sonally, there is the poring over my old diaries and the recovering from them of anything that seems interest-ing, or that truthfully displays my quenchless interest in human life. This, then, must be an invalid's excuse for publishing so much about herself. It is not vanity or egotism or greed. It is only an attempt to clutch closely at the friendly hands and hearts of others in this great big lonely world, and to keep on doing so until the moment comes to wave to it all the last farewell.

II

Turning over and sorting my papers for the purposes of this book I have come across some of my girlish attempts at writing, because I have had literary ambitions for as long as I can remember. The one I take to be the earliest is of course a love story. I think it must have been written after our stay in Florence where I went with my parents and my sister Shelagh when I was about sixteen. I was then mad about singing and aspired to become a great prima-donna, an ambition which persisted for years. I got typhoid fever, temporarily lost my voice and had to come home to recuperate. Then, apparently, I turned my thoughts to " literature." The manuscript, rather faded—like myself—lies before me as I write. It is on foolscap paper, beautifully written and spaced, and my handwriting is much as it is now. The heroine, named Clematice, agonizes with love towards one Rodolfo, an Italian nobleman who was, to quote my own words, " very tall, dark, and very handsome, in fact *very* everything nice." The fact that he was Italian, and that the story contains many quite unnecessary Italian phrases, definitely fixes it as having been written after the sojourn in Florence. While actually there, I would have been far too excited and busy to dream of Clematice and Rodolfo. Probably my long convalescence, and my disappointment at having suddenly to leave Italy, was solaced by trying to write. If so, it foreshadowed days to come, because some of my saddest and darkest hours have been brightened, and some of my bitterest losses and disappointments made more bearable, by keeping my diary.

Rodolfo had, of course, a past in the shape of a wife secretly tucked away in France. It took twenty-two chapters to unite him and his true love Clematice in an everlastingly perfect happiness—Marguerite, the first wife, having died in a very obliging, if not very convincing, manner. If I cannot now admire my early attempt at writing stories I can, at least, be proud of a completed task. Clematice's aunt was certainly a portrait of Granny Olivia ; Clematice, with masses of yellow hair, unusual height, and deep blue eyes, was suspiciously like my youthful self. Marguerite had all the dark, flashing, brilliant beauty of my sister Shelagh and the " Elizabethan home " of the heroine was exactly like Newlands which, much as we loved it, is not Elizabethan at all but " Strawberry Hill Gothic " and was erected only about a hundred and twenty years ago by Admiral Sir William Cornwallis. I may add that the whole story is overladen with quotations from Shakespeare, Shelley, Wordsworth and Tennyson. I do not know where its poetic motto came from, but I might do worse than use it for this volume. It reads :

> *I cannot make this story plain*
> *But I would shoot howe'er in vain*
> *A random arrow from the brain.*

Perhaps that is all even the very greatest writers can hope to do when they try to make plain God's ways to man—or, even more vainly, to woman—or express for others what meaning they have found in life and death.

The next surviving manuscript is much later and much more sophisticated. The story has Russia for a background and the writing of it probably followed my visit to the Grand Duke and Grand Duchess Vladimir [1] at Tsarskoye Selo in 1901. The girl, seated in the sledge beside her bridegroom, has said good-bye for ever to her boyish lover, and her heart is colder than the icy atmosphere of the snow-clad Russian forests.

Later literary efforts (as will appear from my diary) reflect my visits, to India in 1896, and to Egypt in 1911. In each one of them is the ever-recurring effort to depict the dishevelled loveliness of nature in different countries and in all her moods. One article of mine I have always liked; it is called *My Garden at Fürstenstein* and was published in *The Book of Beauty* in 1902.

Wherever I have lived I have always made what Italians call a secret garden. At Fürstenstein I had several gardens, each containing only flowers of one colour; later on, I made my " secret garden," my " Babies' garden," and my " garden of friendship." These were all designed by myself and situated in a part of the great Park called the *Schwarzengraben*, meaning the black grave. I did not like the dismal sound of that name, and eventually changed it to *Ma Fantaisie*, and, for a time, when under the potent influence of the East, I called it the Garden of Kama.

I had built for me there a charming cottage—what the Germans call a " land house "—and furnished it with old oak, simple pottery, and favourite odds and ends picked up in various parts of the world. Both Fürstenstein and Pless are palatial houses, full of gold ceilings and decorations, huge crystal candelabra, mirrors, statues and formal furniture, and with them one could not fit in the little homely pieces I love so much.

[1] (1847–1909) Uncle of Nicholas II.; m. 1874, Duchess Marie-Pavlowna of Mecklenburg-Schwerin; parents of Grand Duchess Helen (Princess Nicholas of Greece) and the Grand Dukes Kyrill, Boris and Andrew.

Ma Fantaisie, designed by myself, was perhaps the only thing in Fürstenstein that I completely owned, the only place which in its entirety expressed myself ; I spent many of my happiest hours there with my children, my parents and special friends, and it was the last roof under which I slept the night before I left Silesia for ever.

This love for gardening, which is shared by Shelagh, is one of our most precious and lasting inheritances from little Patsy, who also made gardens wherever she went. I think it is peculiarly English because, abroad, the gardens of most of the great country houses in which I stayed seemed to have been made by professionals or servants.

Now I must say a few words about my own " secret garden " at Fürstenstein.

At the bottom, and on both sides, was a double herbaceous border with a close-cut green grass walk between, and an old sundial in the centre of each path. Statues peeped out here and there from behind clipped yew hedges. On the outside of the farthest border I planted every sort of lilac, azalea, laburnum, syringa, pyrus japonica, pink and white may, and other flowering trees and shrubs, which made a glorious frame of colour about the end of May and beginning of June.

On the inside, on the edge of the grass and all round the garden was a very low old brick wall, bordered by a little curved line of box. I called this my chain of thought, for, hanging as it were from the little red and green chain, were small beds shaped like hearts and shamrocks, and in them I planted some of my best-loved flowers, the flowers that make me dream, such as violets, heliotrope, lily-of-the-valley, moss rose, dwarf carnation, musk, and white picotee—for these I loved most of all.

From each corner of the garden ran a gravel path,

crowned with flowery arches of roses, clematis, and virginia creeper. These paths met in the centre of the garden and were held together by a wire summer-house, also covered with climbing plants : into this my babies used to run to shelter from the summer showers.

At the top of this garden was a green bank, afterwards converted into a rose garden, arranged as steps or narrow terraces the whole breadth of the bank, with climbing ivy running along the front of the steps, and standard roses on the top. At each corner of the bank, right under the branches of the great lime trees, I built a wide terrace with a stone balustrade, supported by a low wall covered with roses—William Allen Richardson and Crimson Ramblers, red, white and yellow.

I like a garden of my own, because it reminds me of my girlhood, and also because I know where each sweet flower grows. But for real joy, for the complete realization of nature, give me space and distance ; no enclosure, but freedom to let my thoughts wander into the beautiful gardens of my imagination.

My favourite garden at Fürstenstein in June was the woods, which were full of many sorts of strange little flowers, and white with lilies-of-the-valley, growing as large and tall as an English bluebell : I used to take a book and lie down amongst their glorious, proud, fair beauty, and live in their perfume, wondering whether I felt terribly sad, or only sadly happy.

Then came the autumn, with its glorious golden tints ; every wall and balcony covered with the leaves, yellow, purple, and brown, of the virginia creeper, matching in colour the crimson setting of the sun, when the sky sheds an orange glow over the whole valley below, and the castle stands out as if made of walls of fire, each window shining like a little bright flame.

Later on, the year seemed to die with one glorious chord of sadness and despair, while the river murmured loudly at the bottom of the rocky hills, winding in and out amongst the roots of the trees, flowing on and on, as it will still flow on, long after I and my gardens are faded and dead. And the leaves fluttered down, gently at first, to the warm dry earth, and each day one could see the branches and twigs of the trees more distinctly through their faded coverings. The old garden retainers—men and women who would be miserable to be pensioned off as long as they are able to look up, curtsy and say *guten Tag* as one passed —continued to ply their brooms, while the leaves fell afresh where they had swept clean a few moments before. But they did not notice ; they had infinite patience, perhaps because they think little ; and they only smiled as my babies kicked the leaves about and then fell bump into the middle of the heaps they had taken hours to collect. Much of the time they rested on their brooms, and preached German sermons to each other, or exchanged the latest gossip of the village, asking each other how old was Hedwig's baby before Hedwig succeeded in getting married to the baby's father Karl.

At Fürstenstein in the end of October the high winds came. I hated the wind and the sunless sky ; the sight of decay made me sad. It brought bitterness and despair into my soul, and the call of death felt very near in the moan of the wind round the corners of the old Castle. The trees bent low ; a cold mist rose up from the river like a pale funeral pall ; while the dark clouds moving so quickly overhead seemed to gather up the scents of the earth, and measure the dying year for its grave.

Then, in very pity, December's snows fell and made a sort of fairy paradise where all before seemed hard and cruel. Not a little twig or blade of grass but was covered with frozen hoar-frost and snow, seeming to lift its little head up straight and proudly and glisten with pleasure in the winter sunshine, when the sky was often as blue as in June. The avenues that before looked so long and grey and dismal became just fairy ways, the trees meeting in one long high arch of dazzling white, like filigree-work in diamonds. One year the frozen hoar-frost on the trees was twenty inches deep : it weighed them down, and broke many of the finest branches.

I love all that is picturesque. Dressed in white, with my five white Arab ponies, in a red sleigh, I used to drive over the country through the crisp snow, or toboggan down the hills. The ponies pulled the toboggans up again, and in this way we often made moonlight expeditions, the silence of the still white night broken only by the sleigh bells.

Standing on the rock of the *Riesengrab* or giant's grave, one could see across the valley and deep charm of the river, the castle, with its twinkling lights surrounded by a ring of shining white trees and hills, with the moon above in a dark purple sky, the glistening snow at one's feet, and the shining twigs over one's head and against one's face—it was like fairyland, and I, or so they liked to tell me sometimes, was the Fairy Princess : I used to smile, for though I was young then I knew that the world speaks through its beauty to our emotions, and yet does so little to rescue us from ourselves.

But I loved Fürstenstein most, I think, when in summer a sudden stillness hushed the slightest sound, and there was a heavy quietness in the air—a lull before the storm. Then the storm came ! Such thunderstorms as I have never seen in England. The sky turned a browny yellow instead of blue or grey,

FÜRSTENSTEIN.
The Great Hall.

and the leaves flew and whirled up against the windows, and the wind, rising gradually, came nearer and nearer, like a great requiem : then followed pitch darkness with terrible gleams of lightning, which flashed like sudden flames over the whole landscape, so that you could see distinctly for a moment a town more than fourteen miles away, and then—again absolute darkness. The storm crashed and roared through the forest, waking the echoes in the hills, and making the old places tremble ; and I used to stand outside in the corner of a wall for shelter, and think of my poor little flowers, and of my roses whose buds I had perhaps counted, of the trees stripped of their proudest branches, and the trim terrace gardens, usually all swept and gorgeously decked out like a lady of the world, with all their paint and powder washed away. I loved the storm and its roughness ; it seemed to me to be so like our own lives.

Life in Germany brought me many glad and happy things. I had great social success and perhaps did some useful political and serious work. My three sons came ; I spent joyous, happy hours amongst friends and loved ones. Yet I think I never quite succeeded in stilling the deep sense of exile that follows nearly all English people who have to dwell in a foreign land. Behind everything lay a quenchless ache for Irish bogs, Welsh mountains—the pregnant peace of English gardens.

III

If I cannot claim to have lived in the midst of great events, I have at any rate hovered on their outside edge. Perhaps, therefore, what I have thought and said may have something more than a merely personal interest. We all cherish the wistful hope—or delusion —that what we were and what we did are somehow significant, and we long to leave behind us some memorial, however humble, that will outlast the years and still keep our memory green—perhaps even fragrant—when all who knew and loved us are no more. That is one reason why I publish another book. A second reason is that part of the period in which I live, and some of the people in the circles in which I moved, have already become historic. My life before the war seems to me so far away that I can read and write about it as if it concerned another being and events in another world.

"Better left unsaid!" But why should anything be left unsaid? I was always frank by nature and cannot understand the absurd reticences which many people seem to consider so necessary. I do not know why we were sent into this world, but I do know that we were meant to *communicate* our thoughts and feelings to each other. I feel that there are heaps of people, especially women, daily making mistakes, choosing wrongly, meeting success or failure or unhappiness, who might perhaps be helped by my record of how I faced—and survived—all these things. One of the most profitable and most constant ways in which my diary has been of help to me is that by looking back through its pages, it has enabled me, to some extent at all events, to judge myself on my own record.

IV

I have said that the friendship of the British Royal Family was our prized inheritance. In my diary King Edward and Queen Alexandra appear frequently, because they were the highest lights in the English social pageant in which I and my family played a modest part.

The place of King Edward VII. in history is now assured. The words, actions and policies of the

Monarch have been weighed by competent hands and their worth assessed. What no one who did not know him well personally could possibly understand or express was the warmth of the King's humanity, the loyalty of his friendship, the simple, childlike unpretentiousness with which he could enter into all the little charming, perhaps trivial, things that go to make up our everyday existence.

Shelagh and I were at Baden Baden at the end of August, 1894. King Edward (then Prince of Wales) was at Homburg. In response to an invitation from the Grand Duke,[1] the King went to Baden for two days to attend the Races. The King and I had a bet ; he lost and I, in theory, was the richer by a dozen hats. Of course I thought the King would forget all about the incident. But he was punctilious about fulfilling all those little social obligations, the faithful discharge of which does so much to endear us to our friends. Having entertained us at Baden in his own inimitable manner I of course telegraphed, and then wrote, my thanks ; in reply I received the following letter :

PARK HOTEL, BAD HOMBURG, *September* 3, 1894.
DEAR PRINCESS PLESS,—
Many thanks for your kind letter received this morning and I am glad my telegram reached you all right. You have indeed had a busy time since your return and I can well understand how tired you must be. What a cheery time we had at Baden, and it is a pity that our stay was so short. I had to wait three-quarters of an hour at Frankfort for my train and we did not get here till half-past twelve that evening ! Till lately the weather has been lovely, but we had a violent thunderstorm last night and it has been raining all the morning. Many of my friends and acquaintances are going and gone, but I shall have to remain here till middle of next week to

---

[1] Frederick I. (1826–1907), Grand Duke of Baden, m. 1856, Princess Louise of Prussia, sister of the Emperor Frederick III.

complete my " cure." I have ordered your hats and hope to send them to you very soon and that they will meet with your approval. Pray remember me very kindly to your husband, and your charming sister who I trust has recovered from her toothache, and

Believe me Very sincerely yours, ALBERT EDWARD.

" Britannia " has to sail on Wednesday against " Vigilant " for " Cape May Cup." [1]

I see that the names of King George V. and Queen Mary occur less often in my diary, but this is not because I did not from my earliest youth know King George quite well. It is rather because when I was a young girl our Sailor King was working hard in the Navy, seeing and studying the Empire at first hand, seriously preparing for regal duties which surely the world must admit he has finely performed. When the Prince became Heir to the Throne in 1901, I was married [2] and living in Germany and I seldom met him. I think it was only during the Great War that the British Empire learned to appreciate King George at his true and unique worth. Perhaps George V. and Albert II. of Belgium are the only two Sovereigns on record who could, while comparatively unknown, have passed through the most terrible ordeal the world has yet seen, and emerged from it as two of the noblest and most familiar Royal figures in history. It is not for me to say what constitutes greatness in a modern ruler ; but if, in the hour of supreme trial, to identify himself completely and unflinchingly with his country's ideal aspirations and its grim determination to win victory through agony and self-sacrifice be not true

[1] This race was abandoned owing to *Vigilant* (Mr. W. George Gould's yacht), losing her centreboard in rough weather in Alum Bay on Monday, Sept. 3.

[2] The authoress married in 1891 Hans Heinrich XV., then known as Prince Henry of Pless, e. s. of Hans Heinrich XI. (1833–1907), Prince and Duke of Pless, Count of Fürstenstein, Baron of Hochberg, Grand Chancellor of the Order of the Black Eagle, etc.

greatness in a Sovereign, then one wonders what is !
Even so, it was not until his terrible illness in the
autumn of 1928 that the whole world, and more
especially the United States of America, realized how
much noble and disinterested elevation of character
is enshrined in the modest, unadvertising personality
of King George V.

I would like to give here one little picture of the
human, laughing young Prince which I shall never
forget. In 1894 King George, then Duke of York,
came unexpectedly to Newlands to see his father, the
Prince of Wales, who was our guest. I had no suitable
rod with me and there were no trout at Newlands. I
therefore sought to amuse myself by putting a large
piece of meat on a hook and trying to catch a big
common fish in the lake. The Prince of Wales and
the rest of the house-party were out shooting. I was
sitting on the grass watching my float when, suddenly,
from the direction of the house down came the Duke
of York and sat beside me. He asked me what I
hoped to catch and said he would like to try what he
could do. I gave him my rod, and, after a time, the
float wobbled in the most thrilling manner—we had
hooked a big fish ? Alas no ! Unnoticed by us one
of the (almost tame) wild ducks on the pond had
dived and swallowed my piece of meat, hook and all.
" Oh, poor thing," said the Prince. In the end we
had to let it go, as we both felt it was not worth a
wetting. Later on it was captured, cooked and eaten.
I wrote an account of its fate to the Prince and,
with His Majesty's permission, will quote a letter he
wrote me thirty-six years ago, in which he refers to the
incident. He will perhaps be surprised that I have
kept it all this time ; I did so because the King nearly
always laughingly refers to the incident whenever we
meet. The writing is clear, beautifully spaced, simple,

yet full of individuality ; in fact a perfect revelation of
the writer's personality, and is almost exactly the same
as His Majesty's handwriting of to-day :

BALMORAL CASTLE, *September* 14, 1894.

DEAR PRINCESS PLESS,—

I received a letter this morning from Mrs. West, in which
she asked me to write to you at once and *order you* to send her
the photograph of myself which I gave you for her at Cowes
and which she says you have taken to Germany. So this
letter is the " order," but I don't suppose you will obey me
as you are a *German Subject* ! ! ! I suppose the Emperor is
the only person who can give you an order. Mrs. West
called you all sorts of names such as " Fat Frau," etc. Fancy
that celebrated duck I caught *by accident* while fishing is dead,
poor thing—and they want 1/6 damages, but they won't get
it. I hope you enjoyed Baden ; my father told me he met you
there. We have just arrived in Scotland, weather charming.

With many kind messages for your husband, Believe me
always yours very sincerely,

GEORGE.

V

The worst of getting old is that we have reluctantly
and regretfully to face the fact that some of our most
ardent desires can never be fulfilled. As long as I
remember I have longed to visit the United States of
America and Canada. A little later on in this book my
diary shows how disappointed I was that I was not
allowed to accompany my husband when he went to
Washington on an official mission in November, 1902.
Then, for a few years we cherished the vain hope of going
to the United States as German Ambassador and Ambassadress. In 1912, when my brother George[1] and I
went to South America there was some idea of our returning by New York and Montreal, but it could not be fitted
in. Once, before the war, and several times since the

[1] Major George Cornwallis-West, late Scots Guards : m. 1900,
Lady Randolph Churchill (1854-1921), marriage dissolved : 2nd,
1914, Mrs. Patrick Campbell.

publication of my Reminiscences, I have received tempting offers to lecture in America, but everyone tells me I could not stand the fatigue and excitement, and I fear that is now true. So now I shall never see the New York skyline from the Hudson, bow to the statue of Liberty (always a tactful gesture), or experience the forbidden delights of prohibition which, however, of itself does not worry me much as I dislike all stimulants ; but I did want to climb a skyscraper, visit the Metropolitan Opera House, see Niagara, Ottawa and Quebec, sail down the St. Lawrence, and eat waffles—whatever they may be. Above all, I wanted to visit Delaware, the State that takes its name from my ancestor Thomas, Lord West. I wanted to see the Delaware river rise in the Catskill mountains and watch it flow into the bay. There is not much about Thomas, Lord West [1] in the family papers preserved at Knole and Buckhurst, but all the world knows that in the reign of James I. he was Governor of Virginia and it is agreed that " in his short reign he saved the Colony from ruin," and—this I quote with special pride—" if one man can be called the founder of Virginia . . . that man was he." I have in addition a personal reason for loving him. He was member of Parliament for Lymington, a charming old town in the New Forest close to my beloved Newlands, in south Hampshire, where the Wests have been settled since before the reign of Henry VIII. Moreover, I wanted to see the Washington monument cast its lovely shadow over the White House ; the Lincoln memorial reflect its unique beauty in the artificial waters created for the purpose—I wanted to meet and talk to thousands of Americans. Alas ! now it can never be.

All the same it is a real consolation that Thomas,

[1] Thomas, 12th Baron (1577–1618), 1st Governor of Virginia, 1609–10.

Lord West won a favourable and prominent place in the history of the United States and that, through him, our name will always live in that great new continent, from which so many of my best friends have come. Oh, and I did want to revive my Victorian childhood by going to Boston to see the piano legs still modestly draped—or so I am told—in frilled petticoats ; and the harbour into which long ago the New Englanders threw masses and masses of perfectly good tea [1] and thus, unwittingly, laid firm the foundations of the British Empire.

VI

Before plunging into my diary I must say something about my German homes.   Pless, the small principality which the Hochbergs inherited from the last Duke of Anhalt-Coethen-Pless about a hundred years ago, is in Poland.   I never cared for the place.   It is situated in a huge coal-mining area ; its immediate surroundings are flat and uninteresting and, because of the conflicting historic, geographical, political and racial struggles of which it has been the unending scene, it is not a happy country in which to live.   Then, when I first went there as a bride, the family lived a life completely isolated from their humbler neighbours, and hardly seemed even aware of the sources of their vast wealth, or the thousands of miners and others who toiled to secure it. Brought up at Ruthin and Newlands by my father and mother in close personal friendliness with all our tenants and servants, such an attitude, then quite general in that part of Germany, seemed to me intolerable.   I resented it and, unwisely showing my feelings, made much trouble for myself and others.   I am quite sure however that the state of affairs I so disliked did much to make that part of the world the socialist,

[1] The Boston Tea Party, December 16, 1773.

indeed communist, area it later on became, and which it remains to this day.

As will be seen from my diary my father-in-law and his second wife Mathilde [1] were wonderful to me and I came to love them both. Yet neither they nor my husband could understand my feelings of hopeless despair at what seemed to me a hateful and unnatural state of affairs. To them I was only a girl well under twenty who should have been content to sing, dance (very occasionally), embroider, and *listen* to her seniors' talk, according them a continuous, almost fulsome silent admiration. Long before suffragettes were ever heard of I refused to accept the dogma that men were by nature so much wiser and better than women. Yet in the circle into which I married in Germany this was a part of the general creed. Perhaps these early unresolved aversions and frustrations gave me a dislike for Pless never afterwards entirely obliterated. Even when my husband succeeded years later and I could do what I liked in Pless it gave me no real happiness or satisfaction.

If these are my earliest impressions and memories of the place, my latest are coloured with all the agony, despair and horror of the war. During my last visits there it was no longer my home, but the Great Head-quarters of the German Armies in the East and the abode of the Emperor. I was a mere guest under my own roof ; could only come when invited, stay for a stipu-lated time, and leave when I was told. True, my husband was there as Aide-de-camp to the Emperor, but he had even less to say than I had. Then, by most of the poor ignorant people around I was regarded as a dangerous English spy, coming there only to ferret out what I could about the Eastern campaign

---

[1] The Princess's father-in-law m. in 1886, as his 2nd wife, Countess Mathilde von Dohna-Schlobitten.

and promptly send it—God knows how—either to England or Russia, or both ! Even some of our own servants in the house believed this and innumerable other absurdities. No ; Pless has no happy memories for me.

VII

As one cannot readily understand a person without some knowledge of their environment I shall now say something about Fürstenstein, my home in Silesia. It will be difficult for English and Americans to understand the almost feudal life we lived there thirty years ago. The Castle, which has belonged to the Hochbergs for over four hundred years—the original castle— was built at the very beginning of the thirteenth century by Bolko I., Duke of Silesia, from whom my youngest son gets his name : it was literally part of the great high rock from which it takes its name ; its successor, the present Castle, was erected partly in the beginning of the fifteenth, and partly in the beginning of the seventeenth century in the Renaissance style. The Library is famous and contains something like fifty thousand volumes. Usually considered one of the finest castles in Germany it has been entirely altered and magnificently decorated and furnished by my husband. Much against my wishes and advice he spent years and wasted a king's ransom on what is now but an exhibition for gaping tourists.[1]

I dislike large and magnificent houses and have always had something akin to contempt for those feeble personalities who feel that they would be ignored by the world unless they possessed great houses, a useless retinue and stupid pomp and state. In such matters my husband and I could never see eye to eye. One

[1] 80,000 people a year pay for admission to the state apartments and the gardens.

FÜRSTENSTEIN.
Corner of the White Drawing-room.

thinks with pathos of the Lancashire millionaire who complained that " he 'ad five 'ouses but no 'ome." I, too, have had many houses in Germany but never anything that I felt was really a home. One cannot " own " such places ; they are too obsessive, too vast, too impersonal. To me, it is distressing and distasteful to feel the human spirit intimidated by a mere mass of builders' stone, by furnishings, pictures and possessions. Once it exceeds a certain size and a certain (modest) degree of splendour a house ceases to be a home and becomes a museum. And how few people really care to visit museums—much less live in one. True, the West family, like the Hochberg family, had a craze for building, which I inherited. But, apart from gardens, all my efforts were of a very modest nature and *Ma Fantaisie* would be looked upon as an impossible residence by one of the head servants at Pless or Fürstenstein.

Fürstenstein was really our home from the time of our marriage, because Vater and Mathilde mostly lived in Pless, or in one of their other places. From the beginning I loved it. Silesia is the most beautiful and romantic part of Germany and its magnificent mountains are only surpassed by those of the Bavarian Alps. The huge crag on which the Castle stands overhangs a deep rocky gorge ; the house is reached by a bridge which crosses this chasm and is, on its other three sides, almost unapproachable.

Mr. Gaisford,[1] the British Consul-General in Munich, was a shy young attaché at the British Embassy in Berlin when I first met him. He was, of course, invited to Fürstenstein and relates how he arrived at the local station and found a large party of important-looking guests getting out of the same train. Modestly

---

[1] Hugh Gaisford, b. 1874. Attaché in Berlin, 1898–1900 : H.B.M.'s Consul-General in Bavaria since 1925.

waiting until they had filled the semi-state carriages with outriders waiting for them, he found himself with nothing but a luggage cart on which to get to the castle. Even then a man of decision, he climbed in and, as he describes it, eventually found himself in the outer servants' quarters somewhere in the interior of the mountain. He was conducted through archways, cellars and huge stone halls, handed on from one servant to another (and higher) servant until after a walk of a mile or so he was ushered into a part of the house obviously used by the members of the family. The house is said to have five or six hundred rooms; I don't know as I never counted them. What I do know is that from every window it commands superb views over the world-famous *Waldenburger Gebirge*, one of nature's masterpieces. The Fürstenstein, that is the Prince's rock, itself rises three thousand feet above sea level and the views from the castle towers are wonderful. The wild, spacious land of this part of Silesia is indescribably beautiful. Perhaps, as my readers get glimpses of it in my diary, they will come to love and appreciate its magnificence as I did. In spring, which comes late in that eastern European land, when all the fruit and flowering trees are in blossom it is an intoxicating tumult of loveliness; in summer its beauty is in its richness almost overpowering; in autumn when the woods sing with ten thousand notes of colour it translates the spectator to heaven; in winter with crystal trees peeping through miles and miles of snow it is one vast fairyland. Perhaps there are parts of America and Canada more splendid in winter; but in no country could each season spread before wondering man an equally lovely tapestry and, snatching it away, spread a lovelier in its place. I say snatch, because there the seasons can change with the utmost rapidity.

Speaking generally, Silesian scenery reminds one of Thuringia, the Black Forest and, in parts, of the Scottish and Bavarian Highlands. It is a magnificent sporting country and there one finds hunting, shooting and fishing of every sort, and, of course, climbing, ski-ing, sleighing and all winter sports. Its great lakes, comparable only to those of Canada, provide fish for nearly the whole of Germany. In the olden days gold and silver were mined there. Now people go to it from all over the world for its Bads, which seem to cure every ill in the world—except mine ! Salzbrunn, so well known, is Pless property. It was designed, laid out, and the hotel built, by my husband. Its golf course is one of the best in Europe. Alas ! the whole enterprise (which cost masses of money) was only finished shortly before the war. We have therefore never yet enjoyed any return on our huge investment. During the war the hotel was used as a home for convalescent soldiers.

If, against this background I have attempted to sketch, you envisage numberless great estates and, amongst the greatest, Fürstenstein with its guards, foresters, House Marshal, grooms of the chambers, innumerable footmen, outriders, postilions, and all the rest of it, and the endless going and coming of visitors from all over Europe, you will perhaps realize what a terrible incubus to freedom such conditions can be. I know now that poverty can be a crippling, corroding thing. And yet, I think, so long as it leaves one freedom of the mind and soul it is less devastating in its effects than conditions such as I have described.

In spite of our riches we never seemed to have enough money. During his father's lifetime my husband was kept " very tight," as my own dear father used to try and keep George. One bad result of this I think was that Hans never truly learned the value of

money, or how to spend it. The expenditure at Pless
and Fürstenstein used to frighten me because I was
brought up in narrow circumstances. There was no
check on anything ; the Hausmarschallamt [1] used to
control and order everything in the various house-
holds, and all outside affairs were completely under
the Comptrollers, or General Directors as they were
called, at Fürstenstein and at Pless. For instance,
I never paid a bill ; they were all paid for me. Wherever I was, whenever I wanted money, my head-maid
or my Secretary or courier just telegraphed for it and
it came by return in a registered parcel. How could
one have any real feeling of responsibility.

When my husband started altering Fürstenstein in
1909 matters became even more impossible to super-
vise and control. The gardens and stables consumed
money wholesale ; the Salzbrunn hotel was being
built ; new mines were being sunk and—Europe was
marching towards war. The new state apartments
of the Castle, begun in 1909, were not finished till
1915. One would have thought such an experience
would have cured Hans of his building craze ! But
no ! Between 1919 and 1927 the terraces were entirely
reconstructed and many new ones were made. Being
on top of a mountain innumerable terraces are a
feature of the place and are very costly to keep up.
Then we had miles and miles of winding roads and
avenues, unbelievably lovely ; but how I used to
hate the waste of money which I felt could have been
spent more beneficently.

The nearest big town to Fürstenstein is Breslau,
fifty miles away. Naturally we had to go there a
great deal and, although it is a fine old historic city,
I never cared for it—but then I never do care much
for cities for any length of time. Situated picturesquely

---

[1] The office of the Comptroller of the Household.

on the River Oder, Breslau, like nearly all old German cities, has an interesting and attractive Rathaus or town hall, a fine Cathedral, a stately castle (where the Viceroy, Prince Hatzfeldt, lived), innumerable picturesque old streets and corners, and lots of socialists and bad smells.

When, years later, I got up concerts in Breslau for my charities many well-known artistes were most generous and gave their services. They usually stayed with us, and I shall never forget how once, after a concert, feeling we all needed some fresh air, we went fishing on the *Daisysee* (a lake in the woods christened after me) with two of our artistes who did not bother to change out of their evening clothes and top hats ! Little affairs like this used to shock the good Silesians so much that they could hardly sleep in their beds at night. And Lower Silesian " Society " was, and is, so terribly, terribly Prussian !

Of course we had often to go to Breslau for functions of all sorts. On principle, we avoided as much as possible taking any prominent part in the life of the city. It was the residence of the Viceroy of Silesia, and we had no desire to usurp his social functions. Moreover, towns like Waldenburg, Salzbrunn, Freiburg, and many villages were near our own doors and, therefore, had more claims on our time and attention. All the same we could not avoid going to the provincial capital a great deal. For one thing my husband was a member of the Provincial Parliament. Then the Imperial Manœuvres were often held near there ; very often the Emperor and other of our Imperial or Royal guests arrived there instead of at one of the nearer railway stations, and had to be met and received in state, or semi-state, according to their rank. We had our own special train which was kept there and used for official occasions or long journeys. If we did not need the whole train then we used one or two coaches attached to ordinary trains. I must confess that this is a luxury I really appreciated. One's own bed, bed-linen (I never use any other), the light by one's bedside as one likes it, one's own maid and servants. I dislike the smells and fustiness of even the most costly *wagon-lit* and hate the touch of beds and bed-covers used by other people. Hotel rooms always seem to me to reek of the nasty part of the personalities of all their previous occupants ! It was frequently impossible, or perhaps too fatiguing, to return to Fürstenstein after late evening functions in Breslau, so we stayed at hotels and I always hated it when I thought of my own lovely rooms only fifty miles away. When motors came in I would at all costs, very often in evening dress, tiara and Orders, traverse the miles of lonely country no matter how late or cold it might be. I found that on the journey home I frequently recaptured that inner peace and serenity which, all over the world, big social functions seem specially contrived to destroy.

During the shooting season my life was fearfully busy. Our guests were surprised and disappointed if I did not start off with them about half-past ten, instead of only joining them for luncheon. We came back about half-past four and I had to rush up and put on a tea-gown, and with pouring out tea and sitting with them all for a little while, I hardly ever got away in time to finish my letters before the post left at seven. I never had time to rest.

In Germany so often *il faut souffrir pour être poli*. I always had to place our most exalted guest next to me at dinner. The same man every night during his visit. And I was so often bored. Once at Cap Martin I told the Empress Eugénie about this, and I remember her darling face and voice when she said : " You should

do as we used to do at Compiègne. Draw lots.
Have each name written on a slip of paper and let
each guest draw one." The Empress did not warn
me that the innovation aroused much indignation in
French society, and brought a storm of criticism on her
lovely head.

Later I did introduce this practice, saying before-
hand privately to my guests : " Tell the servant to turn
up a corner, or in some other way mark the paper
containing the name of the lady you prefer to sit
next."

But my husband did not like it and we went back
to the old regime. For many years I existed as a
German wife living under German rule, who must
alter no arrangement in house, garden, or stables,
without asking permission. I obeyed and smiled and
made many true friends. At any rate it was a good
piece of acting and as such was a success ; I was quite
pleased and proud of it—but it did not make me happy.

VIII

I think it also made for restlessness that the whole
of Silesia, and its neighbour German Poland, has such
a hectic historic past. Here is a country with examples
of prehistoric stone sculpture, so ancient that one
cannot even guess when they were made. There are
remains of fortresses at least four thousand years old.
History is everywhere enshrined in stone. Perfect
Renaissance cities like Görlitz, lovely Baroque and
Rococo towns, innumerable old castles like Bolken-
hain, memorials of the wars of Frederick the Great,
of the war of Liberation against Napoleon, and of the
still earlier traces of the unending feuds between Russians, Poles and Prussians—all combined to make
something great yet unstable, changeless yet ever
changing.

And then the mixed population. We had to have visiting-cards in German, Polish, French and English. That was for the educated people ; amongst the uneducated there were so many mixed dialects, such uncouth accents, that even a professor of languages could hardly understand them. Picture all this. And then picture poor Daisy, from little Newlands, in little Hampshire, in little settled old England, tumbled just anyhow into the middle of it all, and learn in the pages that follow how she kept her end up, and may perhaps even claim, in a measure, to have won through.

CHAPTER TWO

1895-1896

I CANNOT find any traces of my diary for the year 1895, and do not even remember if I kept one before that date. Perhaps it will turn up some day. I am, however, reminded of something that happened in June of that year by seeing it announced that Lord Crewe [1] is to write the biography of his father-in-law, the late Lord Rosebery. It should be a wonderful memorial. A book about a distinguished writer and statesman by one who, although related, is sufficiently distant to be detached and who is himself a statesman and a distinguished man of letters. All who know Lord Crewe are aware that personally he is gallant and delightful and, as a " bachelor " Viceroy,[1] he was a perfect host. It was, I think, my first visit to Ireland as a " grown-up." From Dublin I went to Blenheim, where I received the following letter :

VICE-REGAL LODGE, DUBLIN, *June* 30, 1895.

I *was* unlucky, dear Princess H. H., not to see you in London, but I ought to have remembered you were going to Blenheim. We talked of so many things that this somehow slipped my memory. . . . I am engrossed in the melancholy business of packing up and saying good-bye to this place, always rather a depressing affair, and it is raining like mad, so the outlook is not cheerful for the moment. Thursday will see the last of one here, and I hope I may get a glimpse

---

[1] 1st Marquess of Crewe (Lord Houghton), b. 1858 ; m. 2nd, in 1899, Lady Margaret Primrose, y. d. of 5th Earl of Rosebery : Lord-Lieutenant of Ireland, 1892–5 ; Ambassador in Paris, 1922–8.

of you before you take flight. I can't understand why it is
you like Germany so much better than England. I'm afraid
you soon will never leave your adopted country, and become
exactly like a Berlin lady. They are very prim, aren't they ?
so it's a terrible prospect.

Ceremony being the order of the day, I will beg you to
" accept the assurance of my distinguished considerations."

HOUGHTON.

All my friends know what a great admiration I had
for Lord Rosebery [1] as statesman, writer and great
English gentleman. Deep down in his nature there
was an aristocratic strain that hated the dust and
turmoil of politics. Then, he was an orator, not a
demagogue, and he lived in a period when the statesman and writer was being hustled out of the arena
of public life by the politician and demagogue. It is
the besetting sin of democracy that " it needs must
hate the highest when it sees it," and it will be
the cause of its ultimate failure as a ruling force.

When writing my former book I asked Lord Rosebery if he had any objection to my publishing some
of his letters to me. He was far from well at the
time, but replied promptly, and his short note is so
characteristic that—although strictly out of its proper
place—I may perhaps quote it here. Let it stand as
a memorial of a friendship the memory of which I
shall always prize :

THE DURDANS, EPSOM, *April* 21, 1928.
MY DEAR PRINCESS OF PLESS,—
I do object ; but it is not worth while forcing my objection
on you. Yours very sincerely, RY.

In imagination I can overhear the little slightly
sardonic smile with which this master of the King's

---

[1] 5th Earl of Rosebery, K.G. (1847–1929), Sec. of State for
Foreign Affairs 1886 and 1892–4, Prime Minister 1894–5.

FÜRSTENSTEIN.
My Sitting-room.

In apple-blossom pink and green, walls covered with hand-embroidered silk, pillars of pale pink marble.

976

English dictated his brief note. Of a grave and old-fashioned courtesy, I can never imagine Lord Rosebery forcing his objections on any woman.

II

In the spring of 1896 Hans and I went to India. It was my only visit to that most fascinating part of the Empire. The Prince of Wales (King Edward) let it be known that we were to receive every attention —and it was so. My uncle Pat Heremon FitzPatrick [1] and my brother-in-law Fritz Hochberg [2] accompanied us part of the way. We did all the usual things. Lord Elgin was Viceroy; [3] we stayed with him at Government House, Calcutta, and he was most kind, passing us on from one Provincial Governor to another, and opening doors for us everywhere. At Madras we stayed with Lord [4] and Lady Wenlock, he being then Governor. He was a sort of relation as his mother was a Grosvenor; Lady Wenlock, who was charming to us, is an aunt of the present Lord Harewood. At Cooch Behar we stayed with the Maharajah, [5] and did many wonderful things, all of which have gone out of my head while I clearly remember one silly incident. Roller skating had about then become the rage and when learning I fell and hurt my nose and face rather badly. Lying in my room swathed in bandages the Maharajah asked leave to come and pay his respects. I could not see him nor he me, and was rather touched when he bent and kissed my toe through the blankets. Both he and the Maharani

[1] Colonel Heremon FitzPatrick (1860–1929), m. Mary Lindsey of Hollymount, who d. 1895; 2nd, in 1908, Grace, widow of Colonel Maloney and d. of Francis Brooke of Summerton.
[2] Count Fritz Hochberg (1868–1921).
[3] 9th Earl (1849–1917). [4] 3rd Baron (1849–1912), s. 1880.
[5] Maharajah Sir Nirpendra Narayan (1862–1911), m. in 1878 Sunity Devel, d. of Chandra Sen.

976

became our firm friends. I brought home my five lovely white Arab thoroughbred ponies which made something of a stir in Germany. I had great trouble getting them to Europe and Aleck Stewart, the English stud groom at Fürstenstein, had to go down to Marseilles to meet them and bring them home to Silesia. As illustrating the absurd nature of gossip and its utter unreliability I may mention that, years later, my boy was asked seriously by a friend if it was really true that his mother went about in a carriage pulled by " five naked Arabs ! "

Hans really went to India for big-game shooting and did extremely well. I put the last shot into a beautiful tigress, so they said she was mine. Her skin hangs now at Fürstenstein and I have had no pride in having put a bullet into it.

In India we of course made the acquaintance of nearly all the great Princes, many of whom became our friends ; chief among them being the Aga Khan, famous for his fine eyes, his sportsmanship, his magnificent presents to ladies, and his loyalty and devotion to the British Empire. He is the spiritual head of one important branch of the Moslem community, and during the Great War his loyalty and support were invaluable. Nor must I omit to mention specially the Nizam of Hyderabad [1] whom both my husband and I liked very much and who entertained us with great magnificence.

I must try and record one other Indian memory that shall remain with me as long as I live. Very early one morning, about three o'clock, we started on our elephants after big game just as the day was dawning and the rising sun tinted with a golden flush the white mists on the hills ; then the jungle birds began to hum, and the insects rustle in the long

[1] 1866–1911.

grasses, while a strange whisper seemed to hover around, and every leaf as if opening gently from its night's slumber, began to flutter. All nature was gradually awakening, and one spoke low, feeling almost as if one ought to walk on tiptoe, and be soft and gentle to everything alive. I used to forget I was going tiger-hunting until a lurch suddenly reminded me that I must stick on my elephant pad for dear life.

In some places the undergrowth was so thick that we had to cut the branches as we went along and they fell into the silken silver cobwebs that covered the whole ground. I felt sorry for the great jungle spiders (being at a safe distance from them), and, absorbed in my surroundings, cared little for the excitement of hunting tigers and big game ; for I love all nature, and every leaf that touched my face as I bent my head to avoid the twigs was a friend ; everything that was growing was fresh and wet with dew, and nature, as it awoke, had touched my face and kissed me. . . .

These are the sort of magic happenings that one garners subconsciously and stores up for refreshment in the after years.

Life on board ship makes for reflection and its uneventfulness encourages one to write. Therefore on our way back from India, I started keeping my diary and have continued it regularly (more or less) ever since. More reliable and truthful than memory, it must now take up my tale.

May 7, 1896. On board ship.

We left Aden at half-past eleven at night, having got there at four o'clock ; the German Consul, rather a nice man, came out in his launch to meet us, and then lent us his carriage in which we drove to the water tanks ; it is about twelve miles there and back. They are very interesting and around them grow the only trees on this arid peninsula—and they only to about eight feet in height ; the tanks are hewn out of the solid rock and look rather like stage scenery ; there is in the centre of one a huge projecting piece of rock the entire surface of which has worn quite smooth by the water ; it was all certainly very interesting and rather pretty. We drove back through the tunnels which here run right through the mountain and are lighted with, I think, gas. There was a glorious sunset, quite red behind the great rough rocky hills and reflected in the sea—on which there were little sailing boats ; and, along the sandy beach passed a train of camels, a yellow line against the background of the blue sky ; it would have made a lovely painting for a clever artist. I should not care to live in Aden, it must be very tiring to the eye—nothing but sand and rocks.

Fiend, my little puppy, is great fun and makes for all the gentlemen's (if such you can call them on this ship) shoes, and tugs at their shoelaces till he gets them undone. I don't know what *Susie* will say when *Fiend* arrives at Fürstenstein. Perhaps, being a gentleman, she will like him.

We get to Suez in four days and are due in Trieste on the 15th, so I shall see them all in England about the 18th or 19th when I hope to go to dear Newlands ; I have not been there in the spring since I married ; I shall see all the rhododendrons out and all the other dear spring flowers which seem to grow more luxuriantly at Newlands than anywhere else. How I always loved the spring there, how free and happy and childish I used to be then, so happy that I felt as if my heart would burst. . . . Everyone who has any happiness generally feels it more in the spring, it is the beginning of the year and, to my mind, an omen of all that is lovely and pure in the world. And I shall hear little Patsy's and Shelagh's voices in the garden, and feel Poppets'[1] hand on my shoulder as he walks with me.

May 9, 1896. On board ship.

Much cooler this afternoon, thank goodness ; it has been intolerably hot in the cabins but is now a few degrees cooler. The days pass too quickly for all I want to do, and the dinner is so ridiculously early—at half-past six. I read history and German with Hans in the morning, and then sing for an hour

---

[1] The family pet-name for my father.—D. OF P.

and a half ; in the afternoon read French and write, and in the evening again read history.

Alas, my nose isn't right yet. I don't believe it ever will be, there is a little red line across the tip, from the cut, and it is still a little swollen, and my bottom lip is still hard in the middle. I shall see a doctor when I get to London.

May 11, 1896. In the Suez Canal.

It is now deliciously cool and I can scarcely believe I have ever been so hot as I was during the last few days. I am *so* surprised as I thought the Canal would be much broader, with at least room for two or three vessels to go abreast, instead of which we are only about fifteen yards away from each side of the bank. I feel quite happy to see real Egyptian soil again. We get to Port Said about five this evening. How much more golden the sand is here than in India. Egypt is really a much more picturesque and fascinating place than India. The whole colouring seems to me to be so much brighter. I wish I could get a brush and paint.

May 12, 1896.

I have a horrid cold and sore throat and do hope it will be well soon so that I shall be able to sing to them all when I get to Newlands. We stayed from five in the evening until three the next morning at Port Said : they had to take in a lot of cargo and also coal. We went for a walk and to see the shops before dinner, and afterwards, to what is called the Alhambra, but there was nothing of interest going on, only a small band, and some girls. Around a roulette table about forty dirty-looking men were playing with franc pieces. It was very cold driving ; we went to several native *cafés chantants* but they were all very quiet, only one girl in each café, and each girl uglier and more repulsive looking than the other. We made one dance for us ; it appeared a most painful process, as she simply moved her chest and " tummy " about, up and down and then from right to left ; it looked horrid. Another girl, looking rather like a little monkey, and prettier than the others, followed us about and said she would dance if we came to her " room," but that the men wouldn't do. I went with Leny, the German consul from Bombay—he and his wife are on board, homely German people—and the Austrian Consul from Port Said. The native part where the cafés are, consists of a lot of wooden houses ; the doors were open and I could see there were two or three small bedrooms, next to each other. Port Said is supposed to be a rather wicked place I believe. They made such a noise on board last night that I did not get to sleep till about half-past three, so I am very tired now. Good-night, diary.

May 16, 1896.

In the train for Vienna, where we arrive to-morrow.

We had intended leaving Port Said by the early morning train but the doctor did not come on board till much too late ; all ships coming from India must remain in quarantine until seen by the doctor. He did come this morning at six, but as it was simply pelting with rain of course none of the passengers were on deck. He had the impertinence to go away again giving as an excuse that " as he saw no passengers he supposed they were all in bed and he wasn't going to wait in the rain." I happened from my cabin to see him arrive and leave, and he never attempted to see the Captain, or gave the slightest sign that he was on board. Everyone has written to complain. I was furious and, when he returned, told him he might be a doctor but he wasn't a gentleman. All the passengers were delighted as the two people who might have done something—the German and Austrian Consuls—behaved like lambs. Men are such moral cowards.

At Trieste this morning I went to bed and had a rest, and then we had a good lunch ; it was very nice to get a good cup of café-au-lait and fresh butter. Then we drove in the pouring rain to the Castle of the Empress of Austria [1] called, I think, Miramar, situated right on the sea ; it is a perfectly delicious place, and the terraces are lovely ; in fine weather it must be a dream.

I got two letters from my darling Poppets and a lot of paper cuttings about George's coming-of-age ; also some prints out of the papers of my picture at the Academy. It seems a nice picture, though not very like me, but then one cannot really tell from prints. They seem to have done everything beautifully at Ruthin for George's coming-of-age ; I am miserable that I was not there. . . .

---

[1] Princess Elizabeth of Bavaria, m. 1854, Emperor Francis Joseph I. (1830–1916) ; assassinated at Geneva, Sept., 1898.

May 21, 1896. In the train.

I shall be in London at half-past four to-morrow afternoon. Poppets and little Shelagh will meet me ; I wish little Patsy were going to be there too.

There is a ball to-morrow night at Mrs. Arthur Wilson's. I suppose I shall go with them. I have a new dress I got in Vienna (I got several) but I am sure I shall be shy at a London ball ; people have not seen me for such ages, perhaps they won't ask me to dance.

I have had a very happy three days in Vienna ; Count (Heine) Larisch [1] behaved charmingly. The boys, Hansie and Fritz, are well ; only Hansie seems very low-spirited, I wonder if he really loves Shelagh ; I believe he does. Dear little girl, I am longing to see her. Count Heine was to have given a ball last night but the brother of the Emperor died, so it was abandoned. We went after dinner to Baron Rothschild's where I heard the most perfect private band I have ever listened to ; each player an artist. I went one night to the Opera, *William Tell* ; it was beautifully done, and the house was full ; what looked rather funny was that some ladies were in evening dress, as they were going on to ball afterwards (where I also went) : others were in high frocks and some in the boxes even wore hats !

We had a follow-my-leader ride one morning, about fifty people came out, including ten ladies. Count Heine led ; [2] we galloped hard for an hour and jumped little hurdles and some of the jumps on the race-course. I was mad with delight to be on a great big horse again—a horse called *Shelagh*, one of Count Heine Larisch's own particular favourites. It was almost like a real hunt. Poor little black *Fiend* isn't well, I had to give him to a vet. ; he is a real little monkey ; Alma (my maid) was trying just now to make him lie down and be comfy and he got cross and bit her finger so hard that it bled.

That awful man who was on the ship is in the train ; he

---

[1] Heinrich (Heine), 6th Count (1850–1918), m. Countess Henriette Larisch von Moennich ; his two elder sons are Johann (Hansie), b. 1872, and Friedrich (Fritz), b. 1875. In 1912 Johann m. Miss Olivia FitzPatrick, a first cousin of the authoress.

[2] Count Larisch was a keen fox-hunter and frequently hunted in England where he was well known. He was Master of the Hounds at Pardubitz and was succeeded in that office by his son the present Count.

came and spoke to me just now at dinner. I scarcely looked at him, but he stood there for several minutes talking. We went yesterday to the races ; I made a few bets—and lost.

July 21, 1896. Fürstenstein.

In the beginning of September the Emperor will be at Primkenau [1] for the Manœuvres. I wish he would come to Fürstenstein. There is to be a big ball in Breslau for him and the Empress ; we shall of course go, and take Patsy, Poppets and Shelagh, who will be here then. It may prove to be a good chance for Hans to have a private talk with his " God Almighty Sovereign." Duke Ernst Günther (the Empress's brother) is going to write and advise me how this talk can best be arranged. I do hope Hans will take his proper position before the Emperor, and not look shy as he always does, and *stand-offish* ; one never can afford to cut off one's nose to spite one's face, and I think that, in Germany to quarrel personally with the Emperor, is to cut off more than one's nose. A great many men have to work under a Ruler with whose politics and mode of government they do not fully agree.

July 25, 1896. *Sunday*. Fürstenstein.

I have not written for a long time ; but I have been very busy. Moreover, I am writing three little stories, so have not much time for my diary. Patsy saw the first one while I was at Newlands. I wrote it on the ship coming home from India ; she wants me to have it printed ; I do not know what she will think of the other two ; probably they are great rubbish and very badly written.

Mathilde and Vater are here, in the best of tempers, they really are charming. We—she and I—spoke last night of religion ; I told her pretty plainly that, if Hans insisted, I would, perhaps, become a Catholic ; she did not seem surprised, and after a while kissed me with tears in her eyes. I do not know how Hans will manage Vater, as many years ago they made him sign a paper saying that he would never turn Catholic ; if so, the property and so on would all go to Conny. [2]

---

[1] The Silesian residence of Ernst Günther, Duke of Schleswig-Holstein (1863–1921), brother of the German Empress ; he m. in 1881 Princess Dorothea of Saxe-Coburg-Gotha.

[2] Count Conrad Hochberg (b. 1867), eldest brother-in-law of the authoress.

That paper can never be destroyed as it is in the hands of the
Government ; but what might be done is to draw up another
agreement declaring the first one valueless, and to make his
brothers Conny and Fritz sign it.   I dread to think of it as we
are all such good friends now, and it would be dreadful to
have a family quarrel !   But I could never sincerely be a
Lutheran Protestant like my husband's family.   Why, one
does not even *kneel* down in church ; the congregation seem
to have no respect whatever for their church ; in fact it is
not like a holy service at all.   Yet I am not certain that the
Catholic religion is not the right one, the one that Jesus
meant us to follow, when He said Saint Peter was the rock
on which His Church was built. . . . · Please God it will all
end all right, but sometimes I feel very miserable and long to
be a girl again at dear Newlands, true to my English Protestant
faith and looking forward to taking the Holy Communion
every month.   Since I married all religious peace of mind
has left me ; Hans is miserable if I go to a Protestant church,
and more so if I take the Communion—indeed he is almost
brutal to me about it.   It is impossible for a husband and wife
to have different religions I think, and Hans is so happy in his
beliefs ; and besides, once the point is settled, it will be easier
for him to shape his·future attitude towards politics and about
going into Parliament and so on.

It is a glorious day and I wish I did not feel so absolutely
miserable and home-sick : the whole family is at Newlands
now. . . .   I think many people will be here this autumn ;
all my dear ones from home come at the end of next month
I hope.   They are all very well.   Gerry Cadogan [1] has proposed to Shelagh, but of course it wouldn't do ; he has only
a thousand a year.   Now I am going to continue writing
my story.

August 5, 1896.   Fürstenstein.

I have just come back from the station having been to see
Vater and Mathilde off ; they have both been so nice and I
really think they have been happy here.   Mathilde is truly nice
and we get on well together.   Hans talks of going to Cairo this
winter and up the Nile again : I am not very keen to do it.
I want to have a little of the Berlin season ; we certainly ought
to go there and I must attend at least one Court this year ;

---

[1] 6th Earl Cadogan, s. 1915, m. 1911, Miss Lilian Coxon.

later, I should like to have a little house in London and go from there to nice shooting-parties.

August 25, 1896. Tuesday. Fürstenstein.

We came back from Pless the day before yesterday to receive the dear Grand Duke of Mecklenburg ;[1] the Grand Duchess (Anastasia) is in Homburg so did not come. He has to leave to-morrow. Lulu[2] and her husband are also here, and Prince and Princess Hatzfeldt.[3] I am just going to drive the Grand Duke to Salzbrunn with my five white Arab ponies. All my own dear people arrive on September the eighth. It is now arranged that on the 29th we go to Primkenau to Duke Ernst Günther for the Cavalry Manœuvres ; the Emperor I now hear will not be present ; all the same, it will be very interesting, and I shall ride. The Count of Turin[4] will be there ; we travelled in the same train from Vienna and he came into our carriage and talked and talked ; I had got up at six that morning and had had a very tiring week in the mountains and longed to sleep. I talked to him of the Pope, and the " blacks " and " whites " of Rome ; he got quite excited and Hans got more and more uncomfortable and made signs to me to stop ; but it seemed to amuse the Count and instead of leaving us, as I thought he would, he remained seated, and winked with his eyes, and gesticulated with his hands. They talked of the Duke of Orleans ; Hans says we shall see him King of France.[5]

We spent a very nice time at Solza ; the longest day of all was when we set off at two in the morning for Spital am Pyhrn ;[6] and

---

[1] Friedrich-Franz III. (1851–97), Grand Duke of Mecklenburg-Schwerin, m. 1879, Grand Duchess Anastasia Michailovna of Russia (1860–1922) ; the Grand Duchess was the mother of Crown Princess Cecile of Prussia, and sister of the Grand Dukes Michael, George and Alexander, who frequently appear in these pages.

[2] Countess Louise (Lulu) Hochberg (sister-in-law of the authoress), m. 1881, Friedrich (Fritz), 2nd Prince of Solms-Baruth (1853–1920).

[3] Hermann, 3rd Prince of Hatzfeldt and 1st Duke of Trachenberg, b. 1848, m. 1872, Countess Natalie Benckendorff. The Prince was Viceroy of Silesia.

[4] Prince Victor-Emmanuel, Count of Turin, b. 1870, brother of the Duke of Aosta, and cousin of King Victor Emmanuel III. His father, Amadeus, was King of Spain, December, 1870–February, 1873.

[5] Philippe, Duke of Orleans (1869–1926), Head of the Royal House of France and Pretender to the Throne.

[6] In Tyrol, some 40 miles east of Ischl, where Count Larisch had extensive chamois shooting.

only got back for lunch ; it was pitch dark and raining when we started ; we got on the top of the mountain at five and the view was glorious. The house party included a Baron and Baroness K., both ugly and uninteresting ; Mr. and Mrs. Townsend, the American attaché in Vienna, she is handsome and just escapes being . . . . ; then of course Countess Larisch, our hostess, her husband Count Heine, and their two sons ; Mr. and Mrs. Gordon Cunard [1] from the Pytchley country, and Mrs. Lawley [2] his sister ; we were all very happy and homely and danced in the evenings after dinner. Solza was formerly an old monastery, and the church attached to it is lovely ; the most beautiful gilt Baroque carvings ; it was built in the seventeenth century ; there are skulls of several saints and their bones are all set into velvet and surrounded by precious stones, big pearls and sapphires, and so on. Many of the monks were buried under the monastery, but there was a fire which burnt up all the coffins ; then the bones and skulls were collected and put into a sort of little chapel outside ; there are three steps down to the shrine, and a lovely iron gate in front which is always left open ; it looks so lonely and weird ; I did not go in, but examined each skull from outside and I wondered which one I would most resemble when I am dead. I couldn't help shuddering with horror at the thought that I shall be like that some day ; and then it made me think of little Patsy and Poppets and all those I love so much. Truly there are many strange things that must happen.

Just finished lunch ; the ponies went very well, and the people in Salzbrunn bowed most beautifully as we passed. The Hatzfeldts have left ; Lulu and Fritz have gone out with Hans to see the foals ; I am going with the Grand Duke this afternoon to shoot roebuck ; I am sure I do not know what I shall talk to him about all the time. . . .

September 7, 1896. Fürstenstein.

The Emperor and Empress have been to Breslau, and have gone. The Emperor arrived at Breslau from Dresden and the Empress from Potsdam. The Empress [3] drove with Princess

---

[1] Now Sir Gordon Cunard, 4th Bt., and Lady Cunard (d. 1927).

[2] Now Lady Lawley, G.B.E. ; d. of Sir Edward Cunard, 2nd Bt., m. in 1885 Hon. Sir Arthur Lawley, G.C.S.I., who was secretary to Duke of Westminster, 1892–6.

[3] (1858–1921) Augusta Victoria, Princess of Schleswig-Holstein-Sonderburg, m. 1881, William II., German Emperor.

Charlotte of Saxe-Meiningen [1] in a postilion carriage drawn by six black horses. They took up a position in the centre of the dais, where we all sat. The weather behaved beautifully and the escort of Cuirassiers of the Guard looked marvellous as the procession drove to the Square where the new statue of the Emperor William I. was waiting to be unveiled. The Emperor alone on horseback stood in front of the statue ; the band played the National Anthem, guns went off, and the Emperor remained at the salute. As he did so his breast-plate, and helmet with the crowned eagle on the top, shone in the sunlight. The Emperor did not make a speech but the Mayor of Breslau did. And at a signal, several men pulled a string and the yellow and black curtains fell, revealing the statue. It is a mediocre work, very high with steps leading up to it, and then a great marble block on which stands the bronze equestrian statue of the old Emperor. Prince Henry of Prussia was present, and the Princes Ludwig Ferdinand, and Rupprecht, represented Bavaria. Of course General von Hahnke, and General von Gossler (the Minister of War) were also there.

During the day there was not much to do. The next morning, the 5th, there was a Review which lasted more than two hours ; I drove with the Countess Harrach in my own carriage, and Mathilde drove Maria-Agnes.[2]

The Czar [3] and Czarina were there, the latter dressed all in white and silver, and looking charming. In the procession through Breslau I was astonished at the numbers who recognized me. Lots of people bowed and waved their hats to me ; and some whispered " *Oh, wie hübsch* " (Oh, how nice). Of course the streets were lined thick with people. It took fully an hour to drive back to the town from the Parade ground.

Only a few ladies were asked to the official banquet at the Viceregal Palace the night of the 6th ; I went and of course Mathilde, also Lulu who came to Breslau on purpose. Hans always complains of our not being given our proper position, and so on, but I was placed most prominently. I sat between Vater and Prince Hatzfeldt, the chief man in Silesia—he is

---

[1] (1860–1919) Eldest sister of the Emperor William II., m. 1878, Bernhard Prince or Saxe-Meiningen.

[2] E. d. of Count Bolko Hochberg, m. 1901, Charles Count of Pückler

[3] Nicholas II. (1868–1918), m. 1894, Princess Alix of Hesse (1870–1918), grand-daughter of Queen Victoria.

FÜRSTENSTEIN.
My Bedroom.

Lord-Lieutenant or *Oberpräsident* ; I was opposite the future King of Bavaria ; [1] he kept staring at me, then laughed, even before I was introduced to him, and it gave Mathilde and me the giggles ; he seemed a real " farmer Prince," and is known by that name in his own country. After dinner we talked to everyone, and then went on to the Opera which was well done ; I sat with Mathilde and Lulu on the left of the Royal Box, and Hans in a box with Lord Lonsdale and Lord Charles Beresford ; it was so funny meeting them both at Breslau ; the former is coming here to stay. The Emperor and Empress were charming to me ; also the Czar and Czarina ; the latter asked after Patsy ; the Czar talked of the buffalo Vater had sent alive to Russia to his father ; [2] The Czar looks very ill and weak, but the Czarina looks very healthy and has a most charming and clever face with deep blue eyes, and low straight eye-brows ; her head is small and her hair brushed up from her forehead, only a few curls on the temples and just twisted up at the back ; she had loads of lovely diamonds and great big sapphires. The German Empress also looked very well with enormous diamonds and a blue frock—both Empresses were in blue. The Count of Turin was there and came and flirted as usual, told me my hair was wrong, my turquoises on my dress were crooked, that I looked much nicer with the turquoise blue wings in my hair than with my crown on, and so on ; and then said that I was the prettiest woman there. Mathilde looked very well and so did Lulu my sister-in-law.

It was great fun at Primkenau, but I only rode one day at the Manœuvres, as, the next day, nearly all the soldiers had left—having to march to somewhere near Dresden. I rode *Empress* and she went beautifully, only pulling a bit ; but everyone admired her and I was the only mounted lady there. It was a lovely sight—three thousand men on horseback all with lances. Now I must go and sing. Patsy, Poppets and Shelagh are here, also dear Gordy Wood.[3] I will write later.

September 19, 1896. Fürstenstein.

Only a few lines as I want to finish my novel and lately I have not had a moment to write. The 14th, 15th, 16th and 17th we had dances here, the one on the 16th being fancy

---

[1] Ludwig III. (1845–1921) ; Prince Regent, 1912 ; King, 1916.
[2] Alexander III., b. 1845, d. 1894.
[3] See *Daisy Princess of Pless*, pp. 67, 77.

dress. We only arranged it that very afternoon; it was a great success; all the ladies powdered. I, Patsy and Shelagh wore some of the Maharajah's [1] jewels; I wore the emeralds. He dressed up in a native dress of blue and gold with a turban and a lot of diamonds. The Grand Duke Michael of Russia [2] looked splendid in the lovely old Japanese coat I bought in Breslau the other day, with a turban and a long sword : Mr. " Nimrod " Sen,[3] the Maharajah's brother-in-law, wore a white native dress and made a sash and turban of some embroideries I brought from India. Another man went as a cook; the Count of Turin, as a Neapolitan fisherman, wore a pair of white leather breeches from the stables, a loose red silk blouse and one of Countess Torby's red silk stockings on his head, with some red pom-poms of mine hanging at the end of it ; Gordy looked capital in a Japanese dressing-gown and red slippers, a piece of pink calico round his head, with a sham pig-tail we bought in Freiburg sewn on the top, and his face all painted up. Some of the men got quite a good effect with bits of coloured satin sewn on to the lapels and cuffs of their dress coats; many wore knee-breeches. I lent things from all over the house, and so did Hans, who wore his red hunting coat. Shelagh looked lovely in her Warwick fancy dress freshened up, and Patsy wore a black hat, a red velvet bodice, a white satin skirt with lovely old lace on it and pink roses; she looked wonderful. I wore my blue satin with the Indian gold embroidery and a high Medici lace collar, my hair powdered, and a little pink velvet cap with feathers.

The Grand Duke Michael and Countess Torby, Gordy, and the Maharajah are still here ; everyone else left the day before yesterday. The party consisted of the Count of Turin and his two aides-de-camp, Count Fée and Count Carpeneto, the Maharajah with Mr. Plowden [4] and Mr. Nimrod Sen, the Grand Duke Michael and Countess Torby, Count and Countess Dohna ; Count and Countess Harrach and a cousin ; Lotka Hohenau [5] and her husband ; Mr. and Mrs. Townsend ;

---

[1] Of. Cooch Behar, see p. 33.

[2] (1861–1929) Grandson of Nicholas I. ; m. morganatically in 1891, Countess Sophy Merenberg, who became known as Countess Torby (1868–1927).

[3] Nirmal Chandra Sen, C.B.E.

[4] C. W. C. Plowden, Esq., C.I.E., formerly in Bengal Police.

[5] Charlotte (Lotka) von der Decken (who was a connection of the Hochbergs), m. Friedrich (b. 1857), grandson of King Frederick-

altogether we were thirty people ; I feel rather relieved now they have all gone.

Patsy has just come into the room ; the Maharajah is playing the piano. . . .

October 19, 1896. Fürstenstein.

My dear diary, I have forgotten you for a whole month, or rather, I have not forgotten, but I have not cared to write ; what is the use ? It does me no good to sit down and write every silly idea or thought that comes into my head, they would be better forgotten—and yet I still write on.

Yesterday Patsy and Shelagh left for England ; I drove them to the station and drove back with Hans in the buggy ; I cried a little, but he was so nice and did not mind ; I did not cry from loneliness (for I am *very glad* at last to have my husband to myself) but I cried to think that the summer is over now—the one thing I had been looking forward to for nearly three years, namely to have Patsy and Poppets here—that has come to pass—they have been, and are gone. I walked about during the last few days with Patsy and we arranged all sorts of things for the terraces and park : great clumps of azaleas to be planted here, peonies there, lilac a little further on, a wall of laburnum, with roses in between, at the end of it a green lawn ; all for next year. Oh, why do the " next years " come so soon ? Why can't this year, this beautiful summer, last much, much longer ; it has not been a very peaceful summer either. First of all the religious question broke out again. I told Patsy that, for Hans's sake, it would be better if I were to turn Catholic, as it must be dreadful for a husband and wife to have a different religion, and so on. Then she told Poppets and he was very upset . . . after all there must be many roads to Heaven, there were and are many good Catholics, and Hans had stuck to this idea for eighteen years ; I would do all I could to help him, and have advised him *not* to turn Catholic, I mean, as far as the world is concerned (of course his own heart would always remain the same) ; but anything I can achieve must be done by kindness and tact, and it will take time ; if they threaten him in any way or show any hardness to him, he will simply get into an obstinate rage and be received into the Catholic Church at once. O, dear God, help him. I do hope all will come right.

William III. of Prussia. As his mother was a morganatic wife he was known as Count of Hohenau.

It was such a glorious day yesterday (to-day the sun shines but the wind howls) and I drove with Patsy in the morning and with Hans in the afternoon ; he is such a strange man, and can be quite unsympathetic at times. I am going to England about November the 10th ; I want to be at Newlands a little while, as I have to spend Christmas at Pless, and oh, it was a hard fight till I got him to say I might go ; he never can understand the love I have for my own people and my old home. However, he joins me there on the 28th, as we are going on the 30th till December 5th (Shelagh too) to Sandringham to shoot.

On the 28th we are going to Pardubitz [1] for two days' hunting and one day's racing. Count Heine (Larisch) has just wired to ask if we cannot go a day earlier and have an extra day's hunting but I cannot be bothered to do so ; I grudge every day away from here now, as we have to leave on November the 4th for Pless. The Emperor will be there from the 5th till the 7th ; I am practising some songs. I wish I could have a nice little talk with him, and beg him to give Hans something to do : Vater spoke of asking him to give Hans a seat in the House of Lords. . . .

Now I am going to write my story ; I ought to be ashamed of myself for all the time I spend in wasting ink and paper !

November 3, 1896. Fürstenstein.

My dear diary, I am a very faithless friend, please forgive me ; now, as usual, I am in a great hurry. We leave for Pless to-morrow, so you can guess all I have to do ; Missy [2] is here fiddling about, dear old fussy thing, but I don't know what I should do without her. The Emperor arrives on the 5th for three nights, with five or six gentlemen. I should like to ask him if he thinks that Bismarck made his " revelations " for spite, or because he really thought it would be doing a good thing for the country : I believe the former reason.[3]

---

[1] *Jagd Casino*, Pardubitz, a hunting-lodge belonging to the Prince of Pless in Bohemia, now Czecho-Slovakia.

[2] Lady-in-waiting or Hofdame to the authoress.

[3] In November, 1896, arising out of the coldness shown by the Czar when he met the Emperor William II. at Breslau in September (see pp. 44 and 45), Bismarck made a public statement regarding Germany, Russia and Austria which aroused much discussion. At that moment Russia was moving away from Germany and towards France —a foreshadow of the Great War.

I shall be in London on the 12th ; Tommy [1] will follow later in time to take Shelagh and me to Sandringham on the 30th November till December 5th. It has been a delicious little time, Tommy and I to ourselves ; if *only* we had a baby.

The summer is over ; I wonder what will happen next year. The weather has been so glorious I am quite sorry to leave Germany, and yet I long to see them all, darling brother George and dear Newlands, and the lovely sea. Perhaps (if it is not too cold) I may come back here for a little in January. I have just finished dinner ; it makes me feel sick to write. We did not go to Pardubitz after all ; I did not feel quite well, so we thought better not to do so, and I suppose, as usual, my " hopes " will simply end in disappointment—and I shall have given up all that fun (for it would have been delightful) ; moreover it was my only chance of a few days hunting this season. And now good-night, dear diary, excuse writing, but, if I go on, I shall faint in a moment. Good-bye, dear beautiful Fürstenstein, for a little while and thank you, dear God, for this beautiful home and my Tommy and all my many many blessings in life, and help Tommy in his religious difficulties and give us a little baby boy, please dear God. And bless all I love, and help me to be always good—better than I am !

---

[1] The authoress's favourite pet-name for her husband.

CHAPTER THREE

1897

January 27, 1897. *Wednesday*. Fürstenstein.

MY dear diary, forgive me for this long neglect, but really I am beginning to be certain that I had better not keep a diary any more; I have so many other things to do, and recording my doings and thoughts does no good to anyone and only shows what a fool I am. Nevertheless, I will try to begin from where I left off so long ago.

We went to Pless to receive the Emperor who was very nice. He kissed my left hand one night, instead of my right as he said : " I do not kiss a hand with a glove on," and then went straight up to the other ladies and kissed their gloved right hands : he wants Hans to work with Prince Hatzfeldt in Breslau, which I think he will begin to do next spring.

I had a very happy month in England, went to all the plays, stayed a week for shooting at little beloved Newlands ; went from there for three days to the Ilchesters at Abbotsbury and then Patsy and I went to see darling Granny in her little house near Chester ; she was very well and so glad to see us. Hugo has gone with Eddie [1] to America.

Hans joined me in England for ten days and then went back to Pless ; he did so only to take Shelagh and me to Sandringham ; we stayed there six nights ; it was not a bit stiff—on the contrary, extremely nice. In the evenings Shelagh and I sang to the little Princess.[2] One day, after the other ladies had returned to the house, we both rode astride on the Prince's two spare ponies that always follow the shooters. The Prince [3] was delighted ; no one else saw us as we did it in a field.

---

[1] Uncles Hugo and Eddie FitzPatrick, sons of Granny Olivia.—D. OF P.

[2] Queen Alexandra (then Princess of Wales).

[3] King Edward VII.

Another day Prince George [1] said : " Now is your time to ask about the dancing " ; they had bet me I would not dare to suggest a dance—but I did ! And we danced the two following nights ; the Princess was a little bit inclined to be cross at first (the Prince had not broken the ice by mentioning it to her) ; but it all went off very well ; those who did not dance played cards in the ballroom. Princess Victoria and Prince George were delighted at the success of my boldness. There had been no dancing at Sandringham since Prince Eddie [2] died five years ago.

I sent the Princess a great basket of lilies-of-the-valley and violets from London when I got back. She was very pleased and wrote me a little note for the New Year and sent me a " Daisy-chain " calendar—a nice thought.

Young Lord Waterford [3] was there and talked all the time to Shelagh ; everyone remarked it. The Ilchesters are quite anxious for her to marry their son [4] and spoke to Patsy and Poppets about it ; he is a charming boy and one of the best matches in England ; he is too shy to propose, and Shelagh says he is too young and will not encourage him one bit ; he is only twenty-two, but I think she is throwing away a good chance, as a woman is almost bound to fall in love with the man who gives her everything, houses, jewels, horses, every penny she has ; and, later on, her children ; in fact the one to whom she owes everything—just as Hans gives me everything and is so good and dear ; a woman must come to love such a husband and I know Stavordale would make a real nice husband for the little girl. Gordy Wood is still in love with her and is going out to Africa to make money in the hope that she will *wait* ; ridiculous. I am alone now for two nights, Hans has gone to Berlin. Will write again to-morrow.

January 30, 1897. Fürstenstein.

I must tell you about Christmas ; it was very dull. I got to Pless on the 23rd ; all the next day Mathilde, Fritz and Conny were busy in the big drawing-room arranging the

---

[1] King George V.
[2] Prince Albert Victor, Duke of Clarence, b. 1864, d. Jan. 14, 1892.
[3] 6th Marquess (1875–1911), s. 1895, m. 1897, Lady Beatrix, d. of 5th Marquess of Lansdowne.
[4] Lord Stavordale, now 6th Earl of Ilchester, b. 1874, s. 1905, m. 1902, Lady Helen, d. of 6th Marquess of Londonderry.

table with all the presents, so I was not allowed in. I spent the time sending away my own cards and presents. On the evening of the 24th we were marshalled into the room and each of us found a part of the table set out with our presents. I love getting presents but it is impossible to admire the same things continuously from seven o'clock till eleven or twelve and go on saying nice things about them ! Yet, if you take a book and read it is considered dreadful and everyone thinks that you are not satisfied with what you have received. We stayed at Pless for about a fortnight. Oh, those early dinners at six and the long evenings from seven till half-past eleven. Somehow it all gets on my nerves so much that I feel I must go out of the room and have a real good scream—just one long yell.

The religious question was *sur le tapis* all the time and now of course there is war in the family ; and poor old Hans—I told him his father would never give in. They pretend to think that, if he were really sincere, he would turn Catholic and not mind giving up the properties, but feel proud of doing so for the sake of his soul. I would like to see how many Protestants would do such a thing ; *I* wouldn't. . . . We go to Lulu, my sister-in-law, on the 6th ; she writes the sweetest letters and seems to be the only one in the family at all sorry for Hans. . . . How I wish with all my heart that Hans would become an English Protestant. The German Lutheran Church Service is more like a children's Sunday-school lesson ; one sits all the time (not supposed to *kneel* even once) and listens to a man preaching *at* you. Even Missy said to me last night : " You had better not come to church to-morrow, it is a dreadful bad clergyman " ; of course she meant preacher —as a man he is grotesquely good. Oh dear, is anyone's life peaceful, is their one soul ever contented, is any heart ever at rest ? I went to see a lot of poor old people the other day ; one woman had sixteen children, another twelve, and so on ; all poor, poor people—and I with exquisite cambric all ready to dress my baby, lace and ribbons to make it pretty, arms longing, longing to hold it, and yet I cannot have *one* ; surely some things in the world are very uneven.

We start for St. Moritz on the 12th of February and go on to Cannes on March 1st ; Patsy goes with Fannie Wilson to Cap Martin about the same time. It *will* be nice to have her so near me. We were to have spent some time in Berlin this winter but we have not been able to do so as Uncle Enrico,

Aunt Anna Reuss'[1] husband died about a month ago, so we stayed on here. We toboggan all day and I read, sew, paint, and am quite happy, except that I wish this dear, beautiful place were in England. It is very lovely here ; sometimes one would like to go and drive to have tea with someone, or ask a neighbour to dinner (it is a bore *always* to have people staying in the house), but there is not a single soul within miles that one can know, or so Hans says !

To-day is Sunday ; O dear God how I wish there was a little comforting church near where Hans and I could go together to pray ; it is dreadful having no inspiring church near, and being at heart of a different religion to one's husband. I shall go to Breslau, I think, next Sunday just to see what it is like ; I believe they have a Protestant service there in English.

February 1, 1897. *Monday*. Fürstenstein.

I heard to-day from Princess Edward of Saxe-Weimar [2] who will later send me some money for my Jubilee subscription [3] ; oh, it *is* an undertaking and it is all in the English papers now as I have started it there too, and have asked English women married to Germans, or any Germans who care to do so, to send their cheques with their names and addresses to the Crédit Lyonnais. The money is to be given to the Institution of Jubilee nurses. It is all my own idea and Freytag, the head Secretary here, and I work all day at it ; I do hope it will be a success ; I have now a hundred and twenty-nine pounds from about sixty ladies.

Dear Hans ; I cried yesterday and told him how I longed to go to Communion and he said, " then go, darling." I wanted to be in Berlin for next Sunday, the 7th, but we have to go to Lulu on the 6th, and, besides, I want to see Dr. Oldhausen again, and it is useless my going for that purpose until the following week.

When the time actually comes I always hate leaving here ; yet I expect St. Moritz will be fun.

---

[1] Countess Anna Hochberg (1839–1916), m. in 1858 Prince Heinrich XII. of Reuss (1829–66) ; 2ndly in 1869, his brother Prince Heinrich XIII. (d. 1897).

[2] D. 1904 ; d. of 5th Duke of Richmond, m. 1851 Field-Marshal Prince Edward of Saxe-Weimar (d. 1902).

[3] The authoress was organizing a Diamond Jubilee presentation to Queen Victoria from Englishwomen resident in Germany.

February 13, 1897. *Saturday*. Fürstenstein.

I am soon going to bed ; I must get up to-morrow at seven ;
we start for Vienna and St. Moritz ; we are both quite miserable at leaving, but now that it has all been settled, rooms
taken and so on, we can think of no excuse for not going.
We tobogganed here to-day, and drove about and said good-
bye in a most melancholy way to the dear old place just as if
we were not going to see it again in a short six weeks. I
can't imagine why everyone always told us it was so horrid
here in the winter. And I shall have to leave my little black
dog and my embroidery behind ; I have finished my " angel
picture " and am sending it to Patsy.

It has been such a delicious sunny day. Poor Tommy is
downstairs writing to Vater ; I draft the letters for him to copy ;
I cannot always pity him—indeed I sometimes feel very, very
angry. I besought him not to reopen this religious question
with his father . . . and now the old man writes and says he
will change his will unless Hans promises to bring up the
children as Protestant (poor little unborn children that have
caused so much bother lately). Hans is furious, but he must
give in, poor boy, as the German law obliges children to be
brought up in the religion of their parents until they are sixteen ; and Hans must remain a Protestant or the properties
go to his next brother Conny. I have persuaded him to
give in ; surely no God would wish him to give up everything,
all his future and position, for religion, when the Protestant
religion is after all very like the Catholic and perhaps, in a way,
purer and grander because of its very simplicity.

I have now two hundred and eighty-three pounds for my
Fund ; I expect I shall get about another two hundred and
fifty to three hundred from subscribers *here* ; the committee of
the Jubilee Nurses' Fund in London are going to work all
they can to help me in England ; it will either be quite a small
affair, comprising Germany only, or else develop into a very
big thing. There are forty thousand Germans in London
alone. I am so excited about it.

I will try to remember to write regularly, my dear diary,
but I do not think I will put in so much about myself in future.
I am just the same as other women (the silly ones I mean) and
my life is probably much the same (I mean my inner life) as
those of the majority. I hope, though, it may be a little
different from the lives of some ; if so, it will not be anything

CASTLE PLESS.
The Principal Staircase.

to my credit, or because of any real goodness in myself ; the real goodness in my heart is for my dear old silly Tommy ; the rest is, I feel, excited imagination. By the way, Tommy *is* going to start working in Breslau with Prince Hatzfeldt on the 1st of April. I hope it is the beginning of a career for him— if only this religious question can be settled. Now good-night, dear diary.

P.S.—Missy, my nice *hofdame*, is going to marry Freytag ! I saw Dr. Oldhausen in Berlin ; he says I am not right inside and that I shall have to see him regularly when I come back to Germany in April. I can't believe I am really leaving here to-morrow. Yet, while I am away the time will pass quickly I expect ; it always does—*too quickly*.

May 5, 1897. Fürstenstein.

I see my last thought was that the time would go too quickly. Well, I have been back nearly three weeks and I was *very* glad to get home after living so long in hotels. St. Moritz was great fun (I beat all the ladies on my high toboggan which I brought with me from here) ; but, afterwards, I caught a cold which lasted weeks. I fought it for a whole fortnight at Cannes and, in the end, had to go to bed with poultices night and day, and a nurse ; it was congestion of the lungs and I was in bed for three weeks.

Little Patsy, who had felt very well at first, got a nerve attack at Cap Martin where we stayed during our last week ; such a heavenly hotel, right on the sea, on the edge of pine woods with lovely walks. The colouring was glorious, the blue of sky and sea, the tinted grey of the rocks, in which each crevice is filled with some little plant—the earth is a bright terra-cotta colour—almost crimson. The pine trees grow down in places right to the edge of the sea ; but where the walks are higher, you look *down* and watch the waves beat against the wall of rocks and the white foam dash up majestically.

I think my two happiest days were when I walked by the sea, once by myself, and once with Patsy. And then, also, the day we sailed on the *Britannia* ; the Prince of Wales was very kind and asked us several times but I was in bed and could not go ; he called to see me once, and Hans, suddenly coming in, was rather surprised to find a man there ; but the Prince laughed and said : " I am only here *en docteur*." The day we sailed on the *Britannia* (she won) Prince Christian of

Denmark [1] was on board ; he is engaged to marry the Grand
Duke of Mecklenburg's daughter ; he is twenty-seven and
looks like nineteen, so much so that, with my usual blundering-
ness I said to him : " I met your eldest brother, [2] Sir, at Sandringham, Princess Maud's husband." He only laughed and
said : " I am the eldest." He is most amusing and very
attractively mad. One day we all went to call on Madame de
Falbe ; at first the gate porter would not let us in—I don't
wonder as we arrived singing, four of us, including Patsy
and Hans, in a fly meant to hold two. The butler, too, looked
extremely surprised, and no wonder as Patsy and I were laughing so much that we couldn't speak. But at last Prince
Christian's patience was exhausted, first to be scowled at by
the porter at the gates and then by the butler ; so he took out
his card and giving it to the butler said : " You needn't be
afraid to announce us ; my grandfather is King of Denmark,
and somewhat of a swell there." It was rather nice he didn't
say : " I shall be King of Denmark." He took off his hat to the
butler, and bowed and smiled up at the window to Madame de
Falbe's nurse who was looking out at us ; he has the wildest
spirits.

The Grand Duke of Mecklenburg-Schwerin's death was
terribly sad ; I went to see him often till just a fortnight
before he died, and then he was too ill ; I cried as if for
someone I loved ; but then he was such an angel, so patient
through all his years of suffering, such a gentleman, so charming
and serene and dignified ; most people loved him and I certainly did. Dr. Rayer from Dresden, whom I knew, was with
him at the last and I wrote a little " message of good-bye " to
read out to the Grand Duke—but it was too late ; before it
arrived he was dead. " Too late " is an answer to so many
questions of the heart ; to so many regretful sighs ; and it is
the bitterest answer of all.

My subscriptions here have not increased ; four hundred
women to whom I wrote have not answered it at all ; it is this
feeling of—one might almost say hatred (to judge by the papers)
which exists between Germany and England ; one or two
women have even written to say that their husbands will not
allow them to send anything. In London the rich Germans have

---

[1] King Christian X., b. 1870, s. 1912 ; m. 1898, Alexandrine, d.
of Friedrich-Franz III. of Mecklenburg-Schwerin.

[2] King Haakon VII. of Norway (Prince Charles of Denmark), b.
1872, elected King, 1905 ; m. 1896, Maud, y. d. of King Edward VII.

already given to the Prince of Wales' Jubilee Fund and, amongst *themselves*, they are going to present the Queen with an address. I fear they will give *nothing* to my fund, although my Executive Committee have had a letter from me about it printed in all the English papers. . . .

We are taking a house this year in London; I can't stand hotels and lodging-houses any more.

May 14, 1897. *Friday*. Fürstenstein.

Dear little Shelagh's birthday, God bless her and give her a long, happy, and prosperous life. It is pouring rain and the day before yesterday we had a real hail and snowstorm, but I see it has been the same in some parts of England. I am afraid it will spoil their " Chester race party " at Ruthin. A wet summer is prophesied. I only hope it won't rain on June the 22nd, the Jubilee Procession day.

I go to London soon now, we have taken 9 Hill Street, an excellent centre, but I am afraid the whole thing will cost a lot of money. We take the team with us and buy another horse there ; Aleck[1] and I are going to try to find one of the same beautiful stamp as *Empress*. Then we shall hire an extra horse for night work ; my hack from India is *en route* ; Shelagh will have her own hack. I *won't* think of the expenses, I am young and we both love fun. I shall make the best of this Season and my house, and it will be so nice having little Shelagh with us ; I should be too shy to go about alone— without her.

My subscription list in London is not succeeding at all ; none of the Germans will give a penny ; I really believe that the ill-feeling against England amongst the middle-class narrow-minded jealous German people living in England is even stronger than it is here in Germany. At any rate I have done what I can and have been working continuously in both countries for the last six months ; I can do no more.

I am to be given the Bavarian Order of St. Theresa in time to wear at the Jubilee ; Nathalie Hatzfeldt has been invited to be present because she was Mistress of the Robes to the Empress Frederick. . . .

I have taught little *Tussie* a lot of tricks, she jumps over *Peter* now, who submits but does not like it, as she occasionally puts her small paw in his eye ; she also jumps through my

---

[1] The English stud groom at Fürstenstein.

hands, and sits up on *Peter's* back. *Lion*, another dog, is a dear little savage and will not even try to learn to be good. I have a lot of letters to write so, dear diary, you must be content with this scrawl. My work is getting on well.

May 21, 1897. Fürstenstein.

On Sunday, May the 23rd, I go to Berlin with Hans, sleep the night there and leave the next morning for London. I shall love to see little Shelagh ; I have not seen her or Poppets for six months, but I shall hate leaving this place ; I always do when the time comes to start. The lilies-of-the-valley are just beginning to come out and I picked the first bit of lilac yesterday. The weather has been very bad, always thundering and raining, everywhere there is flooding and the peasants are miserable as the grain has been washing off the fields, and the young potatoes are rotting.

I arrived in London on the 25th morning and take Shelagh to a ball that night ; I shall feel dreadfully shy and countrified. I feel as if I shall not get any partners. Hans follows me from Breslau in about a fortnight. I have to look out for a horse for his team. I do hope I shall find a suitable one or he will be so disappointed. Two men from Breslau are coming for the night, and the *Landrat* comes to dinner ; goodness knows what I shall talk to them about. Prince Hatzfeldt came last night, and left to-day for a shooting-box near Breslau belonging to Uncle Bolko Hochberg ; the Emperor is to be there. I asked the Prince to be sure and say to the Emperor that Hans is working very hard in Breslau, finds it is very interesting, and so on.

How I wish the sun would shine ; I caught two beautiful trout yesterday ; I go very often to my *Daisysee*, it is something to do when I am alone : Vater gave it that name.

Mr. Moulton and Count Hatzfeldt [1] are coming to see me in London on the 27th about my subscription list, which is in England a failure ; the feeling now between Germany and England can really be called nothing less, I think, than hatred.

They are altering the Schloss-Platz [2] ; when finished it will look lovely.

---

[1] Count Paul von Hatzfeldt (1831–1901), m. Helene Moulton of Paris (1846–1918) ; German Ambassador in London, 1885–1901.

[2] The great open space in front of the Castle of Fürstenstein.

June 9, 1897. Newlands, Hampshire.

We have been here three days, a happy country life after a fortnight's rush of London gaieties. I took little Shelagh out every night ; we leave here to-day in time to be present at the Opera this evening with Prince Christian [1] who comes to dinner ; to-morrow night we go to a play. Hans has not yet said when he is arriving but I expect he will be here soon. We go to Taplow for Ascot to the Savile Crossleys. [2]

I have become quite a bicyclist. It is pouring rain, and looks as if we were in for a wet summer. Dear old Bruin Vivian [3] is here, full of fun and spirits. Oh dear, I do hope Tommy will like the little London house and be happy this season. The Devonshire House fancy ball is the great topic of conversation now. I am going as the Queen of Sheba with two girls and several men in attendance. Now I must get up.

---

[1] Prince Christian of Schleswig-Holstein (1831–1917), m. 1866, Princess Helena of Great Britain (1846–1923), third sister of King Edward VII.

[2] Now Lord and Lady Somerleyton ; Lady Somerleyton was a daughter of Sir Henry de Bathe (d. 1907), 4th Bt.

[3] Honble. Walter Vivian, b. 1856, s. of 2nd Baron Vivian.

CHAPTER FOUR

1902

October 15, 1902. The Castle, Pless.

AGAIN I begin a diary : [1] a waste of time perhaps, yet in years to come it may interest me to remember all that I did and thought (or perhaps not all !) at the age of twenty-nine. I am in the middle of the second phase of my life and alas, I begin to write in a spirit of sadness, with many illusions gone, most of my ideals broken (for I have come to believe that nothing really exists except in one's imagination), and most of the gold has rubbed off the dazzling frames that held but phantom pictures. I am fair and tall ; I look well when I have spent some time in front of my glass with my head-maid Marie near to cheer me with compliments. Some think me lovely, but there is no accounting for taste : my husband, who is playing the piano as I write, says that I am " all that he wants " : such a declaration should be sufficient to satisfy the desire of any good and modest woman : but possibly I am neither good nor modest.

We live in a hectic age. At least I imagine our grand-mothers lived differently in their days : now the functioning of one's body, brains and even beauty, is keyed up to a high pitch of excitement and energy. It is difficult to keep the pendulum of heart and eye and mind synchronized, as it were, with the steady action of one's conscience. . . .

I am perhaps not quite an ordinary woman because I still see the need of fighting and do fight, whereas so many seem to give up the battle and are satisfied to float along upon the tide of existence. I have a great longing to make people happy ; I try to do what is right, and yet it is not with any religious motives that I dream of living with heart and hand

---

[1] The Princess does not appear to have kept a diary between July, 1897, and September, 1902.

full for the poor, the miners and the needy socialists about here : indeed I sometimes fear that my God is one whom no man or woman shall ever see.

I conceive of myself as a bloom sprung from the same tree from which my ancestors and predecessors grew, as did also my baby ; [1] only in my child (please, God, spare him) and in his children shall I live on when I am dead. The *same* flower never blooms twice ; although others may spring from the parent root. Since nothing else in the world, whether animal or vegetable, lasts for ever or rises again after death, why should we who are also of this world's dust, expect an individual life hereafter ? Religion was a power that kept the world clean and orderly before modern enlightenment revealed alternative viewpoints : now education, developing slowly through the years, shows us new aspects of good and bad, and we learn—or should learn—to regulate our moral life as naturally as we learn to think, talk, feel or eat.

I am going to write to the Bishop of St. Asaph [2] and ask him to send me some good books to see if reading them will help to strengthen my faith : sometimes I feel I want only a kind *human* hand to help me and lead me in the right way. Nevertheless, religion is such a rest, and my spirit is so often tired. My little son has been very ill this last week : I prayed, and it was with thankfulness and a sense of great comfort that I rose from my knees ! Thank God he is better.

I have spoken about religion to many men coming straight from the war in South Africa : [3] good, honest, intelligent men, who have themselves been near death and believe in nothing, and shake their heads and say : " We join the dust again, and that is the end of everything." Hans has quite other ideas ; although at heart a Catholic he now accepts unquestioningly the narrow Lutheran faith he has inherited ; he never reads ; he does not even allow himself to think, so on such matters I can never talk with him : and perhaps this is best in the circumstances.

It is now two years since I started to go about among the working people : before that I was always being told it was not " princely " to do so and that if I went it would only mean

---

[1] Hans Heinrich XVII. William Albert Edward (commonly called Prince Hansel of Pless), b. Berlin, February 2, 1900.

[2] Rt. Rev. Alfred George Edwards, D.D., now Archbishop of Wales.

[3] Boer War, 1899-1902.

giving money and help of that sort. True, Vater (my father-in-law) has his own infants' school, a school of cookery for girls, school of handicraft for boys, gives Christmas trees and arranges similar entertainments. But I want to get to the heart of the people and understand them and now, in sheer desperation, I have broken bounds. I order my carriage and go where I choose : alms-houses, hospitals, homes for old people, everywhere. In time, my personal interest in my poorer neighbours will be acceptable and, I hope, helpful. . . .

I have been alone the last few days. Hans has been hunting in Pardubitz. It is good to have a rest after months and months of people, late nights and endless entertainments. It began with the London Season and the Coronation [1] followed by five days in Ostend ; then here to Pless ; house full, dancing, riding, dressing-up and so on for many days and months in succession. My little mother has only just left, she and my darling father were here for three weeks. Shelagh and my brother-in-law, Bend Or,[2] have left for South Africa where they intend to spend a month : their baby girl Ursula [3] is just eight months old. . . .

A few weeks ago the Emperor made Hans a member of the House of Lords or *Herrenhaus*. They say this was conferring a great honour ; for myself, I would rather he had been given the post of first Secretary to the German Embassy in Paris, which Count Bülow [4] promised me for him. Put not your trust in Princes—especially if they happen to be Chancellors, say I.

Hans is very anxious to have, some day, the Embassy in Vienna ; they would all like it *there* : but Berlin I suppose think us too young to be given it now, Hans being forty-one : he said to-night : " the best way to get what we want is for me to make a rumpus in the House of Lords, or for you to

---

[1] Of King Edward VII., at Westminster Abbey, London, June 9, 1902.

[2] Hugh Lupus, 2nd Duke of Westminster, and his first wife Constance (Shelagh) Duchess of Westminster, sister of the authoress, whom he married in Feb., 1901. The marriage was dissolved. The Duke is known to his family and intimates as Bend Or.

[3] Lady Ursula Grosvenor, b. 1902, m. in 1924 William Filmer-Sankey, late 1st Life Guards.

[4] Bernard Prince (cr. 1905) von Bülow, Imperial Chancellor, 1900–9.

make the Crown Prince [1] fall in love with you ; that will make them anxious to get us out of the country ! " I do not see either of these schemes a success. The Crown Prince has a very careful and jealous mama ; and Hans, I am afraid, could not make the requisite rumpus to save his life.

I wrote nearly a year ago to Prince Lichnowsky [2] to ask his advice about the matter of the Paris Embassy and copy here bits from his friendly reply.

GÖRLSDORF, POMERANIA, PRUSSIA. 25. 12. 1901.

DEAREST PRINCESS DAISY,—

I was so glad to hear from you after not having seen you for ages. Why did not you let me know when you came to Berlin ? I should have been delighted to see you ! There would have been a general outcry of joy from all the family if they had seen you walk in ! So let me know when you come again and let's have a cheery party. . . .

I am so sorry poor old Hans is not getting on so well as he ought to ! Speaking to you as a real friend I advise you not to do anything about his diplomatic ambitions just now, nor to trouble yourself about making him work at the Foreign Office. That is by no means necessary. Let the poor boy get well first and then speak to your father-in-law about it and make him speak to Count Bülow. Besides, Paris is not free, and Hans is not well.

Let me know when you come to town and we shall talk it over, but don't frighten poor Hans with the idea of having to go and work in an office.

Perhaps it will cheer him up to come and spend some weeks in Berlin and to have some fun there.

I have been busy working and shooting at home for some weeks now. This coming into property gives me a lot to do. . . .

Marie sends her love and so does Redern with whom I am spending Christmas.

---

[1] Wilhelm, Crown Prince of Prussia, b. 1882 ; m. 1905, Duchess Cecile of Mecklenburg-Schwerin.

[2] Charles Max 6th Prince (1860–1928), m. 1904, Countess Mechtilde von Arco-Zinneberg ; German Ambassador to the Court of St. James, 1912–14. His sister Marie married Count Wilhelm von Redern and lived at Görlsdorf. The writer succeeded his father in October, 1901 : the letter cited was written in English.

Now good-bye, fair and fairy princess, and believe me,
Your great admirer,

LICHNOWSKY.

October 16, 1902. Fürstenstein.

Just washed baby and put him to bed ; he fell asleep in my
arms ; having been out all day he was very tired. I went
down this afternoon to the *Daisysee* with Hans, he in a very
good temper ; I caught three trout with a fly. Hans is funny ;
little things invariably amuse him, big things often bore him,
for he is too lazy to think. Yesterday we walked to the
Riesengrab and I talked to him of the hospitals and the poor
people. It was lovely standing there, all the woods clothed in
glorious autumn tints : but it made me feel lonesome, and long
for someone who would be a help to me ; someone to lean
upon. I turned to look at my husband and there he was
digging in the ground to make a little ditch and let the water
fall down over the rock ; he was delighted, and I felt as if I
had two babies to look after instead of one.

October 18, 1902. The Castle, Pless.

We came here yesterday . . . The Crown Prince arrived
at one-thirty.[1] . . . We danced this evening ; there is no
one here but a few of our relations, and some young boys that
were, or are now, with the Crown Prince at the University of
Bonn.

After tea I sang, and the Crown Prince and the youngest
Prince Ratibor, Hans, played the violin ; some songs went quite
well. They are pleased I am here—and I know I do bring a
little life into a party. Yet, if they only knew how I long to
hide and be alone ! But it is nice to see the friendly way in
which dear Vater and Mathilde look at me. They are very
dear to me, and it is a good thing that I get on so well with
them all. I do hope I shall sleep well to-night ; I want it.
These last two nights I was kept awake trying to think out some
way of raising money to have the river [2] round Waldenburg
cleansed.

---

[1] See *Daisy Princess of Pless*, p. 89.
[2] The Hellabach, which was then in a filthy condition : see *Daisy Princess of Pless*, pp. 97, 98, 106.

October 19, 1902. Pless.

. . . we danced and played games again after dinner. . . .
During the evening the Crown Prince grabbed at a bit of chiffon
that I accidentally tore off my frock ; I pretended not to see ;
he crumpled it up in his hand ; I wondered how he would
manage in dancing the Lancers as he had to give one hand
to Mathilde and one to myself ; at last he pulled his handkerchief out of his sleeve, stuffed the chiffon into it and put it back
again. Now why did he do this ? What it is to be young !
Everything here is very well done ; crowds of servants
in gorgeous liveries. I am at last becoming accustomed to
having a red and gold servant escort me upstairs and throw
open the door of my bedroom for me ; but in the old days I
hated it and I used to sneak away, to think, be alone, or watch
for the post with a hard dry throat. How I detested the
servants everlastingly following me about and opening the
doors. . . . Vater is very well ; he is a dear. . . .

October 22, 1902 : *midnight*. Fürstenstein.

A large house party. Very tired, just come upstairs. We
have danced each night and played cards ; but as Mathilde
and Vater do not dance or play cards I thought it best to
order the band for to-night. Everyone arrived yesterday ;
the party consists of my father and mother-in-law ; Prince
and Princess Hatzfeldt ; Count and Countess Czenin—she
was a Kinsky ; [1] the little weeny Duke of Ratibor [2] without his
nice great fat wife ; Count and Countess Trauttmansdorff ; [3]
Count and Countess Sierstorpff ; Princess Ninie Hohenlohe-
Langenburg ; [4] Oscar Herren ; Count Vico Voss. I think that
is all ; a nice party, but I long for them all to leave so that
I can be alone with my precious baby before I go to Pardubitz.
And somehow, having had the house full ever since the end of
August, I am now tired of people.
We shot to-day and got excellent bags ; Hans is quite

---

[1] Countess Marie-Clotilde, 3rd d. of 7th Prince Kinsky, b. 1878 ;
m. 1897, Ottokar Count Czernin von Chudenitz, who was Austro-
Hungarian Foreign Minister, Dec., 1916–April, 1918.

[2] Victor 2nd Duke (1847–1923), m. 1887, Countess Marie Breunner-
Enkevoirth.

[3] Ferdinand Hereditary Count Trauttmansdorff-Weinsberg, b.
1871; m. 1895, Marie, d. of Prince Charles of Schwarzenberg.

[4] Princess Gottfried Hohenlohe-Langenburg (Ninie), d. of Count
of Schönborn-Bucheim, b. 1865, m. 1890.

pleased as this is only the third season we have shot here, and as it goes on, the shooting will be better every year.

I wore mauve orchids to-night with a blue dress ; Count Voss has given me a lovely Venetian vase with life-size orchids *en relief* : I wonder how thick this book will grow before the vase is broken, it is so fragile ; eighteen were made, and perished in the furnace, before this one came out whole. Life, too, works that way. To produce one perfect man or woman millions must suffer and be broken.

Of the people here what shall I say ? Prince Hatzfeldt is the Lord-Lieutenant of Silesia, a frivolous, middle-aged man ; says he is forty-five, looks sixty, and tries to flirt with all the women. Count Sturm Sierstorpff is a loud fat German and a snob, delighted if he can be on " thou " terms with a Prince : his wife is an American, longs for social success and copies all I wear : the Czernins are young, married for love with nothing to keep it on—five years of this has made them a little disappointed : they misunderstand each other : I can see it and it makes me sorry. Ratibor lives for shooting, and *on* his title and the knowledge that his wife is a far-distant relation to the Empress, having been born a Holstein. . . .

October 24, 1902. Fürstenstein.

Everyone left this morning except Oscar Herren : he goes to-morrow. We had to pretend he was leaving to-day at two-thirty or they might have been shocked at the idea of my being left alone several hours with a young man ! Hans of course knew. The shooting yesterday was quite good, and a lovely day. The Crown Prince sent me a postcard this morning signed " Yours for ever " ! I shall write him a nice quiet sensible letter telling him not to do such things.

October 26, 1902. Fürstenstein.

Baby much better ; I drove him myself in the carriage to the station to see Oscar off, and then we came home and both painted little water-colour pictures. On the way back I stopped in the town to talk to some Sisters at a hospital and promised to send them wine and Salzbrunn water. Received a charming little book from Captain Banbury [1] called *From Flower to Flower*. I shall take it to bed with me now, but

---

[1] Charles William, b. 1877, e. s. of Sir Frederick Banbury (Lord Banbury 1924), killed in action, Sept., 1914.

CASTLE PLESS.
Corner of the Large Dining-room.

as I wrote him, it makes me sad ; everything does ; only, no one would think this of me. But there is a difference between being unhappy and being sad ; for sometimes the very happiness one feels in the warmth and light of the sun or in joyous surroundings makes sharper life's unavoidable darts of sudden sadness ; it is perhaps the loneliness of the soul, the groping in the dark for something steadfast and firm to lay one's hand upon. If only Hans would let me lean more on him : he loves me rather as one would a picture on a wall or a decorative piece of furniture in a room.

October 27, 1902 : *midnight.* Fürstenstein.

Have been writing letters since nine-thirty. Missy dined with me. This evening I read through some of my old diaries, parts of which I will copy down here one day before destroying them ; a good deal of the contents is about how many men have been in love with me, what they said to me, and the various degrees of feeling they aroused in me—generally ending in pity : it is almost the same now, I think. Sometimes I pity myself a little : once I did so far too much.

Hans comes back to-morrow ; I am longing to see him and to hear what he has to say about the telegram from the Foreign Office in Berlin requesting him on behalf of the Emperor to represent Germany at the opening of the German Chamber of Commerce in New York. I suppose it is a great honour, but I am afraid the poor old boy will be sorry to leave his hunting in Pardubitz, seeing that last year he was ill and could not hunt and that later, in December, it is nearly always too hard to ride : so again this year he will have had very little hunting. I shall not at all like to be left alone here without him for a month.

I have just written to the Crown Prince a letter full of home truth ; I wonder if he will feel very cross and hurt. I will copy it in here to-morrow.[1] Good-night. Baby very well and happy to-day.

October 31, 1902. Fürstenstein.

Four quiet peaceful days ; beautiful weather except to-day, which was rainy and misty. I did not go out but sat throughout the afternoon looking over accounts with Freytag. A *horrible* task. I shall write to Vater and tell him that instead

---

[1] *Daisy Princess of Pless*, pp. 91–2.

of a Christmas present I should prefer some money to go towards a big Christmas tree and " tea " here in the riding-school for all the poorest children from the villages around, as I really have not a spare penny. So many begging letters, so many things to buy for the poor at Christmas. And then what must the precious Baby do but go and *eat* his shoes !

Hans came back quite happy from Pardubitz, bringing with him Prince Miguel of Braganza.[1] I was furious at first as I wanted to be alone with Hans the one day we have before he leaves. But I went to meet him at the station (the Prince came by road in his motor-car). Next day I took my old Tommy to the station and saw him off : I felt quite inclined to cry, for somehow America is far away, and I feel rather as if I were left alone in Germany. I heard from him this evening from Berlin. This is his letter :

" MY DARLING LITTLE DANY [2] WIFE,—

" I had a very busy day, luncheon at the Castle ; dinner at seven at Richtoven's [3] with the Emperor, Bülow, our Ambassador at Washington, and lots of others. The Emperor was very nice and rather pleased that I have accepted the offer to go to New York. . . . The Americans hoped they would get Prince Henry.[4] France and England will be represented by their respective Ambassadors. Bülow talked a lot of rot as usual, said he did not understand why you did not go with me, and asked me at least a dozen times not to forget to tell you that he said so. . . ."

Yesterday I went over the Miners' Hospital : it took a long time : I gave them books and cigars. Then I went to see Ritter about the river, and Schultz, the Director of the Mines, about organizing some Christmas trees and fêtes, and came home almost dead. S. the nurse is furious because I have taken Baby to sleep in my room : I wonder what nurses imagine mothers are made of. The letter I wrote to the Crown Prince he has not answered, so I am afraid his little feelings are hurt ; but he will get over it !

---

[1] Prince of Portugal, b. 1853 ; m. 1st, a Princess of Thurn and Taxis, and 2nd, in 1893, a Princess Löwenstein-Wertheim-Rosenberg.

[2] The Prince's favourite pet name for his wife.

[3] Baron von, Secretary of State for Foreign Affairs, 1901–5.

[4] Prince Henry of Prussia (1862–1929), only brother of the Emperor William II.

November 13, 1902 ; 11 *p.m.* Fürstenstein.

I came home yesterday after being away eleven days from my precious baby : now he sleeps again in my room ; last night when he called me back to say he wanted his bed moved into " Mummilie's room " and that I wasn't to go away again, I felt that this one little expression of love was worth all the world to me and nothing but he mattered in the whole universe.

Coming home in the train Z., who travelled half-way with me, made me unhappy and almost angry and tired of his love ; and yet I wish now I had kept his letter received to-day, and all the others written during the five years I have known him, for they were perfect examples of devotion. At last he has made up his mind he cannot live like this and he will take his pleasure in Vienna. He will probably live with some woman—possibly even a lady I may know. But this has nothing to do with me ; I did not question him about it, nor do I care more for him because I know that he has been leading almost a saintly life all these years : sometimes I have let him kiss me on the forehead on what he calls " *die Wolle.*" I can't help smiling to myself when I happen to be wearing two false curls : it is not even " my " hair that he is kissing.

I saw Consuelo Marlborough [1] in Vienna and her two dear little boys.[2] . . . She is looking very well and I think fascinatingly pretty, with her funny little turned-up nose and big brown eyes. She had made friends with Z., before I arrived. And her first words to me were : " Of course, Daisy, you know Prince Z. ? I have been saying to myself that I knew you would come and take him away from me." I replied : " You dear little silly, you can't take away in five days a man who has been a loyal faithful friend to me for more than five years." As a matter of fact I had sent him ahead of me from Pardubitz to Vienna to take care of her ; she leaves to-morrow for England, and from there goes to India for the Durbar.

When I left home I went direct to Pardubitz for two hunts ; then stayed the night in Vienna and left the next morning for Keszthely [3] in Hungary where I arrived the same evening

---

[1] D. of W. K. Vanderbilt of New York, m. 1895, the 9th Duke of Marlborough ; obtained a divorce in 1920 ; in 1921 m. Colonel Jacques Balsan, C.M.G.

[2] The Marquess of Blandford and Lord Ivor Spencer Churchill.

[3] Residence of Count (cr. Prince 1911) Festetics de Tolna, who m. in 1880 Lady Mary Hamilton (1850–1922), d. of 11th Duke of Hamilton.

and stayed two nights; then to Pardubitz again for three nights, and then back here, so it was all rather a rush, and I am *very* glad to be home again.

November 20, 1902. Fürstenstein.

Last Monday, the 18th, I went to Trachenberg [1] to the Hatzfeldts for a day's shooting. I did not at all want to go, but thought it was my duty. They all seemed very pleased to see me.

I often wonder if I am living in a fool's paradise built only of the affectionate words so many people use about me, instead of on solid friendship; and I sometimes wonder how they can give me credit for thought or brains considering all the stories that get abroad about me, and the strange things I am supposed to have done and said. People call me " the sun "; one man calls me " Sunshine "; Bertier, that horrid little French artist, has painted me as *Dawn*. When I met the party in the hall at Trachenberg after my arrival they all exclaimed, " Here is the sun! " At Keszthely, little Castellane [2] said : " *Elle est comme un rayon du soleil.*" That is how people who like me speak of and to me; others, who have nothing particularly nasty to say, content themselves with " She is a baby," which, I suppose, means in their eyes a thoughtless piece of frivolity. But if I talked to them of my thoughts, my endeavours, my ambitions, my sadnesses, would they care or understand ? Not they. " Laugh and the world laughs with you; weep and you weep alone." Trite, but true.

Hans left New York yesterday and will arrive in Berlin on the 27th. I do not know what to do as on that date we are expected at Primkenau to meet the Archduke Franz Ferdinand and his morganatic wife, the Duchess of Hohenberg, and, if the Emperor is in Berlin, he may want to see Hans at once. I have no means of letting Hans know as he is now on the sea. I thought of writing to Count Eulenburg [3]

---

[1] The seat of Hermann, Prince Hatzfeldt, a famous old castle in which the convention between Prussia and Russia against Napoleon was signed in 1813 : the town of Trachenberg is in the centre of the huge forest and lake district of Eastern Prussia.

[2] Count Jean de Castellane, m. in 1898 Dorothea, d. of 3rd Duke of Talleyrand and Sagan and widow of Hereditary Prince of Fürstenberg (1852–96).

[3] August Count zu Eulenburg (1838–1921), Comptroller of the Imperial Household ; m. 1864, Hedda von Witzleben (1843–1928).

to ask him to tell the Emperor, who is now in England.[1] If we cannot go to Primkenau I ought to write to Duke Ernst Günther at once.

I ordered from Hatchard's Conan Doyle's book on the Boer War for the Crown Prince as I found I had not got it here ; they now write that they sent the book and *it was returned*. I shall wire to the Crown Prince and ask him if he did this ; but of course it must be one of those charming aides-de-camp that is to blame. When I see the Emperor I shall tell him, as I consider it most rude. . . .

My visit to Hungary was very pleasant, only I was frightened all through the first night by strange sounds of moaning, and the second night I had Marie my maid to sleep in the bed next to mine : she heard moaning too. The other day Z. said, " The last night at Keszthely I could not sleep ; someone was crying all night." It is a beautiful new house built on to by the present owner, Count Festetics. His wife is half English : her mother was a Grand Duchess of Baden who, when her first husband died, married the Duke of Hamilton : their daughter, Mary, first married the Prince of Monaco ; this marriage, not being a success, was annulled ; the Prince married again—a New-Orleans Jewess [2] who is now separated from him and living in London. Mary married Count Festetics.

As I wanted to get to Vienna in time for dinner and the Opera I left Keszthely at nine in the morning in Count Hoyos' motor-car. They said it was taking a risk as the motor was out of order, but I thought it would be fun, and I should be able to see the country. The roads in some places were no better than ploughed fields, but the villages were most picturesque ; clean, white, thatched cottages, with little verandahs. From the roofs hung heavy strings of yellow Indian corn, pumpkins and onions, which gave a pretty dash of colour. I saw no peasants in native costumes ; they wore the ordinary short petticoats, loose jacket, and a coloured shawl over the head.

We lunched at the best restaurant in Steinamanger,[3] a

---

[1] William II. arrived in England on November 8, and joined King Edward's 61st birthday party at Sandringham.

[2] Alice (*née* Heine) (1858–1925) Duchesse de Richelieu, m. 1889, Albert I., Prince of Monaco.

[3] Some 80 miles south of Vienna.

good-sized garrison town : the place was filthy and the waiters looked like greasy black beetles. The room was full of Jews and dirty people. At one table sat three women with white powdered faces and thick hair drawn low over their ears, dirty fingers with rings, and soiled silk skirts. I think they were actresses or ladies of pleasure—a sad, ironic title to give these poor women !

I had a letter and a postcard from the Crown Prince : so he has forgiven me my " sermon by post."

November 26, 1902. Fürstenstein.

In a few hours I start for Berlin to meet Hans. How quickly the time has passed and *how* nice it is to feel he will soon be home, bless him.

To-morrow we lunch at the Palace with the Emperor : I rather hope that the Empress will not be there, as her presence always makes these stiff " festive boards " even more frigid : somehow I must laugh at the picture I make in my mind when I think of these words of the Crown Prince : " My mother is always in a fever if I or my father go to England." I can see her (surrounded by her six sons) in a black frock with a large waist. (When the Emperor is away she probably " lets herself go.") Besides, she must have an extra supply of breath to enable her to gasp at her fantastic notions of all the horrible temptations that her husband and son have to resist in the dangerous little island : poor dear, she looks more like the Emperor's mother than his wife.

I wired to the Crown Prince to ask if he knew that Conan Doyle's book on the Boer War had been returned, and he answered :

" I am so sorry you having had so much trouble with the book all for my sake : had no idea of it all. I should be ever so much thankful if you sent it to me. With best love.

" WILHELM."

Z. has gone ; it was with difficulty I got him to go at last. Certainly women have more courage and pride than men. He cried and went on his knees swearing eternal devotion all his life, even if he married. I could scarcely even feel even pity for him, and all I could think of saying was : " Do get up ; someone will come in ; you know I have always been your friend and always will be, but honestly I can have no other feeling but friendliness for you." Then he got furious and said I was cruel, and I replied : " Truth may be cruel, but it is always the best, and it would be the guiding star in our lives if only we could keep it always in sight." But . . . I forgot this book was to contain no " love passages " ; but then, it will not be truthful, as so many people love me. However, I must not say too much.

Missy and Marie [1] have been turning tables. I kept one hand on and wrote with the other. The results were extraordinary, as they have never tried it before : for Missy it goes at once, even when she alone has her hands on. It spelt out at different times : " Love God " ; " You will have luck " ; " Be careful " ; I asked, " Of what ? "—" Of man." I asked, " Why ? " " For your own sake," was the answer. Then it said, " Hans is well ; Fritz is ill," and spelt its name, " Gordy." Said it regretted nothing and was quite happy.

Last night we tried table-rapping again. I asked : " Who are you ? " And it spelled, " A friend who loves you." I said : " But am I not too wicked for you to love ? " Then came, " NO " very loud. Afterwards Missy " laid the cards " for me. I never knew she could do this ; it was extraordinary what she said. I wrote it down to see if anything should come true. I am to get two presents ; Hans is surrounded with good luck ; a great surprise is coming that will almost take our breath away ; the Emperor has our interest at heart, but men who are round him are trying to prevent any fortunate result ; jealousy is near Hans and me ; and so on.

Precious Baby has a cold, and now the secretary has just come to tell me of another case of diphtheria : one of the footmen's children. Baby must not go out anywhere now, or if he does it must be far away from where other children are, and besides I trust God to keep him safe ; but I hate to leave him, and when his father comes home the little boy cannot sleep any longer in my room, as I don't think I could persuade Tommy to let us sit up and play together and eat bread and butter and drink milk at half-past six in the morning.

December 11, 1902. Fürstenstein.

What a long time it is since I wrote, but very stupidly I always forget to take my diary with me when I am away from home. I arrived in Berlin in the evening (on November 26th),

---

[1] The Princess's head ladies'-maid.

very anxious lest Hans should have got there before me ; I wanted to be at the station to meet him, but at the Wilhelm-strasse [1] found a telegram saying that the boat was late, and he could arrive only the next morning.

Prince Salm [2] took me to the Bristol for dinner ; his wife gets a baby in February. His grandmother was English, and he is really extraordinarily English. Somehow he does not strike one as being deeply in love with his wife and I therefore told him that I hoped he was going to make a good and kind husband ; for he seemed so pleased at dinner, like a boy with a half-holiday from school.

I was asleep when Hans arrived the next day, very tired, poor darling, and rather liverish after seven days' very bad passage : I wanted him to take me in his arms and be very dear to me, but—he was just as usual ; he might never have been away at all. He found all my clothes wrong and grumbled at everything, and, as hundreds of times before, I was again disappointed. Although I realize that he was very, very pleased to see me and really loves me immensely, though more as a useful friend—I know he could not do without me —it all leaves me lonely and sad and feeling old.

At one o'clock we lunched at the Palace : the Emperor and Empress were both so very nice. I sat next to the Emperor, who spoke English to me.

The next day we went to Potsdam to lunch with Prince Salm and the Archduchess, his wife ; a niece of Queen Christina of Spain, she is not exactly pretty but very amiable, and I should think a dear good little thing. How is it men never seem to fall in desperate love with that type of woman ? After lunch I went skating with the Prince and then went home alone by train. The next morning we came here.

On the 1st December we went to Primkenau to the Duke and Duchess of Schleswig-Holstein to meet the Archduke Franz Ferdinand and his wife, the Duchess of Hohenberg, whom I knew well as Sophy Chotek before her marriage. She was very affable, not a bit changed, and gave herself no airs, although some people say that when he is Emperor he can make her Empress if he likes. I can scarcely believe this

---

[1] Palast Pless, Wilhelmstrasse, Berlin : designed by the French architect Destailleurs, in the style of the period of Louis XIII.

[2] Emmanuel (1871–1916), e. s. of 7th Prince Salm-Salm ; m. 1902, the Archduchess Christa, d. of the Archduke Frederick.

would be possible, but time will show ; and in many ways, and in many places, many strange things will happen.

The Archduke was very nice, fat and quiet (so different from the German Emperor). I should judge him as a weak though very obstinate man, and not overtruthful, but I suppose in a position like his, " Truth must be distributed with strict economy."

The Duchess Ernst Günther was as tiresome as usual ! I really don't think she is quite right in her head, although she is a little better than she used to be. Everyone wrote their name in my book and I wanted her to write hers on the same page as the Archduke and her husband, but nothing would induce her. She said she would spoil the page, that she wrote too badly, and that she would write on the other page. I put the pen in her hand several times, but still she wouldn't, so at last I got cross and said : " You are like a naughty child, Madame, and for that you are really too old." And in front of everyone I gave the book ostentatiously to a servant and said aloud : " Her Royal Highness does not wish to write ; please give my maid this book to pack." She then looked a little surprised !

We came back with the Archduke in his special carriage as far as Breslau, and talked about India and shooting. I hope both he and the German Emperor will come to Fürstenstein in June ; I should be delighted. The German Emperor has not been here yet and I know it would make him angry if the Archduke comes first, as they are so jealous of one another ! Z. put this idea into my head. I said to the Emperor the other day in Berlin at lunch :

" I shall not ask Your Majesty any more, you have refused too often."

We were going to Trachenberg to meet him, but alas, he did not go as he got a bad eye and could not shoot. At lunch the other day his last words to me were : " We shall meet at Trachenberg." I had tried over some songs that I knew he would like, and I had got a new shooting dress ; but it serves me right for being such an idiot. I think he is much fussed about this Tariff Bill ; [1] he told Z. that if it were not passed he would dissolve Parliament. We shall see.

---

[1] The Tariff question was a burning one in Germany between 1900–2 : the inherent rivalry between urban and agricultural interests was complicated by a feeling of the rivalry of British interests. Con-

All the people, and some of the papers, talk of Hans as the new German Ambassador to Washington. I should like it very much.

Ever since we came back the house has been full of people for shooting. The first party was on the 4th, consisting of : Prince Joachim Albrecht, a second-cousin of the Emperor, who brought his violoncello, as well as a gentleman-in-waiting with long teeth ; Prince Miguel of Braganza, Prince Salm, Prince Gottfried Hohenlohe, Count Voss, Count Colloredo-Mannsfeld, Count and Countess Engelbert Fürstenberg, the Princess of Taxis,[1] Lily Kinsky,[2] and her brother Count Metternich.[3] We danced after dinner and played cards. The visiting ladies only joined the shooters for lunch, but I did so earlier : a few of the men returned after lunch to toboggan with us down the *Schweizerei* Hill. Some of the party left ; then Count and Countess Asseburg [4] came on the 9th, also Wimperl Schönborn, Count Adda Sierstorpff, Count Czernin, and Adam Wüthenau.[5]

It was lovely weather all the time our guests were here, the first days only being very cold, generally twenty to eighteen degrees below zero. One night we all went out tobogganing after dinner ; a full moon, no wind, and every tree and twig covered with hoar frost. I had Chinese lanterns hung on the trees all the way down the toboggan run, and as a surprise, had coloured Bengal lights lit at the ends of the avenues and against the sides of the hill. The whole place glowed red and then melted away to pale blue and green ; it was quite beautiful and some of us felt like crying ; and I longed to hug somebody, but the longing ended in a sigh.

Really it was a mad night : each of my five Arab ponies drew two people in a sleigh, flying over the snow. We went

---

stitutionally the Emperor could, with the approval of the Federal Council, conclude commercial treaties without the consent of Parliament.

[1] Archduchess Marguerite (d. of Archduke Joseph), b. 1870 ; m. 1890, 8th Prince of Thurn and Taxis.

[2] Countess Elizabeth von Wolff-Metternich zur Gracht, m. 1895, Charles, 8th Prince Kinsky ; she d. in 1909, the Prince in 1919.

[3] A nephew of Count Paul Wolff-Metternich (who was German Ambassador in London, 1901–12).

[4] Egbert Count von der Asseburg, m. 1879, Countess Marie-Agnèse Solms-Baruth (sister of the 2nd Prince).

[5] Karl Adam, 2nd Count von Wüthenau-Hohenthurm, b. 1863 ; m. 1893, Countess Antoinette, d. of Count Bohuslaw Chotek.

CASTLE PLESS.
My Sitting-room.

to the *Riesengrab* to look at the Castle from the other side of the valley ; by moonlight it looked, somehow, huge, and so far away, but I saw a comforting light in Baby's window. Then we started off over the fields for the *Alteburg* [1] or Old Castle, while the ponies kicked up the snow into our faces. As we arrived dogs barked. We rang the bell and nobody came. Two of the men, against my wishes, burst open the gate ; what I really feared was that the dogs inside might be loose and spring upon us, but one proved to be a little black crooked-legged thing that only wagged his tail, while the other, a big dog, growled and slunk back into his kennel. We made so much noise that the caretaker in his nightgown at last opened the window and put his head out. I told him it was only I and that he need not be afraid ; he did not seem in the least surprised, brought a lamp and carried it in front of us upstairs. Then somebody else took it and we went all through the ghostly-looking rooms. When we came into the Chapel someone blew it out and we were left in the moonlight that shone through the windows. I was really frightened ; I could not help it, so I caught hold of the largest man there and hurried out.

Now Hans and I are alone for a few days before we leave to spend Christmas at Pless. I have so much to do, cards and presents to send off here and to England, besides one, or even two, Christmas feasts each day for the poor people and children : this year Hans accompanies me when I visit them —for the first time in his life !

Yesterday we went to Waldenburg, and two hundred children and five hundred old people got hot chocolate and presents. The clergyman said a few words, some Christmas songs were sung, and then I walked round and gave each person a shawl, petticoat, stockings or something. They all kissed my hand and blessed me, and it made me so happy that I feel I would like to do nothing but this all my life, and if only I had more money I would do lots more, but we *always* spend more than we have : the gardens and stables are enormously expensive !

Last year at these Christmas feasts the old people were kept *standing* for over three hours, and they had walked all the way there, and had to walk back and were given nothing to

---

[1] The *Alteburg*, a modern imitation of a mediæval castle, is built on the site of a much earlier structure ; it contains some interesting old armour, etc.

eat or drink ! I was furious ; one old woman fainted. Now everything is done my way, as generally happens in the end ; but then I know I really am quite sensible sometimes. My greatest fault is that I cannot wait ; I always want everything done right at once.

December 26, 1902. Palast Pless, Berlin.

Christmas at Pless was very pleasant ; they all worship Baby, and my dear old father-in-law *does* love me, so it is really touching, and I am sincerely fond of him. They printed some complimentary verses about me in the Freiburg paper, a copy of which Missy my *hofdame* sent me. I did work hard this Christmas. In seven days I shook hands with four thousand people, including children, and gave each one a present. The big salon at Pless looked lovely lit up for a fête for three hundred children on the last day, with three big Christmas trees by the windows ; the children were delighted. Then Hans and I had tea with the clergymen and their wives and the schoolmasters, and I gave each a photograph of Hansel which seemed to please them.

At one of the entertainments, to which both Duke Ernst Günther and Hans accompanied me, I made a little speech. I kept the notes in my hand, but truly I spoke from my heart, for I love all the old people and I really think they love me ; anyway, never in the past at Pless or Fürstenstein have they had such a Christmas.

At this gathering where I spoke, which took place at Salzbrunn, the parson was shaking with emotion at the thought that the Emperor's brother-in-law should be there too. When we arrived he came forward to the side of the carriage to receive us, and fell flat on his back with his legs in the wheels ; I was frightened lest the horses should move, but when he got safely up I had to laugh ; it was so funny to be listening to a shy man trying to stammer out a speech of welcome and then to see him, top-hat, white gloves, tail coat and all, disappear under the carriage.

The Duke asked an old woman what work her husband did and how many children she had. It was a bad shot, for she answered that she had never bothered herself with a husband at all and had only three children.

Then Missy came to me and said : " The woman behind you in the blue dress is the one whose husband has just had to be put in the lunatic asylum ; say something to her, it will please her." So, later, I turned and in my best German said : " I am so sorry that, particularly just at Christmas too, your husband should be taken so ill in the head, and you have to bear all this trouble alone." And I looked earnestly into her face and pressed her arm, only to be met by a vacant stare of surprise and the words : " Oh, high Princess, you make a mistake ; my husband is not mad for I have none." For the moment I felt quite angry that she wasn't the right woman and went furiously to Missy and asked her why she had shown me the wrong person. Of course she said she hadn't ; I said she had ! Then she *did* show me the right one, and wanted me to go and speak to her, but I really couldn't go again and say kind words about a lunatic husband all over again !

I stayed in bed here all to-day and shall do the same to-morrow, so as to have a rest before I go to England ; for there it means acting, and rushing about all the time ; then back to Berlin for the Drawing-Rooms, Court Balls, and usual functions. Then another visit to England, a visit in February to the Dudleys [1] in Ireland, then perhaps Cannes ; April in Paris, and so on. Oh, what a life ! In May I shall take a rest cure, stay in bed three weeks, eat very little, think of nothing, and do nothing. If I do not " pull up " soon my nerves will go.

December 30, 1902. Newlands, Hampshire.

I got the night train to Flushing, Baby sleeping in my reserved carriage ; about every three hours he called me to tell him stories about bulls, camels, peacocks and lambs, and I had to climb down off my top bed and sit in a footsack in my nightgown and do as he asked. . . .

I left London by the two o'clock train for Newlands with Robin [2] and dear Bruin who is so bright and well. We all three gave our opinion on what is called love ; my thoughts were far away as I looked out of the window of the railway carriage ; I wanted to describe a vision I had seen as through

---

[1] 2nd Earl of Dudley, Lord-Lieutenant of Ireland, 1902–6 ; m. 1st, Miss Rachael Gurney, who died tragically in 1920 ; 2nd, 1924, Gertrude, widow of Lionel Monckton.

[2] Sir Robert (Robin) George Vivian Duff, 2nd Life Guards (1876–1914), 2nd Bt. (s. 1914).

a mist, but they would not have understood it, so I said very little : as for myself, I could not *really* love anyone unless I felt that his influence over me was for good and that my love for him would increase by the spiritual help he would give me, inspiring both heart and soul.

It seems strange to be here somehow in the home that I love so, and only a very little while ago I was at Pless and Berlin. I seem to have to live two distinct lives, and to have a double mind, heart, and imagination ; however, now, with Baby, my whole life has changed.

Little Aunt Min Wyndham is here, a pattern of sweetness and patient content ; she joins her husband Guy [1] in Africa in February. Patsy and her sister are really very different from one another ; but Shelagh and I are also very different.

December 31, 1902. Newlands.

A happy cheerful evening. Patsy, a grandmother, Hans and Bruin both a good deal over thirty-nine, Poppets sixty-seven, and all dancing and playing as if they were sixteen ; Poppets, the oldest, looking about forty-five : it is a more wholesome way of passing an evening than losing money at bridge. Robin had to go, but two more men arrive to-morrow to shoot. Baby came over early this morning and spent nearly the whole day with me without his nurse, and was so good and full of fun.

Hans arrived at five o'clock and we drove straight to Efford to Tommy [2] and Ethel Peacocke (where Baby is staying because this house is full of guests) : Hans is well and cheery and has just been up to see me ; I am writing in bed and he is coming up again in a moment with " two drinks " so that we can toast together the New Year, as he put it. It is nice of him to think of this. I always look upon the last day of the old year and the first of the new as very serious—almost holy —days ; there is so much to be thankful for ; much to regret perhaps, and many reasons for praying on one's knees to God for forgiveness.

And the New Year, just as one hears the clock strike twelve,

---

[1] Colonel **Guy Wyndham**, C.B., late 16th Lancers, of Clouds, Wiltshire, b. of Rt. Hon. George Wyndham.

[2] Thomas Warren Peacocke, Rifle Brigade ; his brother, Warren William Peacocke of Efford Park, Hampshire (d. 1877), m. 1875, a sister of Colonel Cornwallis-West.

as I shall in a moment, is, somehow, rather tragic and almost frightens me. For what will it bring—the year that we are expected to welcome? And how many new souls will be born and how many tired souls go back to their God even as I listen?

I long to go to Church to-morrow but it seems there is no Service—a queer fashion. I have not been in England on this day for so many years that I do not know what the custom is, but it seems to me that in all churches everywhere there ought to be a Service on New Year's Day.

CHAPTER FIVE

1903

January 2, 1903. Newlands, Hampshire.

HANS was great fun on New Year's Eve ; he opened the window and we let in the poor little New Year and then I drank a sip of whisky and soda which I hate, and we kissed each other ; then he mimicked the walk of the English, French and Germans in turn ; told me funny stories and was altogether " less of a husband." I think sometimes it is good for husbands and wives in their respective rooms to be separated by a corridor. For instance last night, he went to change, and then came into my room. . . . He was quite pleased with himself, and then we laughed and talked together and he said : " I shall see you to-morrow— oh, I forgot you were my wife." This sentence explains what I mean ; there was something unusual in his having to come right along a passage past other doors and then leave quietly on tip-toe as if he (and I too) had been doing something wrong ; there is a little air of mystery about it which is amusing, and therefore more tempting.

January 6, 1903. Chatsworth, Derbyshire.

Arrived here late last night, dressed in a great hurry, but got downstairs in good time. The Duchess of Devonshire [1] is marvellous and *looks* marvellous for her seventy-four years. Always very decolletée in the evening with dresses that only a woman of thirty should wear ; and yet she does not really seem dressed too young ; she generally has a wreath of green leaves in her hair (or rather wig !).

---

[1] Comtesse Louise D'Alten (1829–1911), m. 1852, 7th Duke of Manchester (1823–90) ; 2ndly, in 1892, 8th Duke of Devonshire (1833–1908).

This evening, being Twelfth Night, we all danced round the Christmas Tree, Soveral [1] leading the Duchess : then the girls and I ducked for an apple ; I could not get it. And we cut a cake containing charms : little Princess Beatrice of Coburg [2] cut the ring, and the Prime Minister, Mr. Balfour, [3] got a little gold heart—perhaps to make up for the real one that he missed years ago ! After that we danced in the long passage which, however, is really much too narrow for the purpose. I cannot think why they do not use the rooms upstairs, or take the table away from the billiard-room, which is never used as everyone plays bridge ; and there are always a lot of girls here who want to dance.

I sat next to the Duke [4] at dinner ; he was very agreeable and really, no matter what they say, he did *not* get a bit sleepy towards the end.

Now I must say something about the house-party. First of all, there are the Duke and Duchess of Connaught's two charming girls, Princess Margaret [5] (known to her friends as Princess Daisy) and Princess Patricia. [6] They are both gay, simple and approachable and enter into everything with zest. The only other royalties are the Duke and Duchess of Teck, [7] who seem to wish to be polite to everyone. She is such a dear and he was, indeed still is, very handsome. Then there is Mr. Balfour, bland, smiling and with a rare, rather old-fashioned courtesy towards women which is sweet. The others are Violet Mar and Kellie and her husband, Mr. and Mrs. Willie Grenfell, [8] Tottie Menzies [9] (Muriel Wilson's

---

[1] Marquess de Soveral (1862–1922), G.C.M.G., G.C.V.O., Portuguese Foreign Secretary 1895–7, Portuguese Minister in London 1897–1910.

[2] Y. d. of Duke of Edinburgh, the Princess m. in 1909 Don Alphonse de Bourbon d'Orleans, Infante d'Espagne.

[3] 1st Earl of Balfour (1848–1930), K.G., Prime Minister 1902–5, Foreign Secretary 1916–19.

[4] 8th Duke of Devonshire (1833–1908), K.G., Sec. of State for India 1880–2, for War 1882–5, Lord President of the Council, 1895–1903.

[5] M. the present Crown Prince of Sweden in 1905 and d. in 1920.

[6] Became Lady Patricia Ramsay in 1919.

[7] The parents of Queen Mary of England.

[8] Lord and Lady Desborough (cr. 1905) ; Lady Desborough is a daughter of Julian and Lady Adine Fane

[9] Then Mrs. J. Graham Menzies ; m. in 1912 Sir George Holford, K.C.V.O. (1860–1926).

sister), Count Mensdorff [1] of the Austrian Embassy, and Marquess de Soveral, the Portuguese Minister, and Lord and Lady de Grey [2] with her daughter Juliet [3] (by her first husband Lord Lonsdale). Of course Lady Gosford [4] and her two girls, Alexandra and Theo, are also here, Lady Gosford being a daughter of our hostess by her first husband, the Duke of Manchester. There are several other men whose names I cannot remember, but all of whom help to make up a very lively and amusing party.

To-morrow we rehearse before luncheon, so in the afternoon I shall go out and join the guns.

January 10, 1903. Chatsworth, Derbyshire.

I have had no time to write, having had to rehearse hard every day.

We acted last night after only three days rehearsing, while we ought to have had a week ; it all went very well except in my monologue when I was alone on the stage for twenty minutes. I suddenly forgot my cue, and the ass of a prompter, who was not following, lost the page and did not know where to find it, so I had to say : " Please give me the words " ; some of them say that I stamped my foot and said, " damn the man," but I am sure I didn't. The last play *Shades of Night* went very well and I enjoyed playing the ghost which is really the best part. We act again on Monday (the 12th).

To-day, Saturday, nearly everyone left ; only Violet [5] Mar and Kellie and her husband, and the daughter of the house, Lady Gosford, and her daughters, remaining. It is really not a " happy " house to stay in ; it all breathes " society " and nothing else. . . . Many of the people, although I have been acquainted with them for years, I really know very little, as I see most of them only about twice a year (here for instance) ; then, unless I come to London in the Season, which I seldom

---

[1] Count Albert Mensdorff-Pouilly-Dietrichstein, b. 1861 ; Austrian Ambassador in London 1904–14.

[2] Afterwards (1909) Marquess and Marchioness of Ripon.

[3] M. in 1903 Captain Sir Robin Duff, who was killed in 1914 ; 2nd, in 1919, Keith Trevor, whom she divorced in 1926.

[4] Her husband, the 4th Earl, d. in 1922. Lady Alexandra m. in 1905 Honble. Frederick Stanley ; Lady Theodosia m. in 1912 Honble. Alexander Cadogan.

[5] D. of 8th Earl of Shaftesbury, m. 1892, 12th Earl of Mar and Kellie.

do, not again, perhaps, until the autumn in Cowes or Scotland.

Soveral and Lord Gosford argued about the Venezuelan affair [1] ; they say here that the Emperor William is trying to harm England through his policy in South America, thinking, of course, that if he succeeds, it would then go better for Germany in the United States. It is also said that he came over for the King's Birthday only to try to rush England into making an agreement with Germany to support him over Venezuela. It is all nonsense, and as I pointed out, it is stupid for the English Press to be insolent to the Emperor, and for all the people here to believe such foolish things.

Lord Gosford says the Government, as usual, was caught napping, " and if you consider its representatives can you wonder ? " And while he spoke he looked towards Mr. Balfour and the Duke of Devonshire.[2] I agree. The former may be able to arrange such affairs as the Education Bill, but for Foreign affairs he requires rejuvenation, I think, and he never reads a newspaper : both men are absolutely English without sufficient thought or vision to enable their minds to cross the Channel—let alone the Atlantic.

Soveral, the Portuguese Minister, is the oddest character at present in English society : he imagines himself to be a great intellectual and political force and the wise adviser of all the heads of the Government and, of course, the greatest danger to women ! I amuse myself with him as it makes the other women furious, and he is sometimes very useful. He is so swarthy that he is nicknamed the " blue monkey " and I imagine that even those stupid people who believe that every man who talks to a woman must be her lover, could not take his Don Juanesque pretensions seriously. Yet I am told that all women do not judge him so severely and some even find him *très séduisant*. How disgusting ! Anyway, from now on

---

[1] Foreign capital invested in Venezuela being in danger, England, Germany and Italy, after prolonged negotiations, jointly blockaded Venezuelan ports, and, in December, 1902, bombarded Puerta Cabello. Eventually, in 1907, the Hague Tribunal decided in favour of the European Powers. Germany, through the Welsers of Augsburg, established commercial interests in Venezuela as long ago as the end of the fifteenth century.

[2] The authoress and Lord Gosford (1841–1922) shared a current delusion ; the 8th Duke of Devonshire (1833–1908) was a very able, and the 1st Earl of Balfour (1848–1930) a very great, man.

I will not go alone with him to the theatre or to lunch at a restaurant. He hates the German Emperor and I am sure has a very bad influence on King Edward in this direction. It is simply that his prodigious vanity is wounded because he imagines that the Emperor does not care for him, and does not fuss over him when visiting England. Why should the Emperor rush at him ? After all, Delagoa Bay [1] is not the one point around which the whole world revolves.

Everyone here plays golf ; I don't think it is a game I shall ever take to.

It is too ridiculous, all the house-party, including the girls, have received an anonymous letter enclosing a verse from the Bible. The Duchess denies having received one, and Lady Gosford refused to show hers at tea, so goodness knows what was in them. My text is : " For all flesh is as grass, and all the glory of man as the flower of grass. The grass withereth ; and the flower thereof fadeth and falleth away. But the word of the Lord endureth for ever. And this is the word which by the gospel is preached unto you."

This is quite true, but I cannot imagine what good the writer imagines he—or she—has done by sending us all this sort of reminder of " things above " ; to do it thus wholesale makes it seem like a joke. I can't help laughing when I picture myself as a " blade of grass " (a bit of a thickish bamboo, perhaps). And why does the writer imagine we are all so wicked this particular week because we act ?

January 19, 1903. Newlands, Hampshire.

I was on the whole pleased to leave Chatsworth ; the time seemed to drag there ; the last day's acting went off very well except that in *Shades of Night*, Mr. Leo Trevor forgot his lines and the prompter, an idiot (as they all seem to be), never gave them to him, and this time *he* also had to say " give me a word." This consoled me when I remembered what happened two nights before in my monologue. . . . On the Saturday nearly everyone left. I walked with the Duchess in the afternoon and told her all about Germany and her old friends ; she was quite amused and interested, although generally she is not easy to talk to.

On Tuesday night I dined in London with Consuelo

---

[1] Discovered by Portugal 1502 : the subject of repeated disputes between Portugal and Great Britain, the last in 1889.

Manchester,[1] to meet the King. He told me I was *très en beauté*. I always feel rather shy when he talks like that. . . . During dinner he spoke very freely (too freely) about Germany, America, Venezuela, and so on. The Duchess and her sister, Lady Lister Kaye,[2] are Americans, and so is Adèle Essex [3] who was also there, being the only ladies, apart from Mrs. George Keppel. On several occasions they turned apologetically to me, but the King said : " Oh, Daisy doesn't mind : being married to a German does not make her change her national feelings." I thought, neither does it make one insensible, so I let them go on arguing and talking about everything, and when they had finished I *had* my say *at* them, and then dropped my fan and, someone coming to pick it up, caused a change in the conversation.

The next day I lunched with George and his wife [4] ; Winston, her son, was there, Mrs. Keppel, Soveral and others, and an American Senator, a famous orator and traveller, whose name I have forgotten. They again began poking fun at Germany : criticizing her policy towards America, how little it mattered one way or another what Germany thought or did, and similar rudenesses. At last I turned with a bright red face to the Senator and said : " Now tell them what *you* think ; my husband is a German, but please ignore that, only tell them a few positive facts." *Then* he reduced them all to silence ; even Soveral had not a word to say. The Senator stated that in America, politically, Germany had a very powerful hold which made itself silently but firmly felt. One city alone had one million German inhabitants. Germany got what she wanted ; England took what she wanted—which was a great difference. In the United States they had a great respect for Germans and Germany. There were several questions asked and answered and the whole company was

---

[1] Consuelo (1858–1909), d. of Señor Yznaga de Vaille of Louisiana, m. 1876, 8th Duke of Manchester (1853–92).

[2] Natica, d. of Señor Yznaga de Vaille of Louisiana, m. 1881, Sir John Lister-Kaye (1853–1924), 3rd Bt.

[3] Adèle, d. of Mrs. Beach Grant of U.S.A., m. 1893, as his 2nd wife, 7th Earl of Essex (1857–1916).

[4] Miss Jennie Jerome, whose father owned and edited the *New York Times* and was a patron of the American Turf ; she m. 1874, Lord Randolph Churchill (1849–95) ; 2nd, in 1900, Major George Cornwallis-West, whom she divorced in 1914 ; 3rd, in 1918, Montagu Porch. She d. in 1921.

effectively treated to a courteous lesson in matter-of-fact common sense. I was delighted.

That night at a dinner-party, Soveral opened up the argument again ; he was furious with me, and said I had spoken to him at luncheon as if I thought he were a fool ! (He is generally credited almost with genius.) Yet I did most certainly think he was a fool (and not for the first time either) when he said : " *Oh, cet Americain, il n'a dit rien que des bêtises.*" I begged his pardon for having forgotten that Monsieur le Marquis, Minister for Portugal, would naturally know more regarding the feelings of America about another foreign country than any American Senator could know ! . . . The King was again present and, during dinner, touched me on the one great empty place in my heart when he said : " Do you then never wish to have another son ? "

I go up to London to-morrow, Monday, with little Min whom we brought down here with us ; and I leave there on Wednesday, for Germany, Tommy and my dual life : other people, other manners, other thoughts, other clothes, other men, other compliments : and, after all, a good wholesome existence. In Germany there seems always to be the need of a little mystery about everything. I feel somehow like a lady in a harem. I must not drive in an open carriage nor walk alone, nor see a man alone for tea unless I have asked others to come and see me the same afternoon. But I shall be so pleased to see Tommy . . .

January 29, 1903. Palast Pless, Berlin.

I have been here a week. Berlin is the same as ever, only even less amusing. I have to pay calls every day, and there have been endless balls, and people come up to me and say : " You look like a fairy Queen "—" At last the sun shines "— or, " You are the sunshine." But I have got used to it, and now it makes no difference to me, only I wonder, do they really mean it ? Vater and Mathilde seem very pleased to have me here.

At the Court, so as to be different from the other people, I had a fringe of real violets sewn all down one side of my train which was of transparent lace, with gold sequins outlining the design, and lined with pale blue chiffon.

Last night was the gala performance at the Opera for the Emperor's birthday. I was sent a ticket for a box on the

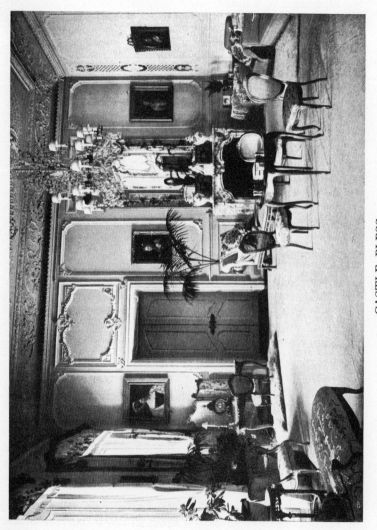

CASTLE PLESS.

Another view of my sitting-room. On left the table where a good deal of this diary was written.

second tier : I wrote to Eulenburg [1] returning it and saying simply I would not go amongst the spiders on the ceiling. So I got another place. The Emperor, the Empress, indeed everyone, was charming to me. I wore blue velvet and sable. Poor old Hans did not come, he did not feel well enough. . . .

How I wish I had kept, or could keep, all the love letters I have received. . . .

I went to a few dinner-parties in Berlin. At the Wedels' big reception, where, as a great novelty, they had the cinematograph, I again saw the Emperor and Empress. She sent for me and we talked quite naturally for some time ; I had sent her a few days before some newspaper cuttings about the " sleeping sickness " in Uganda which, when I mentioned it in January last, she laughed at and did not seem to believe in. Moreover I thought she might be furious, perhaps, as I had written and asked the Crown Prince to come and see me before he went to Cairo. He sent a touching little note saying his parents would not allow him to do so because my baby had just had the measles. Hans said : " Hum ! they are afraid of something else." So I thought it best to say quite naturally to the Empress : " I was sorry the Crown Prince could not come, but I daresay it was better that he did not." As it happens, *thank God* he kept away, as both he and his brother have now got measles at Luxor ; and if he *had* come they would have said I gave it to him. The Empress did not seem annoyed, and only said she hoped I should see the Crown Prince later. The Emperor did not even give me his hand. I prophesied that he would not, as I know he is terrified of measles ; he contented himself with smiling exaggeratedly from a distance and making ugly faces at me during supper, which I did not think very dignified. Once more everyone was charming and really seemed pleased to see me again.

We had a quiet little dinner one night with Sir Frank Lascelles,[2] the British Ambassador : I think he ages prematurely. And I saw much of Prince Joachim Albrecht and played the piano a good deal to his 'cello accompaniment.

The last evening of all we dined with the Imperial Chancellor Bülow. I sang. Countess Bülow is an Italian, the daughter of the Prince of Camporeale. She married, first, Count Charles

---

[1] See p. 70.
[2] Rt. Hon. Sir Frank Lascelles, G.C.B. (1841–1920), British Ambassador to Germany 1895–1908.

Dönhoff ; that marriage was annulled, and she then married Count Bülow. She is bright, clever and amusing, and very kind. But that night made us decide not to go to Berlin again in the winter until we are given some official position, as at this dinner, I went in after a Countess who was a mere " Frau " until last year. Hans had no lady at all. Lulu and Fritz never came to Berlin until, long after she had a daughter out, she was made " *Exzellenz* " and her husband Lord High Chamberlain—when she automatically became first lady at the German Court. It is a great pity as Berlin ought to be one of the finest capitals in the world with an interesting society. As Soveral said the other day : " The Emperor forgets he is not Frederick the Great of Prussia, but only German Emperor."

The Arenbergs, from Brussels, sometimes come to Berlin, but there are many heads of grand old German families, and eldest sons, who never do so as their birth gives them no precedence whatever ; at Court they simply have " army rank " ; and in our case Hans happens to be a Captain in the Reserve. We go in almost last ! [1]

March 29, 1903.   Stanmore Golf Club, Middlesex.

General Arthur Paget [2] brought me here in his motor-car and we played golf (or I tried to) before lunch ; no one else is playing and it is a heavenly day ; we shall be back in London about five-thirty, when I have promised to see Thaddé Kozibrodski for a little while ; he is in London for a week-end and, to be honest, bores me—but then most of them do. As I said to him last night, if one were so very plain as to be without any attractiveness, except perhaps for one man, so that one could go from one part of the world to another and meet with only ordinary politeness, perhaps the prayers and " sweet sayings " of that *one* man might be touching ; but when, as often happens, three men on the same day say exactly the same thing, perhaps in the very same words, compliments lose any charm they might possess, and one gets bored or even angry with their perpetrators.

---

[1] This would only be while he was Prince Henry of Pless ; when he succeeded he and his wife would take their proper places with the Princes and Princesses. Apparently there was no official precedence for eldest and younger sons as in England.

[2] General Rt. Hon. Sir Arthur Paget (1851–1928), m. 1878, Mary (Minnie), d. of Mr. and Mrs. Stevens of U.S.A., who d. in 1919.

I came up from Newlands five days ago and have been
staying in London with brother George, his wife having gone
to Cannes. . . . George loved my precious baby at Newlands ; he is the dearest little boy and so clever and full of
mischief. He comes up to London to-morrow for the night
as I want to try clothes on him and put him into breeches.
I am so excited, and Hans will be surprised and pleased when
he sees him. Hans, thank God, must be quite well now :
he does not mention his health when he writes. His letters
are full of politics and the prospect of his being sent to Washington as Ambassador.

I leave for Cap Martin on Tuesday, and join him in Paris
about the 8th of April.

Shelagh is there, poor little girl, not well, and has to lie up ;
I think she hunted too much after her baby was born. Patsy
is with her, and Bend Or, who went to Eaton for the Grand
National, rejoins them in Paris to-day. His horse *Drumree*
ran badly, broke its neck and had to be shot.

I had a deliciously peaceful time at Newlands ; Poppets
used to drive Baby and me all over the country and into the
Forest, and we stopped and had tea with the neighbours.

The Queen [1] sent for me the other day at six, and she kept
me at Buckingham Palace till twenty minutes to eight ; she
showed me all her rooms, and her jewellery which is arranged
under glass all round her dressing-room, and she was so sweet
and charming. She is going to Copenhagen and is furious
that the German Emperor will be there to spoil, as she says,
their family party. The Duchess of Cumberland, her sister,
had just got there and, on hearing of his intended arrival, left
with her husband and daughters the day before he was due !
So the Emperor did not have a chance of seeing these reputedly
pretty girls ; rumour says he wished to discover if one of them
would do as a wife for the Crown Prince. [2]

The Queen also spoke about the old old story of Schleswig-

---

[1] Queen Alexandra.

[2] In 1913, the Emperor's only daughter, Princess Louise, married
Prince Ernest, only son of Ernest Augustus Duke of Cumberland
(1845–1923), thus healing the long-standing quarrel arising out of the
annexation of Hanover by Germany in 1866. The Duke's grandfather, Ernest Duke of Cumberland (1771–1851), owing to the Salic
Law, succeeded as King of Hanover in 1837 (on the death of William
IV.). Before the birth of the Empress Frederick in 1840, he was the
direct heir to the British throne.

Holstein,[1] and how terribly the poor Danes there are treated. She takes in a little Danish paper published in Jutland giving particulars of all their miseries : forced selling of their old homes to Germans ; burning of their Bibles written in Danish ; school-children torn from their mothers' arms and forced to learn German, and similar atrocities !

I again met the King at dinner one night ; he was, as always, very delightful, but inclined to chaff too much. He told me he thought I was a humbug (probably because he imagines— goodness knows what, and because I would not be " nice " to him) ; I only answered that I was less of a humbug than anyone I knew.

Alfred Rothschild [2] gave a very nice dinner for the Prince of Wales [3] ; he took me in and I found him much more vivacious as a conversationalist than he was a few years ago, when he used to be rather shy. He asked if I wouldn't like to elope with him in a hansom. He was recalling an old joke of ours referring to some years ago, when there was a lot in the papers about him and me intending to elope ! I said that because of the heat of the dining-room and the length of the menu, I would readily elope (round the corner only) with anyone. Lady Lansdowne [4] had to leave the room ; she has developed a weak heart through anxiety, poor lady, since the trying time her husband had at the War Office during the South African War and the criticisms about him in the newspapers.

Now I must go out and join Arthur Paget or he will think me rude ; he has a daughter of twenty-three and a son a little older, but is a very well-preserved, charming man, quiet and dignified. He said at luncheon : " What on earth would a man do with a fine character in these degenerate days ? " I am inclined to agree !

April 3, 1903. Monte Carlo, Hotel Riviera Palace.

I arrived here two days ago and found Patsy very well and looking so young. Little Shelagh in bed still ; she has been

---

[1] Incorporated with Prussia in January, 1867, as a result of Germany winning the war of 1864 against Denmark.

[2] Alfred de Rothschild, C.V.O. (1842–1918), 2nd son of late Baron Lionel de Rothschild.

[3] King George V.

[4] Maud, d. of 1st Duke of Abercorn and widow of 5th Marquess of Lansdowne (1845–1927) ; he was Sec. of State for War 1895–1900, and for Foreign Affairs 1900–5.

laid up a fortnight and will have to remain here for another fortnight and then travel back to London with a nurse and a doctor and take *great* care for many months to come, poor little girl ! Bend Or leaves here to-night to ride in some point-to-point races near Eaton, and will probably return again. I *wish* he would give up riding races ; I hate it.

Lady Ermyntrude Malet has just been in to see me ; they were in Berlin about nine years ago as Ambassador [1] and Ambassadress. Gerald Paget, General Arthur's brother, came too and had a long chat with me. He loved Patsy once, and will be a grandfather in some months, but this has not killed his youthful spirit. Countess Matuschka has just called ; the place is full of Germans, goodness knows how I am going to see them all in this short time, and if I don't, they will probably be " piqued." Now I want to get up and go to sit with little Shelagh.

April 9, 1903. *Thursday.* Villa Kazbeck, Cannes.

I came over here for the night to stay with Sophy and her husband the Grand Duke Michael. They will not answer when I ask what has been the matter with his sister, the Grand Duchess Anastasia of Mecklenburg-Schwerin, whose husband (the dearest man on earth [2]) has been dead about seven years. . . . Shelagh is better ; Patsy is very well. I have lost about ten pounds at Monte ; at one time I had lost fifty, an enormous sum for me. There are a lot of people there but nobody very interesting. The Duchess of Devonshire was at Monte Carlo, and they say that in the gambling rooms was always followed by detectives and carefully watched by the croupiers in case she tried to snatch any money. Dear Gordy's brother was also there, so like Gordy in manner and voice and even in looks ; it made me feel quite strange sometimes. George's wife is here, as charming as usual, and looking very well but *so* fat, gambling and wearing lovely clothes. . . .

What a lovely bit of the world is this wonderful coast ! After glorious sunny weather and a sapphire sea it suddenly clouded over and the sea became green and dark with a sky to match : the dust flew up in clouds on the roads, and no bright-

---

[1] Rt. Hon. Sir Edward Malet, 4th Bt. (1837–1908), m. 1885, Lady Ermyntrude Russell, d. of 9th Duke of Bedford. Sir Edward was Ambassador in Berlin 1884–95.

[2] See pp. 42 and 56.

faced women or the tanned faces of little children peeped over the flower-decked balconies. How well I understand the natives being " a people of moods." One day basking in the sun in the little cafés, or under the trees with the scent of pine and the perfume of hundreds of flowers in the air—a pretty girl to carry their home-grown wine and fruit to them —later, perhaps, the man's arm may draw her to him as they sit for hours forgetful of work or duty or God—true children of nature happy in the physical joy of all around them. But, suddenly, the air changes and the storm comes ; and man can become cruel, vile and utterly regardless—even forgetful of the one he loved while the sun shone and the flowers showed their faces : these people are full of passion and poetry, cruelty and imagination, courtesy and brutality.

On Saturday I leave little Shelagh and Patsy here and join Hans in Paris. I shall be so glad to see him again.

April 28, 1903.   Paris.

We have been here over a fortnight and remain on to see the King of England arrive next Friday, the day after to-morrow. Just now an invitation arrived from Monsieur Loubet,[1] the President of the Republic, inviting us to be present at a Gala performance at the Opera on Saturday. It is very nice of them to ask us, and we shall be delighted to go. It seems sad to think of all the descendants of *la vieille noblesse* sitting at home that day ; most of them are not asked as the Opera House will be full with all the government representatives and their wives, whom one never sees at other times : all the dinners given will be attended by the same people, and the King will not see any of his own friends, or be able to speak with them, even at the Races next Saturday.

May 15, 1903.   Eaton Hall, Cheshire.

We stayed in Paris to see the arrival of the King of England.[2] He was received : and that expresses the enthusiasm that was shown, which was neither warm, nor cold. I can scarcely believe that this visit to France did any political good.

We went to the Castellane's house in the *Bois* to watch the procession ; the King's carriage was so surrounded with

---

[1] Monsieur Emile Loubet (1838–1929), President 1899–1906.

[2] King Edward VII. paid State Visits to Lisbon, Gibraltar, Malta, Naples, Rome and Paris, March 31–May 5, 1903.

soldiers that it was quite impossible to see him. At the Races he remained in the Jockey Club Stand and did not come into the Paddock and speak to the few of his personal friends who were present, as they all hoped he would.

Monday at the Gala Opera the King sat between Monsieur and Madame Loubet, trying his best not to go to sleep, as he had been to a Review early in the morning and had attended a big lunch given by Monsieur Delcassé.[1] He has just paid visits to Portugal and Italy, and with so much travelling, and so many fêtes given in his honour he had every excuse for being fatigued. There was nothing " gala " about the Opera House which, although a pompous building, always looks dull and dingy, the gold enrichments being quite faded ; there were no floral decorations, and few jewels, as so many of the French nobility refused to be present.

To sit there and see the King in a big " Presidential " Box between a little monkey-looking man like Loubet, and his wife who looks like a fat Jewess—no jewels or uniforms near him—seemed somehow to advertise the Republic and make one feel still more strongly than ever the wonder and pity that France has no King nor Emperor—no beautiful Queen. Paris breathes " Court " : somehow all the beautiful old palaces, the *Bois*, the fine streets, and the Palais du Louvre standing stately and empty, seem to cry for Royalty. London, in spite of the frequent sight of a Royal carriage, seems far more a city of merchants like New York, than does Paris, a truly fitting background for Kings and Emperors, women, beauty, poetry, song, all that arouses and breathes emotion. Yet the hands that govern France make laws that breed every evil in the mind of the people, and will ruin the future lives of the children. France will soon be at the bottom of the hill ; and only time will show if it is within the power of any one individual to place her on her feet again ; I am afraid I shall not be here to see.

I forgot to say that in Paris at the Opera the King smiled and shook his head at me and held out his arm and pointed straight at me for Madame Loubet to look at me, which she promptly did through her glasses. I had to laugh and so did the King.

---

[1] Monsieur Théophile Delcassé, b. 1852 ; Foreign Secretary 1895–1905, when he resigned on the Morocco question ; again Foreign Secretary 1914–15.

The Prince and Princess of Wales [1] have been staying here. The Prince had to inaugurate a memorial at Wrexham in commemoration of the local soldiers who fell in the South African War : he went one day to the Races with Bend Or by motor.

Hans and I went both to Ruthin and to the Races by train. Girlie Cawley [2] has been staying here, also Gladys Deacon,[3] Lady Naylor-Leyland,[4] a nice girl who plays the violin, Charlie Wood (dear Gordy's brother), Count Vico Voss and Captain Davies.

We went to London for Mrs. Adair's fancy Ball ; Hans wore a red coat ; I went as a goddess and called myself *Inspiration*, in white and gold with big white lilies, partly embroidered and partly painted on a foundation of white chiffon. It was not a pretty ball as so many men were in plain evening dress, because of the order of the King forbidding uniform to be worn at fancy-dress balls. This is a foreign idea, but I think quite right as it was ridiculous to hear men say, " A fancy ball, bother, then I shall have to wear my uniform."

Hans went to Paris and I came back here to have a few quiet days with Shelagh. Poor little girl, she cried yesterday ; but I told her every woman gets more and more disappointed as she gets older, and no husband turns out to be as one expected. (Hans is as nearly perfect as any husband could be, as long as I help him and dress well and smile at his guests and act the part of a Prince's wife.) . . .

I went back to Ruthin for one night : Bruin Vivian was there. Patsy is lucky, and ought to be joyous in having such a true, loving and lasting friend after twenty years' acquaintance. He is one in a thousand. On the way I lunched with Granny in her new house ; she and Uncle Hugo FitzPatrick seem very cosy ; she is the most charming and holy old lady in the world ; and so picturesque in her big black hat and tulle ruffle round her neck.

Poppets is going to close up Ruthin in a month and is, I think, not sorry : poor old Ruthin, the home of his ancestors for centuries, with its moat and dungeons, and its lovely flower-

---

[1] King George V. and Queen Mary.

[2] D. of 1st Lord Cawley; m. in July, 1904, Capt. C. Long.

[3] D. of E. P. Deacon of Boston; m. in 1921 the 9th Duke of Marlborough.

[4] D. of W. S. Chamberlain of Ohio; m. in 1889 Sir Herbert Naylor-Leyland, 1st Bt. (d. 1899).

gardens amongst the ancient ruins ; it seems now as if the spirit of disaster hovers over it ; the guest bedrooms are not kept up now, the servants live in them ; the carpets are thread-bare and the curtains faded. In the old rooms where we played " house " and had tea-parties I looked about me and thought sadly that the little feet of my nieces and nephews would never patter on those boards. George can have no children by this wife. . . . Naturally it makes little Patsy and Poppets lose interest in the place. Newlands is small and sunny, and there are nice neighbours ; the sea is always a companion, and Poppets has the development of his seaside resort, Milford-on-Sea, to interest him : Ruthin is miles from everyone and everything.

Now I am going out to fish with Bend Or and am taking Hansel—and the nurserymaid to hold on to him ; he is so well, and so wild and full of spirits and little naughtinesses, and is very sharp and clever.

June 3, 1903. Vienna.

We got here this morning after a peaceful fortnight in Für-stenstein. From Eaton I went to London : Bend Or let me go with Baby to Grosvenor House. I stayed only two days. The night I arrived I went to a party at Mrs. Adair's ; the Prince and Princess of Wales were there, the Duke and Duchess of Portland,[1] Mr. and Mrs. Joseph Chamberlain, the Lans-downes, and so on. There was singing, recitations, and music. I sat on one side of the Prince, who was in good spirits, but rather annoyed at such a long evening ; they had dined there and did not get away till twelve ! The Princess looked very well and was wearing a new diamond and ruby necklace.

Then I went on with the Saviles [2] to Mrs. Oppenheim's ball : a dreadful bore asked me to go down to supper and I had to say yes ; he saw I had only just arrived so could not say I was engaged. He writes to me from Zululand, or Honolulu, or some strange place where he commands a Regiment, and I never answer. I took care to have nice Sir Condie Stephen [3] on my other side. Soveral was there and we talked for some

---

[1] 6th Duke, s. 1879, m. 1889, Miss Winifred Dallas-Yorke.
[2] 2nd Baron, b. 1854, m. 1894, Miss Violet Wedderburn ; s. 1896.
[3] Sir Condie Stephen, K.C.M.G., Minister at Dresden and Coburg 1897–1901 ; Groom-in-Waiting to the King 1901.

time ; and I spoke with Patrick de Bathe,[1] one of the Secretaries in the British Embassy in Berlin.

Robin Duff marries Juliet on the ninth of June [2] ; he came to see me at a quarter past ten, before I went to Mrs. Adair's, and I congratulated him.

I went to Marlborough House to have tea with the Prince and Princess of Wales ; it was quite simple, not at all as in Berlin where one is handed over to one lady-in-waiting after another. I was announced straight into the drawing-room where the Princess was reading. Soon we had tea and the Prince came and then all the fine children, real healthy tomboys, even the little baby of five months (Prince George) came down, and I played with him and nursed him. Marlborough House has been done up and is very fine now.

I saw Bend Or when I got back to Grosvenor House ; he had been to Salisbury to ride a race but did not win. We sat and talked a little, then I rested and dressed to dine with Lord and Lady Warwick,[3] a big dinner of forty-five people, followed by a ball. I really had quite a success, even the women were nice to me and said, " Daisy, you are looking lovely," " like a Boucher picture." I wore no jewels and had my hair done broad at the sides with not much fringe, and three curls very low on my neck, a little black patch near my eye. My embroidered frock was white satin, trimmed in festoons of tulle and pink roses, caught up with bows of blue velvet baby ribbon. Perhaps they all crowded round me so, because they knew I was leaving the next day.

I lunched with Alice Keppel before leaving for Berlin ; three or four of the women present had had several lovers, and did not mind saying so—but—I can generally *placer* myself in any *milieu*. Alice is fascinating.

Hans met me in Berlin ; we dined at the Bristol with Ada Sierstorpff and afterwards took a drive in the *Tiergarten*. I felt I wanted fresh air after my long hot journey.

I left Berlin the next day at half-past four and arrived at Fürstenstein at half-past eleven, driving from Königszelt in an open carriage with postilions : it was all very still as I drove,

---

[1] (1876–1930) Was brother and heir-presumptive to Sir Hugo de Bathe, 5th Bt.

[2] Lady Juliet Lowther, oldest d. of the 4th Earl of Lonsdale.

[3] 5th Earl (1853–1924), m. in 1881 Frances, granddaughter of Viscount Maynard.

a hot silent night with few stars—*comme si le ciel dormait* ; the dogs barked as we passed the villages ; and the chirp of the crickets in the field seemed to follow the carriage the whole way.

I thought of them all in London—at a ball probably—the glare, the lights, and the jewels ; yet I did not envy them or wish to be back in a crowd where there is so much artificiality. I think English society is becoming stupid—there is no conversation ; no " bon mots " ; no repartee ; after dinner it is always bridge, or one is obliged to sit tête-à-tête with a man (never three or four together), so there can be no arguments or discussions ; you sit with your man, *c'est bien* ; if he is the ordinary man his conversation is about friendship, and then love, to discuss which is, I think, always an opening to flirtation : if he is an old friend, he will ask, how do you get on in Germany, how many men are in love with you, what do they think of you there (he might be discussing a savage country), and similar inanities. Or another sort of man will tell you all about his hunting, polo ponies, golf or shooting. You will seldom find anyone to sit down with you and have a sensible conversation about current topics, the politics of different countries, what they tend to, socialism, even religion. Soveral is the most agreeable conversationalist of them all—and he is a foreigner.

I always think the sea round England holds her safety and keeps off invaders ; but it also circumscribes the intelligence of Englishmen and makes them narrow-minded and uncosmopolitan. When they talk of going abroad it means a week of dissipation in Paris, or three months in India, Africa, or the Rocky Mountains shooting big game.

It was lovely in Fürstenstein, all the lilacs and laburnums in bloom and the woods white with lilies-of-the-valley ; I sat much in my garden and wrote and read and talked. Hansel is now in breeches, and rides his donkey without being held on. I did not really want to come here and leave the country. We arrived yesterday morning, I had lunch in my room. We are staying in the town house of Count and Countess Larisch, the father and mother of dear Hansie and Fritz.

Last night I went to an evening party given by Count and Countess Lanckorónski [1] ; a beautiful house with the *most*

---

[1] Count von Lanckorónski, b. 1848, m., 3rdly, in 1897, Countess Margaret, d. of 5th Prince Lichnowsky.

lovely things in it, only there was such a crowd of people it was difficult to see them. Three Archduchesses and two Archdukes, the most uninteresting people there, I thought. I was presented to them and put sitting next to the Archduchess Josepha,[1] wife of the Archduke Otto. . . . I tried to make conversation, spoke of the beauty of the house and my pleasure at being again in Vienna. She made a few coldly polite remarks but did not in the least give herself any trouble to talk, and as I certainly was not going to, I got up and left her sitting there. They say she is always like that, and that I did quite right ; but I should not care if I had done all wrong.

Everyone else was very nice to me, I was " superbe," " brillante," and so on, but I was bored even with compliments which I do not care a bit about, so, at half-past ten, I persuaded Hans to take me home. As soon as I got out in the air and felt the wind blowing my hair about I became natural and myself again ; we got home at eleven, and I tumbled into bed with a nice book. Hans went on to the Club, determined to play poker and win—and lost fifty pounds.

June 5, 1903. *Thursday.* Vienna.

We dined last night with the Larisches, a nice dinner ; old Princess Metternich [2] and her son-in-law, the Prince of Oettingen [3] to whom after dinner I said (which is true) " I am so fond of Austrians ; they make one feel homely at once. Really, although Hans is Prussian, my best friends are Austrians, particularly the women. German women are stiff, more reserved, one never gets quite true friends with them." I found out afterwards that the Prince is a Bavarian. Count Goluchowski,[4] the Prime Minister, was there. I went in to dinner with him ; he is very agreeable and talked of Patsy and her beauty as he remembers her years ago in Paris. His wife was not there, she is a sister of Prince Joachim Murat. I talked in French and German and it rather amused me ; I once thought I should like to come here as Ambassadress ; but

---

[1] Mother of the Emperor Karl.

[2] Countess Pauline Sándor-de-Szlavnicza (1836–1921), m. 1856, 3rd Prince Metternich-Winneburg.

[3] Albert 5th Prince Oettingen-Spielberg (1847–1916), m. 1878, Princess Sophie Metternich-Winneburg.

[4] Agenor Count Goluchowo-Goluchowski (d. 1921), m. 1885, Princess Anne, d. of 4th Prince Murat.

CASTLE PLESS.

My Bedroom.

The walls hand-painted on cream silk in the Japanese manner.

I know now I shouldn't ; the town smells, and one always meets the same people, the real society being very small.

The other guests at dinner were Betka Potocka [1] (a Princess of Radziwill) and her husband who is a real Pole, and, when in the country, wears the national dress, including a little pointed felt hat and an enormous pheasant's feather sticking out behind. Count Festetics [2] and his daughter [3] (who afterwards married Prince Charles Windischgraetz) were there ; he is the biggest swell in Hungary. Also a Countess Esterhazy and her daughter, very rich. Prince Gottfried Hohenlohe, Hansie and Fritzie Larisch, and I think that was all. We all sat *en masse* after dinner and conversed. I got tired at ten and longed to fall asleep. Old Princess Metternich told amusing stories with the funniest and ugliest face ; she has a mouth and lips like a nigger's which she paints purple—yet is most fascinating. In youth she was Austrian Ambassadress in Paris, became a great friend of the Empress Eugènie, and the heroine of countless witty stories.

June 6, 1903. Vienna.

At the *Preis-reiten* the Archduke Franz Ferdinand came to my box and spoke with me for some time. Hans said it would produce a great effect in Vienna because the Archdukes—or, indeed, any of the Royalties—seldom talk to anyone ! The Archduke told me he must first of all find out what the Emperor Francis Joseph's plans are and then he would let me know if he and his wife can come to Fürstenstein in June or July. If they do not come I think I shall try to take a little house for Kiel Week ; the German Emperor will be there and he likes one to go ; also I think it would be a diplomatic thing to do if Hans wants to be made Lord-Lieutenant of Silesia now that Prince Hatzfeldt is resigning ; it ought to be considered a grand post, I suppose, but I have no wish to reside at the *Oberpräsidium* [4] in Breslau for even a week in the year.

They now agree in Berlin (I told them so last January)

---

[1] Princess Elisabeth (Betka) Radziwill, m. 1885, Count Roman Potocki (d. 1920) of Lancut, Galicia (then Austrian, now Polish). Her younger sister, Princess Helen, m. 1892, Count Joseph Potocki.

[2] Received Princely rank in 1911. See p. 71.

[3] Alexandra, m. 1905, Prince Charles Windischgraetz (1871–1915) ; 2nd, 1917, Prince Erwin Hohenlohe-Schillingfurst.

[4] The Lord-Lieutenant's Palace : originally, in eighteenth century, it was a palace of the Hatzfeldt family.

that if Soveral calls there on his way to Fürstenstein, he must be received *au sérieux* by Bülow, as he is a strong personage in England, owing to his influence with the King, and he is not friendly to Germany ; but a little second class Order,[1] and a strong clasp from the " mailed fist " will, I am sure, satisfy him and have the effect perhaps of tying his tongue—which would certainly be a good thing.

June 6, 1903.   Vienna.

Comfortably in bed with my feet against a hot-water bottle ; just come back from the " Derby " : it is nearly seven o'clock, for the Races here end very late and the Racecourse is far away. I refused to go out to dinner as I must have a rest before the ball in the Prater to-night. Last night we danced till after three and I got into bed at half-past four. To-night it will be the same I suppose and to-morrow night we leave for Fürsten-stein—thank goodness. I am getting too old for so much " society," I find it impossible to be polite and smile and make conversation for so many hours. All the same I love the Vienna balls, because dancing here is taken as an art and most of the men dance beautifully ; they like dancing with me for I dance well—although I say it.

Coming home from the Races we passed three or four Imperial carriages containing the Archduchess Marie Theresa,[2] the Archduke and Archduchess Otto and their ladies and gentlemen. It seemed so funny to see them standing there amongst all the other carriages to *watch us* all go past. They were such ugly carriages—low victorias with grey horses and the coachmen and grooms in cocked hats with a lot of gold braid, and *over* the hats a yellow oil-silk covering. Indeed, most people here have oil-silk put over their servants' hats and I never saw anything so hideous and unsmart—like cheap sponge-bags—but then the ordinary servants and carriages one sees in Vienna are very bad. Except for the Emperor Francis Joseph Royalty plays a very small and *pianissimo* part here ; one never seems to see or hear them and people walk about under their box at the Races, and similar gatherings without

---

[1] I cannot remember if he did get one.—D. of P.

[2] A sister of Prince Miguel of Braganza, she m. as his third wife, the Archduke Charles Louis (1833–96), thus becoming step-mother to the Archduke Franz-Ferdinand (assassinated 1914).

even taking the trouble to look up and bow or curtsey. It was a bitterly cold day to-day and rained nearly all the time.[1]

June 21, 1903. Fürstenstein.

As usual, I have forgotten my diary for some time ; but as soon as I come home for peace and quiet I seem to have to rush from one thing to another. The baby, servants, gardens, farm, letters, piano, singing, reading, and, even so, I try to find time to paint and embroider. Since we came back from Vienna we have had some glorious days, and then terrible thunderstorms ; I never saw it rain so hard. I am afraid many of the seeds that I sowed will have been washed away. I had lunch in my garden ; it consisted chiefly of salad, strawberries and fresh almonds. . . .

I have seen some old sick women lately and they all pray to die. I wonder if some day, from the sheer fatigue of living, I shall long to die as they do ! Old Rose asks for apples, sour cherries, vinegar, and, although she eats nothing, always has the strangest fancies.

Baby is very well and comes in the motor-car with us when we aren't going too far.

June 22, 1903. Fürstenstein.

I have not talked much with Hans since he returned from Breslau, but he seems pleased. He lunched with Hatzfeldt who, when he was here the other night, spoke of Hans as the future Governor or Lord-Lieutenant of the Province of Silesia when he himself resigns in July " on account of his eyes " : but it is really on account of his open mind on the Polish question which annoys the Emperor. He wrote to Bülow, as did also Christian Kraft Hohenlohe, recommending Hans for the post, but somehow I don't think he will get it : they will say he is too young. And there are many who are, or would be, jealous ; among these is Prince X. . . . Anyway, if the post is given to Hans I suppose I shall settle into it, and try to do my best, but it would be an irksome tie to have to remain *in* Breslau for some months in the year, and to feel one could never travel whilst in residence there, or hunt in England : indeed it would be awful. After the first year or two I suppose I could get away sometimes, but I do not like to travel about too much without Hans.

---

[1] Hence, I suppose, my hot-water bottle in June !—D. OF P.

We go to Kiel the day after to-morrow. I feel that this should be a good move, if Hans seriously wants that post : the Emperor is always good-tempered at Kiel.

June 27, 1903. Ulrichshusen, Mecklenburg.

We arrived here by motor from Berlin. To-day, before leaving, we lunched with Lichnowsky : we talked of Soveral and his influence with the King of England, the Socialist question in Germany, the cleansing of the Silesian rivers, and so on. I made myself as agreeable as possible, and as usual he was very nice.

This is a very weird, but nice place, built in twelve hundred and belongs to Count Voss. It is all in red stone with a long high red-tiled roof : a small house and supposed to be full of ghosts, but as it is now one o'clock I am too frightened even to write of this. Count Vico is doing a lot to the place, making ponds and a garden, and it really could be made very nice. There is a big lake and the house looks directly over it. There is a great deal of water in Mecklenburg and the country is wooded and picturesque ; now and then one sees a hedge which reminds me of England. We leave for Kiel to-morrow at five.

June 28, 1903. Kiel.

My birthday ; I am twenty-nine to-day. It seems impossible, there must be some mistake and here I am dressed up in a yachting suit, consisting of a rather short blue skirt, white shoes, sailor blouse with turned down collar, red tie and red cap. I am sure I dress too young, and yet all the other women wear white, pink and pale blue when they are over forty. I must ask someone to tell me the truth. I hate getting older.

June 29, 1903. Kiel.

I got lots of flowers yesterday, and everyone said I looked so nice. Last night when we went to dance on the *Princessin Victoria Luise*, I had a lace scarf over my head and someone said, " She looks like a baby." Even Hans said, " You look much younger than Adene Eulenburg.[1] So this morning my years do not feel so heavy on my shoulders.

Yesterday morning we went to the launching and christening

---

[1] Alexandrine, d. of 1st Prince Eulenburg, b. 1880, m. 1910, Eberhard Count of Schwerin.

of the *Roon* by Count Waldersee.[1] The Emperor and Empress
and their suite were there : all the men in uniforms and
Orders : my poor old Hans, naturally having no uniform
with him, had to put on " evening clothes and a top hat "
and consequently was perfectly furious and in a horrible
temper. It was a beautiful sight to see this great man-of-war
slide silently without a quiver into the water. " Everyone "
was there, but Kiel " society " is not very amusing. On the
Princessin Luise are the Rederns,[2] Princess Lynar [3] and her
daughter, Princess Eulenburg [4] and her daughters, and the
Emperor's chief gentlemen. The men I saw last night all
looked terrible. Thank God I knew none of them and we
danced only for about ten minutes. This hotel is crammed,
but with people one does not know. The Princess of Thurn
and Taxis is furious that she is not asked with us to lunch
on the *Hohenzollern*, but I saw by the list that she is dining
to-night with Princess Henry of Prussia ; [5] it will be a hen
party as all the men are dining at the Club ; poor May Sierstorpff [6] is not asked to lunch or dinner and I know will cry all
night to Sturm—which she does sometimes. It is very hot
here and not very amusing as the racing yachts belong chiefly
to owners from Hamburg and Bremen and, as no one seems
to know them, we receive no invitations to go racing. In
the mornings when I see them setting their sails, and flitting
about like great birds or butterflies, it makes me just long to be
on board one of them.

The Emperor told Hans he would take us out on the *Meteor*
—but he will probably forget his promise.

Two big American yachts are here, Mrs. Goelet's *Nahma*,
where we dined last night, and the *North Star*, belonging to
Mr. and Mrs. Cornelius Vanderbilt, on which I have promised

---

[1] Alfred Count von Waldersee (1832–1904), commanded the Boxer
Expedition ; he m. an American, widow of Prince von Noer. The
Roon was a cruiser of 9,600 tons.

[2] See p. 63 (footnote).

[3] Miss Parsons (1851–1920) of U.S.A., m. 1871, 4th Prince Lynar
(1834–86), and had two sons and a daughter.

[4] Countess Augusta Sandels, b. Stockholm 1853, m. 1875, 1st Prince
(cr. 1900) Eulenburg, and had three sons and three daughters.

[5] D. of Princess Alice of Great Britain, m. 1888, Prince Henry of
Prussia (1862–1930), brother of the Emperor. The late Czarina was
her sister.

[6] Count von Francken-Sierstorpff (1858–1917), m. 1892, Mary, d.
of E. Franklyn Knowlton of Brooklyn, U.S.A.

to dine to-night. The *Margarita*, which a Mr. S. has chartered from Mr. Drexel (we went to St. Petersburg on her two years ago), was here too, but has left ; I expect they were offended, as no one called on them or received them, but then the arrangements—or lack of them—here are too ridiculous : there is no rendezvous like the Royal Yacht Squadron garden at Cowes ; one never sees anybody so one can make no plans or arrange anything. I hope to have a talk with the Emperor to-day ; I have lots of things I want to say to him. I feel very doubtful whether Hans will be made Governor of Silesia ; somehow he is never nice to, nor on good terms with, the right people ; he hasn't " a way " with him, as the Irish say, and few people really know him well.

June 29, 1903. 11.30 *p.m.* Kiel.

A very nice hot broiling day, a lunch on the *Hohenzollern* which lasted from one o'clock till four ! The Emperor and Empress both charming, and markedly so to me. They all pay me extravagant compliments over my toilette. I would not wear a feathered hat on the sea, so wore a lace and embroidered frock with pink round my waist and a pink white bébé washing hat with pink ribbon. My dear diary, I am really not vain, for honestly I cannot see where my beauty lies. This is what I am really like : I would be much plumper if I did not wear long and well-made French corsets ; blue eyes with fair eyelashes which I make black ; pretty coloured fair hair ; good eyebrows ; straight yet somehow turned-up nose ; short upper lip with the two front teeth rather longer than the others (like a rabbit or a mouse I think) ; thick bottom lip and a very slight double chin—which I keep in hand by dint of frequent massage. There is nothing to boast about in that, is there ? And it is the truth.

Anyway, I had great fun on the *Hohenzollern* and said what I thought to everyone. The Emperor and Bülow were standing close to Lady Ormonde [1] who does not like us, and who had done *all* she could against Shelagh's marriage : both of them stared quizzically at me and laughed. Bülow said :

" Oh, she never looks at me," and again laughed.

Then I went straight up to them and said :

" Your Majesty, may I pick a bone with your Prime Minister ? "

---

[1] Lady Elizabeth Harriet, d. of the 1st Duke of Westminster, m. 1876, 3rd Marquess of Ormonde (1844–1919).

" Yes, as many bones as you like."

" Your Majesty, Count Bülow told a young man (who happens to be here to-day) that I was a great flirt."

The Emperor interjected : " Quite right, quite right."

Then Bülow retorted : " No, I did not say that. It was the day you arrived, when we saw you through the hotel window and you would not come out to us. I said to the young American : ' Oh, you must beware of her, she is very beautiful and very dangerous.' " Then, turning to Lady Ormonde, who hates me, he said : " Is it not so, is she not beautiful and dangerous ? I love her."

It all made me feel rather foolish ; at the same time it amused me as it seemed to make Lady Ormonde search for something to say which she did not find !

After lunch we ladies sat round the Empress. I felt as if I were at a Quaker meeting. They were all so shy with her, but I never am : she lent me her fan because I felt hot ; and I saw she liked it if one kept the conversation flowing quietly ; for nothing is so awful as a dead silence in such gatherings ; someone coughs or giggles, and then a brave one mumbles faintly something which no one hears, and everyone says, Hem ! What ! and it turns out that whatever she had said was not worth repeating ; then everyone looks at everyone else to see who is going to speak next.

Hans had a good chance to speak privately to Bülow and to the Emperor about politics and upon his ideas about combating socialism. In fact we both behaved passably well in our different ways ; yet I think the post of Governor of Silesia is already given to someone else.

The Emperor said he could not come if I gave an afternoon party : " they were at Kiel for serious work, not for tea and pastries." I said :

" Your Majesty finds plenty of time for *bierabends*, and surely they are not serious."

" You are very naughty to say that, you know I never drink beer."

He told Hans I looked charming but was dressed " like a layette." He said to me as I was leaving : " Good-bye, my dear Daisy, don't tread on your layette." I could not make out what on earth he meant as Hans had not yet told me of his remark.

This evening, as all the men are of course at the Club, Princess Henry of Prussia had another hen dinner-party.

She sent her carriage for me. After dinner we again played thrilling games like Up-Jenkins, and then all went out on the launch and saw the illuminations and searchlights, which were really beautiful. From thirty-four men-of-war the searchlights, working together, flashed all over the sea and made our heads quite dizzy ; there were a few fireworks.

To-morrow morning I race at eight o'clock with Mr. Goelet.

June 30, 1903. Kiel.

Got up at half-past six ; a lovely morning with a strong breeze, and just longing for my sail. When I got down to the pier Mr. Goelet met me and said that he was so sorry but he had only just been told that German rules do not allow more than a certain number of hands on board and that ladies count as hands—which of course they do not in England or in America. (I think this is the only one occasion on which women count for anything in Germany, so I had to come home *furious*.) Had breakfast outside on the terrace while a lot of people were having breakfast inside with windows and doors shut. How stuffy Germans are ! Prince Lynar [1] was quite surprised last night when I said : " It is such a nuisance here : the window is just on a level with my bed and my head so I cannot sleep with it fully open." I wrote a lot of letters this morning and sang, having found a very good Bechstein piano downstairs.

July 1, 1903. Kiel.

Yesterday, not being able to race, Hans and I went on board the *Mirage* to lunch with the Ormondes and steam to Eckernförde : there we had a walk and I took some photographs ; got back in good time to dine with the Vanderbilts on the *North Star*, a beautiful boat : my maid brought my clothes and I changed on board. Hans dined at the hotel restaurant, dressed and went to spend the night on the *Princessin Victoria Luise*. Prince Henry of Prussia came to dinner ; then he and all the men left us to go to the *bierabend*.

We women were left alone on board with two Frenchmen, but in about an hour, to my astonishment, the launch reappeared with several men *and* Prince Henry, who disappeared

---

[1] The 5th Prince zu Lynar, b. in Rome 1875, m. in 1917 Countess Victoria von Redern. His mother was Miss May-Amelia Parsons (1851–1920), an American.

down below with Mrs. Cornelius Vanderbilt, our hostess, a fascinating (though snobbish) little American, but with much charm ; I always imagined the Prince stiff and shy, certainly without a *soupçon* of flirtation but—still waters run deep : I think, too, he saw a good deal of her during his visit to the United States.[1]

Hans seemed pleased with his sail on the *Princessin Victoria Luise*, and said the Emperor was charming, made him sit beside him at lunch, and was very civil. He seems to think that there is quite a chance of his getting the post of Governor —but I don't think so.

Mrs. Vanderbilt told me that she said to the Emperor : " It is the Plesses we want in America ; why do you not send them, it would be a great compliment to us ? " The Emperor only answered vaguely, but he said to her : " I am fond of both of them : I promised my mother to befriend her and always shall ; she is my charge." . . .

How I should hate to be May Goelet,[2] all those odious little Frenchmen, and dozens of others, crowding round her millions.

July 5, 1903. M . . .

Arrived here by motor at seven : large fine house, heaps of people, but I was bored to death : as a rule I always do dislike going to other people's houses, but I love to have guests in my own. The journey by train from Kiel to Berlin was horrid ; I never felt such heat, not even in India. We left Berlin the next morning by motor expecting to arrive at Fürstenstein about tea-time, but did not get home before half-past eleven at night ; we punctured four tyres, broke two springs, then a pipe went wrong, and the benzine did not find its way to the engine which started to jib and hiccough up-hill. But I did not really mind as it was a lovely day and a beautiful moonlight night. Strange to say, at Kirschberg we met two more motors. I suppose in a few years there will be hundreds, and in a few years after that, we shall all be skimming over trees and church steeples in flying machines : Hansel will probably go off on his honeymoon in one !

To-morrow I shall have to walk about and be pleased with

---

[1] Prince Henry of Prussia was in the United States, Feb. 23– March 11, 1902 : the Emperor subsequently presented a statue of Frederick the Great to the city of Washington.

[2] Miss May Goelet, m. on November 10, 1903, 8th Duke of Roxburghe.

everything ! Some things are very nice, the hall with the carved staircase, and a big room with Gobelins tapestry ; but the bedrooms and the dining-room are like those in a first-class hotel. I envy them the electric light ; it would be *so* easy to put it into Fürstenstein : the engine is there, and the company at Waldenburg will *give* us the cable if we take so many lights, so it costs only about two thousand pounds to put in the fittings. I wish Vater would do it for us.

I do not care for our hostess ; they were given the title of Graf only a year ago, and now she walks about on the tips of her toes, smiles condescendingly sometimes, and has a " lady-in-waiting " carrying her cape, " showing visitors to their rooms," and so on. She tries to be *trop grande dame*. Dear old Hatzfeldt wrote to me and said : " You know I am your friend ; then may I advise you to be very stiff at M." I cannot quite make out what he means. I should never switch off my real self in the house or company of anyone, considering myself *born* a lady and fit company for Kings and Queens, and also, I venture to think, for little German Counts and their wives. It is too tiring not to be natural and I consider that a real lady need never " rub it in " by a false stiffness or by " giving herself airs " as one says in England. *Noblesse oblige*, but to me that seems rather a motto for our inner life and thought, and has little to do with outward signs such as the manner of shaking hands, putting one's nose in the air, or pretending to be more important than one is.

July 9, 1903. 1 *a.m.* Fürstenstein.

Baby was in wild spirits this afternoon ; he was naughty and I put him in the corner ; he never said a word but stayed there about a quarter of an hour ; then I went to him and said :

" Oh, Baby, I never thought it was possible for a little boy to be so naughty when his Mummy loves him so."

He looked quite solemn as he replied :

" Didn't you ? I fink it kite poshble," and he again turned his face to the wall.

Later (with only a few tears) he was quite good. Oh, what a joy he is—greater than anything in all the wide world. I sing him all sorts of little American " coon " or plantation songs : the refrain of this one is pretty I think :

CASTLE PLESS.

Two Corridors, that on the left showing Sporting Trophies.

Funny leetle feller everybody knows,
Don't know what to call him, but he mighty like a rose,
Looking ·at his Mammy with eyes so shining blue—
Make you fink dat Heaven is coming close to you.

July 16, 1903. Fürstenstein.

An ordinary day, what I call a " German duty day." I
will describe it. A walk to the *Riesengrab* in the morning,
the men in front, the dutiful wives trotting after ; then lunch,
with Ritter the head agent present ; after luncheon we all
kissed each other and said *mahlzeit*.[1] Then Vater's secretary,
who used to be Hans's tutor, came from Salzbrunn ; they
sat and smoked and talked. I got restless and sat on the
balcony looking at the papers (*longing* to play the piano but
afraid to make a noise). Then Mathilde went to write letters
and I came upstairs and got right into bed for an hour ; I
felt so tired, it has been *such* a hot day. Later we had tea
on the terraces and dawdled there for two hours, and at last
they made up their minds to go for a drive, so we drove through
the *Salzgrund*. We got home late, so dinner was not till a
quarter to nine. After dinner I could resist no more my
piano, so I hummed while playing with the soft pedal down.
Hans, furious, said I had better sing ; he said that I was
drowning the conversation, so I really didn't know what to do,
but felt inclined to cry. I looked at a great perfumed lily
in a silver vase at the end of the piano, and wished I could
be in a soft, sweet-scented, peaceful country where perhaps
people grow and live freely—nothing forced or unnatural,
tamed or " squeezed in." I hate to dawdle and do nothing
as one does when my in-laws come here, although I am very
fond of them : it upsets my liver, I think, and makes me cross.

To-night—the river indeed sounds like the sea.

July 17, 1903. Fürstenstein.

It has been raining, and I feel a little better and not so
grumpy.

To-day I got a letter from Violet Mar and Kellie asking
me to help her with some theatricals in October, but alas, I
had to decline as we are going over soon for Cowes, and Vater
would have a fit, I expect, if I went again in October ; and I
long to go, as I love acting. Milly Sutherland [2] has asked me

---

[1] I.e. good digestion.
[2] Millicent Duchess of Sutherland (Lady Millicent Hawes), widow
of the 4th (1851–1913), and mother of the present, Duke.

to sing at a concert at Trentham; and Louise Beaufort [1]
to open a bazaar at Badminton (which is a beautiful place);
all this in October and the dates would have fitted perfectly.

Oh, well, I must try to be less spoilt and not wail for all
that I cannot have. But alas, with the years that pass by I
sometimes feel more homesick than ever, and wish once more
with all my soul that this beautiful place were in England.

July 18, 1903. Fürstenstein.

. . . Hansel is the greatest darling on earth now. His
particular game is to make dreadful noises and pretend that a
bull, bear, or monkey is coming, and that he must take care of
Mummilie; so he cuddles my head down into his neck to hide
my face and holds me fast with his two little arms round my
neck. When we got home from fishing this afternoon we
found that Prince Joachim Albrecht [2] had arrived. He stays
till Monday. Poor dear, he told me he has about two hundred
a year to live on, and he misses his mother terribly; she
died about five years ago. His father is a stiff, stern, narrow-
minded man, but with a kind heart hidden deep inside the
stone into which his upbringing and education have almost
moulded him.

July 20, 1903. *Sunday*. Fürstenstein.

We all went to Service in the private chapel in the morning.
Because I felt sad I longed for a nice service in an English
church, with a beautiful organ and hymns, and freedom to
kneel down to my God and feel *alone*.

Instead of that we all sat perched side by side on high state
chairs, and it made me want to laugh. The service lasted
only one hour. The smell was horrid; all the poor people
in their best stuffy Sunday clothes, having walked here in
the heat. And then the kitchen is underneath the chapel and
I kept on smelling the menu I had just looked over with the
cook. I felt inclined to laugh, too, in the course of one psalm
where it is written *macht deiner lichter hell* (I can't spell it
aright but it means ' make thy lights bright '), for, at that
moment, one of the attendants, in a long blue cloak with a

---

[1] The Dowager Duchess of Beaufort m. 9th Duke (1847–1924) in
1895.

[2] A great-grandson of Frederick-William III. of Prussia; b. 1876;
his mother, a Princess of Saxe-Altenburg (1854–98), d. when her
second son was twenty-two.

long stick and a snuffer at the end, went to the altar and
extinguished the two candles ! Dear Vater trying to sing
is enough to upset anyone ; it is like a nest of bumble bees very
close—or far distant thunder !

Prince Joachim Albrecht went away and returns to-morrow ;
he went off again with my handkerchief ; it is quite strange
that Vater and Mathilde really do not seem to mind a bit his
boyish, open flirtation. Vater kissed me last night and seemed
quite pleased, and before the Prince left this morning Mathilde
went to him and said : " I think my daughter-in-law really
wants her handkerchief " : afterwards she said to me : " he
gave it me without a word, making me feel quite sorry."
Later Willusch [1] got it somehow and gave it back to the
Prince !

July 24, 1903. Fürstenstein.

We talked politics this evening, Vater furious against
Chamberlain ; says he is always having his knife into Germany. Then we talked of the Boer War and Prince Joachim
Albrecht—who is here again—talked a lot of nonsense ; he is
the type of German soldier who thinks there can and ought to
be no other career for any man but to bear arms all his life for
his country and therefore to know no freedom. He spoke of
" the absurd ways of the English in battle," their bad tactics,
and so on. . . .

I am thoroughly cosmopolitan in my ideas ; I know well
enough the faults of England and admit frankly that the
English leave the things undone that ought to be done—but
I know, too, the extraordinary narrow-mindedness of the
average German, the type of soldier who has never seen a
fight, not even with a savage tribe ; who has never travelled ;
whose body, indeed—whose soul and heart one might say,
move only at the command of his superior officer.

July 25, 1903. Fürstenstein.

This evening (as usual) I sang and the Prince played his
'cello : how childish all Royalties are as a rule. He now
has three of my pocket handkerchiefs. He got so close to
me on the sofa that, Mathilde says, Vater made a face at him
and he moved away. I did not notice all this. I notice so

---

[1] Count Wilhelm Hochberg, b. 1886, step-brother of the Prince
of Pless.

little, really. To-morrow morning we have to go to the opening of the Bakers' Exhibition—a frightening prospect as it is I who do the opening, with a speech in German.

August 4, 1903.   Cowes, at a little villa we have rented.

To-day we went out sailing and nearly won ; it was blowing a hurricane ; even I felt ill and had to go down below for an hour. Little Patsy was ill all the time. This evening I dined at Egypt House ; the King and the Prince of Wales arrived after their Squadron Club dinner to play bridge ; but I came home early and now I am going to sleep, very tired, and my bed is nothing but hard " humps."

August 6, 1903.   Cowes.

Yesterday the others went sailing and were all rather ill. I, knowing I should be bored with the people on board, stayed at home and lunched at Egypt House, and then played croquet. Hans, Patsy and I dined with the King and Queen on board the *Victoria and Albert* ; no one else there but the Prince of Wales and Princess Victoria and the aides-de-camp in-waiting. I sang after dinner, the little Queen turning over the pages of my music.

To-night I again dine at Egypt House to meet the King and Queen. ·I would much rather be dining here at the villa, laughing with all the others, and afterwards sitting in the Squadron gardens to listen to the band.

I bathed this morning and it was delicious ; I found I could *really* swim a little, but the water was none too clean, with salad leaves and bits of paper floating about—quite horrid !

August 10, 1903.   Cowes.

Have had no time to myself all these days getting up at half-past seven to go racing, coming home too late to rest, and then dinner. We have had little dinner parties ·here and lots of fun, and afterwards went out and sat in the Squadron gardens and listened to the " Hungarian " band.

On Friday we were to have sailed on the Emperor's boat, the *Meteor* ; it was a calm still morning, and as we were getting into the shore-boat to go out to her, a note was put into my hand ; we pushed off and after a while I thought I might as well read it. It was from Admiral Eisendecker saying that, there being no breeze, it was not a " *Meteor* day " ; she would, therefore, lose the race and spoil her record which has been so good, consequently he was not going to take her out ! So back we had to go, very disappointed ; but ate some more breakfast, having hurried so much before. Hans says the Admiral did not sail because we were taking Miss Gladys Deacon ; but I scarcely think this is possible. After all, if the Crown Prince did give her a ring once, that's all over long ago. . . .

The Russian Ambassador, Count Benckendorff, Natalie Hatzfeldt's brother, has been staying at Egypt House with his Secretary of Embassy ; [1] rather the tables turned—an Ambassador staying with his Secretary. The party includes the Duchess of Manchester and her sister, Miss Emily Yznaga, two Mexican Americans about forty or fifty years old ; Lady Howe and her husband ; [2] Count Albert Mensdorff, Chargé d'affaires at the Austrian Embassy ; Captain Seymour Fortescue [3] and—I think that is all.

I shall walk up after dinner and wish them all good-bye, as we leave for Newlands to-morrow. This has been a very pleasant week and the weather delicious. I love the sea, particularly for bathing, and I think I should soon know how to swim ; at present I dare not go out of my depth. Cowes is such a weird little town, very bad hotels with very bad food, but no one seems to mind. The roads are so narrow that I don't think two carriages could pass each other, and the streets are packed with people—niggers, clowns, Punch and Judy shows, conjurors, and plenty of bands, barrel-organs with monkeys ; girls with yachting caps trimmed with gaudy ribbons on one side of their heads and dirty white shoes, singing to the accompaniment of a small piano or concertina, played generally by a man ; while a few yards away the King and Queen, Dukes, Lords, and ladies, are conversing in the Squadron garden or on the R.Y.S. landing stage.

But all this noise is in the town. The Club is charming and quiet, and the crowd that wait outside to watch the people come in and go out are respectful ; they go to *see* and admire and criticize ; one hears one's name mentioned as one passes ; they show—indeed *are* full of interest towards

---

[1] Monsieur Kozello-Poklewsky.

[2] 4th Earl (1861–1929), m. 1883, Lady Georgiana Spencer Churchill (1860–1906), d. of 7th Duke of Marlborough.

[3] Capt. the Honble. Sir Seymour Fortescue, b. 1856, s. of 3rd Earl Fortescue ; Equerry to King George V. since 1901.

what they call " the gentry." So different from Kiel where
you find nothing but beer gardens and where if you *do* happen
to pass by, no one takes the slightest interest in you, except
perhaps to turn and stare, and puff a whiff of horrible cigar
smoke into your face.

August 16, 1903. Lochmore, Sutherland, Scotland.[1]

I must go back nearly a week. Poppets was delighted to
see us when we got home and we spent one quiet day at Newlands. On Thursday morning Hans and I went up to London,
leaving that night to come on here. We arrived after a horrible
long journey and a drive of thirty miles by motor in the rain
along the most narrow and dangerous roads—and I arrived
without Hans. He got out at Crewe at half-past eleven at
night; absolutely refusing to come any further. He had
neither guns with him, nor, so he said, proper shooting clothes;
and Lord Cairns,[2] whom he had met in the Marlborough
Club, worked him up against Scotland, telling him that it
rained all the time there (which so far has proved true); also
that he could get no newspapers and send no telegrams. This
of course is exaggeration. At first, when he said he would not
come, I was furious and disappointed and thought it so ridiculous after getting his tickets and seeing all the baggage in.
He was so like a baby and really *so sad* at the idea of being
bored during a whole week in Scotland that I had to let him
go, after he had trumped up a beautiful excuse which he
proceeded to propound with great effect : " Dany, I will go
to Ostend, you have always wanted me to take sea baths ; very
well, I will go and take them, and then come back to dear old
Newlands strong and well and ready to do my duty and we will
have another baby." I did then believe that it is possible to
laugh and cry at the same time. How I hated to be left alone,
and longed to put out the muddy artificial light and watch the
moon through the window, holding Tommy's hand and just
talking " little nothings that make a world of thought." I
wanted to feel he would be happy with me here amongst the
hills and heather even in the rain, even if there was nothing in
particular to do.

How seldom people find their happiness on a darkened stage ;
they must turn up all the limelights to find it. To my mind

---

[1] Scottish residence of the Duke of Westminster and his first wife
the sister of the authoress.

[2] 3rd Earl Cairns (1863–1905).

love, sympathy, friendship ought to be sufficient in life—not of course to live entirely for them ; that would be selfishness ; but I would just take love and clasp it in fair weather or foul, tempest or calm ; to have it for my sun shining on life's path, even if the sky overhead be darkened with rain-clouds : but Hans would not stay and my soul must get used to its loneliness.

This is a nice house surrounded with a few scant trees, but the scenery is lovely—splendid jagged rocky mountains and great expanses of water ; one loch stretches to the sea seven miles from here. We drove this afternoon ; it poured nearly all the time, while the tops of the mountains stood out above a diadem of soft white mist. We fished in one of the lochs yesterday and caught a lot of sea-trout with a fly. To-morrow I shall try for a salmon in the river, but they are almost impossible to catch : then I shall ride up to another " shooting-lodge " and join Shelagh and Bend Or for the night as we are to go stalking very early in the morning ; the other people will be left here—Leila Crichton [1] and her husband, Agatha Thynne [2] and Mr. Garnett.[3]

August 18, 1903. Lochmore.

Shelagh and I came back to-day from Kylestrom ; it is a charming little " lodge " on the sea-coast, nestling amongst a few trees in the most glorious scenery amidst high rocky mountains and lochs. We two and Bend Or rode over yesterday in about one and a half hours ; he stays there to-night ; the rest of the party came up for luncheon ; later we all came back here because there was scarcely room at the lodge for everybody. As Shelagh and I rode home about seven, the view from the top of the hills was truly magnificent. Far away the sea was calm as crystal and the setting sun seemed to be plunging right into the water ; here and there we saw great big lochs dotted with islands ; some of these lochs spread out low at the foot of the hills, others were high up between two mountain peaks, which gives a curious effect as they stand out like mirrors in the whole panorama. We both rode on gentlemen's saddles, which I had never seriously done

---

[1] Lady Mary Grosvenor (now Lady Mary Stanley), m. in 1903 Viscount Crichton (1872-1914) ; their son is the 5th Earl of Erne.

[2] M. in April, 1904, 3rd Lord Hindlip.

[3] Wm. Thos. Garnett, D.L., of Queenmore Park, Lancs. ; Diplomatic Service 1902-20

before. It was almost dark before we arrived but I was so
filled with the solemnity and grandeur of it all that I forgot
to feel afraid, and lost all thought of myself ; in that frame
of mind I could have adventured a gallop into Hell. As I
cantered along even Shelagh, who is a perfect horsewoman,
called out : " Don't be too brave."

Shelagh and I leave on Saturday. She goes to Ireland
for the Dublin Horse Show ; I to Newlands. . . .

October 18, 1903. Fürstenstein.

The autumn has almost passed ; the house has been full
of people and is now empty : the summer flowers are over,
summer hats and frocks put away, fires are lit and we come
home to tea instead of taking it with us to the *Daisysee, Eulenge-
birge, Riesengebirge, Friedland*, and other lovely spots. We
motored very often to different little rivers to fish, which
delighted Poppets, but unluckily he was here only for about
a week ; he could not spare more time away from England,
as he had spent three weeks in Homburg—which did him
a lot of good ; he got thinner and younger—it is almost ridiculous how young he looks although sixty-nine—he might be
fifty-five ! Little Patsy, too, was so well and cheery, the
people almost took her for Shelagh ; her figure is marvellous
and one cannot be dull or sad when she is in the house. . . .

I have still some flowers in bloom—tiger-lilies, violets,
beautiful begonias and even roses. The late autumn tints
are marvellous ; little Hansel is out all day, and has the warm
colour of sunshine on his cheeks.

November 3, 1903. Eaton Hall, Cheshire.

I left Fürstenstein on the 20th of September for London,
where I slept the night at Grosvenor House, and left the next
evening for Scotland to stay with Lord and Lady Mar and
Kellie at Alloa House, not far from Perth. We acted *A
Pantomime Rehearsal*, one of the most amusing pieces that
have ever been written ; the rehearsals and the two perform-
ances were great fun.

When in London Patsy and I went to a fortune-teller in
Bond Street ; she was extraordinary ; told me the past
absolutely, and described Hans and the baby ; she also said
I shall have another baby before I am thirty-one,[1] and that

---

[1] The Princess's second son was b. in Feb., 1905 ; her father-in-law
died in Aug., 1907.

dear Vater will not live three years more. She also said that I have a great power and magnetism over people which will increase so much that I shall have to take care. Some of my friends will remain true to me for ever ; they will stand by me always no matter what happens. I must avoid making people unhappy ! At the age of thirty-four I shall be lifted off my feet by some extraordinary power—I suppose in some person ! Then she astonished me more than ever by saying : " You have a sister who will come more into your life than she has ever done." (I cannot see how this can ever be : we live so far apart.) " And I see a gloom round her—she will not be a happy woman." [1] I cannot bear to dwell on this last prophecy, and I will not believe it, and pray to God it may be otherwise.

November 4, 1903. Eaton Hall, Cheshire.

This evening I sang, and we laughed a lot and I did an imitation of a German governess at a girls' school. As Mrs. de Winton and Doll Hartopp [2] arrived to-day, we were seven women and only two men at dinner ! I have a piece of work and the most lovely bundle of silks and I have gone quite crazy on embroidering. To-morrow the others hunt and Aunt Min and I go over by motor to spend the day at Llanarmon Tower. I do hope it will be fine.

I cannot help laughing at a little story about Shelagh. She said to Min the other day : " Darling, what are ' high teeth ' ; the nurse keeps on talking of Ursula's ' high teeth.' " Min thought for some time and answered : " She doesn't mean high teeth, she means eye teeth, which are at the side ; the nurse must drop and pick up her aitches in the wrong place." Then Shelagh was furious and said : " Min, how awful ! " The other day a lot of old women from Chester came to tea, and asked : " How many teeth has the dear little baby girl got now ? " So I answered : " Oh, eleven, but only two high teeth ! " What *will* they think of me ? I noticed one of them kept eyeing me queerly the whole time afterwards.

---

[1] The fortune-teller was no fool and, of course, must have known us well. Our photographs were never out of the papers, especially Patsy's and Shelagh's.—D. OF P.

[2] D. of 1st Baron Nunburnholme, m. in 1895 Sir Charles Cradock-Hartopp ; 2nd, in 1905, 3rd Earl Cowley ; 3rd, in 1914, Major Duberly.

I laugh now when I think of it. They probably went home and told scandalous stories about the Duchess of Westminster's inability to manage her aitches !

November 9, 1903. Newlands.

A heavenly day, but then I always feel this little peaceful place is not far from heaven.

This morning we *sat out in the sun*. Patsy read, and I tried to print some photographs ; it may be more economical, but it is a dreadful nuisance and then they do not look half so nice as when the photographer does them. Poppets painted a little water-colour sketch for my scrapbook. This afternoon he drove me all round by the sea and showed me a lot of new villas and houses that are being built at Milford. The trees have grown up well round some of the houses. I wished one were mine, that I could move into it with Baby and rest, and have my piano, books, embroidery, painting and camera. Patsy said this morning : " I wish you could have a quiet time here now, but I don't suppose you would like it." I was surprised ; I thought she knew me better.

When in London I shall stay at Grosvenor House as it is always such a rush of bootmakers, dressmakers, milliners and hairdressers when one goes to town for only a few days. Tony Shaftesbury [1] (Shelagh's brother-in-law) has asked me to stay with them ; but, with so much to do, I would rather be free, and for this reason prefer Grosvenor House.

November 18, 1903. Fürstenstein.

I spent three days in London, and returned to Newlands on Friday, stayed till Saturday, taking a special train back on the Sunday with Charlie Wood and Freddy Guest [2] to get to London in time for me to catch the eight-twenty-five from Victoria for Berlin. Our " special " got us up at five.

Soveral came to see me in the evening, vainer than ever, saying : " *Mon chère enfant, vous ne vous connaissez pas*. If we were to meet more often or I were to come to Fürstenstein it would be dangerous, in fact, fatal to both of us." I took " rude care " to explain to him that I was not the least in

---

[1] 9th Earl ; m. 1899, Lady Constance Grosvenor.
[2] Capt. Rt. Hon. Frederick Guest, C.B.E., D.S.O., 3rd s. of 1st Lord Wimborne, b. 1875, m. in 1905 Miss Amy Phipps ; Sec. of State for Air 1921–2.

love with him, only liked him as a friend ; but I believe he was not convinced.

I arrived in Berlin on Monday evening and did not sleep a bit during the journey. Hans met me at the station. I dined at half-past eight with Count Vico and Wimperl Schönborn and we went to the Metropole Theatre ; everything seemed so vulgar and dirty after the pretty women and smart clothes one sees on the English stage.

We left Berlin yesterday afternoon and arrived here at eleven. I woke up this morning to find everything white with snow ; and only last Sunday we were sitting in the open at Newlands and marvelling at the roses still in bloom on the walls and in the gardens !

The Crown Prince is not coming here as the Emperor has ordered him to attend a *Hof Jagd*[1] instead. I received a letter from the Prince when I arrived in Berlin. His sudden change of plans gives rise to much discussion. One story is that he rode in a race (which he is not allowed to do) on the very day of the operation by which the Emperor had the polypus taken out of his throat ; and that the Emperor, on hearing of it a few days later, was so angry that he put him under arrest, and has stopped his leave for a year. Another story is simply that the Emperor ordered him to attend a definite number of *Hof Jagds* ; and the Prince's Colonel, although giving him leave to come here, said he would therefore miss a *Hof Jagd* ; that the Emperor on hearing this said no—the *Hof Jagd* was a duty and must be performed ; therefore he must give up Fürstenstein. Yet another story ! Prince Salm who arrived to-night (his wife remains in Potsdam as she is expecting a baby) said : " Do not be cross or misunderstand me, but I think both the Emperor and Empress are afraid of the Prince coming here and being with you ! " This may seem a compliment, but I do not take it as such ; I am sick of having my appearance, which is quite ordinary, being thrown into my face as an excuse for some strange behaviour of the Court. Anyway, they shall not see me in Berlin this winter. I am angry now and defiant, and one thing I *will* do is to go and stay at Potsdam with Prince Salm and the Archduchess his wife, when the skating begins, and they shall ask the Crown Prince to lunch without saying I am there, and he shall go home and *not* mention that he

---

[1] A Royal Hunt.

met me; yes, and come *again* if I choose. If they are such idiots I shall just fool them all. I think the Emperor's behaviour most rude.

November 21, 1903. Fürstenstein.

To-day we shot about eight hundred head. I shot about thirty pheasants and some hare; it snowed hard in the morning but was fine and nice in the afternoon. Having got very wet, I sent for another pair of boots and stockings and changed in the tent when the men had left. I had to lower my " panties " to get at my suspenders and Mathilde and " Ma " Asseburg helped me; to think of my doing this with them about ten years ago! *Mais nous avons change tout cela.*

This evening " Ma " and I dressed up in my dancing dresses and danced skirt-dances before them all, cake-walks, and Spanish dances. Prince Salm played tunes on the pianola which is most useful and delightful to have. Eight years ago my dear old father-in-law did not like to walk with me in Berlin unless I wore a little black gown; now after I had danced and delighted him, Hans said: " Vater was off his head and said you were so graceful." All that Mathilde said when I took her to her room, was: " Try and remember when you hold your skirt to catch only the top skirt of the crêpe-de-chine, for once or twice you caught the underskirt too, and one could see up to your knee." But she did not really seem the least shocked. I can scarcely believe they are the same people; my brother-in-law Conny who used always to say to me : " *Daisy spricht doch Deutsch*," now writes to me in English, to thank me for his " charming visit " to Fürstenstein. Well, if no one belonging to the outside world about here liked me and everything felt wrong, I should still have the comfort and satisfaction of feeling that Hans' relations like me—bless them!

Hansel, thank God, is very well, and how he loves me! And Mathilde is too dear and nice with him. I am sure I don't know whether it is shocking or not but I have my bath with him every evening; he is not four years old yet so I do not think it can matter.

December 3, 1903. Donaueschingen,[1] Baden.

I have had no time to write earlier although we have been

---

[1] The residence of Maximilian Prince of Fürstenberg, b. 1863, m. in 1889 Countess Irma of Schönborn-Bucheim.

CASTLE PLESS.

The Prince's Sitting-room.

here nearly four days. The house is fine and contains some good tapestry and pictures. It is built on the edge of the town, which is a pity. About half an hour's drive away is a beautiful park where the stags and wild boar are ; a very large enclosure and a great long drive through it, like the long drive at Windsor ; dented in the middle, with a high hill at each end. An ideal site for a large house. There is a little house perched on the farthest hill-top which a previous Fürstenberg built for his mistress : the couple must have had for each other more than a passing fancy as the house is very lonely, but has a magnificent view all round ; there is something very grand and silent about it. And yet the little house itself is so simple.

The shooting to-day was of the best ; in one drive they shot with about twelve or fourteen guns seventy-five foxes ; this afternoon we shot driven deer and hinds and wild boar. I shot three wild boar and five deer : two or three I killed while they ran, which I had never tried to do before with a rifle, and was much surprised when they fell. In the morning I killed three foxes, but I hated the whole thing ; especially (because of my remembrance of the dear hunting days) did I hate shooting the foxes.

The Duke and Duchess of Schleswig-Holstein left last night, also Count Wimperl Schönborn. In the evening I dressed up in a hat of Irma Fürstenberg's and one of her brocaded petticoats, and sang and danced coon songs for them. Count Sturn Sierstorpff and Fitch Colloredo [1] also dressed up and we danced the cake-walk. All the other evenings we have played cards.

The nice little Duke of Wurtemberg, who will one day be King, is here. He lost his wife, sister to the Archduke Franz-Ferdinand, two years ago and has five little children ; he is only about forty [2] with a nice face and brave sad eyes like those of a young man grown prematurely old.

Before I came in I just rushed to the green-houses as I had heard so much about them, but they are very poor. The orchid-house has nothing in it but the brown orchid, and a few chrysanthemums and cyclamens ; no roses, violets or bulbs of any sort. It is extraordinary, but I have never seen what I call " a garden " in Germany or Austria, except that of

---

[1] Count Ferdinand Colloredo-Mannsfeld, a cousin of the present Prince, m. 1909, in New York, Nora Iselin.

[2] Albert Duke of Wurtemberg, b. 1865, m. 1893, Archduchess Marguerite of Austria (1870-1902).

Ferdy Rothschild at his Vienna house, and at his villa outside Vienna.

December 30, 1903.　Newlands.

What weeks it is since I have written in my diary, and now I seem suddenly to find myself here again. After I left Donaueschingen and returned to Fürstenstein, I was ill in bed for ten days, with Doctor Ismer and the little dentist from Waldenburg in the house for a week, because it was feared I would have inflammation of the jaw. The dentist in Breslau took twenty-five minutes to pull a tooth out and tore all my gum away and left splinters in my jaw. I held my old Tommy's hand all the time ; I nearly fainted and had to stop in the middle and drink brandy. He came the next day to Fürstenstein and said everything was *ganz normal*, and then went away and left me. A day later I was in such pain that we got the dentist from Waldenburg, who extracted two little bits of splintered jaw and took away little bags of matter.

I was just well enough to crawl through the different feasts for the poor people. Freiburg, Polsnitz, Waldenburg, Upper and Lower Salzbrunn—I would not have disappointed them for anything. I love the old poor people. One old woman while she was very ill, indeed dying, said : " I should like to live another year just to see once more that Princess." She recovered, and we talk together often.

Mathilde sent me a nice little brooch for Christmas. Vater, I am glad to say, gives us double-windows for the big drawing-rooms. Bend Or sent me a lovely pendant with a big emerald ; Shelagh two silver vases. Hans is going to give me Hansel's miniature in a diamond heart on a bracelet.

Ethel and Tommy Peacocke are here, and Reggie Hoare. Also Mr. and Mrs. Guy Chetwynd ; [1] he is Lady Anglesey's brother, and son of Lady Hastings ; she is an American, and very pretty.

How I wish Hansel were here and that we were going to have a nice quiet two months in England. I shall not go at

---

[1] Sir Guy Chetwynd, 5th Bt., b. 1874, s. of 4th Bt. and Lady Florence, y. d. of 2nd Marquess of Anglesey and widow of last Marquess of Hastings ; m. 1902, Rosalind Secor of U.S.A. (who divorced him 1909 and died 1922) ; 2nd, 1917, Constance Amor. His sister Lilian m. her cousin the 5th Marquess of Anglesey (1875–1905).

all to Berlin this winter, not to Court anyway. I am much too angry about the Crown Prince's cancelled visit and his extraordinary behaviour (which was not his fault), particularly as an aide-de-camp, writing to Hans, had said : " The Crown Prince will not be able to get any more leave for this year ! " Yet three months later, he was shooting at Klitschdorff, Hans' sister's place. I suppose the Emperor really thinks he may fall in love with me and all that nonsense ! Well, perhaps even to take that risk would be better than to keep his son away from the society of ladies and to force him, in consequence, to mix with American actresses and that sort of person ; anyway, I am not going to any Court function this year, and I only hope (even if I am flattering myself) that they will notice my absence. Bülow and the Emperor imagine I am only a pretty woman and think that if they tell me that whenever they see me, or pay me some extravagant compliment, it is all I want ; but from now onward I intend to show them that I expect something quite different—and I will get it some day.

CHAPTER SIX

1904

January 10, 1904. Chatsworth, Derbyshire.

WE have been here since the fourth, staying one night in London on our way from Newlands, when we went to the theatre with Soveral; Hans had to leave yesterday for Germany to be in Berlin for the Opening of Parliament, and I leave to-morrow to go to Eaton. The King and Queen also leave, and probably everyone else.

The Queen is as charming and beautiful as always, and the King very well and in good spirits. A possible war between Russia and Japan does not seem to cause him anxiety. . . . . The King has his bridge with Mrs. Keppel who is here—with lovely clothes and diamonds—in a separate room, and in the other rooms people are massed together, also of course playing bridge. Generally, to amuse the Queen, I am made to go and sing and dance in the corridor where the band is, with Muriel Wilson,[1] Maudie Warrender,[2] the Duchess's grand-daughters (the Acheson girls), Mensdorff (who will be nominated Austrian Ambassador in London in a short time), Soveral, Lord Howe, who is sentimental and likes to sing, and several others. The party is much the same as last year : cousin Mary Elcho, a most charming and clever woman, and her husband [3] ; Lord and Lady Howe, the Willie James's, the Grenfells, the Mars (and Kellie), the Arthur Sassoons, and Princess Victoria. The Duchess of Manchester has just left. Then there are a lot of men, Sidney Greville and John Ward (in-waiting) ; Bertie Tempest, Frank Mildmay and others.

---

[1] D. of Arthur Wilson (d. 1909) of Tranby Croft and niece of 1st Lord Nunburnholme ; m. 1917, Major Richard Warde, Scots Guards.

[2] D. of 8th Earl of Shaftesbury, and sister of Lady Mar and Kellie, m. 1894 Sir George Warrender, 7th Bt. (1860–1917).

[3] Now Earl and Countess of Wemyss ; Lady Wemyss is a sister of Colonel Guy Wyndham and therefore related to the authoress.

Yesterday we all motored over to Hardwicke, the most beautiful old Elizabethan house ; it is unique and was built by Bess of Hardwicke to entertain Queen Elizabeth. The tapestries are marvellous. The roads were lined nearly all the way with people and children waving flags and calling hurrah !

This morning it is raining and snowing, so I think this afternoon I will sit quiet and do my embroidery.

The present Duke of Devonshire always lived at Hardwicke when he was Lord Hartington.

January 12, 1904. Eaton Hall, Cheshire.

Arrived here yesterday from Chatsworth.

The last evening there was very cheerful : the Queen danced a waltz with Soveral, and then we each took off our shoes to see what difference it made in our height. The Queen took, or rather kicked hers off, and then got into everyone else's, even into Willie Grenfell's old pumps. I never saw her so free and cheerful—but always graceful in everything she does.

Everyone except myself left for London in the King's Special train—the Queen kissed me when parting.

Little Patsy was here when I arrived, but left this morning.

This morning Shelagh and Bend Or went out hunting. I went by train in half an hour to Flint and spent the day with Granny and Uncle Hugo ; Walter Brooke,[1] Minnie's second boy, is staying there. Granny is extremely well and amuses herself very much among the neighbours ; she has them to tea, and goes out to lunch, and to-morrow she attends some private theatricals. After lunch she walked about with a pen in her hand saying : " Now, darling, what shall I mark for you to have at my death ? " Then she wrote " for Daisy " on several articles, including a little painted picture of Patsy at the age of fourteen. Then I said she could leave me her chair, the one she always sits in ; it was so funny, somehow, and Hugo was so comical all the time that we all died of laughter, for in the same breath we were settling when she would come to Fürstenstein and all sorts of strenuous activities.

. . . Oh, diary, I haven't a friend in all the world I think to whom I can go and lay bare my soul and spirit and beg for a little grain of comfort against all the miserable disappointments this world brings one : not that I mind what society or one's acquaintances do or say. I expect nothing

---

[1] Major Walter Headfort Brooke.

but sham and lies from them.   But to be disappointed in those one loves, that is the hardest to bear—and in one's own family. . . .

January 20, 1904.   Newlands.

I left Eaton on the 14th and went to stay with Gwen Lowther : her husband is Lord Lonsdale's brother and will inherit the Peerage as Gracie Lonsdale has no children.   I stayed with them for the Melton Hunt Ball which was not very amusing.   I like to go to a ball to *dance*, and Englishmen as a rule do not dance well ; besides, here they never reverse as they do in Vienna.   I danced with little Jack Brinton, Heine Larisch, Bertie Sheriffe—who is married now to a nice woman with money and has two funny nice little babies.

The next day, Saturday, I went to London, having promised to dine with Count Metternich [1] and go to a play, but when I got to the Embassy I found we were dining alone, he had asked no one else : but we were quite cosy.   We talked away and really laughed, and he is renowned for being so dull. After dinner I tried to button the straps over my instep, which I saw were open, when Metternich got out of his chair with his cigar in his mouth, went down on both knees on the carpet and proceeded to try : I thought he would choke as he was getting redder and redder.   I said, " Take your cigar out of your mouth," which he did, and then fumbled again with the tiny diamond buttons.   I felt, after all the poor dear's trouble, if he didn't succeed it would be tragic ; so was delighted when he *did* button them and get off his knees with a crack in one of them and a smile of victory on his crooked jaw !   He is awfully nice, and a real gentleman.   Later, we went to a German play beautifully acted called *Der Zapfen-streich*.[2]   It is forbidden in Germany.   I learnt three new expressions—one was *Ach mein Freund spuck auf die Frauen* (oh, my friend, spit on the women).

Saturday I went to a matinée at the Palace with Maud Warrender and Willie Grenfell, but felt so seedy I had to leave.   I nearly fainted while I was alone in the electric brougham, and had to stop at an hotel and lie down for a little, and then went on again.   It was just chance that I got home to Grosvenor House without fainting, by praying hard, " God,

[1] Count Paul Wolff-Metternich, b. 1853.   German Consul-General in Cairo 1896, Ambassador in London 1901–12.
[2] *The Last Post.*

don't let me faint," and keeping my head close to the open window. I don't know now whether it was God or the open window; perhaps both! I think I caught a chill. I was five days late, and so pleased as I thought perhaps it meant a baby!

Monday I lunched with Consuelo Marlborough; her new house [1] will be beautiful, only I can't stand the dining-room; it is not high enough and the windows have always to be covered over with stuff as they are right on the ground and the people in a dirty little back street can look in. We went to the theatre in the evening, she and I, Mensdorff and Captain Banbury.

On Tuesday I lunched with Soveral at Willis's, and in the evening went to the theatre with him, Consuelo Marlborough and Lord Charles Montagu.[2] In the afternoon I went to Princes' and skated with Captain Banbury.

I write in bed with the window open in front of me and the sun shining; the doves cooing this morning woke me up. I thought it was the cry of a child and it gave me quite a start and brought back to me the voice, years ago, of my little baby girl as she sobbed herself to death with convulsions. This is certainly the most peaceful, dearest place on earth. I should like to lie in bed all day by the open window and just *rest*. But I must get up, dress and go out; make jokes with Reggie, and sing this evening with Dicky Braun. . . .

January 24, 1904. Grosvenor House, London.

Arrived here at eight-thirty in a slow Sunday train which took over four hours. I had an engaged carriage, which was lucky as people kept trying to get in. I had written to C., an old friend, about some shares of mine which he still holds for me, and in opening my bag to take out a book of poems, my eye was caught by his handwriting; a letter had come from him by the second post and Marie must have just put it into my bag.

It was strange as when I shut my eyes, and think of Cairo, I walk in the desert sand with him; or I lean from the window of my room to look at the purple sky, the bright moon, the

---

[1] Sunderland House, Curzon Street, London.
[2] S. of 7th Duke of Manchester and his wife Louise, who afterwards m. 8th Duke of Devonshire. Lord Charles m. in 1930 Hon. Lady Meux, *née* Sturt, w. of Admiral Sir Headworth (Lambton) Meux.

shadows of the palm trees. I see him waving us good-night, and I hear his steps and the clink of his spurs down the silent path. Then he was a soldier; now he drudges in the City to make gold which ever retreats as he comes near it. Once he was lucky and made a lot of money. Nearly four years ago Patsy banished him, and I shed tears; he asked too much, so he had to go, and for a moment I was miserable. But he wasn't really worth a tear; I know it now. Yet women are contrary beings and even worthlessness does not make them hate a man; often they pity him instead, and pity, it is said, is akin to love. On arriving here I found another letter asking if he might come and see me. I shall let him come to tea before I leave—if there is time.

Now I am going to read a little and try to go to sleep. I cannot think, somehow, what is the matter with me lately; it is not discontent, for God is so good to me; and my precious baby, and Hans, and all whom I love, are well. I owe money, true—but I could not go bankrupt as Vater would always pay, but I feel something in me that aches to emerge and meet something deeply responsive. I feel a longing for peace and something perfect, something profound, great, grand like the peal of an organ as its notes rise in an anthem to God, some one thing alone to live for, one ideal to help me to do great works in the world and make people happy. If I had a lot of money it would give me power to do good, and perhaps my mind would be content if I could make hundreds of sick and sad people well and happy; as it is, I have a cramped feeling. I have a longing to cast something from me, and that is why the East generally appeals to me so much : its glorious temples and buildings, its Sphinx and Pyramids, its great expanse of barren land, its ocean of sand, its many tribes with their different codes of life and religion, its buried histories and buried kings, men and women of character working out their own destinies, great for good or for evil. I copy this :

I want the lonely level sands
Stretched out beneath the sun,
The sadness of the old, old lands
Whose destiny is done :
The magic and the grace that cling
About the mountain's crest,
Where tombs of many a glorious King
Guard faithfully their rest.

Not lightly would I speak of love
Or depreciate his power,
But every star that wheels above,
And each enamelled flower,
That sends persuasive influence
To touch the human mind—
Appeals to some strange inner sense
That love can never find.

January 26, 1904.   Tranby Croft, East Yorkshire.

I arrived here only to-day and went straight to the theatre at Hull and we started rehearsing ; came back and had a rest, and rehearsed again after dinner : we are doing *The Pantomime Rehearsal.* I ought to have come yesterday but Captain Banbury who came to see me in the morning, persuaded me to delay and go to skate in the afternoon at Princes' and to the theatre with him in the evening ; so I did. And it was rather fun being incognito in London. We went to the Hippodrome where we would meet no one we knew. Society goes there only in the afternoon. I went wearing a hat, and it was such a relief not to have to dress up ; it is not supposed to be quite right to go alone to the play with a man, although lots of women do, but it rather depends, I think, on the man.

February 3, 1904.   Fürstenstein.

Have just written this to Poppets : " The curtain goes up and down on so many different scenes and acts of my life, with such very short intervals, that I find myself suddenly as it were standing alone amongst scenery I know well, with a part to repeat that I have often spoken, and yet a sort of tired dazed feeling comes over me : I forget my words, and know only that I must smile, laugh and *seem* happy ; and no one notices that I am in truth weary of many things, or that I *miss anything*—as the words at the end of the song *Forethought* express it."

Hans got to Berlin on Tuesday morning from Nice, and we came here together, arriving in time to help eat little Hansel's birthday cake and give him the Noah's Ark I had brought for him, and the hunting horn from Captain Banbury ; he has grown a great deal and is, thank God, so well. It is beautiful weather here, quite springlike, but I would prefer snow and tobogganing.

At dinner Hans said to me : " I have found out why they did not make me Governor ; Bülow said I was too Catholic, and took too much the side of the Poles." I was glad to hear this, seeing that it supplies a reason for not giving Hans the post, as I could not clearly understand why they did not. And Bülow, acting on the policy of the present Government towards the Poles (which I believe to be right), naturally did not nominate Hans. Oh well, if Hans does not do something between now and when he is fifty he never will. . . .

. . . O God, my life wants protection in more ways than one. Therefore, O God, have pity for my many and great faults, do not forsake me, keep me under Thy protection, for Thy Son's own sake. For no one knows my soul ; it stands alone, and sometimes it would fain pass away to a life of peace where only good is felt and known.

February 9, 1904. Berlin, Palast Pless.

On arriving here I went at ten-thirty to a picnic Ball at the Hotel Bristol, which was quite amusing. I left at three-thirty, but the others all stayed till after five. Last night was the Court Ball. The Empress was not there, she has a bad leg, a varicose vein I am afraid. I did not think the Emperor looked at all well, he was so pale ; he only spoke to me about the Waldenburg River and said it was all the fault of Vater's coal ; which I denied, that not being the chief fault. He said nothing about the Crown Prince not coming to Fürstenstein.

At first the little Crown Prince was frightened, but soon became quite happy, and we talked so long that I got quite nervous for his good name ! The latest story (which I told him) is that the Empress requested me not to come to Court because of him ! He is giving a ball to-morrow night. I told him I would go if there were any other married women, and he assured me there would be ; soon after I regretted my promise as I did not realize the Ball was to be in Potsdam at the Neues Palast, but now I think of it, it will be rather interesting to see the Palace all lit up at night with wax candles as in old times.

February 15, 1904. Berlin, Palast Pless.

It seems as if I had been here *years*. One lives through the night and sleeps in the day ; by this I mean that as I dance nearly every night till three-thirty, I sleep in the morning till twelve. At the Court Ball the other night, to my great astonishment, I was put sitting next to the Crown Prince at supper, although all the Princesses and Ambassadresses were

RUTHIN CASTLE, NORTH WALES.
The West Terrace.

there. I suppose the Crown Prince repeated to the Emperor (as I guessed he would do) all the gossip I had just told him. And therefore, to show the people how senseless their gossip is, the Emperor arranged that I should sit next to his son, which I think was very very nice and sensible of him.

The Crown Prince's own Ball at the Palace in Potsdam was really charming, a beautiful Louis XV. ball-room, and lit up only with wax candles.

Yesterday afternoon I asked the Crown Prince to come to tea, also Fräulein von Meister, who brought her guitar, and the two Ratibor boys, who brought their violins, as did the Crown Prince ; the Duchess of Ratibor brought her trumpet ; we " made music," and a good deal of noise besides, from five to seven, and I was rather tired.

To-night the Emperor dines here with Vater, a *Herren-Essen*, something to do with shooting ; I believe it is called *das Fest des Weissen Hirschen*.[1] I go to the Circus with the Sierstorpffs, Count Vico Voss, and a large party—to be out of the way.

To-morrow is the last Court Ball, and the next day I return to Fürstenstein and little Hansel. I've had quite enough of Berlin, although this time, because we snarled and said we would not come here this winter, I have been treated with much ceremony, always sent in correctly to supper at Court Balls, and many people have said to me : " Oh, I am so glad you have come, we can't get on without you."

Next year, please God, we shall take a villa at Beaulieu and live all these cold dismal months in the sunshine and flowers of the Riviera, and I shall take little Hansel with me.

February 16, 1904. 2 *a.m.* Berlin.

Just returned from the last Court Ball, to-morrow being Ash Wednesday. We all went afterwards to the Hotel Bristol and had some cold meat and something to drink : Irma Fürstenberg and Prince Max, his brother Charles Fürstenberg and his wife (who was May Festetics), Count Colloredo-Mannsfeld and his son. To-night's ball was very nice. I went in to supper with Max Fürstenberg (who has been made " *ober*-something-*meister* ") and sat opposite the Crown Prince—again a very high position, I suppose arranged by the Emperor. At the same table was Countess Redern,

---

[1] The festival of the white stag.

Count Bülow the Prime Minister, the Princess of Wied,[1] the Austrian Ambassador,[2] Rita Reischach,[3] and Prince Lichnowsky. I asked the latter when the promised appointment of Ambassador (perhaps to America) was going to be given to Hans—and added pointedly that he and Count Bülow made promises that they did not keep. I said it in chaff, but wanted to feel the ground a little.

I talked across the table to the Crown Prince and Count Bülow and made them all laugh about the old Ministers from Copenhagen who dined on the *Princessin Victoria Luise*, on which we stayed for the Kiel week two years ago, and how I had told them I was a Fräulein Schmidt and lived in Hanover, and they all brought me bouquets before I left ; and then, when they found out who I was, went to Hans and " excused " themselves to him.

The Emperor has not been the same to me this winter ; he seems shy. I cannot think he is cross about my letter referring to the river at Waldenburg. But I shall write to him from Fürstenstein and ask him straight out ; he and Count Bülow both talked about me to Mathilde and said what nice letters I wrote ; and all the Americans (we lunched with the American Ambassador to-day) tell me that he always says nice things about me. I leave here to-morrow and shall be very glad to get to my beloved Hansel.

February 23, 1904. Fürstenstein.

Am alone, Hans left for Berlin yesterday to dine with his Regiment to-night to meet the Emperor ; he returns, I think, the day after to-morrow.

It has been like spring to-day and Baby and I and the new nursery governess Miss Copeland took a walk in the *grund*. She is delighted with everything, and after a few scenes and screams and tears Hansel has now settled down with her quite happily. It is a disappointing winter as I was so looking forward to skating and toboganning here, and one can do neither. But I hope in a few days, if it continues to thaw, we shall at least be able to ride.

I am afraid poor *Peter* is dying of old age : he must be sixteen ; he is not in pain but gets weaker every day, although

[1] D. of Duke of Wurtemberg ; m. 1898, 6th Prince of Wied.
[2] M. de Szögyény-Marich.
[3] Princess Marguerite Hohenlohe-Schillingfürst, m. 1887, Baron von Reischach, Marshal of the Imperial Court.

we dose the old dog with brandy and beef tea every two hours.

I am very busy with my embroidery and music, reading to Hansel, and then it takes quite an hour to read through the papers about this horrid war between Japan and Russia.[1] I live in dread that other nations may be drawn into it, as Turkey and Bulgaria are now fighting.

February 28, 1904. Fürstenstein.

Count Vico arrived this morning ; to-morrow afternoon Lady Elcho—Guy Wyndham's sister—will arrive with her son and daughter who are studying in Dresden.

I feel miserable to-night. I was so proud of the way I had arranged the red salon downstairs with lovely embroidered cushions, old brocade-covered sofas and chairs from upstairs, and some furniture out of my boudoir and dressing-room. I made the change as it is now too cold to sit in the big salon, and my beautiful piano would have been ruined near one of the windows there. The red salon looked so nice, but when Hans saw it he insisted on the space in front of the doors being left bare so that two people could pass in and out together ; so all the cosiness vanished ; it seemed ridiculous and I was angry. Then Hans began about his ancestors not doing it, and said he would not have cottage arrangements in his castle. Added to this Count Vico, with his German taste, did not approve of the white rugs ; I only wished another woman had been there to help me to " sit on " both of them. Hans hates it if I bring a picture, book, or photograph downstairs : he wants everything arranged against the wall and Count Vico likes a table with chairs all round—real German, called " home taste." I nearly cried with disappointment. I know I behave like a child, and I am an idiot and everything you like—but I was so pleased ; and then never to get credit for anything, and to be told " I make nothing but blunders " : and Mary Elcho being used to beautiful homes in England like Stanway, and Gosford in Scotland, I wanted to have everything as nice as possible here for her to see. Also Todd, our Scottish head gardener, has given notice because I told him he must be nice with the people, and not rough, particularly as they are very socialistic here and he, not being German, was unpopular. To crov n all, dear old *Peter* died this evening. However, Hansel is very well.

---

[1] The Russo-Japanese War, 1904-5.

March 16, 1904. Fürstenstein.

It is eight o'clock and a glorious sunny morning ; I could not sleep all night. I have just been to the nursery and had breakfast with Hansel whom I must leave on the 18th when I go to join Patsy at Grasse ; the De La Warrs [1] have lent her their villa, so we shall stay there until the Grand Duke Michael and Sophy Torby can take us in. I shall love to get to warm weather and be near the scent of flowers, but I hate leaving my beloved little boy. He is so much more to me, even in the short time since his nurse left. I lie on his bed every night till he goes to sleep and he holds one of my fingers. I am with him all day ; he rides his donkey really very well now.

The other day passing Salzbrunn churchyard he said : "Mummie, what are those mounds of earth and crosses and stones and things ? "

I said : " They are just remembrances, darling, put up by friends and relations for the happy people who have gone to God."

But he was not deceived and said : " Mummie, shall I be put in the ground some day too ? "

It is a long time since I wrote in my diary, but the days have been so full of healthy exercise that I have scarcely been in the house. Until four days ago the ground was white with snow and we sleighed and tobogganed all day. Mary Elcho and her nice boy [2] stayed a week.

March 23, 1904. Villa Mont Fleuri, Grasse, Alpes Maritimes.

I lie in bed with the windows wide open ; a little breeze stirs the palm leaves, the flower beds and banks are full of bulbs, daffodils, narcissus, and violets, and there are two little white doves that sit in the olive branches and coo, thinking of their nest and the spring. It is a dear little villa with a delicious garden winding up the hill on which the villa is built ; an old gardener looks after it all while a woman cooks in the kitchen, chiefly macaroni. In the morning a nice fresh egg, a warm roll and a little jar of honey comes up to my room ; it seems as if I had been here weeks and I arrived only on the 20th. My journey was very comfortable ; Marie and I had each a little

---

[1] 8th Earl (1869–1915), and his wife Hilda (who m. J. W. Dennis in 1922).

[2] The late Lord Elcho, b. 1884 ; missing, presumed dead, 1916 ; m. 1911, Lady Violet Manners.

compartment with a door opening between us and I read and sewed and lay down a great deal.

Poppets arrives to-day sometime. Little Patsy is so well and full of spirits. She is sitting in my room humming to herself and looking at photographs. We have been out every day in the motor, the twisting roads, and corners, give me fits, and passing all the other motors which, coming towards one, look like some horrible animal with big round eyes and a roaring voice.

All the plum and peach trees are in full bloom and the yellow gorse and broom. I should love to take a villa in this part of the world next year and be able to have my little precious boy here.

Hans saw me off at Berlin and bought me some flowers at the station and was *so* nice.

None of the luggage that I sent by the agent in Waldenburg to save excess carriage, has arrived yet ; it is a great nuisance, as the seven boxes I have with me seem to contain nothing but shoes, nightgowns, and evening dresses. Now I must get up and shall go and lie in the sun and eat oranges—but I really cannot go out in the daytime in an evening frock or a nightgown ! Why do the maids pack all the *same* things in one box ?

March 25, 1904. Grasse.

At last my clothes have arrived at Nice. I have had nothing to put on but a short cloth skirt and some cotton frocks and the last two days it has been pouring with rain and very cold. Yesterday in spite of it all, we went by train to Monte Carlo. I lost thirteen louis ; darling Poppets won five pounds and was so pleased. We really laughed at ourselves as the whole journey was a dreadful undertaking. We left the villa at ten-thirty, got to Monte at one, left there at five and got here at eight. We arrived at the station to find no flies, so had to *walk* home for one whole hour in pouring rain.

To-day we walked about in this dirty strange little town through long narrow smelly streets with little sort-of-cupboard shops on either side ; we went to the scent factory and saw them making the scent ; a corner of the floor was covered with violets. We watched the oil they are put into and turned in. Then, when it has absorbed all the scent of the flowers, the oil is mixed with alcohol and becomes perfume. We also went to the sweet-shop ; preserves of every sort and at all stages, half-cooked, boiling, getting cold. Baskets-full, shelves-full, and all rather untidy. It was not very *appetitlich*. Here again the floor was strewn with violets that were going to be crystallized.

March 26, 1904, 11.30 p.m. Grasse.

We went at eleven to Miss de Rothschild's [1] villa and saw the lower part of the garden which she calls her tropical garden ; it is too beautiful : palms, aloes, bamboos of every sort, freshly sown grass and great beds and patches of spring flowers. She is terribly fussy and most particular ; in feeding the ducks Patsy put her foot just on the edge of the grass border ; the old lady saw it at once and said : " Oh, please be careful, you touched the grass." To-morrow we lunch there at twelve and drive up to the mountain garden which runs right up from the front of the house, or rather back (for the front door is really at the back). She has several miles of land and it is quite worth seeing ; she has every sort of creeping and " tumbling " plant ; nasturtiums growing up into the trees, and over the walls. I shall write and tell Hans of this, as he was so furious when I planted them in the rocks at Fürstenstein. (I have not heard from him yet : he hates writing.)

This afternoon we drove into Nice or rather motored there and had lunch ; then we went to a flower show, where Patsy and I went crazy over the flowers. I ordered a lot of plants of carnations and roses, but they will probably none of them do well in Germany ; I can only try.

We dined at the villa and played bridge ; to-morrow is our last night here. On Monday we go to Monte Carlo for two nights and then we shall make a short tour in the motor to Genoa and home by Turin. Poppets wanted to go to Florence (he was born there and loves it) but it is really too far. We shall be away four days and shall then go to the Torbys at the Villa Kasbeck, Cannes.

March 29, 1904. Villa Kasbeck, Cannes.

Sophy and the Grand Duke seemed very pleased to see me. Last night Lord Wolverton [2] and Lord Hardwicke [3] were dining here ; to-night the Vanderbilts dine ; so I must go and

---

[1] Miss Alice de Rothschild, sister of the late Baron Ferdinand de Rothschild ; she owned the Villa Victoria, Grasse.

[2] 4th Baron, Vice-Chamberlain of H.M.'s Household 1902–5 ; m. 1895, Lady Edith Ward, C.B.E., d. of 1st Earl of Dudley.

[3] 7th Earl (1867–1904), Under-Secretary for War 1902–4.

dress. I will write a little item of interest when I come up to bed to-night. We lunched at the Golf Club to-day, a lovely drive. Prince Joachim Albrecht was there enjoying his " leave " from Germany and, in fact, rather wild.

We are just starting off in the motor now to Nice to see the motor races. Then we go to Monte Carlo for a little, and I hope to have luck again. I have not had a line from Hans and I have written three times and wired often ; he has wired me once.

Nearly one o'clock in the morning ; just back from a dinner with Lord and Lady Savile. Gambling is in the atmosphere here ; I lost at poker but again had luck at Monte Carlo, winning twenty-seven louis. We did not stay to see the motor race, but the record of the world was beaten to-day by Rigolly, driving a Gobron-Brillie car in the third Henri de Rothschild Cup race ; he attained a speed of over one hundred kilometres an hour—a world's record—quite extraordinary.

April 1, 1904. *Good Friday.* Villa Kasbeck, Cannes.

I wanted to go to Church but *had* to go to the dentist or else he could not finish my teeth in time. Drove with Sophy and the Grand Duke to the Golf Club for lunch ; he is so ridiculously affectionate, blowing me kisses and calling me " Daisy " all the time, and before we started in the motor I wanted a safety pin so he turned to Sophy and said, " Get me a safety pin," and I am blest if she didn't run upstairs and get one (although I tried to stop her) and handed it to him for me !

April 10, 1904. Toulouse (in bed).

We left the Villa Kasbeck on Tuesday, and went to Monte Carlo for two nights ; lunched one day with the Malets (former Ambassador in Berlin) and also with the Charles Wilsons.[1] Charlie Wood and Cyril Foley were in Monte Carlo. I gambled each evening and for a short while in the afternoons and won a hundred louis, which is a lot for me. We went to see the Villa Isolata on the little island just off the coast. I should love to buy it, or lease it, if the owner would only build on to it, as at present it has only four rooms.

We started on our motor-car trip last Friday and got as far as Marseilles, stopping very often ; two tyres burst, and so on ; the car is not in a very good temper just now. We slept there

---

[1] 1st Lord Nunburnholme (1833–1907), m. Florence, d. of Colonel Wellesley.

the night, a very dirty hotel, the streets were crowded, I never saw so much traffic or so many people walking about ; I imagine it continues all night, as, sleeping with my window open, I heard carriages and horses continuously.

We left the next morning at ten-thirty, arriving at Nîmes at 7 p.m., having stopped an hour and a half at Avignon, which is full of curiosity shops. I bought four cupboards and am so pleased as I have none in Fürstenstein, and these are nicely carved *Louis Seize*. Patsy and I would have liked to stay there much longer.

April 13, 1904. Biarritz.

I have got so behindhand with my diary that I can scarcely catch up ; but after a long day motoring, then a change, warm bath and dinner, one feels so pleasantly tired that it is impossible to think or write. The other morning I woke up and looked round my room, it was very large and I could *not* remember where I was. I heard my maid knock at a door, I saw two doors at the further end, and knew there were two on each side of my bed ; and I simply lay and wondered by which door she would come in, vaguely conscious that I had to get up, dress and go in the motor-car, but to what place I did not know, and where I had come from the night before I could not remember : this stage of " idiotness " lasted only a few seconds I am glad to say.

From Nîmes we went to Toulouse through very ugly country nothing but ploughed land and grape vines—acre after acre and mile after mile : we arrived about dinner time and went to bed very early. The next morning I wanted to cash a cheque but it was against the rules of the hotel, and they said it could be done at the *Société Général*, so Patsy and I walked off there to an enormous building and were asked to sit down in a glass room while two polite men explained that it was difficult for them to do what I wanted, as of course I might *say* I was the Princess Henry of Pless, but they wanted something more than my word. I said :

" You can see the initials on all the articles in my dressing case if you like."

" But how are we to know that you have any money in the Bank ? "

" There you are right ; I often haven't."

I then inquired if there was a German Consul in Toulouse, they said :

" No ; but do you know the English one, he is a dentist ? "
I said :
" I do not know him but I do not care if he is a butcher ;
he might perhaps believe me."

The two polite, incredulous gentlemen then proposed that I
should go to call on him with them, but this honour I refused,
and said the whole thing was too much bother; they could go
themselves if they liked, and if the result was satisfactory,
I should be much obliged if they, or someone else, would come
to the hotel in twenty minutes.   When I got back one of the
men was already there with the money ; he had not been to
consult the dentist, but he took down my address, and also
the name and address of other hotels where I had written
cheques.   What fun it would be if the Bank returned the
cheque, as I may have overdrawn now over the journey and
not know it !

April 16, 1904.   Poictiers.

I must write some more about our experiences at
Biarritz. . . . We arrived at the Villa about six o'clock,
dusty and tired, to be received by a group of about twenty
guests, Russian and French Princes and Princesses, Italian
Marchese, a Jew or two, an English Duchess, and, of course,
a rich American widow.   Patsy and I both refused to be introduced all round or to stay amongst so many over-smartly
dressed women ; we were too tired to dress up ourselves, so
we just washed and had some tea in our own bedrooms, and
went for a walk by the sea.   We had heard so much about this
marble villa and the gardens.   The house looks like a Théâtre
de Variétés, the hall like the bar at a Casino, the garden is a
mass of weeds, and everything most uncomfortable.   No towels
or matches, impossible to have a night-light, and the lady's
maids furious because in the housekeeper's room, they had
to drink out of bowls instead of cups.   We stayed at the villa
for two nights.   Oscar Herren and Count Vico Voss came to
dinner.   Oscar lives at Biarritz with his parents.   The next
night we all dined with Prince Orloff at the Casino.   I played
baccarat and held the cards *nine times*, much to the delight and
surprise of the people at my side of the table.

One afternoon we went to Bayonne, only fifteen minutes by
motor, and saw the fair ; we went in to one show for which
each person paid a penny for a ticket, and there to our horror,
surprise, astonishment, amusement, disgust—in fact every

feeling that the sight of any spectacle can arouse—we saw a *Passion Play*. I had never seen one before and certainly never expected to do so for a penny at a fair in France. It was sincerely and beautifully done, in a series of tableaux ; a woman sang, and a man played the piano. The curtain went up on the Christ on the Mount of Olives ; then followed Christ before Pontius Pilate ; Christ in the Wilderness ; Christ carrying the Cross ; the Crucifixion ; the Descent from the Cross ; the Resurrection. And between each tableau, when the curtain went down, the piano began to play *Sourire d'Avril*, *Tararaboomdeay*, any tune ; but the whole thing gradually grew on one, and one felt more able to take it in the same spirit in which the two priests and the few other people present seemed to receive it. It was the conflicting elements in it that seemed so hard to understand : a common show ; Mary the Virgin selling the tickets ; then, after seeing Christ and the two thieves hanging on the Cross, their limbs torn in agony (very well acted) the curtain descends and at once tingles in one's ears the valse *Amoureuse* with the words *Je suis lâche avec toi, je te veux*. Somehow, since I have seen more of France as a country, I begin to think the French people are great talkers and advertisers—even to advertising their own religion.

From Biarritz we went to Bordeaux ; in the evening we went to the Opera and heard *Rigoletto* very badly given. I forgot to say Reggie Hoare joined our party at Biarritz.

We left Bordeaux at twelve, in the pouring rain, for Poictiers, but it got very nice during the day : we had to stay the night in a horrible dirty hotel, but the bed was comfortable and, as always, I had my own sheets.

I began this in bed before we left this morning. Now we have airrved at Tours, charming rooms and everything very nice. I went to a curiosity shop at Poictiers and bought for Hans a big Arab gun inlaid with silver and coral ; also an Empire silver coffee-pot for which I paid only five pounds ten : and Patsy says that in England I could get twenty pounds for it ! The turquoise bracelet that I bought at Monte, and for which I paid eight hundred francs, a man at Biarritz said he would give me twelve hundred francs for !

We had a lovely drive here to-day although it rained now and then ; we lunched at Chinon, and saw the Castle where Joan of Arc went to see Charles VII., to tell him of her vision ; we stopped at the Castle of Azay le Rideau which was once taken by a dreadful Count de —— who kept a *pension* for boys.

Bend Or was there for a time and once came direct from Azay
to Fürstenstein ; he pretended to start off with a servant and
two horses on a tour in France, instead of which he took the
train to Germany and came to see Shelagh ; the *pension* did
not prosper and the venture ended in a horrible scandal.

April 28, 1904. In the train.

I spent a week in Paris fussing about clothes, and left with
everything half finished as I did not want to remain there
alone, and my little mother left two days after we arrived.

I dined out and went to the theatre, also to two evening
parties. How Society *en masse* bores me, crowded rooms and
unsympathetic people to speak to—one can scarcely call it
talking ; one opens one's mouth occasionally to answer their
stupid questions, or banal observations. In France, particularly,
the men who crowd round you can talk such absolute rubbish ;
and if one is speaking quietly and trying to collect one's
thoughts with one person, man or woman, others are certain
to come and try to join in the conversation.

The theatres are abominable ; no theatre is prosperous or
a play complete unless there is a bedroom scene in the second
act ; the hero is always in bed with his wife or his *vieille amie*,
his *ancienne cocotte* ; and then they get out of bed and dress
on the stage ; he puts on his trousers, she her drawers and
stockings ; one cannot help laughing, but the " tone " of the
whole thing is horrible. Poor France, such a lovely country,
such enthusiastic people, *bons enfants*, chivalrous, hard-working,
true in their faith ; and Paris the decayed kernel in which the
worm ever hides ; with its immorality and its rotten government ; the Revolution seems to have drained all the good as
well as the bad from the hearts of the people ; their strength
seems gone, they realize the shame to their country, but are
too weak to carry the banner of Hope ; and there is no one to
lead them.

It is no use having illusions about life. Life, as we live it,
is commonplace unless one chooses to renounce the world,
and live out of it, and therefore be different from others. We
are like birds that flock together, sheep in a fold, bees in a hive,
we crave for companionship and sympathy, but there is something in one that is always alone ; and so we walk together on
the same uneven road, trying to avoid the rougher parts, trying
not to slip and stumble too often. There *is* another road which
we are told is best, but it is uphill and on it we should find

ourselves almost alone : our friends—or those we call our friends—would not be there with us.

It is difficult to know what is really sin and what is not. To my mind " the leaving undone of things one ought to have done," is really the great sin rather than " the doing of things one ought not to have done." I think when we come to judgment we shall be asked, not what harm or sorrow we may have brought upon ourselves and one or two people we may have met, but how many people we made happy, how many people's sorrows we made less, what real good we did in the world.

Oh, how I long to be young (I am already thirty) to feel the sun in my hair, to feel the cool wind through my thin summer skirts, to smell the breath of spring and the lilac, to hold the world soft and kind, truthful and grand in my heart, instead of hard and jagged, cruel and full of lies ; while the cries of pain and suffering, lost illusions and broken ideals drown the sound of the wood pigeon, the nightingale, and the voices of spring.

April 29, 1904. Fürstenstein.

Hansel was asleep when I got here at eight-thirty ; he had only arrived from Pless and was very tired ; I stayed in bed this morning till twelve o'clock, and then gave him some new toys. He has grown so much. The weather is mild and all the trees are in bud, everything is much earlier than usual. I think the lilacs will be out in about ten days ; I walked about with the head gardener this afternoon. I love this place in a way, and take the greatest interest in it and yet, try as I will, I cannot feel like " coming home."

May 4, 1904. Fürstenstein.

We went fishing to-day in the *Daisysee* ; I caught the biggest fish I remember, three pounds, and in excellent condition. It rained at intervals. Hansel came with us ; he asked questions all the way, wrinkled his little forehead and opened his eyes wide to make me understand and realize every word he was saying.

Yesterday was lovely and we drove to the *Schwarzengraben* to arrange my new trout stream. In the morning a poor miner's wife came to see me : in two years they had made debts of three hundred marks, and now the Law was coming to take their furniture ; they had been so happy ; the husband was good ; when they married they got furniture for a hundred and fifty marks and had not yet been able to pay it. Three hundred

MYSELF.
In Fancy Dress.

marks in two years—good heavens! And the woman was crying on her knees and holding my hand. I longed to give it to her at once, but thought it better to let it go through the hands of the head'man at the mines; otherwise I might have all the miners coming to me. But I gave her something to go home with, and I hope the rest will have been arranged, and that she is now happy. One of the gardeners had his eye put out with a twig some time ago and he has not taken proper care of it; the injury is not properly healed so I sent him off to Breslau again to-day.

Hans has to go to Berlin on Saturday for a few days for the sitting of the House of Lords, so I shall be alone. I shall have Hansel to sleep with me, my beloved little boy.

May 5, 1904. Fürstenstein.

A clean page tempts me to write, although I just came up in the middle of dinner as I did not feel well and am in bed after putting my feet in mustard and hot water; now I feel better. The smell and fumes of smoke, and ammonia, which I inhaled this afternoon for two hours, while going with Hans to look at a coal mine and a new coke manufactory, must have upset me.

It was as cold as winter to-day; I drove in a footsack and fur coat. I noticed the people on the roads seemed much more polite than they used to be, but still there is a wrong principle at work. All the heads of the different departments employed by Vater think themselves little gods; they are good servants and clever honest men, but Vater individually is not felt at all, and of course Hans has really not the power to do anything.

A new Miners' Hospital is going to be built; naturally Vater will have to give more than any other coal owner; to begin with, most of the others are Companies; Vater has over nine thousand labourers in the mines, not counting all the outside officials and heads of departments and their assistants. I asked who is building the Hospital and who will decide which is the best plan to adopt; to which Schultz, the head of the mines, said, "Oh, a committee will be formed and of course I shall have a lot to do with it," and so on. It was always *Ich* and *Wir* as if Vater did not come into it at all.

They think these matters are too trivial to interest the *Herrschaften*: the Prince is only asked his opinion about the opening of a new mine, or about investments when these amount to several thousands of pounds. But some day we will change all that. I want the agents, labourers, miners, woodcutters, poor people, old men and women, and even children, to realize that I, Hans and the staff at Fürstenstein are here to advise and help and sympathize ; to give, or lend money.

I received rather a nice answer to some remarks I wrote in the train to a real friend as I was on my journey to Berlin from Paris. My thoughts and ideas had got troubled and puzzled after reading a certain book, and I wrote rather bitterly, indeed ungratefully, when I think of all that Providence has bestowed upon me, but I get so tired sometimes. Here is the letter :

" I hope the clouds have passed and that you are yourself again ; why look at the dark side of life when one is made, like you, to enjoy the happy, sunny side. Did not God make the world as it is ? Did He not make you young and beautiful, to live to be happy and to do good and make others happy ? Why then criticize too much ? Do you think the world you would have made, if you had been in His place, would have been better ? You can, and you will, be able to do *so* much good ; don't waste your time and thoughts over the dark colours of life, and if ever you are in a black mood again, think that a little shade there must be, where there is so much sun."

May 7, 1904. Fürstenstein.

My old Tommy has just gone to Berlin so I shall be without him for four or five days and I feel rather lonely ; I have had ambitions for him, but they are over ; perhaps Hansel will some day fulfil them. The other day in Berlin Hans was asked to be present at a very little dinner to meet Countess Bülow and Countess Redern. His answer to the old gentleman who asked him was : " Invite two prettier women and I will come." To begin with the answer was rude, and then to refuse to dine with the wife of the Chancellor is ridiculous ; and particularly so as Countess Bülow is Italian, very clever, knows the world and has seen a lot, is a delightful companion and conversationalist, and has great influence with her husband ; and how on earth does Hans expect to be asked to their house when he is in Berlin and treated well and to be given the post of Ambassador, or Governor, by a man whom he scarcely knows, and whose wife he does not take the trouble to be polite to ! Nor will he see Prince Rz. . . . It is unreasonable to quarrel with and shun people from whom you want a favour. If only Hans would make friends of, and mix with, intelligent people and talk on the topics of the day ! He is not at all stupid, and thinks he is much cleverer than anyone else, but in conversation he generally comes out with some new and absolutely incomprehensible idea, or else contradicts everyone flatly. As Vater says, " *Hans always says Nein.*" Somehow my ambitions are dead. I shall try to do good my own way and alone, bring up my beloved little boy, pray for another child, and enjoy the spring and summer as they pass in this lovely outside world of nature. Politically, I can only hear and see a sort of roaring demon of *wars : poverty : plague : lunacy : disease ! !*

Japan is beating Russia on sea and land. It is extraordinary ; I wonder how it will end ! It seems almost incredible that Japan could tackle and beat that great vast army ; and yet now it seems as if it might be so.

May 8, 1904. Fürstenstein.

Wrote this morning, and had a long afternoon with Hansel. We went out together with the donkey and the groom and walked all over the woods at the back of the home farm and picked violets. We tried who could pick the most, and then we sat and listened to a distant band playing in Polsnitz at a socialist gathering ; then we played hide-and-seek. I arrived home with a face flushed scarlet, having run with the donkey nearly all the way home. Hansel rides quite well now and has a firm seat ; when alone with him I sometimes feel as if I were a girl of ten.

May 9, 1904. Fürstenstein.

Wrote this morning, and looked through wallpapers and stuff to do up Mathilde's little salon as a surprise. I shall wait till Hans comes before I settle, as perhaps chintz is not the right thing to put in a boudoir, but it does look so nice and I have such lovely patterns from London.

In the afternoon I drove with Hansel and Miss Copeland to Salzbrunn to inspect the hotel gardens ; Todd, head gardener here, followed in another carriage. Kraft, the hotel gardener, showed us lots of things, and we drove along the beautiful new avenue, ending up in the garden where he grows his cuttings, seedlings, bulbs ; I got him to give me lots of things, and two big palms, for which he can find no room in the hotel at Salzbrunn.

May 15, 1904.   Hotel Bristol, Berlin.

Yesterday there was a ball at Countess Beroldingen's whose daughter married Fritzie Larisch [1] two years ago. The Crown Prince was there ; a Prince of Wurtemberg, very good-looking but *bête*, a brother to the dear little Duke of Wurtemberg whom I met at Donaueschingen ; Prince Joachim Albrecht, and others. It was a very small party and there was nobody very pretty. The Crown Prince told me that the Emperor sent him a furious wire when he rode in the *Hoch Springen* on an Irish horse, and won the first prize, the Emperor's Cup. He said, which I thought very sporting and youthful : " Well, I suppose I shall be forbidden ever to ride a race again or ride in a jumping competition ; but never mind, I have won my father's cup at the first attempt, and I have won three other races, so that must last me for life." I went in to supper with the Prince of Wurtemberg ; on my other side was Count Lerchenfeld the Bavarian Minister in Berlin.

To-night we had a very cosy dinner at the English Embassy and played bridge ; only the Münsters, [2] Count Gleichen [3] the Military Secretary, and Prince A. H. whom I detest, and snubbed all the time, as he has not a nice word for anyone, even for people who were once his friends. Florence Lascelles is to be married on the first of January. [4] Poor Sir Frank will miss her dreadfully as his wife died about five years ago. Dear old Lady Edward Cavendish, [5] his sister, is still there, having come for the wedding.

May 23, 1904.   Fürstenstein.

A week of peace, arranging my garden, playing with Hansel, picking lilies-of-the-valley in the woods, fishing, and walking in the fields to admire Hans's foals, his new cattle and sheep. Yesterday it rained hard, the gardeners and farmers I expect were pleased as the ground was getting very hard. I felt sorry for the birds and their nests which must have got so

---

[1] Count Frederick Larisch, m. 1902, Countess Marie von Beroldingen.

[2] Alexander 2nd Prince Münster (1858–1922), m. 1890, Lady Muriel Hay (1863–1927), d. of 11th Earl of Kinnoul.

[3] Major-General Lord Edward Gleichen, Grenadier Guards, British Military Attaché in Berlin 1903–6.

[4] To Sir Cecil Spring Rice (1859–1918).

[5] D. of Rt. Hon. W. S. S. Lascelles, M.P., m. 1865, Lord Edward Cavendish (d. 1891), son of 7th Duke of Devonshire ; Maid of Honour to Queen Victoria 1863–5.

damp, but their occupants could not have minded much, as in the evening they were singing their fullest little notes with a tremolo as if their hearts were beating with joy.

I had a sad letter from Patsy yesterday telling me they have to let Newlands this year for the summer months and probably every year ; they cannot afford to keep up the two places ; I cried, as I am most dreadfully disappointed. I *love* that place and wanted to send Hansel there in July for sea air, and to spend some time there myself ; and my poor old Poppets loves the place too ; so it seems hard that at seventy-one he should be turned out of the house he loves : also, all the building going on at Milford-on-Sea interests him. But being Lord-Lieutenant of Denbighshire, and the real family seat being Ruthin, I suppose he feels it his duty to live there, or else give up all his county work and responsibilities in Wales.

Shelagh is taking a house on the river this year : being in the family way, she is not going to be in London. I wrote to her and Bend Or to propose that they should take Newlands instead and to say that I would sell my pearl and diamond necklace and give three hundred pounds towards the cost. I do hope they will agree to the proposal and accept my offer ; on a lovely day like this one would do anything to make those one loves happy, and I *long* to do so. Of course it would be a lovely arrangement for me, as then Hansel and I could go there too.

May 26, 1904. Fürstenstein.

I spent the whole of yesterday on the *Daisysee* with Hansel and Count Vico. I sat in the boat on a heap of cushions and a rug round me and watched my float bobbing up and down ; fish were rising everywhere but we only caught four, three of them with small live fish out of the river for bait. Count Vico left for Berlin and Prince Z. arrived here at eight, Hans only at ten, as he again missed the train ; he does not seem to be able to catch a train lately. Prince Z. and I drove after dinner to meet him at the station in a carriage with postilions ; such a warm moonlight night ; coming home we saw a falling star : I never have seen such a big one, it was like a rocket and fell right across the sky.

To-day I sat nearly all day in my garden and wrote, read, and did my embroidery, while Hansel made cakes and puddings with sand and water. Prince Z. went stalking in the afternoon ; he seemed cured !

Hans looks happier than ever, and so glad, poor old darling, that I am late ; it really is very funny. I sit and pray all day that I may be in the family way, I should be so delighted to have again in my arms a dear little soft warm baby. . . . I am very quiet and scarcely move, no exertions except one game of croquet in the day.

May 28, 1904. Fürstenstein.

Prince Z. left last night after dinner ; Hans and I went for a drive in the postilion carriage seated hand-in-hand ; it was a glorious moonlight night and I smoked a cigarette and felt very peaceful though rather dissipated. To-day I lay in a hammock in the garden through all the long sunny hours. I do not feel well and have pains in my inside which does not seem right somehow under the circumstances ; I shall ask the doctor. In the mornings I read German with Frau Endermann, the schoolmaster's wife, and in the afternoon play a game of croquet with Hans. Hansel played in my garden nearly all the time and rocked me in the hammock. I have just come in from a moonlight drive again ; my old Tommy seems so well and happy now and is so pleasant to talk to ; I am never bored with him. We drove to Salzbrunn, the road is broad and light and there are dear little cottages on the roadside with gardens ; and the air smelt sweet ; I held his dear nice warm hand, and tried *not* to think of New-lands, and to listen to what he was saying. I should like to write a lot more but really feel too tired, and I long for a good night's rest. I always wake about four, and toss about for hours until it is nearly time to get up ; and I read always till about one ; but to-night I will not ; I am in bed now. Good-night.

May 31, 1904. Fürstenstein.

Writing in my private garden ; a perfect evening, the garden people have just done watering, the sun is gradually sinking and the birds are giving a concert, each trying to outvie the other in a better song ; the chorus they make is beautiful. In one box tree I watch a little mother bird fly backwards and forwards with food for her young who are lying very squashed together in a very lop-sided nest. I am so afraid that when they get older and move about some of them will tumble out.

Hans went to Berlin last night for Miss Lascelles' wedding. I excused myself because I have caught a chill. Doctor Ismer came to-day and said he of course could not say for sure any more than I could, but . . . I shall stay very quiet; of course I have to give up Homburg and the Gordon Bennett Motor Race; my absence will disappoint my darling brother George, and I shall be *very* sorry not to see him. To Kiel I may go in the motor (not in a train) if I feel well enough; by then I shall be sure one way or the other, but I must not go to England in the third month, so shall perhaps go only in August.

The little bird has flown off the nest and is singing in a tree just in front and quite close to me. I can see its tiny throat swelling, and the proud jerk of its head. I wonder if by this time next year I shall be watching my own little off-spring learning to crawl.

Hansel and I have just been for a walk and looked at the young chickens, geese and ducks (I wonder why one doesn't say gooses for more than one goose); I scolded the women who milk the cows for not having their big pinafores on, that I ordered for them to wear when they milk. I also sent them to wash their dirty hands; it is impossible here to make the people clean and neat and nice. I suppose I am getting old and resigned, but I have laid down my weapons and feel inclined only to live in peace with those I care for or love; read, play, paint, work, count the flowers and the rain-drops, walk in the sun or the mist realizing that everything in Nature is true and beautiful.

Perhaps it was partly conceit that made me want the people to like me, and yet I feel it really wasn't. Last night, a lovely moonlight night, I drove my old Tommy to the station, so cosy and happy together—I was of course alone coming home. We met crowds of people both coming and going (there was a fair in the town) and none of them thought of saying good-evening or good-night; only, on the way back, as I drove through the square in front of a great globe of electric light, some women ran near the carriage and said *gutenabend*, while a man took off his hat and shouted in English, " good-evening." I had felt lonely, returning alone to this great empty house with not a soul near, but those few words of greeting made me feel happier. I like the people round here to forget I am Princess Henry of Pless, and talk to me as to a fellow-mortal; and the night was so beautiful, I longed to hold out my hands and say : " Let me be amongst you, come to me, let me help you, be with me and I with you as my mother with her village friends at Ruthin ; don't send me back to the top of my hill again, give me some word of greeting." A German has a good solid heart for his *Frau Kinder*, and *Vaterland*, but his heart stays at home and does not pass his cottage gate ; beer draws it out for a short while and it shows itself in songs of the country about soldiers, or fir trees (*Tannenbäume*), ending in a climax with a *Hoch* for the Kaiser—or for the most prominent socialist leader. Perhaps when I have much money, and our people come direct to me for help, we may get nearer to each other.

Hansel and I only got back to the house at a quarter past seven, both feeling very guilty for coming home so late. (He ought to be in at seven.) To-night I shall go again for a drive in the moonlight, and have promised to take Copie (Hansel's nursery-governess), laying down as a condition, however, that she must not make conversation with me.

Now I must go and wish my darling baby good-night ; why do my thoughts suddenly wander back to Newlands ? I can hear my father's voice : " Mai ! Daisy ! For goodness' sake go and dress for dinner ; *do* you know what time it is ? " while Patsy and I walk leisurely up from the lake.

June 2, 1904. Fürstenstein.

Hans came back this morning. I felt better to-day ; went with Hansel in the donkey cart to see the young pheasants and ducks ; then Hans and I played croquet : he is very well and said they all missed me at the Lascelles wedding.

I have come back from " Bohemia " ; and dressed for dinner to-night, and this morning had lunch indoors ! These last few days I have had no lunch, only a cup of soup when I felt I wanted something. Two evenings ago I took some sandwiches in the postilion carriage with Copie, and ate them in the moonlight on the *Wilhelmshohe*. Yesterday I was out all day with the gardeners " building castles " and making plans for enchanted places and things (which I shall probably never see). Then I came home and put out half the lamps in my boudoir and had dinner by the open window. Sometimes I do love living naturally—or like an animal if you will ; living in the sun in my garden, eating when I am hungry and then only one thing, and not having to come home punctually for dinner and lunch, and sit down seriously twice a day in front of a menu and white tablecloth, and be stared at by large footmen. And the days seem so much longer, somehow, if one does not come in to lunch. Yesterday afternoon we went to pick lilies near the *Daisysee*, and had tea in the woods : Hansel, I, Missy (Freytag's wife) and Copie ; the latter fussed all the time at the many caterpillars and other animals which crawled and flew about.

The middle of June, 1904. Fürstenstein.

I *am* getting a baby and feel too ill to write down each day what I do ; lately I have tried to get up in the mornings, only to go back and lie down again in the afternoon : I find I feel better if I stay in bed till about two o'clock with the windows and doors open in a draught of delicious air (which Copie thinks most dangerous), and then I get up and drive out somewhere, although sometimes I have to disappear and be ill behind a tree.

Prince Z. came again and left ; we quarrelled all the time, as he seems to have fallen suddenly in love with the Russians (six months ago he hated them) and has begun to despise the Japanese. I love neither, but I certainly believe the Japs to be a people of finer and more cultivated mind, having ideas, and ideals, in life, and living up to them ; while the Russians, when they are not almost dumb ignorant animals, are demoralized from top to toe, Grand Dukes, Government and all. I thought this when I was in the country three years ago.

Hans did not care to go to Homburg for the Gordon-Bennett Race without me. I should like to go to Kiel to see King Edward and the Emperor together ; the former will be so different in those surroundings ; I shall want to laugh ; while the Emperor will be trying to make himself as agreeable as possible in a loud voice, and the Americans will be tumbling over each other to be the first to glow, and swell, under the smile of Royalty. We hope to be able to stay with Mrs. Frederick Vanderbilt on their new yacht ; [1] the Cornelius Vanderbilts on the *North Star* will also be there ; I wonder if they are " jealous relations."

I cannot of course go to London in July ; it will be the third month and I cannot travel then. I wrote a long letter to Metternich and told him that I hoped he would let us come

---

[1] *Warrior*, 1,226 tons, built at Troon 1904.

to the Embassy another time. Hans was going to stay with him and I with Consuelo Marlborough. Perhaps we shall go over in August; it all depends on how I feel.

I was thinking the other day how perfect everything in nature is, except mankind! One would not change one note in the song, or feather in the plumage of any bird, the scent or colour of any flower; but how many things one would like to change in human beings! This ought to be the happiest, proudest, most beautiful time in a woman's life, when she knows that she has conceived and that she will give birth to a child: instead, she has to suffer almost continuously, and, often most horribly, at the one supreme moment of the new birth; and for months before she has to hide her person from the eyes of the world in shame of her disfigurement. It makes me feel now as if there were nothing beautiful in the birth of a child because of the way God has imposed it on us; the agony, pain, sickness, the surgical intervention, destroys all the poetry, grandeur and exaltation that parents ought to feel at the birth of a child; the first feeling is of relief, " thank God it is over." Last night it seemed to me to be cruel that God should make man and woman for one purpose and that to populate His world (or why did He form them so), and then forbid them to eat of the Tree of Knowledge. Surely if His power was supreme He could have kept back the devil who spoke to Eve and tempted her. And when the sin was committed, what more cruel than His curse on the man and woman He had made—to send them from the garden of peace to battle with the world, the woman condemned for ever to conceive in pain, the man to earn his living—and his dying —by the sweat of his brow. Must we conclude that God finds it dull to be in Heaven and therefore makes us the subject of His mirth?

July 26, 1904.[1] Fürstenstein.

I have not used the diary lately, having felt inclined to write nothing but remarks on my state of my health. Uncle Bolko from Rohnstock and Aunt Leonorchen and other relations staying there come over very often. To-day ten of them come for lunch and stay for dinner; Aunt Anna Reuss, Vater's sister, is among them. I have ordered the terraces to be lit up

---

[1] The Princess did not keep her diary between August and December, 1904.

THE CROWN PRINCE WILLIAM OF PRUSSIA.

1913.

to-night, and Bengal lights, and a few of the Salzbrunn band to play in the distance as a surprise for them. I feel much too seedy to be really pleased, but as they are coming I want them to enjoy themselves.

I pine for the sea, it is so dreadfully hot here, and has been even hotter ; last week we could not go out till after seven in the evening, and had almost to stay in the dark so that no sun should penetrate to the house ; there is no grass for the cattle or foals ; soon we shall have to stop watering the lawns as there will be no more water in the ponds ; the corn was scorched at the roots before the grain was ripe and in some places has not grown higher than two feet ; near Schweidnitz and in the lower country the peasants had to cut the young corn and wheat to give to their horses and cows. There has not been such a season for more than forty years.

I shall stay a night in London, and then go to Ruthin or to the sea near there, and meet my little mother. Hans takes all the luggage and goes from Bremen straight to Southampton for Cowes, and meets me afterwards, I hope at Ruthin.

CHAPTER SEVEN

1905

January 22, 1905. Bruton Street, London, W.

OH, the months that I have not written, but I have gone through so much morally and physically and have been so seedy all these months that I have not had the courage to write. How shall I begin ?

At this moment I am in bed resting before dinner as we have several people coming : Consuelo Marlborough, May (Goelet) and her husband Roxburghe, Marie Hope Vere, Count Metternich (the German Ambassador) and others. I feel weary ; I expect the baby to be born in about a week or ten days. I have had to buy a lot of new clothes for it, and I love to look at the tiny things ; please God, all will go well and that my little one will be strong. I shall nurse it for the first weeks ; the English doctor here quite agrees to this and will not take the baby from me as did the doctor in Berlin when Hansel was born.

I will try in a few words to pick up the threads. When I left Germany in July I went to the sea at Colwyn Bay. Hansel paddled and loved it, in Wales, close to Ruthin. Hans and Count Vico (with his motor) and Patsy joined us there, and we went on the most lovely excursions ; I never dreamt that there were parts of Wales so beautiful. Then I stayed a few days at Ruthin, the home of my early childhood ; it is large and cold and I have not the same tender love and memories for it that I have for Newlands. From Ruthin Hans and I went to Scotland to Lochmore, to Shelagh and Bend Or ; this year Hans did *not* get out at Crewe to go to Ostend ! He enjoyed himself very much, shot several stags, and I caught three salmon and a lot of sea-trout ; the weather was divine, no rain to speak of, and lovely views. Shelagh's great boy [1] weighing eleven pounds was born the 13th of November ; she is very well now, and has already started hunting again.

---

[1] Edward George Hugh, Earl Grosvenor (1904–9).

This little house is quite nice, but oh the callers, notes, and telephones ! This moment they have let goodness knows whom into the drawing-room and they will have to let them out again, for I told the servants to say not at home !

I was interrupted ! Now, where was I ? Yes, in Scotland. Well, we went straight from there to Germany, accompanied by Patsy and Poppets. . . . All the autumn and winter we had people in Fürstenstein ; in October Lord Lonsdale came, Sir Neil Menzies,[1] General " Bully " Oliphant,[2] Lord and Lady Mar and Kellie, Maudie Warrender and her sister, and masses more ! We did some motoring and played poker and bridge in the evenings. Then the shooting parties began. I got *very* tired of people as of course I was feeling seedy most of the time. Did very little at Christmas, and I thought it a good thing for the people to " miss me " for once.

We came to England just before Christmas which we spent with Shelagh and Bend Or at Eaton. There were a lot of people there, Robin Duff and Juliet, Girlie Cawley, Pat Fitz-Patrick ; poor Lord Cairns, who, though quite well then, went straight to Paris where he died suddenly of heart disease.

January 25, 1905. Bruton Street, London, W.

I feel so much lighter to-day and can move more easily in bed and the nurse who arrived two days ago thinks that before Sunday the little thing will have arrived. We have just returned from dinner at the German Embassy ; Metternich included Poppets in the invitation : he arrived here to-day from Newlands. I drove him and Hansel about this afternoon ; the precious little boy goes to Shelagh at Eaton to-morrow, I shall miss him dreadfully, but please God when I see him again I shall have a strong healthy little baby-brother (or sister) to show him. Patsy comes to-morrow.

My guardian spirit helps me, as it does *so often*, even prompting me what to do and say at critical times.

January 29, 1905. Bruton Street, London, W.

This is quite a nice house, and would be nicer if the house-maid left " in charge " did not have hysterics at intervals ; we think she drinks.

---

[1] 8th Baronet (1855–1910), m. 1905, d. of Sir James Grant-Suttie, Bt.

[2] Sir Laurence Oliphant, K.C.V.O., of Condie, Perthshire, m. in 1878 Honble. Mary, d. of 1st Lord Gerard.

The nurse says the baby *must* arrive to-night or to-morrow. I am sure I wish it would ; it is weary work waiting and I dread the whole performance. For the second time the King has told people I am doing far too much, I ought to be quiet. Last night he told Metternich. I wish people would mind their own business. And anyway, what does His Majesty know about it ! He and the Queen sent me each a pretty Christmas present.

I am in bed having a rest before dinner.

March 7, 1905. Newlands.

I came down here on Sunday for a fortnight of quiet and rest in this peaceful spot by the sea. My little boy is five weeks old to-day, and Hansel already loves him.

The christening was just a week ago, on the twenty-eighth of February : he was born on the first. The little Queen Alexandra was his Godmother and the Prince of Wales his God-father and they both came to the christening at the Chapel Royal. The other godmothers were my darling Granny and Patsy, and the other godfathers, the German Crown Prince and my brother, so the poor little mite bears the names Alexander George Friedrich Wilhelm Conrad Ernest Maximilian !

It is delicious here with my two little sons, and only Patsy and I besides. Poppets, I am sorry to say, had to go to Ruthin on business.

Hans comes on Friday for the night, before he returns to Germany for the House of Lords sittings, and the Pro-vincial Parliament in Breslau. . . .

Sometimes lately my mind seems to have failed me. I have prayed at theatres, prayed in hansoms, prayed as I heard the wind in the chimneys, or the rain on the window-panes, prayed silently at the sound of a barrel-organ in the streets which reminds me always of myself as a little girl years ago in London. I have prayed at all times that I might be shown what is best and right to do. . . .

There are some things that, like a poisonous drug, enter into one's spirit and one is never quite the same again ; one pre-tends that there has been no change and nobody marks the difference. I can never forget an offence done to me, but outwardly I forgive easily, and always, for if the person (even if it were my worst enemy) were to be really sorry and regret their words or actions I could not bear to see them suffer, or be un-happy, knowing myself what it is to be unhappy and alone. . . .

March 10, 1905. Newlands, Hampshire.

The days go very quickly ; out in my Bath-chair in the morning, a drive in the victoria with Hansel between us in the afternoon, in the evenings bridge. Tommy Peacocke and his wife Ethel sometimes come and dine here, and last night we dined with them.

Hans came from London for the day. I went to meet him this morning in the motor-car which Maitland Kersey [1] sent down for me to use for ten days.

I had a nice letter yesterday from the Emperor telling me the sanitary arrangements would be carried out round Waldenburg and the adjoining towns, and that the necessary money would be granted by the State.[2] So at last the *grund* will be clean, and the poor people in their homes, already dirty enough, will at least be relieved of the horrible smell that now goes up through their windows. I hope Vater, and everyone, will be pleased at the result of my " obstination," and determination ! But " where there is a will there is a way " is a good old English proverb. I would like to add, " There is often the will but one must show it the way."

I sometimes feel I am standing at cross roads without the faintest idea which is the *right* one to take ; not that I *fear* anything, or wish to avoid the rough places, but I do not know whither either road will " land " me ; what goal I am expected to try for and reach ; or whom to stop and help by the way-side.

This morning was beautiful and warm, spring weather with sunshine and blue sky, but this afternoon it poured, and to-night it is blowing a hurricane, which it has done now for four nights. I *hate* the wind ; it makes me wonder if I shall ever commit suicide, and I lie in bed and pray for those at sea, or for those whose soul has been rent from them by misery or disappointment. To-night my maid is sleeping on a sofa at the foot of my bed ; I could not bear to be left alone at night in the dark. The little boys are very well ; the little baby has such big blue eyes.

April 2, 1905. Villa Kasbeck, Cannes.

I arrived here this morning on a visit to Sophy Torby and the Grand Duke. I left Newlands with little Hansel and the

---

[1] Major Henry Maitland Kersey, D.S.O., late Hertfordshire Yeomanry.

[2] See p. 168.

nurse, who is new ; she seems very nice and was with Princess
Frederick Leopold of Prussia [1] for eleven years.   In London
we stayed at Claridge's and little Hansel had to have a small
operation.   He was *so* good and brave, but cried dreadfully
when he awoke from the chloroform : I saw him, when he was
still under the effects of it, lying there quite quiet with a little
pale face and heavy eyes and I felt miserable for him and knew
more than ever how I adore him, and it was misery to have him
clinging to me in pain afterwards, poor precious mite.   But
it all passed very quickly really and in four days he was on
his feet again and before the end of the week back at Newlands.
Hans came from Germany for my last five days in London
and we dined out and went to the theatre together ; he seemed
very happy.   He went alone to Eaton, the Grand National,
and then to Lady Gerard [2] for the Melton Races.   When I
leave here I meet him in Paris.

I saw lots of people in London, and before going to Newlands met the King twice at dinner ; always very nice, he was
delighted to see me. . . .   At one of the dinners I said to
him : " How extraordinary it is to think that now the dressmakers are doing their best to make us look as if we wore
crinolines while my grandmother (Patsy's mother) remembers
the time when she used to see *her* mother's maid sprinkle
with water the dress on the bed so that it should cling well to
the figure ! "   The King said, " Well, when you women start
doing this again, let me know, and I will come and see it." . . .

. . . Somehow it seems a waste of time to write this diary
now, as I feel *some day* things will happen that will be *really
worth remembering*.

Staying here I shall be *entourée* with Grand Dukes and
Grand Duchesses ; but they interest me, particularly during
this awful time of war, and the Czar has not yet even started
to make peace.   To-night we dine at Villa Vendôme with my
host's sister, the Grand Duchess of Mecklenburg-Schwerin ;
it was there the Grand Duke, her husband, died of typhoid.

April 2, 1905.   Villa Kasbeck, Cannes.

Just come from dining at the Villa Vendôme.   I would
have given anything for a few Englishmen including my darling

---

[1] Louise-Sophie, Princess of Schleswig-Holstein (sister of the late
Empress of Germany), m. a second cousin of William I. in 1889.

[2] Widow of 2nd Lord Gerard (1851–1902) ; her sister-in-law,
Honble. Mary Gerard, m. General Sir Laurence Oliphant.   See p. 157.

father, the greatest gentleman one can meet, to have been there. I can understand still better now why and how the Japs are beating the Russians at every turn.

There were no other guests but Sophy, the Grand Duke Michael and myself. There is staying with the Grand Duchess Anastasia her other brother, the Grand Duke George and his wife, daughter of the King of Greece ; [1] also her son, the present Grand Duke of Mecklenburg-Schwerin and his young wife (a daughter of the Duchess of Cumberland) ; her second daughter, Cécile, who will marry the German Crown Prince on June the 6th, was there too, as well as some ladies and gentlemen-in-waiting. The dinner was awful ; badly served, and every meat and vegetable looked brown. After dinner some played bridge and others poker. I lost a little money. The Grand Duke George quarrelled with his sister and *roared* the whole time. . . . He shouted and yelled and behaved too dreadfully ; at last the Grand Duchess got quite red and said : " That is not really my brother. I made a mistake in introducing you."

Sophy, coming back in the carriage, said to her husband, " George behaved in the most extraordinary way again tonight." I could not help saying to the Grand Duke Michael before coming up to bed : " I like you ever so much better than your brother George, you are by far the nicer, both outside and inside." And *entre nous*, Michael himself, poor dear, is not anything particular, *mais mis contre son frère*, there is no comparison ; Michael seems to have got nicer and quieted down ; perhaps he feels the effects of this ghastly war. I really like best the other brother, the Grand Duke Alexander.

April 20, 1905. Paris.

Arrived here on Monday, having left Cannes on Sunday, or rather Monte Carlo, as I stayed there on Saturday night with the Sierstorpffs and the Grand Duchess Anastasia and won altogether over two hundred pounds, a great deal for me ! I leave here on Friday. I shall try to go to Church in the morning ; have only had three days to get my clothes, but did not order much as all the things I had last year and never could wear are still good enough for this year ; the fashion has not changed much.

---

[1] Marie, d. of King George I. of Greece (1845–1913) ; her husband was shot in St. Petersburg in 1919 ; in 1922 she m. (morganatically) Commander Pericles Joannides.

April 23, 1905. Easter Sunday and Hans's birthday. Newlands.

My husband is at Pless. I arrived here yesterday.

We went to Church to-day to Brockenhurst to hear Mr.
Chambers preach again ; I did not care for the sermon : I
suppose it had to be rhetorical for the occasion, and was
therefore not so human as his sermons generally are.

Poppets has got up a concert here at the Village Hall for
Friday, an afternoon and evening performance, and some professionals are coming from London. I have to sing, and regret
it because I have caught a cold (this horrible change of weather
and east wind) ; and besides, after having had a baby, one's
voice is not really right again for some months. Both the
boys are well, although Hansel looks a little pale to-night ; I
think he ate too many Easter sweets, and the wee boy is still
sorry for his little self after his vaccination; the marks are not yet
healed. I shall not leave for Fürstenstein until he is quite well.

On the 27th there is to be a county ball given at a neighbour's house, a drive of an hour and—country neighbours at
the end of it. Awful idea ! It is with a feeling of self-pity
that I picture myself being bumped against everyone, with
the arm of the country curate round my waist. And can't I
hear their silly questions ! " Do you like Germany ? " " Do
you live in the same way as we do here ? " " It must be
dreadful to dine at six every night." " Does the Emperor
really hate England ? " and " Are not the women in Germany
ugly ? " " Do you really eat *sauerkraut* ? " and similar
inanities for ever and ever amen !

May 30, 1905. *Monday.* Fürstenstein.

Am alone here, Hans having gone to Berlin last night for
the House of Lords sittings. I follow on Friday the second
for the wedding of the Crown Prince and other festivities. I
have just finished dinner in my boudoir ; as I entered, the room
did not look to me half so cosy as did a cottage at Polsnitz where,
from the roadway, I saw Jachevitz and his wife having dinner
by the open window. Oh, what joy to be alone for a few days !

As no one else can see into my soul, I alone realize how I
feel the intense wonder, grandeur, and generosity of life.

Yesterday I went with nurses and children to the *Silbersee*
to fish ; we had tea amongst the lilies-of-the-valley and Baby
lay on my coat. This afternoon we went to the *Schwarzengraben*
and had tea. I started at the top of the little stream, and when

the children went home, I fished right down, and then walked
back through the woods. I wanted to walk alone, but a new
Unterjäger from Lonitz who was on duty would not let me ;
he seemed to think it wasn't safe and persisted in marching
behind me all the way. I spoke to him now and then, so as
not to hurt his feelings ; his presence did not altogether prevent me from collecting my thoughts and relishing the song of
the birds, and the smell of the woods. The firs looked so big
at night, and it was like walking through a magic land. I should
be so happy quite alone here ; now and then solitude is such
a rest, and when one is by oneself every little incident leaves a
mark on the memory. If I had met even a dozen robbers,
they would not have frightened me ; indeed, while that mood
lasted, I should have been pleased to meet them ; one cannot
feel afraid in Heaven. I should have greeted them with a
smile wishing them a life of happiness and warning them only
to be careful not to tread upon the lilies, and gone my way.

Hans wired this morning to say that my presence was desired
in Berlin to-morrow at an *Empfang* at Countess Brockdorff's
and for a soirée the next night at Lulu's, Hans's sister, the chief
lady at Court ; but a week in Berlin will be more than enough,
so I wrote to Countess Brockdorff and said I was ill on the sofa,
and wired to the same effect to Lulu ! . . .

Oh, why is it that I can *feel* the higher side of life, the grandeur,
peace and silence of woods and silent nights, the hopeful sunshine of the morning, the song of the birds seeming to say :
" Come on, come on, work and sing to the glory of God and
the world " ; and yet I feel all this only when I am alone !

June 16, 1905. At Sea.

I write in a little brass bed in the " de luxe " cabin on board
the *Hamburg*, a Hamburg-Amerika liner which stops at Dover
on its way to New York. The short sea voyage in the summer
is far pleasanter than the long dusty train journey.

I had a small party at Fürstenstein for Whitsuntide. It
included Princess Salm (the Austrian Archduchess), a dear
little woman, married just three years, and Prince Gottfried
Hohenlohe. Prince Gottfried, just as dear, nice, and amusing
as ever, but each time fatter, stayed three days, and left Berlin
for Petersburg the day we did.

In Berlin we dined at the Automobile Club with Prince
Christian Kraft Hohenlohe and Prince Salm. Minnie Paget [1]

---

[1] Wife of General Sir Arthur Paget ; see p. 90.

dined there too, looking very ill, poor thing, and not able to walk without a stick and someone to hold on to the other side. I drove her home to the Achenbachstrasse, about fifteen minutes' drive, and she told me that if she remained a cripple another year she would poison herself.

Prince Gottfried thinks the Czar is sure to meet his fate at the *hands of a murderer*; the feeling of anxiety and suspense in Russia must be dreadful : I made him promise not to drive anywhere with any Grand Dukes as I don't want him to be blown up.

Hans and I went to Berlin for the wedding of the Crown Prince.[1] It was so dreadfully hot there that it was quite impossible to sleep. For the Gala performance at the Opera I sat in the large box with all the Princesses : it was like a furnace. In the foyer afterwards there was a mass of Royalties and even those whom I only knew slightly seemed very pleased to see me. The Duchess d'Aosta [2] said to me : " Oh, do wait, my husband is so anxious to talk with you " : and I had met him only twice before in my life. The Grand Duchess Vladimir was so gentle and nice but her face was very sad. I asked her to Fürstenstein, but she cannot fit it in. The Grand Duke was not present, not daring, I expect, to appear in public after the terrible naval defeat of Russia—their second Fleet annihilated.[3]

July 19, 1905. Again on a Hamburg-Amerika liner.

We left Dover four hours ago. How quickly the time passes. I have been to England—London, Ascot, Newmarket, dinner parties and lunches ; have talked with the King and Queen, Princes and Princesses, have seen my friends (and probably my enemies), have sung at two concerts, have smiled, talked, laughed, and, once or twice, almost cried inwardly ; and now I return to Fürstenstein and my darling boys.

It was very nice staying at the German Embassy, Count Metternich let us do exactly what we liked ; we dined and lunched out nearly every day and poor dear Count Metternich— as far as he knows how—has fallen in love with me, so I think he misses me now that I am gone. He is so weird but so

---

[1] *Daisy Princess of Pless*, pp. 109 *et seq.*

[2] Princess Helene of France, m. 1895, the Duke of Aosta, cousin of the King of Italy, and brother of the Count of Turin (see p. 42).

[3] Russia was finally defeated by the Japanese in the naval battle near Tsushima in May, 1905.

nice ; it is really too funny. I made him give a ball [1] and had to look through all the accounts this morning before I left as his servants rob him too dreadfully, or so he says. I took him to Newlands last Saturday. He held two ropes which were attached to us while Patsy and I bathed, and then he took off his shoes for me to walk back in and himself walked in his stockinged feet over the shingle. I gave him lots of useful hints, and am trying to find him a butler and a secretary. He said : " Yes, if you were always with me I might be able to do something, for I have no ambitions, but you have." Then he said : " Tell me candidly what people say of me in this country ? " Poor dear, I couldn't tell him most people think him a bore, so I only answered : " People do not see enough of you, you must entertain them more and make yourself more agreeable." This he is quite prepared to do, and wants me to help him, but I am not in London often enough to be of any real use.

Nevertheless, I hope in time to push Metternich through it all and make his Embassy popular, for I like him so ; he is so nice and such a gentleman though very silent and quiet and in public sometimes never opens his mouth ; he has grey hair and a crooked jaw, and looks much older than his age, which is, I believe, only forty-five. Ascot was very hot and crowded.

Last night I went to a party at Lady de Grey's when Caruso, Scotti and Madame Destinn sang. Afterwards I drove back in the motor with Prince Francis of Teck. He said : " I suppose you and Muriel Beckett [2] are now the two most beautiful women in Europe ! " I am beginning to think that I really must be good to look at, as men are so attentive to me and all the women (perhaps because I see them so seldom) are so nice to me. Captain Holford [3] who was in-Waiting on the King told me he overheard someone say at a Court Ball : " What is the good of all the others coming ? She knocks them all out."

Shelagh's ball at Grosvenor House for the King and Queen was a great success.

Oh, this boat is *awful* ; if I had known I would never have

---

[1] See *Daisy Princess of Pless*, p. 120.
[2] D. of Lord Berkeley Paget ; m. 1896, Honble. Rupert Beckett.
[3] Lieut.-Colonel Sir George Holford (1860–1925), Equerry to His Majesty 1901–14 : m. 1912, Susannah, d. of Arthur Wilson of Tranby Croft, and widow of J. Graham Menzies ; owned Dorchester House Picture Gallery.

come on it ; it is crammed full of awful American-German Jews. I only know one person on board, a young man who is going to learn German at Potsdam ; he is Ingham Whittaker's [1] brother, and seems a nice gentlemanly boy.

I expected to get to Hamburg to-morrow by four o'clock and now they calmly say the steamer is late and will miss all the connections to Berlin ! If only they had a Marconi telegraphic machine on board I could let Hans know, and also wire to Cuxhaven for a special train from there to Hamburg, and not have to go to an hotel. The sea is very calm, but the boat is filthy ; they have been longer than usual on the journey from New York and everything is high, meat, chickens and lamb ; fortunately they took on some fresh fish at Dover so I shall live on that. The noise, and horrible second-rate German, English and American accents one hears is enough to drive one mad. There are no " de luxe " cabins so I have one with two small beds, and the maids have one opposite mine ; these, they say, are the best cabins they have ! *All* the passengers travelling first class look as if they ought to be travelling fourth—or eighth—if there was such a thing. Major Maitland Kersey saw me off and gave me flowers and books, as also did Caryl Ramsden.[2] Oh, the Jews that are tramping up and down in front of me ! I feel that if I get up from this chair I shall go and quietly drop somebody overboard. There are dozens of screaming children too, and all the mothers and fathers are talking broken English to them, I suppose to teach them the language, and something is biting me : I am sure they all have fleas !

August 4, 1905. Fürstenstein.

Mathilde, Vater, Anna and Willusch still here. I say " still," because it seems as if they had been here months and I back from England a year, and yet it is only about a fortnight. For the first hour or two I am with them it is like walking on ice—so carefully and self-consciously. . . . I even had to move my beloved piano into another room as if I played a little between lunch and tea or after dinner Hans came and asked me to stop as it disturbed the conversation. And not once have

---

[1] W. Ingham Whitaker of Pylewell Park, Lymington. His youngest step-brother, Hugh, b. 1885, m. 1913, Lady Helen Wilbraham, d. of 2nd Earl of Lathom.

[2] Lieut.-Colonel Caryl John Ramsden, late Seaforth Highlanders, b. 1868, m. 1919, d. of Senator Scott of Kentucky, U.S.A.

To Daisy
from: J.

John S. Sargent 1913

THE DUKE OF BERWICK AND ALBA.
From a Painting by Sargent.

I been to fish in one of my little trout streams, because our visitors do not care about it, and I naturally have to stay with them morning, noon and—no, fortunately not night. . . . But now I have got them acclimatized, or at least I have got them to smile and laugh, and be a little cheerful ; one must simply make up one's mind not to think ; but go on behaving rather like a *sensible* idiot ; and talk only of motors and one's various relations, and then play games with Willusch and Anna who are seventeen and eighteen but might be taken for babies of seven and eight. They never read—in fact I can't think how they live : it must be a great rest, though, to be able to exist without thinking.

Our new Comptroller who replaces the late Doctor Ritter, seems most intelligent ; so far I am delighted with him, and his wife seems sensible and inclined to work for the poor.

I am writing in my garden ; the head gardener has a passion for white ; white daisies, white dahlias, white lilies, white roses—and I think a garden should be full of colour !

In about a week, when my relatives leave, I am going to take Hansel and Baby to the sea ; Hansel is growing so fast, and is quite a little man and rides beautifully. The baby is a darling now and he is such fun.

October 6, 1905. Berlin.

Shelagh, Granny, Muriel Parsons,[1] brother George and Jennie and masses of people have been to Fürstenstein to stay. We had paper-chases, motor-trips, dances, a fancy ball, shot partridges, fished, played golf and croquet—in fact all the usual things. Amongst those who came were Count Mensdorff, Countess Raher and her daughter (her husband is Secretary for Foreign Affairs at Copenhagen), Prince Francis of Teck, the Grand Duke Michael of Russia—Sophy couldn't come as her father the old Duke of Nassau was ill and has since died —Count and Countess Henckel, the Matuschkas, Fritz and Nancy,[2] Mrs. Bingham, Prince Emmanuel Salm, the Sternbergs,[3] Duke Ernst Günther Holstein and the Duchess (who now seems more human and intelligent than she used to be),

---

[1] Lady Muriel Parsons, d. of 4th Earl of Rosse, m. 1906, Colonel Harold Grenfell, C.M.G., M.V.O.

[2] Count Fritz Hochberg, m. in January, 1905, the Honble. Nancy Burke-Roche, d. of 2nd Baron Fermoy.

[3] Leopold, 6th Count von Sternberg, b. 1865, m. 1895, Countess Franziska (Fanny) Larisch von Moennich, d. of " Count Heine."

Betka Potocka who brought with her Mr. Oliveira (a Mexican, the son of the Brazilian Minister in London). Doctor Lehrhammer also came—and sang for us—but I cannot remember them all now.

Granny the old darling was more delightful and dainty than ever and full of fun and spirits in spite of her eighty-two years. And little Shelagh was her old self again, full of fun, and wore all her pretty clothes and took a delight in everything, making herself look lovely, and wearing her diamonds. She really loved being at Fürstenstein again.

Fritz insisted on my letting C. come to Fürstenstein to do my bust ; he is one of the most famous sculptors of the day. And he came but alas, his " clay " got lost on the way ; he waited for it four days while they searched railway stations and towns but it could not be found ; so I do not expect now I shall ever sit to him. Anyway, I do not care for him ; he is not a gentleman (I had never thought that a genius *could* be anything but a gentleman !) and makes the most ridiculous, almost offensive, compliments and speeches to me ; and to secure a good picture one must be in sympathy a little with the artist I feel, and not be thinking all the time, " I must keep this man in his place."

During the past few days I have seen more of Berlin than I ever did before. I have been to several beautiful picture galleries ; oh, the Rubens—far more beautiful than those in the Dresden Gallery. I wired to Eulenburg for special permission to see all the Royal Castles, so we went to the Palace in Berlin (I had never seen the bedrooms), Charlottenberg, Neues Palast, Stadt-Schloss and Sans Souci in Potsdam, and were met everywhere by royal " men housekeepers," and enjoyed ourselves immensely.

The Finance Minister, Her von Reinbaben,[1] came to see me in Berlin. I thought I should be very shy but we got on beautifully, yet I am afraid, in spite of the Emperor's letter, that all my smiles and prayers will not help in getting any money towards cleaning the Waldenburg River, because, as he rightly says, if one place gets help all Germany will come forward and expect it, and some parts of East Prussia are even worse off than we are. But sooner or later it will have to be done, and it *will* be done. Now I am going to have a rest before dinner ; the cook at this hotel is dreadful.

---

[1] Prussian Minister of Finance, retired in 1910 after a sweeping attack on the administration of Prussian finance. See p. 159.

October 25, 1905. Lancut, Galicia.

Have been here alone for three days with the Potockis, and meet Hans to-morrow at Castolowitz for the Sternbergs' shoot, given for the Archduke Franz Ferdinand.

I was for about ten days alone in Fürstenstein writing my letters, playing with the children and getting some old clothes done up in Breslau.

Hans came back from Parduwitz for two days ; then I went to Pless with the boys and stayed a week, a week of holy quietness and German stiffness ; although they are so nice and I love them, Germans don't know how to live ; even Anna, the daughter, sighed and said : " Oh, Daisy, I can't be myself in this house." At any rate it was nice and soothing to my nerves and dear old Vater got up a shoot on purpose for me—he and I alone and about a dozen *Ober-Jagdmeisters* ! It was all arranged as carefully as if the Emperor had been there. We shot about two hundred hare, and a few other things. I rode, too, every morning with Anna and made the horses really gallop ; she was delighted and so, to my surprise, was the *Ober*-something-*rittmeister* who of course rode behind us. On the way here I spent a night at Solza with the Larisches. They did all they could to keep me longer but I had promised to come here, and dear Betka Potocka is so nice and always comes to Fürstenstein every year, and I had not been to stay with her since I came a long time ago with Shelagh and Pat. Besides, it is a beautiful home full of lovely things, and lovely flowers. Some imagine the Poles to be a rather wild people, I cannot think why, but there is such an idea abroad ; in reality, they are all so quick and cultured, very good linguists, and the women are like Austrians, full of life, dress in Paris, and travel a great deal. This house is full of pictures and china brought home by a Countess Branicka ; [1] her family was connected with Marie Antoinette. It is beautifully kept up now by Betka and her husband, who have taste *and* money.

We shot yesterday and to-day. There are about twelve people here, amongst these being Prince and Princess Salm, Count Zeparie, a Hungarian ; Count Castellane, [2] Dolly's husband (her first husband, Prince Fürstenberg, died and she had no children, so she gave up everything and married a

---

[1] Countess Potocka's brother, Prince George Radziwill (1860–1914), m. 1883, Countess Marie Branicka, b. in Paris 1863.

[2] See p. 70.

Frenchman of the typical sort, with frilled shirt, pale face, thin boots and cold feet—a little man four feet high !). There are, too, a Count and Countess Esterhazy—she was a Borghese ; and Count and Countess—something ending in ski ; she is a niece of Roman Potocki ; I can't remember the others.

I wrote a letter to the Emperor from Pless [1] . . .

It will be queer, but now, after the Russo-Japanese war, and in view of England's treaty with Japan, it is not unlikely that Russia and France will make a treaty with one another !

Gottfried Hohenlohe has written me a very interesting letter—more or less in English of which the following is a part :

" Well, I am back in this blessed country ; things are going worse than ever and if someone does not soon put an end to the reigning state of anarchy it *will* and *must* be the end of everything.

" In spite of all the things that happened in the Army I still believe that the Czar could count on nearly all the troops, could restore order with their help, and then begin a new regime ; people are so sick and tired of all those troubles that if the Czar *se met enfin à la tête*, and shows *sa bonne volonté de remettre à tout prix l'ordre*, he will have much more of the whole people behind him than some think. But if things are going on only for two months more in the way they go now, it is the end of the Army too ; for how can you expect to maintain order and discipline in the Army which, nowadays, is nothing else than a part of the whole population, if everywhere else there is nothing but disorder and anarchy.

" I was received a few days ago by the Czar ; he looked smaller, yellower and more helpless than ever, and this time he did not see things *couleur de rose* as usual, but was ' *aigre* ' and furious against everybody and everything. We had a long talk and he said : ' *J'ai assez fait de concessions, mais maintenant on veut positivement que je sanctionne l'anarchie. Il faut plus céder—je l'ai déjà fait trop.*' Then he added : ' *Est-ce-que tout ça ne vous rappelle pas un proverbe qui va admirablement à la situation d'ici !* '

" I thought for a moment and then replied that we Austrians had a saying that if you give your little finger people at last want the whole arm. He laughed and said : ' *C'est juste aussi, mais mon proverbe quoique vulgaire dépeint encore mieux la situation ; il dit : Si tu invites des cochons à ta table, tu peux être sûr qu'ils*

---

[1] See *Daisy Princess of Pless*, p. 111.

mettront les quatre pieds dans les plats. C'est ce qui m'est arrivé ces derniers mois.'

" I don't think the Emperor could characterize more plainly what the Duma has done till now. Only I am afraid that poor little Emperor will never succeed in being energetic, even if he wants to !

" Please don't mention all that to anybody as nowadays *une indiscretion se produit si vite* and it would not be pleasant for me if that conversation of mine with the Emperor would be known.

" I am in Tsarskoye Selo living in my old rooms at the Grand Duke Vladimir's ; he is not here and neither is the Grand Duchess so I live for myself.

" I dined with Boris [1] yesterday, he is a good boy and I really am rather fond of him, but if you think of all those creatures being Grand Dukes and doing *nothing at all* at the present moment, it *is* disgusting.

" The little Salm was very nice ; she is such a charming little thing and adores you. I am sorry for her that she did not marry in Austria for one cannot be more Austrian than she is and that means that one cannot be really happy in Prussia, especially as the wife of an officer in Potsdam. At least I think so !

" Now good-bye, dear old thing ; I would have written you sooner but had no chance to send the letter safely out of ' holy Russia.' I think very much of you, as I have many lonely rides and walks in those splendid parks, greener and fresher than anywhere else, full of remembrances of times gone by. I often dream of the good old times here when it was still worth while to be a man (in every sense of the word, especially under Catherine II.). Nowadays all that, all the personal qualities are more or less of no importance, the principal thing is a big and well-filled pocket . . ."

October 29, 1905. In the train to Berlin.

It was very nice at Castolowitz.[2] I went to bed for two hours when I arrived and then I and the other ladies went out to lunch with the guns. It was a lovely day. The second day it rained but we went out all the same, and when

---

[1] Second son of Grand Duke Vladimir, b. 1877, m. morganatically in 1919.

[2] Residence of Count and Countess Sternberg, in Bohemia, now Czecho-Slovakia.

we came home after tea I sang in Fanny's boudoir ; they liked it and I made one or two almost cry ; so I sang my best for over an hour as I felt my audience sympathetic. The Duchess of Hohenberg and her sister Henriette Chotek [1] love music. The former has three children. We shot nearly three thousand head of game, chiefly rabbits ; the Archduke's mixed bag of pheasants, hares and rabbits totalled sixteen hundred and thirty. I was in very congenial society, Austrian men and women are *so* nice.

October 31, 1905. Queensberry House, Newmarket.

What a change in place and address. I arrived in London last night an hour and a half late ; the crossing to Flushing was dreadful. I was not ill but everyone seems to have been. I had a late dinner with Lily and Charles [2] Kinsky, who are also staying at the Embassy. This morning Count Metternich came and watched me trying on hats. Maudie Warrender and Oscar Herren also came to see me. I went to lunch with the latter at Willis's Restaurant, not an extraordinary thing to do in England, but in Berlin—to lunch alone with a man !

I do not know who is staying here, only a small party I expect. So far I have only seen Julia [3] and Mr. Maguire, Edith Wolverton, Adèle Essex and General Scobell. I had some tea and came up here for a rest. Now I shall write to Hans.

November 1, 1905. Newmarket.

Just back from the Races ; sunny day but windy ; lost a few pounds ; some of the women looked very well but all those hats trimmed with cock's feathers looked dreadful in the wind. I lunched with the King, Edith Wolverton, Alice Keppel, Mrs. Ronny Greville,[4] old Mrs. Tharpe, Horace Farquhar [5] and Arthur Sassoon (the Jew page boy) who gets up after each course to make bets for the King and the others while they are at lunch.

---

[1] Y. d. of Count Bohuslaw Chotek, m. 1921, Leopold Count Nostitz-Reineck.

[2] See p. 76 ; the Prince, in 1883, won the Grand National at Liverpool on his own mare *Zoedone*.

[3] Honble. Julia, d. of 1st Viscount Peel, m. 1895, James Rochefort Maguire, C.B.E., M.P. (1855–1925).

[4] Dame Margaret Greville, m. 1891, Honble. Ronald Greville (1864–1908), e. s. of 2nd Lord Greville.

[5] 1st and last Lord Farquhar (1844–1923).

They got on the subject of Russia and the brutality of the Russian Cossack soldiers ; the King at once changed the subject because of me I suppose ; it is horrid.   It makes me feel like a foreigner here—as in Germany—when politics are discussed. The King did not mention Hans or Germany, and, for the first time in any place where I was present, he scarcely spoke to me ; he must hate the Germans.

November 4, 1905.   Salisbury Hall, St. Albans.

Came here from London to stay from Saturday to Monday. George and Jenny have made this little house delightful ; it is full of pretty things, and the garden will be very nice.   On Friday night I dined with Count Mensdorff to meet the Connaughts ; lots of people there.   Went afterwards to the Opera in Maudie Warrender's box.

I have just written a long letter to the King about England and Germany.   I wonder if he will be furious : it is a congratulatory letter as well, as the ninth is his birthday.

The Emperor has not answered me ;[1] I never for one moment expected he would, but it seems rather strange—he was not going to Pless to shoot, and now suddenly he changes his mind and announces that he will go there on the 26th !   I wonder what he will say when we meet.

November 8, 1905.   Newlands.

A delicious day as warm as spring and a nice shoot.   I shot fourteen duck and a few pheasants.   Gerald Paget is here, brother George, Maitland Kersey, and Mr. and Mrs. Sloane Stanley.   I received a wire this morning from the Comptroller of the Household asking if I could accept Their Majesties' command to come to the Banquet at Windsor Castle in honour of the King of Greece.[2]   Of course I shall go ; I wish it were to stay the night, as returning to London so late by rail will not be pleasant ; however, I suppose they will have a special train.

As I posted it from London, the King must have received my letter yesterday ; the result is, so far, satisfactory.

---

[1] See p. 174.
[2] George I. (Prince of Denmark) (1845–1913) became King of the Hellenes in 1863 ; m. in 1867 Grand Duchess Olga of Russia (1851–1926).

November 11, 1905. Newlands.

I had a letter from Sir Francis Knollys [1] in answer to mine
to the King ; it is the first time he does not answer a letter
himself ; but I suppose as King he is too busy, or perhaps X.
has forbidden him to do so ! Anyway I shall keep it ; he
says he has not in the least changed towards me, and that he
has no feeling of dislike towards the German Emperor (which
of course isn't true). . . .

The Banquet was a great success, and the King was very
nice ; the Queen—charming as always.

November 29, 1905. Pless.

I arrived very tired in Fürstenstein on the 18th after travelling for two nights. Baby and Hansel met me on the stairs,
each with a little bunch of flowers for me. . . . I had a few
happy days alone with the children and made toffee and baked
apples in the nursery ; it is alone with them that I am happiest.

A few days ago I received from Count von Bülow a reply
to the letter I wrote to the Emperor more than a month ago.
Here it is, written in English :

Der Reichskanzler.   BERLIN, 23 *November*, 1905.
DEAR PRINCESS,—

From your letter of the 22nd of last month, to His Majesty the
Kaiser and King, which His Majesty has handed to me, I have
seen with great satisfaction, how very much you bemoan with
me the present condition of the German-English relationship,
and how warmly you wish with me a betterment of this state
of affairs. Many places in this letter are as though written
from out of my own heart, and I wished that my countrymen
could share your convictions, according to which, no real hate
against Germany exists in England. But justly, one cannot
blame part of the German public opinion if it has gradually,
only very gradually, arrived at actually believing in a deeply
rooted hostile feeling against us. In contrast with the Press
of many other countries, the larger English newspapers have
always been rightly considered as politically well disciplined,
and fully conscious of their moral responsibility. But what
ought German public opinion to say if important English
papers, some of them for years, give way to the most un-
just slanders about German Politics, and in constant personal

---

[1] 1st Viscount Knollys (1837–1924), Private Secretary to King
Edward and King George 1870–1913.

slanders of our Kaiser and his co-workers, being at the same time extremely friendly towards almost all other countries?

With such a position of affairs, even the most well-wishing and most gratifying intentions as yours, must unfortunately remain without practical results for the present; and only from a gradually juster view on the part of the English, may all German true friends of England hope for an alteration of the present conditions. His Majesty the Kaiser uttered to me, he had got lately too many discouraging impressions from the English side to be able to make up his mind now on his part to take the initiative in the direction desired by you,—an initiative which after all could again be misjudged.

Once again, warmly thanking you for your interesting and so well-meant explanations. I remain, dear Princess, Your sincerely devoted,   BÜLOW.

December 1, 1905. Pless.

Apart from Natalie and Hermann Hatzfeldt, our party to meet the Emperor consisted only of members of the family. The Emperor called me " my dear child " or else " Daisy " the whole time. . . .

I wanted to show the Emperor some press cuttings, but Baron Tschirschky asked to have them, saying : " For God's sake don't show them to the Emperor, or goodness knows what he might do ! "

December 10, 1905. Dresden.

I came here with Nancy and Fritz the day before yesterday— my wedding anniversary ; it seems impossible to believe that I have been married fourteen years.

We really came to hear the new Opera by Strauss, *Salomé* ; but did not like the theme or the music. The head of John the Baptist is brought up on a silver dish, and Salomé talks to it, kisses it, and lies on the floor with it, the idea being that she as well as her mother Herodias, loves the Prophet ; but the whole story was distorted and not in keeping with what is written in the Bible ; I think one must hear the music several times before understanding it.

We leave here on Tuesday for Halbau.[1] The shops are lovely and full of nice Christmas things. We left Fürstenstein at nine-fifteen and got here at four-ten, stopping three-quarters of an hour on the way to shop in Leignitz and have lunch ;

---

[1] The Silesian residence of Count Fritz Hochberg.

the chauffeur drove well, but much too fast ; we nearly went into a ditch while rounding a corner. I wonder how soon we shall be travelling in flying machines ! Fritz and Nancy seem very happy, they are both so full of ideas on every subject, and so companionable ; it is good to be with them.

Christmas Day, December 25, 1905. Pless.

I see in this book how changeable my handwriting can be ; sometimes the change is due to the different kinds of pen available, or the size and position of the table I happen to be writing on, or the speed of the writing. I daresay a handwriting expert would not only read into it a variety of moods, but even fasten a changeable character on the writer ; but this conclusion would not be quite exact : my character, alas, remains the same ! I only wish I could get quieter and more satisfied. All day long my soul cries out within me to some unknown protector : " I am lonely, understand me, take care of me, hold my hand, be my guide ; I am so tired of standing alone, and I have had to pretend so long, so long ; let me see sunshine ; give me peace ; take me to a country of fair flowers and fresh Springs, where in love and harmony men and women work their common way to a higher destiny ; away from the world of lies, criticisms and forced smiles." But to wish to change is perhaps, after all, to have a changeable character !

And what is the good of these reflections, I am *alive*, . . . I must take up my staff, must think of my boys, and work on, and take an interest in everything that will one day interest them. God help me.

After I left Halbau I had a very busy time in Fürstenstein. Every day for a week I had one or even two Christmas feasts for the old men and women and children. I suppose, in all, I gave food and presents, such as petticoats, shirts or stuffs for dresses, to two thousand old men and women, and some thousand children in addition ; but their joy and kind words repaid me many times over. They all *sat* at tables and had lots of cakes and as much hot chocolate as they could eat or drink. The servants' Christmas was very nice too ; we all sang round the tree and every servant seemed to get the presents that he or she most wanted. I shall miss dreadfully my two maids Marie and Hedwig when they get married. I do not know what I shall do with two strange maids.

We went to-day to give toys, coffee, nuts and apples to the

Prince of Pless
(in uniform).

Colonel and Mrs
Cornwallis-West.

Major
Maitland
Kersey.

Seated : Queen Sophie
of Greece.

The
Authoress.

Duke of
Connaught.

Queen Marie
of Rumania.

Archduchess Crista of Austria
(Princess Salm-Salm).

General
Sir Ian Hamilton.

Seated on ground :

Br.-General
Geoffrey Brooke.

IMPERIAL MANŒUVRES.

Silesia, 1905.

poor children here ; there was a tree in the riding-school ;
but *what* toys ! I was *ashamed* to hand them round—and the
poor mothers so tired, some of them having carried their
children for miles, got nothing. The toys could not have
cost more than one penny or a halfpenny each, *really*. Fritz
and I simply looked at each other and sighed ; this was Pless,
not Fürstenstein. I feel *nous allons changer tout cela* some
day ; I do not mean this unkindly, but in the natural course
of events it must happen.

Hans is furious because the Emperor has made Vater a
Duke on the occasion of his Jubilee as Prince of Pless ! All
the boys are annoyed—I mean Conny and Fritz ; Fritz says
that it will make his mother turn in her grave at such an
insult to her eldest son and grandson. I must confess, myself,
that as the title gives no additional rank or position, I cannot
understand why Vater should accept it, or rather, why he should
use it ; for accept it he must, I suppose. But after being Prince
of Pless all these years, suddenly to begin to call himself Duke
of Pless seems too funny. Natalie and Hermann have not
changed their title, they remain Prince and Princess Hatzfeldt ;
neither did Christian Kraft Hohenlohe ; nor old Prince Bismarck after being created a Duke.

As I told Hans in Fürstenstein, the Emperor has heard of
his Catholic leanings combined with his Polish sympathies ;
people are jealous of us . . . the money we are supposed to
have . . . There is no " good feeling " towards mankind in
aristocratic Germany, they are all snobs, and hate anyone who
has more of anything than they have ! The Emperor might,
instead, have given Vater a Regiment, or the Black Eagle in
diamonds, or anything else . . .

Vater says that if we show we feel hurt, it will only make the
jealous people more pleased, and the Emperor, if he meant to
be rude, will see that he has succeeded, whereas if we show
nothing, no one will think there is *anything* for us to resent ;
he even proposes that Hans should go with him to Berlin to
thank the Emperor for this new dignity. But Hans won't,
and I really cannot make out which of them is right. Hans has
made up his mind not to go to Berlin this winter or to receive
the Emperor at Fürstenstein in the summer when he comes to
Breslau for the Manœuvres ; there is no real necessity for me
to go to Berlin this winter as I went there for the Crown Prince's
wedding. As to the future—I think we will see a good deal in
the future.

Considering the present bourgeois Society of Berlin the Emperor does wrong not to encourage nice people to go there, and some day I shall tell him a few more home truths ; also, I shall open his eyes about some of his *men* friends—with whom he ought not to consort !

New Year's Eve.   Eaton Hall, Cheshire.

It is a quarter to twelve and I am waiting for Geoffrey Brooke [1] (Aunt Min's eldest son) to bring me something with which to " drink the New Year in." I am in bed ; we were all too tired to stay up till twelve o'clock. 1905 will soon have passed and 1906 be here. I always hate to lose the old year even if it brought to our eyes tears of sorrow and little lines to our face ; at any rate it has been with me and I know what it was like. But this New Year, I know nothing of it, I can guess nothing, it makes me nervous, for it is always silent, and yet it knows already things that are secrets to me.

Poor little Patsy could not come, she has a bad cold and is at Newlands, so I came here with Poppets from London. I arrived the 28th morning ; left Pless the 26th and slept the night at the Wilhelmstrasse. I rehearsed all the 28th and 29th. I really think my monologue will be a great success ; it is beautiful with the orchestra, and Herbert Tree,[2] the actor, came to see a little of it while I rehearsed alone, and liked it enormously. Dicky Braune who wrote the music and his brother-in-law Simpson Ladell are both coming to Chatsworth to conduct it. I go there on Tuesday. I had permission from the King and Queen to stay here over the New Year, as I really did not want to be alone at Chatsworth, much preferring to be with my sister and relations at Eaton. Girlie Cawley (that was) has just been in, and Geoffrey brought some whisky and soda which I hate, and we drank the health of the New Year. The bells have just done chiming : now I shall go to sleep. . . .

---

[1] Lieut.-Colonel Geoffrey Francis Heremon Brooke, D.S.O., M.C., 16/5th Lancers, first cousin of the authoress.

[2] 1853–1917 : knighted 1909.

CHAPTER EIGHT

1906

January 1, 1906. Eaton Hall, Cheshire.

BEND OR has given me a lovely pearl pendant for a New Year present, just a big pearl with diamonds each side beautifully set by Cartier.

Hans has not wired to me to-day although I wired to him. Fancy a new year has begun ; the fortune-teller woman has told me a lot that would happen this year ; I wonder if it will come true. I wrote Hans a long letter yesterday and told him what Mathilde had said—which is what I feel myself : To show he minds the title of Duke given to Vater not being hereditary would only look snobby, and delight those people who are already jealous of us. He must *say nothing*, only, some day, when it is offered to him, he can refuse it, as I should most certainly persuade him to do, unless another territorial designation was given with it. I want to go to Berlin for a week and tell them all how much nicer and more amusing it is in Fürstenstein ; this will be quite enough to annoy them, as the Court loses two handsome pieces of furniture when Hans and I do not deck its polished floors ! Whereas we lose nothing as Berlin now is dreadfully dull.

January 8, 1906. Eaton again.

Arrived here again this afternoon with Violet Mar and Kellie and her husband, after nearly a week at Chatsworth, where I had no time to write.

I arrived at Chatsworth on the Tuesday ; at dinner sat next to the King and immediately afterwards rehearsed my monologue ; rehearsed again all Wednesday and acted on Thursday and Friday. It went well, although it was a very big undertaking, and perhaps too poetical for the fashionable audience. Mr. Hawtrey [1] acted a little piece one evening

---

[1] 1859–1923. Knighted 1922.

179

with Muriel Wilson and Maudie Warrender : although one of the best professional actors he was very nervous ; he congratulated me enormously, and I got a charming letter from Miss Rosina Filippi the day I arrived wishing me every success, and saying how delighted she was with the rehearsals.

The King still walks lame from his fall in a rabbit hole last November ; he strained some sinews but is getting on well. The Queen was very well and full of fun and looks the same as she has done for the last sixteen years !

I was made the chief source of amusement ; I had to tell them stories of Germany, dance, sing, do tricks with a glass of water on my head (before the men came out of the dining-room after dinner) and show how high I could kick, which is higher than my own head a good bit. Princess Victoria held up her fan for me to kick. All the women were charming to me—but what they said or did when I wasn't there, I am sure I don't know nor care.

I never had a greater success at any Chatsworth party. Soveral was cross because I walked about a lot with Captain Holford, aid-de-camp to the King, and lots of funny little things happened. . . .

January 21, 1906.   Newlands Manor, Hampshire.

After nearly a week at Eaton, the party consisting of the Marlboroughs, Chesterfields, Lyttons, Mar and Kellies, and Lady Sarah and Mr. Wilson,[1] and a week in London spent at the dentist and the dressmaker, I am *here*, the dearest place in the world to me. It is spring weather and yesterday I picked some primroses in the woods and sent them to little Hansel. Hans hasn't written for ages although I have written to him asking if there is any particular hurry for me to return ; at any rate *he* isn't in a hurry as he hasn't answered. But I can't stay away longer from the children so shall leave for Germany next Saturday.

The Eaton party was nice and quiet after Chatsworth : Shelagh and Bend Or went out hunting every day. We went to a public meeting in Chester when Sir Henry Campbell Bannerman [2] spoke.

---

[1] Lieut.-Colonel Gordon C. Wilson (d. 1914), m. 1891, Lady Sarah Spencer Churchill, d. of 7th Duke of Marlborough.

[2] (1836–1908) Was Liberal Prime Minister from December, 1905, till his death in April, 1908, when he was succeeded by Mr. Asquith (1st Earl of Oxford and Asquith).

I dined out in London and went to plays ; last Thursday I went to open a Club for young men (chiefly for clerks, merchants, and shop hands) at Dulwich, half-an-hour by motor on the outskirts of London ; Consuelo Marlborough came with me ; they gave us bouquets and I made a speech, quite a nice one ; I was terrified at first but I wrote it all down before going. I told them how necessary it was, besides physical exercises such as cricket and football, to educate their minds, to encourage in themselves any particular taste or talent they might possess, to be nature's gentlemen, which were the best sort of gentlemen, requiring no frock coat or a pocket full of gold. I asked them to remember always that they were proud Englishmen and honest worthy subjects of His Majesty the King. Then Consuelo returned a vote of thanks for the reception we had received, and after seeing them dance a valse (it was a ball and ladies were present) we left in a storm of wind and rain and the motor full of flowers.

We went fishing to-day with nets all round Hurst Castle and caught a lot of little fish and a few shrimps which I ate for tea. I hear there is no snow at Fürstenstein, which is a pity as real winter there is charming ; otherwise out of doors there is nothing to do. But I expect it will come.

January 28, 1906. Hotel Bristol, Berlin.

The night I left London I dined early with Count Metternich in his own little private room ; poor old dear, he liked having me for once all to himself ; and I attended a matinée with Patsy and we went behind the curtain afterwards to talk to Sir Charles Wyndham [1] the actor. Then I went to see Consuelo Marlborough ; she was getting on very well after her operation ; then to see poor Minnie Paget who has been laid up on her back now for nearly two years, hip, leg, ankle, knee, all smashed to bits through falling down a lift ; she is so brave, I love her so. It was a week of " rush " in London with visits to dentist and dressmakers . . .

To-morrow a ball at my German in-laws ; on the 31st a Court Ball ; and oh, how tired my heart is ; and yet I know things must ever go on like this. I have been cast for a part on this world's stage and when the curtain goes up I must come forward, face the audience and speak my lines. . . .

Deep in my heart I keep hearing—is it an echo of genuine

---

[1] (1837–1919).

life somewhere in this world, or intimations of some past or
future existence that was, or shall be, mine in close communion
with some ideal love ?   My *true* beloved—whose hands will
hold up my face, whose voice will sound ever caressingly in
my ear : " Come, little one, away from it all to a home in
the woods near the sea, in some far, fair country . . . where
you will ; a spot where you can be up to greet God's sun in
the fresh awakening of each morning, and go to bed by the
light of His moon—no electric lights from glittering candelabra !   The scent of the flowers at evening floating in through
open windows ; the thrill of crisp air over white snow—no
artificial perfumes in gilded salons !   Home and peace ; aye,
game to shoot, horses to ride, bodily work to do—not the
perpetual harassing of the brain to answer notes, send telegrams, chatter through telephones . . . live only for and in
the worship of God, tending the new lives that spring from
us."—But I must drop this nonsense. . . .

The hotel band downstairs is still playing : may it make them
happy !   And to-morrow I shall again wear diamonds and dance.

Yet my soul lives in my distant dream-house, a little house,
but big as the kingdom over which love reigns ; for now I am
alone, alone, in an alien country, trying my best to do my
share fairly—to do my best ; and no one knows, but God and
myself, what is in my heart.

February 5, 1906.   Fürstenstein.

Alone after dinner ; Hans had to go to Berlin for two
nights.   I have been here since the 29th, as, on the next day
after Mathilde's ball, the Court suddenly went into mourning
for the King of Denmark,[1] and I came here at once to the
children.   The ball was " awful " except that I was very glad
to see Irma and Max Fürstenberg, also Pia Fürstenberg and
her husband (Count and Countess Fürstenberg from Westphalia) ; she looks well but is a *mauvaise langue*.   I danced
with dozens of men one after the other, all of whom grabbed
me firmly, turned me twice round the room and then dropped
me ; if I was giddy and ventured to say : *Wo bin ich ?* they
only looked surprised, smiled, and said " Pardon."   I really
couldn't be bothered to explain that as I had been neither in
Berlin nor Vienna last year, I had not become accustomed to
being held up one moment and left the next suddenly to
stand alone without even a word of warning !   Between

---

[1] Christian IX. (1818–1906), father of Queen Alexandra.

their horrible spurs and their uncouth handling of me they tore the whole of my dress, and all the pale blue paillette embroidery was in bits ; they even trod upon and tore the tulle from the waist band !

Leopold X., a relative, led the ball ; he has been married two years ; his wife has a little money but is dull and frightful ; he is very tall and good-looking, but I should think stupid. He started a violent flirtation with me in a common (I imagine, a German soldier's) way by pressing his leg against mine at supper and then suddenly trying to get his leg over mine ; we sat rather cramped at round tables ; I heard his chair creak and wished he would fall over and upset the table. I did not dare move, but talked all the time to my supper partner, Count Reischach, the new Master of the Horse to the Emperor. The " distant cousin " got paler and paler and tight round his nose, and afterwards kept on whispering over my shoulder as my back was generally turned to him : *Je suis fou de vous ; ich bin wirklich ganz verückt*. I was mad with rage and told Vater.

Hansel and I have been tobogganing all the afternoon. I drove Hans to the station. I must try and keep him. I cried myself to sleep last night, or rather at six this morning. I felt so sad and miserable that I nearly went to fetch Hansel to come into my bed . . .

God ! diary, don't you understand *what* it all means to a woman like me, fêted and admired by everyone else, and who has a determination to fight the evil in life ; a terror of being disappointed ; a longing for what is *good* and noble ; happy walks and talks with husband and children ; hating to be dependent on the presence of guests in the house to win a smile. . . .

The clock ticks as I write ; there is wind and snow outside, my soul is lonely and my mind afraid, and I dread the night for I sleep so badly, always worse here than anywhere. . . .

I got a doctor to-day from Breslau to see the precious baby's ear ; he has developed a red growth behind it and under the lobe and he will have to be chloroformed and operated upon. Hansel's birthday was on the second, and he has the sweetest little mouth and great big blue eyes, and the darlingest little face. I can only pray to God for Baby and hope for the best. I shall get the best operator from Breslau. I wish it could be done before Hans comes back ; I would rather be alone, and I dread it dreadfully ; I shall go now and give him his last bottle which he takes when half-asleep. He tries to talk now and says : " Dad-dad, bo-wow, and Dé-see, Désee," all the time whenever he sees me ; he won't try to say " Mummilie." Please God bless him and be his Big Brother always.

March 6, 1906. Fürstenstein.

Since I last wrote Providence has been so good and kind to me. My precious baby is well now, there is only a little mark left, behind, or rather under, his ear. During the operation which lasted an hour I went out and walked as hard as I could ; Hans joined me afterwards at the home farm and we went with Hansel to watch him skate ; it was only the second time he had skated and he did it beautifully. The nurse said that, even the very first time, he went out on the ice without any hesitation and took to it as a young duck takes to water.

Walking with Hansel as we passed a spot whence the castle is visible, I said : " Those are yours and Baby's windows, the doctors are with Baby now, let us pray to God to make little Baby better," and we prayed together. Afterwards he said to me : " You know, Mummilie, dear God can see perfectly well for himself without your telling him, so why doesn't he make Baby better without waiting for us to ask him ? " Of course I explained the need of prayer as well as I could. . . .

We stayed in Berlin ten days on the occasion of the Silver Wedding of the Emperor and Empress, and also for the wedding of their son, Prince Eitel Fritz,[1] which took place on the same day. The whole ceremony was just the same as for the wedding of the Crown Prince, except that for some reason or other I was made to pass the Throne and also go in to supper with the Princes and all the old Excellencies. I gave little presents in silver to both the Emperor and Empress.

The Empress was very kind when we met at the Opera, and asked all about Baby. I made her laugh, much to the astonishment of the on-lookers ; and at the Court she received me with a smile, whereas the Emperor sat up with the two ends of his moustache almost sticking into his eyes, and as I passed seemed to say : " I allow you to have the honour of looking at me." . . .

The sun is setting on the *Riesengrab* . . .

---

[1] Second son of William II., b. 1883, m. in 1906 Duchess Sophie of Oldenburg (dissolved in 1926).

April 2, 1906. Villa Kasbeck, Cannes.

It is now five o'clock in the morning and I am sitting by the open window listening to the birds singing and the croak of the frogs. I was awakened half an hour ago by great flames and saw the Japanese screen quite close to the bed, on fire ; the night-light set it in flames ; it was useless to pour water on it as there was not enough. I went to call the nurse in case it became serious because of the children, and then the governess, and she carried the screen out when it had nearly finished burning, very proud of herself.

Dined last night with Mr. and Mrs. Clayton, she was Jeanne de Fougière. I left immediately after dinner to play poker here, leaving behind me the Grand Duke and Duchess Vladimir, the Grand Duke and Duchess Kyrill (she is looking so well and happy now) playing poker.

When I got back here I found a telegram from Hans from Vienna saying he had broken his thigh, or his thumb, I could not make out which, but fear it must be his thigh. He has his horses there and is hunting with the Drag at Malaczka. They never write a telegram properly here and it was all spelt wrongly, so I pray God it is not true, as I cannot think he would say " nothing much " to a serious accident. I wired at once and shall try to speak on the telephone to the hotel at Vienna to-day.

After this small bonfire, my losses at Monte Carlo—about forty pounds—and this horrible uncertainty about Hans, it is difficult to think of peace, and yet I feel it, for I see the little fishing boats, that a short while ago had their lanterns still lit, are slowly gliding home, a faint grey shadow is rising over the sea and the sails of the boats are reflected in the still water, although, as yet, there is no daylight anywhere. Only nature is awakening and it seems as if really the world can only have been made for God, not for the dusty, hurried, tainted men and women creatures who have built the ugly houses (that I see as I write) in which to live, and who are now asleep in them !

As for Monte Carlo it seems a dream of some other life I knew long ago, it surely cannot exist in this delicious morning air alive with the song of the birds. I sang last night in the brougham coming back here after dinner, and then I suddenly stopped like a bird when a stone is thrown at it, for as I got near this house I felt something was wrong.

April 5, 1906. Villa Kasbeck, Cannes.

Have had very good news of Hans, thank God he has not broken any bone but dislocated his thigh ; he wires he has no pain and sleeps well, poor old boy. I am very sorry for him and leave here on Sunday. It was impossible to get places earlier ; all the trains are crammed. It is after midnight and I have just come back from a dinner with the Saviles, the Grand Duchess Anastasia, her brother the Grand Duke George, and so on. I won three hundred francs at poker. Yesterday afternoon I went to Monte Carlo with the Grand Duchess Vladimir (he has gone back to Russia) and the Grand Duke and Grand Duchess Kyrill, Mr. Etta the aide-de-camp and an old Italian. The two men stayed the night, but we women motored back after losing some money gambling, and listening to *Veronique*, very badly given.

It has been pouring again to-day ; the next day after I wrote about the little fishing boats there was a storm at sea, and one of them—probably one of those I saw in the morning —was sunk, and the sailors drowned.

I have bought the most lovely frocks and pinafores for Baby, some only cost twenty francs !

May 10, 1906. Hotel Sachen, Vienna.

I came here at once to Hans whom I found lying in a nursing-home : he has broken his leg, but until I came I didn't know that the injury was *above the knee*. Poor old boy, he is so good and patient, and thank God he has no pain and sleeps and eats well. He has had no pain since the second day after the accident, which is a great mercy. I arrived five days after it happened. Vater met me at the station. They (my in-laws) all came from Pless on the 23rd for Hans's birthday. He is not bored as he has his papers, plays cards and sees lots of friends.

After being with Hans a week I went to Pless for five days to see the children, both well, and oh, I love them and miss them so. Then I have been for four days to Fürstenstein to look over accounts and see about the gardens ; our expenses there are enormous, the stable alone costs five thousand a year ; Hans will go on breeding; and I must say the five four-year-olds he has now in the stables are beauties. It is his hobby and he will not give it up. The gardens cost two thousand a year ; I shall try, in fact insist, on Todd doing it eight hundred pounds a year cheaper. The *chef*, too, I saw and spoke to ; he is a robber (like all cooks) ; I found that from April 3rd till the 24th he had bought nine hundred and ninety-one eggs, although Hans, I, and the children and six servants, were away. We have again to ask Vater for six thousand pounds. I wish to goodness Hans *would* make up his mind what to do to reduce the expenditure and stick to it. This year, though, it will be very difficult ; there is the expense here, doctors, his living at the Sanatorium and I here (he likes me to be with him), and although I *long* to be quietly in the country with the children, I don't like to leave him ; and then in September there are the Kaiser Manœuvres close to Fürstenstein and that means a house full of people. Well—we shall see !

I wanted so much to have singing lessons here, being for once forced to stay some weeks in a city, but all this time I have not been able to as I have had a bad throat ; even now I can scarcely say " come in " if someone knocks at the door. My days here are all the same ; lunch with Hans, a drive or a ride in the Prater ; I have a horse here, besides which I have ridden five of Count Larisch's and his son's ; then back to Hans till it is time to return to the hotel and dress for dinner. Sometimes I dine with Hans ; last night I did so and we played poker together : I lost three hundred kronen.

There have been two balls, one at the English Embassy given by Sir Edward and Lady Goschen ;[1] the floor in the ballroom was dreadful and very dirty. The other, in a very fine palace here, was given by the Archduke and Archduchess Frederick, the parents of little Princess Salm. (Countess Chotek, now Duchess of Hohenberg and wife of the Archduke Franz Ferdinand, was once lady-in-waiting to the Archduchess Frederick.) I stayed only one hour, just to see for once what a Royal Ball in Vienna was like.

All the Archdukes, except the host, were very rude, not even asking to be introduced ; but I am told they never do here. One little Prince who looks, and is I am sure, half-witted, and whom I met at lunch three years ago at Nice at the Duchess of Coburg's, and several times at the Grand Duchess Kyrill's, and at her sister's, never even said, " How do you do ? " to me ; he is brother to D. When I had been there half an hour and got introduced to an Archduchess and tried

---

[1] Sir Edward Goschen (1847–1924), Ambassador in Vienna 1905–8, in Berlin 1908–14. He m. 1874, Harriet Hosta (d. 1912).

to do the right thing all round (which I am hopelessly unable to do unless Hans is at hand to tell me who people are), the Archduchess Frederick made a movement and some of the ladies, including myself, were made to follow her into a room and to sit around a big table, about seventy-five of us, to drink tea and eat cakes—without any men—and I was engaged for the quadrille !

May 14, 1906. Budapest.

I came here with Betka Potocka the day before yesterday ; we roasted during the four hours' journey. We dined that night at the Park Club with Count Sigray and lots of other people ; the Club was busy with other " dinner parties " and afterwards the dreadful German practice of introducing began ; it always puzzles and bores me and without Hans I felt lonely and shy.

May 16, 1906. Budapest ; outside on the balcony of my hotel.

It is half-past four, just home from a ball ; the sun is rising, there is a pink glow over everything, and all the cocks are crowing ; ships on the Danube (which is so close I could throw a stone into it) on which all the men are busy loading and unloading, or getting ready and tidy for passengers later in the morning, when, as always, all the boats will be crammed ; I do not know where they go to from here.

Budapest is really a most fascinating place ; the women are kind and natural, the men—inflammable.

To-day there are races. We dance all night and rush about all day ; I believe I have been here only three days but it seems like three weeks. Everyone is more than charming to me !

The sun has now quite risen and people are walking about, and carts and horses busy ; all the lights have been put out and the Palace to my right on the hill stands out gloriously against the higher hills behind ; dawn is fascinating and a symbol of hope ; the birds are all chirping. I trust there are many happy people in this quaint city, but, somehow, I doubt it.

May 28, 1906. Vienna.

I have been in bed since I returned from Pest ; the day after I got here my sore throat and cough began again and the

Dining-room.

Sitting-room.

SCHWARZENGRABEN OR MA FANTAISIE.

doctor said that if I did not go to bed I should have congestion of the lungs. I got up yesterday for the first time for
a little in the afternoon and then, again in the evening, when
some people came. Lily Kinsky, Princess Demidoff,[1] Count
Sternberg and Count Reventlow played bridge, while Countess
Reventlow, Count Hoyos, Fanny Sternberg, Prince Schwarzenberg and myself played poker ; I won seven hundred and fifty
kronen. Christian Kraft Hohenlohe came and stayed for a
little while and Count ' Fairy ' Metternich, Princess Lily's
brother, also came.

To-night a few people are coming again just to play poker.
This afternoon I went to see Hans, feeling dreadfully weak
when I walk ; my temperature is not normal and the doctor
says it is the result of the influenza but does not tell me what I
ought to do. I found Hans walking in the garden on crutches,
poor old boy ; thank God he can do that much now but it is
horrid to see him lame like that. He says the new bandage
is wonderful, and he feels his leg better every day. He has
been up now for four days, but of course I had not seen him
for eight days or more.

When I came home at five and changed into a loose tea-
gown Prince Gottfried Hohenlohe came, also his cousin
Christian Kraft Hohenlohe (Duke of Ucjest) ; they stayed here
till nearly eight talking on every sort of subject, and German,
Austrian, French, Hungarian and Russian politics. Gottfried
Hohenlohe's other brother,[2] appointed Prime Minister only
three weeks ago, has resigned to-day, as he does not agree
with the Emperor over the Hungarian question ; he did not
want to grant their proposals whereas the poor old Emperor
has given way over some things ; of course everyone here
is furious with the Emperor and delighted with Hohenlohe.
In the " House " Prince Schönborn got up and said : " At last
we have a Minister who speaks out his own mind and the truth."

The German Emperor comes here on the 6th ; there will be
a big dinner at Schönbrunn to which only a few ladies have
been asked ; I am glad I am invited. I have never yet seen
the two Emperors together, and the speeches will amuse and
interest me.

---

[1] The wife of Elim Prince Demidoff, b. 1868 ; he was at one time
Russian Minister at Athens.

[2] Prince Conrad Hohenlohe-Schillingsfürst (1863–1918), m. in 1888
Countess Françoise Schönborn-Bucheim (a sister of ' Irma Fürstenberg').

July 5, 1906. On board ship.

I am on this very nice comfortable boat going to England with the children to stay at Newlands and bathe in the sea. Of course I am delighted, though I hated leaving behind poor old darling Hans, but, if we do not go to Newlands now, no other time is possible as, at the end of the month, there is Cowes and Goodwood, where he wants to go with me, and at the end of August we have the Manœuvres at home.

We stay at Grosvenor House for one night with Shelagh ; Bend Or has gone off to South Africa for six months and Shelagh is to follow him. Baby has just shed tears, having mislaid his doll somewhere—the most wonderful brown gollywog ! It has lost all its hair, its head hangs loosely held on with cotton, its trousers are red calico, torn and stained, and it has (or had) a white shirt.

I have to be in London on the tenth to go to the Opera with Shelagh, and on the thirteenth I present Nancy at the last Court. Countess Eulenburg, wife of the Emperor's Lord Chamberlain, is on board with her son and daughter ; she is going to England to the seaside. . . .

July 10, 1906. Newlands.

The day we arrived in London I took Hansel and Baby to a children's party at Buckingham Palace ; I received the invitation just after I arrived, Soveral having told the Queen I was expected. The children had no time to rest, only to be washed and dressed. Smith and Esther went in one carriage with the two babies, and I, Shelagh with little Ursula, and Hansel, went in the other. It was a lovely party out of doors, a miniature circus, a conjurer, surprise fireworks which after rising high in the air fell down and contained little presents ; they served a big tea. The King said Hansel was the image of Hans. The Duke and Duchess of Sparta [1] were there with their children. We talked for a long time ; she said she loved England—and how easy and happy it all was compared with Germany ! The true motto of England, she said, was : " live and let live," but in Germany it seemed to be : " you must do and think as I do, or die." Of course for many years she has not been on speaking terms with her brother, the German Emperor, because she joined the Greek

---

[1] Succeeded in 1913 as King Constantine and Queen Sophie of Greece. The Queen is, of course, a sister of the Emperor William II.

Church, and this, while it pleased her husband, displeased her brother. The Duke is a dear ; a big, fair man.

Prince Gottfried Hohenlohe was at Fürstenstein the last few days before I left. I am much devoted to him, he is a real friend. It is ten years since I first met him at Castolowitz. I only pray he may come to no harm now in Russia. . . . I wrote to him yesterday and said if he could look into my eyes and really see what was there, he would find evidence of a great sorrow unsuspected by anyone, a longing for things unattainable, a disappointment with the knowledge of the world that ends in disillusion. . . . Little Patsy brought me up a rose and some sweet peas ; I should like to put out the lights and lie by the open window and hold the bunch to my face and lie still, still, still, and listen to the silence. . . . But to indulge too much in dreams and sentiment is not wise. I wonder if in the next world one's soul, and thoughts, and actions, will be free, and all in harmony ?

July 14, 1906. Taplow Court, Maidenhead.

I went to London on the twelfth, dined with Consuelo Marlborough and went to the Opera for Puccini's *Madame Butterfly*. The Duke is away doing a throat cure ; we had with us a Liberal Member of Parliament, Mr. A. E. W. Mason, the author of *The Four Feathers* (a clever book), and the Duke of Alba,[1] young, brilliant and good-looking.

At the Court the other evening I represented Germany ; the Ambassadors and Ambassadresses, Ministers and their wives went in according to the printed programme. I was surprised that I was given such a position but there is no German Ambassadress, and it was for that reason I suppose that they selected me. I wore gold and mauve shot tissue and my diamond pearl and turquoise tiara, the new Russianshaped one. Nancy and I sat together on the Diplomatic bench and watched all the people pass the Throne ; it was most amusing, some were very funny, and some miserably shy. I got rather sleepy watching but woke up later, had a standup supper with Soveral, drove home with Metternich, took off my train and blue feathers and went for half an hour to Lady Huntingdon's Ball.

---

[1] Santiago Fitz-James, 17th Duke of Alba & 10th Duke of Berwick, b. 1878, m. 1920, Marchesa Maria del Rosario de Silva. A greatnephew of the Empress Eugénie. Spanish Foreign Minister 1930–.

I drove down here with Consuelo Marlborough in her motor. Lovely peaceful place and beautiful flowers, host and hostess both charming (Lord and Lady Desborough, until last year Mr. and Mrs. Willie Grenfell). The party consists of the Duchesses of Portland and Marlborough, Mr. Balfour, ex-Prime Minister, Lord and Lady Essex, Mr. Evan Charteris,[1] Lord Grenfell [2] whom I met in Egypt three years ago, General Scobell, Mrs. Asquith,[3] and one or two young men ; also Lord Ribblesdale [4] who, poor dear, lost his eldest son two years ago ; he has not been the same man since.

August 11, 1906. Cowes (staying with Consuelo Duchess of Manchester).

The time has passed very quickly, the London season is over, Goodwood is over, Hans has arrived, and I seem to have had no time to write in my diary.

After I left Newlands on the Monday I stayed in London till Friday : went to one ball which bored me, and to dinners each night to meet the King or the Prince and Princess of Wales. As usual I was sent in to dinner before the Duchesses, even before the old Duchess of Devonshire ; I wish they would not do that. One very nice dinner was at Marlborough House with the Prince and Princess of Wales ! I went in with the Prime Minister, Sir Henry Campbell Bannerman, whose politics I dislike and whose government I wish I could upset. I said to the Prince, who had taken in Countess Benckendorff the Russian Ambassadress : " You sent me, Sir, in to dinner with the one man in England whom I would not choose." But I found him clever and agreeable to talk to, and of course I had to be polite. Shelagh also dined and looked lovely in a white satin dress ; her figure is beautiful.

I spent Saturday till Monday with Mrs. Hartmann, at White Lodge, Richmond. The King came on Sunday, also several other people including Mrs. George Keppel, and we played croquet.

---

[1] Honble. Evan Charteris, s. of 9th Earl of Wemyss, b. 1864 ; m. 1930, widow of Lord Edward Grosvenor.
[2] 1st Lord (1841-1925).
[3] Now Countess of Oxford and Asquith.
[4] 4th and last Baron (1854-1925), m. Charlotte (d. 1911), d. of Sir Charles Tennant ; his e. s. (1878-1904) killed in action in Somaliland, and his 2nd son d. of wounds (1887-1915). He m. 2nd, in 1919, Ava, widow of John Jacob Astor.

Goodwood week at West Dean Park, Chichester,[1] was pleasant but tiring, very hot at the races ; I lost my money at
poker and on the racecourse. Nancy was there and looked
very nice, *so* handsome with her grey hair. We were about
twenty-seven in the house.

Prince and Princess Salm (the Archduchess) have been
here for this week ; she is such a dear little thing ; their visit
was quite a success and they enjoyed themselves ever so much.
They left this morning. The Empress Eugénie called this
morning, a charming and lovely old lady ; I did not know her
before. Count Mensdorff the Austrian Ambassador is also
staying here.

I went to the Royal Yacht Squadron gardens and listened
to the band this evening with the German Ambassador, Count
Metternich, who dined here ; he is very nice when he likes to
be, and is really fond of me. He is not a bit understood or
appreciated in England : I am glad he does not hear all the
things that are said about him. For instance the other night
(while the Salms, who are Germans, were still here) the
King dined here ; I went in to dinner with the Prince of Wales
and sat opposite the King. The King talked to me the whole
time and chaffed and laughed. . . . At any rate he said, in
speaking of Metternich, that he was a " D.D.," adding :
" Do you know what that is ? " I said : " Well, I suppose it
means damn something." He laughed and said : " Such
words I don't use before ladies ; no, it means ' dull dog.' "

The King also chaffed me a great deal about the many
pictures of me in all the papers, especially the one of me and
Soveral at Goodwood ; some editor photographed us in every
attitude while we talked ; of course we knew nothing about it.
The King said : " It is very vain of you to advertise yourself
like that—why, everyone can buy your photograph now for
sixpence." I said : " Has Your Majesty thought it worth
while squandering sixpence on me ? "

But we are always really good friends and, as a little girl,
I loved him like an uncle.

September 23, 1906. Ulrichshusen,[2] Mecklenburg.

It is nearly a whole month since I last wrote here, although
I had intended keeping this diary up to date ; but I honestly

---

[1] The residence of Mr. and Mrs. Willie James. Mrs. James afterwards married Major J. C. Brinton.

[2] Residence of Count and Countess Vico Voss.

have had little time lately. As soon as I arrived in Germany I had a house full, for the Review in Breslau and the Manœuvres. In the evenings I arranged for all the terraces in Fürstenstein to be lit up by little lamps outlining the paths and grass banks ; I would not have Japanese lanterns hung up as they spoil the style of the place. Count Esterhazy and Count Apponyi, who were two of our guests, brought a famous gipsy band with them from Budapest, the best band in Hungary ; it has recently been to Marienbad to play for the King of England.

My party in Fürstenstein for the Imperial Manœuvres was quite successful though difficult to organize as people were always arriving at different hours and then often missing their trains, and failing to let me know exactly when they would arrive.

The Duchess of Sparta came alone for five days, as the Duke had to hurry back to Greece on urgent political business. The Crown Princess of Rumania came bringing her sister the Princess of Hohenlohe-Langenburg : the Crown Prince of Rumania was taking a cure somewhere, and the Prince of Hohenlohe-Langenburg was busy in Berlin getting over his disappointment because the proposal to appoint him Under-Secretary for the Colonies was rejected by the Reichstag. The idea somehow makes me want to smile as I cannot imagine why the few colonies possessed by Germany should necessitate the appointment of an Under-Secretary. Christa Salm came, also without her husband, as he was attending manœuvres near Berlin, so I expect my character will be still more blackened for enticing to my house four Royal princesses without their husbands there to protect them from the dangers of a wild Hungarian band and moonshine on a summer's night !

The Duchess of Sparta said that she knew that the Emperor always spoke nicely about me, and had remarked that if he had his way, there was one person whose statue he would like to see erected—and that person was I : she also said that it was the Empress who objected to either the Emperor or the Crown Prince going to any place gay or amusing, or where they would meet pretty women. However, she advised me to go on asking the Crown Prince to Fürstenstein.

September 26, 1906. Castolowitz, Bohemia.

We left Count Voss's old-fashioned dark picturesque château the day after I wrote last in this book ; we at last tried the patience of the motor-car too far on the terrible Mecklenburg roads, and it broke down after behaving for months like a heavenly chariot, so we had to return by train, sleeping in Berlin and leaving the next afternoon for Fürstenstein.

At Berlin in the morning we drove to the big Kunst Museum of pictures and statues ; very few pictures were really fine (except some old ones) while some of the " new school " were simply dreadful, or worse, as they made one die of laughter.

Cousin Adelaide,[1] Mrs. Hope Vere, Lady Kilmorey [2] and Prince Francis of Teck [3] were already in Fürstenstein when we arrived, and the following day we all came here except Patsy, Prince Francis, who has not brought his guns from England so did not care to come and shoot with someone else's, and Lady Kilmorey who preferred to stay behind. I had wired to order a reserved saloon so we travelled very comfortably without changing and were able to smuggle in all our cartridges ! My new guns shot quite well to-day and they are nicely made. Poppets shot very well. It was a lovely day, such a treat after the dreadful weather we have had lately ; and Hans is really getting on well and walks better every day. Our host and hostess are as usual dear and kind and hospitable, so I have been happy and shall now go to bed and sleep.

October 6, 1906. Fürstenstein.

My darling Poppets left to-day, also Fräulein Suttes, who came to play for Signor X., a poor little Spanish Mexican who has lost all his relations and money and is now trying to make singing his profession. I have given him letters of introduction to people in London and America, and have promised to write to Madame Melba and Caruso, but I am afraid he will have no success ; his voice is throaty and sounds like that of a gondolier in Venice ; very few notes are quite true and pure.

Cousin Adelaide also left to-day and the Signor left for Halbau. Prince Francis of Teck, Lady Kilmorey and Marie Hope Vere left a few days ago. Fanny Sternberg came for a night and brought her boy Jaroslav whom she left here

---

[1] Lady Adelaide Taylour, d. of 3rd Marquess of Headfort.

[2] D. of E. Baldock, M.P., m. 1881, 3rd Earl of Kilmorey (1842–1915).

[3] (1870–1910) Brother of Queen Mary of England ; his eldest brother m. 1894, Lady Margaret Grosvenor.

while she went for three days to Halbau the boy joined her at Nieder Salzbrunn to return to Castolowitz to-day ; he is Hansel's age, but smaller ; they had great fun together ; we all went down to the *Schwarzengraben* and fished for crawfish and took Aleck's (the head groom) little boy—and of course Baby ; he is a perfect darling, tries to sing and talk, and is full of fun and so big and strong ; he looks like a child of three and he is only two in February.

October 17, 1906. Fürstenstein.

Little Patsy left to-day for London and Ruthin, where she joins Poppets. I motored with her to Waldenburg to catch the train to Berlin ; she has a very nice maid and Stumper, a servant from the Wilhelmstrasse Palast, has been told to meet her there, as he speaks English. I miss her dreadfully ; we had such a cosy little time the last few days.

On the 11th Hans left to shoot duck at Count Vico Voss's place and he only came back on the 15th ; while he was away we cut down trees and started to make a homely little garden by the river in the *Schwarzengraben* ; it will be delicious, little old paths and a wooden railing with flowers all up it, and hedges of sweet briar and lots of roses growing in the trees. I am building a little thatched cottage too, one big room and a kitchen. I have not dared tell Hans ; he would get furious at once, although it is doing no harm and I shall pay for it myself. I also had the new *Forstmeister* (head forester) there one day and he measured it all out and for two thousand marks (which Vater gives us for Christmas) I could make a great big lovely lake there.

Count Vico has left his motor here so Patsy and I and Hansel have been using it. We went to see Count and Countess Henckel and her children near Breslau, and also nice old Countess von Zedlitz,[1] whose mother was English ; anyone could tell she had English blood as she had all the windows open in the house and was not afraid of standing near one of them. And from her we went to see Count and Countess Pückler ; his wife was a Russian, a Princess Korski, and twenty years older than he. He sang for us as he has a good voice ; he has also some artistic taste and he picks up old china, miniatures and so on. They all seemed very pleased

---

[1] Robert, 6th Count Zedlitz-Trützschler, Governor of Silesia, and a *Hof-Marschal* at Court, b. 1837, m. 1862, Agnes, d. of Herr von Rohr-Levetzow.

to see me—and yes, perhaps if I were to see more of these people they would really get to like and understand me. As Patsy said, for neighbours they are very nice ; which is true, as neighbours even in England are sometimes awful. I feel that these people are afraid to come to see me, thinking that my house is always full of a younger and more fashionable society than they know (which is a fact) ; but, all the same, there are times in the year when I should like to ask them. Only Hans never will agree ; they bore him, he says, and so he cannot realize how much more homely it would make it for me if I felt that we had a few neighbours not " in society " who liked and understood me. Some homely people to go and have tea with and take the children ; of course if I had a motor it would all be so easy as we could go further afield. But Hans says that he cannot afford to buy one, and he will not make economies in the stables which cost, counting the breeding of the foals and brood mares, five thousand a year, which is ridiculous and almost wicked I think, when I know lots of people who have only three thousand a year, and have even to keep up a sort of show on that sum.

October 21, 1906. Fürstenstein.

Have had four days all to myself with the children ; Hans is in Vienna. I have had breakfast with them two mornings at eight, but, to-day and yesterday, I did not feel quite well so stayed in bed later. I hate leaving for Lancut to-morrow where I am to meet Hans. I have got a saloon which is more comfy and not so very much more expensive as we shall be several travelling.

Yesterday I lunched at the *Schwarzengraben* with Hansel and planted some lovely red autumn leaved oak, shamrock, elm, besides lilac and laburnum. I marked every place myself ; my new little garden will, I hope, be lovely.

Hansel said to me point-blank at lunch : " Mummilie, do you know what I would do if anything happened to you ? I would kill myself—with a sword ! " He is not seven yet, the precious little boy ; I wonder how many times he will say that to other women before his age is four times seven !

November 2, 1906. The Sanatorium, Königgrätzerstrasse, Berlin.

I have been here now five days and am getting accustomed to it ; at first I thought I could not stand it : rooms that get no sun, and the walls and furniture of a chocolate or terra-cotta colour, but now I have got lots of flowers and some chintz covers from Fürstenstein which makes everything at once look brighter ; and from my bedroom I can see the sun over the roofs of the opposite houses, so I have the comfort of knowing when it is there. I don't sleep a bit well and I don't feel any better, and I *did* think I would have lots of time to myself to read, but the few hours I am not out, I am " being cured " all the time. I am to have plenty of air, so to-day I lunched with the Salms at Potsdam ; he came and motored me there and they both came back with me. Christa Salm and I went for a walk in the afternoon in the gardens of the Marmor Palace and met " the Baby " ; of course I mean the son of the Crown Prince and the Crown Princess ; he is only four months old but is a beautiful child and looks and smiles at you just as if he understood everything and wanted to talk. Truly, I have never seen a child like him ; it made me feel quite jumpy, and I have a feeling that he will grow up to be some-thing extraordinary, or else die.[1]

I stay here till the 19th, I suppose, and only get back to Fürstenstein in time for our first shoot. The children could not go to Pless as scarlet fever broke out there ; Smith wrote that little Hansel was very disappointed, but is happy again now. I miss them dreadfully. Baby is a darling, but I would never spoil my children ; for instance, mine must do at *once* what they are told.

Hans is in Parduwitz now, he went there from Pless, whence he wrote me this typically German episode : Travelling to Pless with Count L., an old gentleman from near Breslau, some of the others in the same carriage with him thought he must be drunk, as he lost his words and talked nonsense ; so when they got him to Pless he was put to bed and the doctor sent for. When he arrived he said it seemed a strange ill-ness ; he could not really say what it was—it looked like a slight stroke ; on this everyone became excited and his old maiden sister with whom he lives, was at once wired for. She arrived, but did not show much anxiety, which was sur-prising. Later the truth was quietly given out by the valet who said : " Ach, it is not much ; the Herr Graf is always taken like that when we kill a pig at home ; this week we killed one, and the Herr Graf has eaten too many sausages."

---

[1] This boy, Prince William of Prussia, is now the great hope of the Hohenzollern Party in Germany.—D. OF P.

The Daisysee.

The Garden.

SCHWARZENGRABEN OR MA FANTAISIE.

Nancy is in Berlin for three days staying at the British Embassy ; she came to see me this morning—I like her.

November 16, 1906. Sanatorium, Königgrätzerstrasse, Berlin.

Thank goodness I leave here on Monday the 19th and meet Hans in Fürstenstein ; he came to Berlin for two nights and has now left for Pless ; he dined with me twice and was very nice. For the last fortnight Professor Renvers has been injecting stuff into my legs with a long needle and a syringe ; it was rather painful and made my legs ache.[1]

I have seen no one here but the Salms and Count Ada Sierstorpff. I went once to the Automobile Exhibition, and have had a singing lesson every afternoon, which has delighted me. But I have never slept well, and do not feel one bit better, in fact worse, so low and restless and sad at the thought of all the parties coming ! And I should so like a peaceful time with the children.

November 17, 1906. The Sanatorium.

Went this afternoon with Christa Salm to see the Crown Princess : no lady-in-waiting present. We three had tea together. She was much interested to know who was coming to Fürstenstein and was delighted when I told her. Christa remarked : " Daisy is coming later on to Potsdam to stay with us." The Crown Princess exclaimed : " Oh, how nice —what fun we would have if you were always here."

The Doctor said to me this morning : " Now go home and rest ; you are a person of whom everyone expects something ; you give too much of yourself, and no one gives you as much in return." And it seemed so at the Crown Prince's Palace this afternoon ; I was expected to talk, to be amusing, to look charming. To have a reputation of being " something " —something different from other people—is rather tiring.

The Royal baby is a darling, so well and bright ; we stayed in the nursery for hours ; then the Crown Princess showed us all over the house. She arranged it ; some things are nice and some awful. It looked very different from what it did when the Empress Frederick lived there ; she had some lovely furniture.

---

[1] The beginning of the illness from which I have suffered more or less continuously ever since. Now, because of neglect and hard work during the war, I cannot walk at all.—D. OF P.

November 26, 1906. Fürstenstein.

I returned here the day before my shooting guests arrived ;
now they have all gone since two days. In the party were
Nini Hohenlohe [1] and her husband ; Count and Countess
Clary (he is Austrian Minister at Brussels) ; Count and
Countess Herberstein (she was an Apponyi) ; Lorry and Heinrich Hochberg ; [2] Gottfried Hohenlohe from St. Petersburg
(he is Austrian Military Attaché there) ; the Grand Duke
Boris, second son of the Grand Duke and Duchess Vladimir ;
his aide-de-camp, Monsieur Demidoff ; Fanny Sternberg ;
Fritz and Nancy ; Christa Salm and her husband from Potsdam ; Prince S., the black-eyed officer from Vienna with
whom it is said every woman falls in love—I consider him
an idiot—and I think that's all. It was glorious weather
and everyone appeared to enjoy themselves. We shot fifteen
hundred head the first day, and eight hundred the second.
I forgot—the Duke and Duchess Ernst Günther of Holstein
also came. Nini and Gottfried Hohenlohe told me all about
the Emperor's visit to Donaueschingen. [3] The Emperor began
talking about Fürstenstein, and Daisy this and Daisy that.
He said : " They play hide-and-seek on all fours in the dark ;
Daisy nearly put her mother's eye out at this game, she has
been almost blind ever since. Another game they have is
sliding down the stairs on tea-trays ; my friend Philie told
me all this." This " friend " is Philip Eulenburg, once German Ambassador in Vienna, a person no decent *man* will talk
to, and to whose house no one will go ! One can guess the
reason—it seems horribly prevalent in Germany. A Count
A.B., married since ten years to the sister of a Grand Duchess,
has, for similar reasons, just been dismissed from the Garde
du Corps and his uniform taken from him ! . . .

Poor Prince Joachim Albrecht has just been sent off to Africa
as he had a liaison with a woman in Berlin whom, it is said, he
paid a Baron to marry, I suppose thinking it would be more
proper in his position to have an affair with a Baroness. At
any rate the Emperor on finding it out was furious. Prince Z.
asked him : " But I do not understand, Your Majesty, *what*

---

[1] Princess Gottfried Hohenlohe-Langenburg (née Schönborn-
Bucheim).

[2] The daughter-in-law and son of " Uncle Bolko."

[3] The residence of Prince and Princess (Irma) Fürstenberg ; the
Princess is a sister of Princess (Nini) Hohenlohe-Langenburg.

has Prince Joachim *done* ? " The Emperor answered : " *Er hat mit dieser Frau gelebt.*" Prince Z. replied : " *Aber Majestät mit wem soll er dann leben ?* "

I was to have gone to Dresden yesterday to join Fritz and Nancy for Christmas shopping, and then on to Potsdam to stay with Christa Salm and rehearse some songs and dances for the acting at Chatsworth in January, but I really felt too seedy ; I have had headaches every day and feel tired, so have postponed going till later perhaps. The day before yesterday was divine ; we went to the *Schwarzengraben* and as I did not want to be away from Hans a moment, as he was leaving that night, I took him with me. I was terrified at what he would say ; but he was delighted, the darling, with my new garden and walked about and gave advice and took interest in it all. " My new madness in the middle of the wood " he called it ! He soon went home to do business with the General Director but the children stayed with me and dear Smith the nurse ; at five we were having tea *in the dark* except for a lovely moon which rose over the fir-trees ; it was broad moon-light when we drove home at half-past five, and Baby loved it.

Yesterday was glorious, quite hot ; I lunched on the top terrace and lay in a hammock, Hansel next to me without a hat or coat and only a light flannel shirt ; we played there all the afternoon ; this morning I jumped out of bed thinking it would surely be the same—but it was cold and misty.

Hans will be away shooting all this week.

December 30, 1906. The German Embassy, London.

I must take to writing in pencil in this diary, as the very idea of using pen and ink seems to make it too serious a work. If I have time to write, and have lots to say, it then amuses me, but I seem to live in a whirl of letters, clothes, conversation, and trains, and during the precious moments I have alone, I feel inclined only to sit down and close my eyes, or open them to the sun, and freedom of thought. . . .

I see I have not written for a month ; we had several other shooting parties at Fürstenstein ; then I caught a cold and had with it, I think, a touch of influenza and was in bed a week ; then came Christmas at Pless and all the different feasts. I gave cakes, chocolate, clothes, nuts, apples and so on to about two thousand five hundred people, including about seven hundred children. I got so many smiles that if they were real, they ought to keep me happy all next year. I would

have enjoyed it all more if I had felt better. I did not take
Hansel this year; the smell in the rooms and the heat is
sometimes too awful, and he is so fit that " I left well alone."
The weather was divine, frozen hoar frost on all the trees and
every little twig and branch and blade of grass. Baby always
went out, even with the temperature below zero.

On Christmas Day Hansel dressed up as Father Christmas
with a red cloak and grey beard and said a German poetry and
songs without a mistake; Baby was dressed with a wreath of
mistletoe round his head (his hair is curly), artificial holly
on his white muslin dress and silver threads on it and a pair
of wings as a Christmas angel—he looked a darling.

Hans arrives to-night, he is so dear and nice and gentle
since his accident; I love him to be with me, and I know he
loves me better than anyone, but I wish his leg did not make
him walk lame; I shall make him see Sir Alfred Fripp again.
We go to Eaton for the New Year, and then to Chatsworth as
usual. The King and Queen arrive the day before we do but
they both understood that I naturally wanted to spend New
Year's day at Eaton : the Queen sent me a lovely little brooch
for Christmas. . . . Poor darling brother George has had
influenza and is at Bournemouth to recruit.

There is no sun in London, only snow and dirt and fog.
I am afraid Hans will feel very homesick when he gets here.
When I think of what going back to Fürstenstein means now!
My beloved boys standing on the stair to greet me, and their
noise and laughter and little pattering feet in the passages ;
the first eight years of my married life seem like a dream of
misery, homesickness, and longing. . . .

CHAPTER NINE

1907

February 13, 1907. Newlands.

I really believe that Catholicism is for the West, Buddhism for the East. . . . Civil and social life is ruled by law, then why should our religion not be subject to rule ; the Catholic Church insists that every single soul that belongs to her must obey the laws of the Church ; this removes the wonderings and questionings that trouble people's souls. They do not have to cudgel their brains, they do not reason, they are happy in leaning on the strong pillar of their faith ; whereas our own religion is divided into numberless sects, all quarrelling and jealous of one another. But I cannot change now, I am too old and have seen and heard and judged for myself too long ; my mind is not simple enough to surrender itself to the perfect calm to be found in acknowledging the supremacy of such a Faith. In some respects, as to the condition of a future life for instance, I am inclined to be a Buddhist. The love we find and make in this world, however perfect and unselfish it be, cannot persist unchanged in the full light of another and higher state of existence ; therefore we shall neither remember those who are still on this earth, nor even see and recognize in another world those whom we met in this : we start again afresh in greater strength and unselfishness and a purer love. The souls we have loved here, we may love and meet again because we have once loved them ; but our intercourse with them will not be tainted with the remembrance of this heart-breaking little world ; we shall not recognize them in their personal limitations. My love for my little Patsy and Poppets, Hans, the children, and all my dear friends, will be boundless ; I shall feel them in me, they will feel me in them ; all our feelings resolved into one tender peaceful love, all shadow of misunderstanding dissipated. I shall not be able to say, this is Poppets, that other is Hansel ; the thought is sad now, terribly sad ; and yet we must find comfort in the promise that the love and peace of the future is " past all understanding." We shall understand—then.

March 21, 1907. Villa Espalmador, Beaulieu, Alpes Maritimes.

Am in a big row-boat with the precious children, Smith the nurse, and a nice cheery brown-faced sailor. I came here with Patsy twelve days ago. Adèle Essex found the villa for me, one of the very very few that are properly drained ; it is right on the sea with a garden full of flowers—violets, freesias—and orange trees. There are four bathrooms and everything is very clean and comfortable. . . .

I have lunched out once, dined out once, and yesterday the Grand Duchess Vladimir came to lunch, the Grand Duke Boris arriving as a surprise. I asked Christian Kraft Hohenlohe, Julia Maguire and her husband, Gladys de Grey and Consuelo Marlborough to meet the Grand Duchess ; so we were eight. We lunched on the terrace looking right on to the sea ; it was delicious and Gauget gave us a very good *déjeuner*. I have not had a gamble yet or been near the rooms ; I wanted to have a good rest and start to go about only when Hans comes. And oh, the joy it has been to be quite alone with the children ; I find that *not* to be in one's *own house* is a rest somehow. We have fished together in the morning, then I have had a rest before lunch, and gone to bed every night at ten and got up about half-past seven or eight, and had breakfast with the children. In the garden I have a hammock to rest in and breathe the salt air, and every afternoon I have gone for a walk with Hansel and we have taken tea with us and had it out among the rocks at Cap Ferrat which is near here, and very lovely ; there is never a soul about ; we carried only a bottle of milk and some bread and butter.

March 29, 1907. Villa Espalmador.

Alas, my peaceful days are over for some time. Hans came on March 25th and we had breakfast together on the terrace ; he is in very good spirits and pleased with everything. I am *so* glad. Bend Or arrived on Tuesday morning unexpectedly ; his chauffeur arrived the day before, so I guessed he was coming and put him up in the day-nursery as the children are in it so little ; they are out all day and have their meals in the library. Bend Or is so cheery and nice and quite natural, which he is not always when in his own house. Christa Salm and her husband arrived last night and Count Metternich to-day, so the villa is full. . . .

I shall not have much peace in my garden, as even if I do lie in my hammock, I shall hear voices ; in order to rest and feel really content and happy, for the time being I want to hear nothing *human*. I do not mind the bark of a dog, and I love the little chirp of a bird (here one never hears a bird singing outright), the sound of the waves, and the distant clip-clip of the gardener's scissors as he cuts the grass under the palm trees, and the swish of the wind in the tops of the bamboo trees. The other day I lay so content rocking in my hammock and listening to the little voices of nature which cast a spell of peace and serenity on a sunny day.

This afternoon the others went to Nice to see the Duchess of Coburg [1] and her daughter the Princess of Hohenlohe-Langenburg (the one who was at Fürstenstein).

I have to make copies of some unpleasant letters I drafted for Hans, one being to the King of England. . . .

April 5, 1907. Villa Espalmador.

It is a week nearly since I wrote in this diary, a week mostly spent in amusing my guests. We dined several times at Monte, once with Adèle Essex, and once here, when all the Coburg family came to dinner and brought Prince Arthur of Connaught, such a nice intelligent boy overflowing with sensible conversation. He has travelled a lot, to America, India, and elsewhere. Recently he was sent by the King on an official mission to convey the Garter to the Emperor of Japan. I could not help smiling at dinner when he said, speaking of his parents in India : " Of course my father was there merely as an English General and my mother simply as his wife ; but when I represented the King it was quite different. I never moved without a salute of guns nor walked on anything less than a gold or embroidered carpet." He did not say it in swagger but in a tone of boyish pride.

The " three husbands " as I call Salm, Bend Or and Hans, have had some wild times ; one night they sent Christa and

---

[1] Duchess of Edinburgh (1853–1920), b. Grand Duchess Marie of Russia, m. 1874, the Duke of Edinburgh (1844–1900), who succeeded to the Duchy of Coburg in 1893 ; mother of Queen Marie of Rumania, the Grand Duchess Kyrill, and the Infanta Beatrice of Bourbon d'Orleans.

me home and stayed at Monte till five, and got home here at six ; they went to a ball . . . or so they said.

Christa Salm and her husband leave to-morrow ; she told me lots of gossip from Berlin about myself and the things I am supposed to have said and done. . . .

Well—thank God my windows are open, the sun is pouring in, and I can see the white foam of the waves dashing up against the rocks at Cap Ferrat, so though the world is full of lies and shams and traps, that some men and women are longing for one to fall into, I feel that my life is my own, and I do not need even to expose one bit of my mind or soul for them to throw dirt at.   Yet it is a joy to live (and even to look pretty) just for one or two people besides myself ; for my boys, perhaps even for the grass and flowers, and the air I breathe ; to smile and look one's best and still try to feel good and do good, is a way of giving thanks to the Creator for the gift of life and love. . . .

I pray that God will not withdraw His protecting arm from me ; it has often before warded off the enemies that tried to trouble my peace and rest. . . .

April 14, 1907.   Villa Espalmador.

We are all going on a motor trip.

Jennie, my sister-in-law (Lady Randolph Churchill), who married George and still loves him immensely, poor dear ; she is uncommonly nice and still very handsome, but of course the difference in age is a sad and terrible drawback (no babies possible) ; well, she is coming with us.   The Duke of Marlborough, her cousin by marriage . . . also comes ; then Lady Essex and her uncle Mr. Grant.   She is a charming and very pretty woman of over forty (but does not look it).   Hans loved her for years when she was a girl but did not marry her because she was American and had no quarterings—a particularly important item in the German marriage market.

April 15, 1907.   Avignon.

We left Beaulieu at ten-thirty, stopping half an hour at Nice for lunch and about forty minutes at Aix to see the tapestries.   We got here in torrents of rain and a thunderstorm.   I had a bath and some bread and butter and a cup of coffee.   Marie, my maid, came in the car with me which was more comfortable for her than to travel with the other maids, arriving hours after me.   Jennie and Marlborough arrived only at nine, they ran out of essence or whatever the stuff is called that makes the motor go. I think essence is a most inappropriate name for a substance that smells so horribly.

We all had dinner together and now it is ten and I shall jump into bed. After dinner we wanted to have the table moved so the Duke pushed it and down the whole thing went. Dessert, wine, butter, olives, dates, plates : the corner of the room into which everything fell looked like a pig-sty. I was too horrified at first to laugh or say anything, it was such a crash, but somebody said it was the quickest way they had ever seen a dinner cleared away ; it really was rather funny as nothing was left on the table but the cloth. The Duke was miserable ; by the way he looked at the debris one might have thought he was peering at his own life, which at the present moment is in much the same state.

May 1, 1907. Villa Espalmador, Beaulieu.

The first of May—the very words sound like the beginning of a poem wrought of the stuff of dreams—a maiden's dreams called forth by the voice of love. As I write I can see the little stream in the shady wood bubbling in and out amongst the many stones and caressing the green ferns that nod their heads at it. Surely every lamb bleats at least once on the first of May, for how can any young creature play voiceless amongst the buttercups and daisies ! Now begins the summer ; now the real new year begins.

Hans has just left and I feel most dreadfully sorry. I had planned so many picnics by the sea with him and the children. He had to go for the *Herrenhaus* sittings ; also, dear Vater is again not so well. Yesterday, though, we had a lovely afternoon. We all went, Baby too, to Cap Ferrat and sat in what I call my nest in the rocks ; we watched the waves dashing up, and had tea. Then I sang and Hans whistled second voice, and then we made poetry—in fact we all laughed and behaved like children. How few such afternoons one has in a year ! Hans was very happy. Two days before, he and I drove to St. Hospice (quite close) and then walked all round it and, in our imagination, we bought it (it *is* for sale), and built a beautiful Greek villa there, all marble and pillars ; Hans said, seriously, it would make a very good investment as if I were to die, and Hansel did not care for it, he could always sell it off in lots !

May 17, 1907. Hotel Vendôme, Paris.

I left the villa by the blue sea three days ago feeling very, very sad ; it was hot summer weather and everywhere a mass of roses. I felt very lonely, the children having left in the morning for Germany, and although Hans had promised to be here on the 14th, I dreaded the possibility of arriving alone in Paris. I was therefore delighted when I got to the hotel to see Joseph's grinning face, and I found Hans in his bath, and in very good spirits. . . .

We have just come from a party . . . Mademoiselle Farrar sang, and a horrible little Jew recited, both professionals ; she was a lady and the man a pig. He was so filthy and disgusting that if ever I knew he was going to be anywhere in future I should not go there or I should leave before he began. One or two people were shocked, Helen and her husband Potocki, and Hans too. The Jew person said that he had a friend who lost one of his gloves and he told his dog to go and fetch it, he gave the dog his other glove to smell, *et figurez-vous j'ai attendu et enfin mon bon chien m'a apporté les pantaloñs du cuisinier*. Oh, how I *hate* Paris society, it makes me want to cry, or kill someone, to think that I should waste one smile or one pretty dress on such people. They are poisonous, and they poison, not only each other (which is small pity), but the whole feeling of the country and the people.

Last night we went to a *café chantant* which was also disgusting.

May 20, 1907. *Midnight.* Paris.

Just back from a party at Princess Murat's ; the Grand Duchess Vladimir, the Grand Duke Kyrill, and other Royalties : everyone in their best clothes and wearing tiaras. I wore my round turquoises and diamond crown and my gold (Indian) dress. They were all very flattering. Hans is in love with me again, poor old boy, he is so dear and nice to me now ; when I think of some of the past years, it seems like an absurd nightmare. I have waited long, but peace and understanding have come at last ; I pray God it will last. After the party we went to the Opera and saw the end of a dull ballet, and now I am in bed very glad to have all my fine clothes off.

Last night we dined at the Ritz with Wimperl Schönborn and afterwards went to his apartment which is charming, with an old Italian Renaissance hall. About thirty people came in after dinner and we danced a little, but I did not stay late.

Hans went to the races and I was sorry not to go and see all the new fashions ; I had nothing new to wear except a hat. I am not getting any new clothes as I shall not be in London this season and it is really not worth buying things for this one week here. We shall probably leave on Sunday.

Dear Vater is at Albrechtsburg Castle, their place near Dresden, no better, in fact worse, I am sorry to say ; I wish one knew what was best for him to do.

Hans will not be back till far into daylight ; I expect he has gone to a bachelor's party and a supper of cocottes.

June 22, 1907. Fürstenstein.

Mathilde wrote this morning a nice little letter and said how much Vater liked Hans being there, as he had such nice ways with Vater ; he has nice ways with everyone now, so gentle and thoughtful, and yet full of jokes. . . .

Last Sunday Hans and I and Hansel went to Church and the clergyman's whole sermon was about the " splinter in your brother's eye and the mote in your own." Hansel sat dumb and full of astonishment with his eyes and mouth wide open. I carefully explained it all to him afterwards, as I was afraid he might begin searching in Baby's eyes for little bits of wood and things !

July 14, 1907. Hotel Continental, Dresden.

It is useless for me to excuse myself for not having written since June 22nd, for after all, I feel this diary to be worthless and badly written ; anyone else who may ever care to read it (after I take out some of the pages) will also think so. I must christen my diary with some name and make believe it is a " dotty " friend who likes to know what I do and think, so perhaps in this way I shall write better and more often. What name shall I choose ? *Désirée, Caro Mio Bene, My Friend, My dear Unknown,* or *Unseen.*

A fortnight ago we came here. Vater is really better I find, but of course it is impossible to say how long it will last ; so I had to give up the idea of going to England and Scotland at the end of this month, as from Lochmore in Sutherlandshire to Fürstenstein is a journey of four days, and it would be impossible for me to get back in time if anything were to happen ; besides there is no way of receiving or sending a telegram in Scotland on a Sunday, and anyway the house is hours distant from a telegraph office. I am *very* disappointed as I wanted to have a quiet little time with Shelagh.

What have I been doing lately ? Well, I have been riding, singing, painting in my garden, doing some embroidery,

fishing, and building in the *Schwarzengraben* ; for that *one*
room and little kitchen there have been about eight workmen
for four months—ever since the last days of March ; it is
perfectly absurd. Of course they get paid by the day and so
they dawdle on.

The restful time I have had—seeing only a few people and
having no social duties—and massage have done me a lot of
good ; I sleep much better and look younger ; and this pleases
me for, my dear, I have had a birthday on the 28th of June,
my thirty-fourth birthday. The Comptroller, Herr Keindorff,
made a speech at the official luncheon we gave and afterwards
I took all the wives on the terrace. . . .

I also went to a Birthday concert in Waldenburg the other
night and sat in a box with Frau von Treutler, Countess
Zedlitz and a lot of old women ; the big china manufacturer
too, Herr von T . . . (just made " von ") was there ; he looks
like a fat black pig, and his wife squints. If only you could
have seen them, and yet they are the " nobility " of the place,
people who are happy and find their peace in " fearful innocence
and household laws." The concert was terrible, only two
performers who sang and recited for two hours ! On the 20th
of this month I am giving a concert in Salzbrunn and am singing ;
I have got a lady, a *Hofsängerin* from Leipsic, coming for
nothing ; Count Pückler, and a Herr von Schimmel, a good
'cello player from Freiburg, who came to Fürstenstein to play
for me the other morning at eleven-thirty wearing a beautiful
frock coat, white waistcoat and white *kid* gloves !

. . . I am not going to England this year—to Cowes with
Shelagh on her yacht, to Newlands, to see my friends or go to
plays. I have got into a subdued frame of mind . . . My
thirty-four years are telling on me : I cannot fly from one
thing to another as I used to do with joyful excitement ; I
seem to get into a groove and not wish to move suddenly out
of it. Perhaps it is that I am not feeling very well ; or it may
be the depressing green of this wall-paper without any pictures
—Germans adore depressing colours.

But the chief thing is the comfort I derive from feeling the
presence of Hansel asleep here in the room opposite mine,
and from thinking of the precious baby waiting for me in
Fürstenstein (why cannot I ever get myself to call it "home" ?).
A walk anywhere with the children means far more to me than
even a journey to England, and to have them holding my hand
is a greater delight than to have a King offering me his arm to

QUEEN MARIE OF RUMANIA AND PRINCESS ILEANA.
1913.

take me in to dinner, as I should have had at Cowes. The babies don't notice or care whether I look pretty or not, and for them Marie does not bother me to curl my hair and wear jewels ; so I can be quite natural. And in my old age I suppose I am getting lazy, and besides . . .

August 4, 1907. Heiligendamm, Mecklenburg (on the Baltic).

Charlotte Reuss [1] and her husband (he has been ill) are here with two of their sons, aged fifteen and eighteen, two dreadful boys with vile manners ; I wonder what on earth they will grow up into. Prince Friedrich Wilhelm,[2] brother of Prince Joachim Albrecht (who was sent to Africa), is also here. This boy will also have to be sent somewhere I think to improve his manners and his education, for although he is quite nice in a way, clever and good-looking, he has not the faintest idea of how to behave in the society of ladies and gentlemen. He drinks tumblers full of champagne, pledges the health of all the young men continually, thus forcing them to drink far too much. The last three nights, not being very well, I have not dined at their table ; which was just as well as I should have been furious. I hear the Prince has been amusing himself by competing with others in throwing glasses and bottles on the floor and breaking them to bits, and Charlotte encouraged them and laughed ; she is a Mecklenburg, too, and a cousin of the present Grand Duke.

The day before yesterday when I was resting the Grand Duchess Anastasia came and sat with me ; she hates being here . . . and she can talk of nothing but her desire to be at Cannes or Paris. We motored to her place the other day and had tea by the sea ; the reigning Grand Duke and Grand Duchess [3] were there ; she is a pretty little thing but stupid, he is nice and quite intelligent I should imagine, but, without intending it, is rather stiff in manner and so is not at all popular in his country.

---

[1] Charlotte, a Duchess of Mecklenburg-Schwerin, m. 1886, Prince Henry XVIII. of the cadet branch of Reuss-Köstritz (1847–1911). Her two sons both made morganatic marriages.

[2] Prince Friedrich-Wilhelm (1880–1925), a distant cousin of Wilhelm II., m. in 1910 Agathe, d. of the Duke of Ratibor, and leaves four daughters.

[3] Friedrich-Franz IV., son of the Grand Duke Friedrich-Franz III., and of the Grand Duchess Anastasia, m. in 1904 Alexandra, Duchess of Brunswick-Luneburg.

The Crown Princess is here staying in one of the Grand Duke's villas. I had tea there the other day ; the baby is really a darling (very like the Crown Prince, which is a pity) ; she " expects " again in October and looks, in spite of this, extraordinarily well.

Now they have made the tea ; I must go and pretend to be hungry. I lunch with Smith and Hansel and mostly dine at Charlotte Reuss's table. I wish I had never begun to do this as for the last two nights my quiet dinners upstairs have been so cosy ; I have read the papers and then played the piano and gone to bed early, but now I have no longer any excuse not to dine downstairs (as my cold is better).

Baby had a little cold but is better, thank God ; Smith has a sore throat so I sent for a doctor ; he told her to stay in, which of course she hasn't done, and in writing her name on the prescription he said : " *Wie alt sind Sie*," much to her indignation : she did not agree that because she had a sore throat it was necessary for her to reveal that she was thirty-five.

August 7, 1907. Heiligendamm, Mecklenburg.

Hans arrived here on the 6th. Poor darling, he has been grumbling at everything : the hotel is dreadful (which is true), the cooking is worse (which is true) and the weather is vile (which is also true) : it rains every day and precious Baby is again in bed ; he can't shake off his horrid cold. A lot of ugly second-class looking men (but they may be delightful, every one of them for all I know) have arrived to play tennis ; also some lady players, one an English girl, and another a German who wears *Reform Kleider* even when she plays tennis, so she is not very graceful.

The Crown Prince arrived last night, I have just been with him and the Crown Princess for a little drive in his motor. He asked me if I would dance to-night, and if I still wore dresses that tore so easily ! We dine with the Grand Duchess Anastasia, and her son and daughter-in-law ; I want to play poker after dinner if we can get a fifth, otherwise I suppose I shall have to dance. I danced three times last night with three different men, but really they were all so awful I felt cross and not inclined to allow any of them to put his arm round my waist ; why should I ? When I think of London and Vienna and all the nice men I know, I don't want to make any new acquaintances, or talk to any new people : I know too many already. So I came to bed early : Hans stayed on a little longer.

August 10, 1907. Heiligendamm, Mecklenburg.

The weather has changed, and please God the change will last. All this morning I was on the tennis ground and have become really excited over the game; to see it well played is delightful. The Crown Prince is playing with an English girl against two other people, but he is only a beginner.

Last night was spent quite frivolously; we dined in a private room and then played poker. The Crown Prince and Crown Princess then arrived and after a while we went down and danced ; I waltzed twice with the Crown Prince, we danced a quadrille, and then they left and we went upstairs and played a little more poker. I lost three hundred and sixty marks, but I do not mind that as the horse (in Count Trautmanndorff's stables) in which I bought a half-share last year, won the big prize at Kottingbrunn (near Vienna). After all the expenses are paid, and the keep and the entering for other races, we shall each of us be about eight hundred pounds to the good out of the two thousand pounds we won.

I had a long talk with the Grand Duchess Anastasia this morning ; she has to go to Paris now to meet her father, but I begged her to be back in time to receive the Crown Prince and Crown Princess at Gelbensande ; it will make a very bad impression in Germany if he does not go there, to his mother-in-law's house (twenty minutes by motor from Heiligendamm). She seemed quite reasonable, but hurt because the Crown Princess did not keep her promise to go there for a ten days' visit. . . . She might manage things much better, but she is fussy and rather tactless ; yet one cannot help liking her. Now I am going to sing.

August 14, 1907. Heiligendamm.

Just got a wire from Hans, " *Vater heute halb zwei schmerzlos gestorben.*" [1] It is all so sudden and dreadful I cannot realize yet, or think. My poor old darling Hans arrived in Dresden, alas ! two hours too late. Oh, it's misery ; I only pray Vater did not ask for him. . . .

August 23, 1907. Heiligendamm.

Hansel and I left Fürstenstein yesterday and slept in Berlin at the Wilhelmstrasse [2] and arrived here this evening. Hans

---

[1] I.e. Father passed away peacefully at half-past one to-day.
[2] At the Palast Pless.

has gone to Pless, and from there he says he has to go to England for a few days. My little Mother arrives to-morrow in Hamburg by sea from Harwich. I was very glad to leave Fürstenstein even for a few days, and let the dark shadow pass from it before I go there again, and start a new life if not outwardly at least inwardly. I feel sure Hans will act very quietly and steadily, I can't make out *why* people imagine him to be so different from what he really is.

August 28, 1907. Heiligendamm.

Patsy arrived yesterday. We did not go to Hamburg to meet her as it was pouring rain and the roads are too bad for a motor, so I sent a footman to do so, and she came the next day by train.

This afternoon we went to Schwerin to see the castle. There was a celebration there for the unveiling of a monument to a former Grand Duchess of Mecklenburg. The Emperor was present (the Empress has hurt her leg in a fall so could not come). The Grand Duchess Anastasia telegraphed asking if Patsy and I would like to go, and we did. The Crown Princess of Denmark [1] was there and showed us all over the castle while her mother sat and talked to Count Vico. Then we went up and saw the young Grand Duchess and the Grand Duke ; after that we went down again for tea, and, as I was crossing the corridor, whom should I see but the Grand Duke and Grand Duchess Vladimir of Russia coming up the stairs (she was born a Mecklenburg) ; she was very much surprised and pleased to see me. We then went into another room where there was more tea and more Grand Dukes and Grand Duchesses. I told the Grand Duchess Anastasia that she just got me in there to puzzle and annoy me. I was introduced to the stepmother [2] of the Grand Duke Vladimir ; and to the (morganatic) Grand Duchess Paul,[3] middle-aged, with dark red hair, is much talked about, travels extensively, stays in hotels,

---

[1] E. d. of Grand Duchess Anastasia, became Queen of Denmark 1912.

[2] Czar Alexander II. (1818–81), m. 1st, Marie-Alexandrovna, Princess of Hesse (1824–80) ; 2nd, in July, 1880, Princess Catherine Dolgorouky, cr. Princess Yourievsky. The Grand Dukes Vladimir and Paul were his sons by his first marriage.

[3] Grand Duke Paul (1860–1919), m. 1st, Princess Alexandra of Greece (1870–91) ; 2nd, morganatically, Olga Karnovitch, divorced wife of Eric de Pistohlkors (cr. Countess of Hohenfelsen (a Bavarian title), and, in 1915, Princess Paley).

is said to be very extravagant, and has been painted in Paris
with scarcely any clothes on ! So gossip has it. Then another
old lady said she had met me in Vienna (I thought she must be
a lady-in-waiting) and I said vaguely, " Oh yes." She then
asked to be introduced to Patsy ; I hadn't the faintest idea of
her name, so she said very haughtily, " Princess Windisch-
grätz." [1] Goodness knows when or where I met her before.

We had not even tidied ourselves after motoring, but just
looked at ourselves in a glass in a passage which gave me no
comfort : an ugly three-cornered hat, a black veil hanging
round my head, and of course, a black dress on. They
said I looked like a nun.

It is a lovely castle [2] situated high up on a hill, surrounded
by water and approached by four bridges ; the furniture and
decoration are insignificant, but the building as a whole is
fine and imposing.

August 31, 1907. Ulrichshusen.

. . . At present I feel in a daze, I can't believe that all the
property belongs to Hans and that we are rich ; I still feel
afraid to touch or order anything. . . .

September 6, 1907. Fürstenstein.

We arrived here very comfortably from Berlin in a saloon
carriage. Yesterday I showed Patsy everything ; we went
on the terraces, and to my garden which is full of flowers,
tobacco plant and gladioli, late pansies which I hope will
soon be a mass of colour (I love them so), roses (still !), and
autumn daisies (like me) ; the new white garden seats have
arrived and look very nice. In the afternoon we of course
went down to the *Schwarzengraben* or *Ma Fantaisie* ; the building is scarcely more advanced than when I left. It is really
shameful the time they have taken. The woodwork is not yet
painted and until the shutters are in I can do nothing as I
don't like to take any furniture and china down there without
being able to lock it up. The dam is also not finished, the men
are still working at it, and the plaster in the bathing pond,
which I am going to have painted pale blue so that the water

---

[1] Princess Alexandrine Windisch-Grätz, d. of Prince Hughes
Windisch-Grätz and his wife, who was Duchess Louise of Mecklenburg-Schwerin.

[2] Built 1845–57 in early Renaissance style ; in the twelfth century
a palace of the Princes of Mecklenburg occupied this unique site.

will look deep and clear, is not yet finished. Patsy has good taste and helped me to arrange some things in my boudoir. My dressing-room here will look lovely with the gilt Louis XV. furniture and decorations, and all my Morland and Angelica Kauffmann prints and pictures.

Hans arrived this morning looking very well and full of happy news ; he had been to Newlands during his short stay in England and gone with Poppets to Bournemouth to look at hotels and villas to give him an idea what to do in the future at Salzbrunn. He persuaded Poppets to come here and I am so glad the old darling will arrive at Promnitz on the 20th and shoot some stags ; Patsy and I will go there to meet him, and I will send him a cheque to-morrow as he really cannot draw a large cheque and the expenses of coming and going will be considerable. This afternoon we went again to *Ma Fantaisie* and cut down some trees. I would have walked with Hans but he did not feel quite well, so he went about the paddocks with Aleck. We have laughed this evening : he has been so funny and full of nonsense. Hans came to me and said : " Daisy, have you sung yet since Vater died ? " I said : " No, I haven't had time." Then he said : " Do you think I might play—but I don't know any holy music." The old darling ! I told him to play just whatever he liked and that I felt if dear Vater knew he would only be pleased. Marie, my maid, also asked me this morning if they might play the piano in the housekeeper's room as Freytag had told them not to. I said of course they might play the piano, but that they were not to dance.

September 11, 1907. Pless.

We came here on the 9th to be with Mathilde on the 10th and the other two sisters and brothers, as that date is Vater's birthday, so that she should not be alone. To-day I go with Hans to Promnitz to arrange things there a little cosily (if possible) for Patsy and Poppets when they come ; to-morrow I go back to Fürstenstein. It is glorious weather, warm in the sun ; there is a little fresh feeling of frost in the shade but no wind.

I now occupy the rooms on the ground floor which are known as the Emperor's suite. There is nothing cosy or private here, and I feel as if I shall never be able to find a little hidden corner to rest in.

Mathilde will leave here altogether in the late spring of next year and go to Dambrau, Conny's place, which he will let to her for as long as she cares to have it.

The sums of money which Hans has to pay out is twenty thousand pounds a year to each of his three brothers, eleven thousand to Mathilde, and eight thousand a year to each of his sisters ; and he must put by thirty-five thousand pounds a year towards a sinking fund out of which these incomes will later on be paid. It means that every year Hans has to pay a hundred and twenty-two thousand pounds out of income, and we have also to keep up these two big places and staff them.

September 11, 1907. Promnitz.

Just come up from dinner and am in bed ; I left Hans downstairs with Fritz Solms, Heine Reuss [1] and Willusch. This afternoon I went with Hans whilst he shot. We stood behind a beautiful artificial wall of fir trees built with loop-holes ; his rifle had of course a telescope on it, and I fail to see how anyone could miss with such an apparatus. Hans himself said it was drawing-room shooting. I can see no sport in it, the only skill required being that of choosing one particular stag to shoot at and no other ! To shoot stags in such a flat country and behind a manufactured shelter, without first stalking them, and just for the sake of their heads, is a sport only fit for dotty lame old gentlemen. And in fact stag-shooting in Germany is carried on mostly out of vain emulation ; each owner of a deer forest wishes to kill the largest stag in order to win the Emperor's cup. I find even the roebuck-shooting in Fürstenstein more sporting as there one walks up and down hills and has to find what natural shelter one can behind bushes and trees.

We are not going to occupy Mathilde's and Vater's rooms as they are downstairs, on the wrong side of the house with no view or sun. Our own rooms upstairs have a little tower and a balcony overlooking the lake. I think it would be a good thing to make Mathilde's bedroom and dressing-rooms into one and use it as a dining-room, and use the large dining-room, which looks like a Gothic banqueting hall, as a big hall to sit in. I could get quite fond of this place. Of course there is no trout and salmon fishing as in Scotland ; it is not so sporting, but it rains less, and the woods, the moss, and the bracken are lovely.

---

[1] The son of " Aunt Anna Reuss," Prince Henry XXVIII. of Reuss (1859–1924).

September 28, 1907. Promnitz.

Minnie and Guy arrived here the other day coming viâ Warsaw from St. Petersburg ; [1] they have brought Olivia, their youngest child, a very pretty girl of ten. They are delighted with this place and Minnie is looking so well. We are *all* sorry to leave to-morrow, it has been perfect weather, and we have boated on the lake and punted up the river much to the surprise of the *jägers* and people who have been used only to seeing Mathilde walk round the house and now and then take a short drive. All the *Försters* and *Oberförsters* seem quite pleased with me, I am glad to say, as they are a charming class of men brought up from childhood in the woods and no town smoke or influence has been near them ; they all come and tell me about everything and seem so keen to arrange some duck-shooting and fishing for me. To-day they all paraded ; we had the six *Oberförsters* to lunch and Hans gave each of them a stag's head shot by Vater. He made them a little speech and then the head man (I forget his name) said a few words and they called a *Hoch* for us. Hans fastened a *Hirschfänger* (a long knife) round the waist of the oldest Head Forester ; it was one given by Vater to Hans when he was a little boy.

October 14, 1907. Newlands.

When the time came we were all very sorry to leave dear Fürstenstein ; the weather was very good. The last night after dinner I went to say good-bye to my garden : the tobacco plants smelt delicious and the sky was full of stars.

I stayed the night in London at the Embassy but only saw Metternich for a moment as I did not lunch downstairs but stayed in bed till two, then shopped in the afternoon and dined with Shelagh. We went to the theatre, I hid behind the curtains in the box letting no one see me, although I do think it is ridiculous that one can dine out, and yet not go to a play when one is in mourning ; after all dear Vater was no blood relation of mine ; in England a daughter-in-law would not be prevented from going to the theatre after two months ; but then in Germany mourning, like everything else, is taken in extremely large doses.

To-day we went to Church at Lymington, a nice service and good preacher, and in the afternoon we walked to the sea and along the cliff ; I loved it and I adore this place.

[1] Colonel Guy Wyndham was Military Attaché at St. Petersburg 1907–13.

. . . I have been singing to Poppets this evening and he said : " You really have a marvellous voice, Daisy." I almost thought so myself, it was so full and clear—but the room is easy to sing in and the piano a perfect Bechstein.

December 5, 1907. Fürstenstein.

I wanted to sing for the gramophone company (they will give me one shilling royalty on each record sold) but my voice is not quite right even yet—after the fog in London in October : so I must wait. It would be great fun if I made a little money every year for the Cripple School. Some day I want to build a convalescent home, but I am afraid this will never be as Hans wants to make such enormous changes in the house, and I cannot see how we may have both.

A furrier came here the other day from Leipsic and Hans said I might buy some sables, a long boa and muff : these cost twelve hundred pounds. He is so kind now and thoughtful. I don't mean on account of *this*, but in every way : only one thing is missing—the old story. . . . I am thirty-four and yet some days I feel younger than I have felt for years. It is perhaps that my soul is more at rest. Besides, I have no ambition left in me. I simply want to be myself, that's all, and help Hans in any ideas or undertaking that he may have. . . . I don't want Ambassadorships or intimate friendships in high places ; after all, what are they worth ! Anyway, I am certain to get such things without even troubling—I feel it. God has put so much luck and opportunity, so many of the good things of life in my way. The only thing I would love to do again is to travel. . . . When the boys are bigger I shall certainly do so. . . .

December 6 *and* 10, 1907. Potsdam.

Christa Salm was so glad to see me ; this is a little weeny house on one of the lakes and my bedroom is very small. I am in bed now, a very comfy bed and such a funny little homely room : a window at the back of my bed over the dressing-table, and two windows on the *floor* with the roof slanting so far down to them that I cannot stand up there.

The most charming host and hostess : I feel happy and peaceful ; she is so good and unselfish, a most thoughtful little lady, so young in her ways, and loves pretty things. Why is it that Austrians are so different from Prussians ? Here I am " at home," far more so than I would be in any German house

I know : and indeed it isn't that I am prejudiced—why should I be ? Germany and Germans have, on the whole, been very kind to me. But the two races *are* different. Austrians are much more like English people. Christa gives herself no airs or graces (which as an Archduchess she might justifiably do) ; she is just charming and dear and natural, and the only real woman friend I have in this country.

December 12, 1907. Potsdam.

Just back from dinner with the Crown Princess at the Marmor Palace : only Christa and I, no lady or gentleman-in-waiting. We dined in a little cosy room with very subdued light, the walls hung with a sort of yellow silk and silver lace, and the chairs and sofas covered with chintz. It was a strange mixture but the light not bright enough to distinguish much ; it seemed like what I should imagine a *chambre separée* to be like in some restaurant ! We talked clothes, and babies, and people ; it was most cosy. The Crown Princess looked so well and so pretty ; her second son is only a month old.

After dinner we sat at the end of a long room and looked at a lot of *Farbergeld* enamel things, some little links and pencils —so cheap ; the Crown Princess is going to send us over to-morrow what she doesn't buy so that we can take some. Christa went downstairs to talk on the telephone to her father the Archduke Frederick in *Vienna*.[1] He will pass through Berlin on Monday on his way to the funeral of the King of Sweden.[2] While she was downstairs the Crown Princess began to talk about her mother. . . . I told her all I knew . . . the Grand Duchess Anastasia . . . did not wish to put herself into the position of begging for the favour of a visit from her daughter and son-in-law.

Patsy and Poppets have both written me about the Emperor's visit to Newlands ; he was very charming and talked a lot about Hans and me. Patsy told him about my plans for cleaning the river, my work for the poor, how my in-laws cared for me, and so on. The Emperor said : " Yes, I am very fond of her, she has plenty of brains and I follow her career with interest." He also said, which Patsy said surprised her enormously, that he found Hans very much changed and softened. . . . I

---

[1] At the time I thought this wonderful. Now one telephones all over the world as a matter of course, and even without using wires or cables.—D. OF P.

[2] Oscar II. of Sweden, b. 1829, d. December 8, 1907.

To dear Daisy
    in affectionate remembrance
                of Pilar
                            1931.

PRINCESS PILAR OF BAVARIA.

cannot think he noticed this—he has been told it. He also said : " I am sure he expects me to make him a Duke but he has first to prove himself the high-minded, noble man his father was." I *know* it is Hans's Polish sympathies, the religious question and the lies of jealous people that have kept the Emperor away from Fürstenstein. As for the Duke's title we *don't* want it unless it is attached to another territorial designation.

Prince Hatzfeldt made me quite cross the other day when he said : " Hans *must* be in Berlin on New Year's Day to congratulate the Emperor at ten in the morning." This means we shall not be together on New Year's Eve, which I hate, and we shall not be able to listen to the old clock striking twelve, and open the window and let in the New Year. I absolutely refuse to be alone then ; I shall either come to Berlin and be with Hans, or go to England and be with Patsy and Poppets and Shelagh and Bend Or. Hatzfeldt then leant forward and said : " I cannot say for certain, but perhaps the Emperor will give him an Order." An Order indeed ! I don't care a hang that he should be given second class Orders and things, and chains to wind round his neck ; some day he should get the Black Eagle and, until then, I want *nothing* for him. I think the whole idea of the Princes having to leave their wives and families on New Year's Eve is all wrong. And I shall not let Hans do it every year !

December 13, 1907. Potsdam.

This morning I went to leave cards on Countess Tiele, but as she was at the window we settled to do it on our return home. It ended in Marie (my maid) leaving a card there this afternoon ; the Countess is Mistress of the Household to the Crown Princess. Marie, and Christa's maid, Amalia, went to the Neue Palast and left cards there for me on Countess Brockdorff and two other ladies of the Empress's suite ! Strictly incorrect, I feel sure, but both maids were very proud. I walked with Christa to the Neue Palast to write my name in the Crown Princess's book, but she hadn't got one ! We met the Crown Prince coming home in his motor with a lot of young officers ; he stopped, got out, and took us into the stables to see two new race horses he has just bought. Christa left us soon as she had to hurry back and change for lunch with the Empress. Then the Crown Prince showed me all the horses and carriages (including a little weeny pony for the eldest son to ride).   He told me he had had our carriages copied ! I innocently said :   " What colour ? " And he answered : " Dark blue inside and red wheels."

We then walked alone to the Palace and he showed me his private rooms and some pictures he had recently bought. Then the Crown Princess came down and we went to the nurseries, passing through a corridor where an artist is paint-ing a picture of the eldest child—perfectly dreadful.   The nurseries seemed delightful, but Christa says they never get the sun.   The little baby looks exactly as his brother did at the same age, and the eldest little chap is delightful, has a clever little inquiring face, not a bit like a baby's ; he looks much older than his one and a half years ; indeed his head looks like that of a child of five.   He had been ill, yet the new nurse, a German, took him out of his bed and put him on the table with only his nightgown on for us to look at : I said, " He is suffering from a chill : for goodness' sake let's cover him up —coming straight out of his warm bed."   Then the Crown Prince cuddled him up wrapped in a blanket.   It was very nice to see.   They are devoted to each other, and when she came into the room after he and I arrived they embraced, and patted each other's cheeks at intervals every three minutes. I turned round and looked at books or photographs while they did this.   During our walk he did not mention the subject of my conversation with the Crown Princess the evening before.[1]   I walked home alone in ten minutes : Prince Salm came to meet me, we had lunch together, and the two little girls came and sat with us.

Christa came home about three o'clock from her luncheon with the Empress and we drove in the motor to Babelsberg,[2] a palace which is going to be enlarged for the Crown Prince and Princess ; it is in a lovely position, quite a big park round it, but the old house, where the late Emperor Wil-liam I.[3] and the old Empress Augusta lived, is dreadful—early-Victorian Gothic ; but as the Emperor wishes it to remain untouched and as no one could now live in such surroundings, a new house will be built adjoining it.   Inside, the old house is exactly as the Emperor William I. left it.   The *bed* too, with the night table and chair ; a plain room with a few

---

[1] About the Grand Duchess Anastasia of Mecklenburg-Schwerin.
[2] See *Letters of Empress Frederick*, by Rt. Hon. Sir F. Ponsonby, p. 17.
[3] D. March, 1888, aged ninety.

prints, a dirty bed hung with grey and mustard-coloured stuff ; next door his study—only a small round table and stiff chairs. The whole house is dismal and stiff ; it seems as if nothing cosy, much less sumptuous, or even clean, had ever been in it ; it is pitch dark ; carvings on all chairs and everywhere. That dreadful, bad " gothic " style ! How differently they lived in those days.

Christa amused us about her luncheon with the Empress : only ladies-in-waiting present, and one of the sons. The Empress showed her afterwards all her private rooms, as they lunched upstairs, and Christa thought of the book, *Guillaume II et sa vie intime*. She said she could have screamed when the Empress took her into her bedroom and showed the one big bed and four beautiful new screens, one on each side of the bed and two across the room ! The Empress explained : " These are a surprise for Wilhelm when he comes back to-morrow ; they are intended to make the room look small as he dislikes a large bedroom ! " Christa said : " But the bed is in a niche—and over there opposite is what looks like the canopy for over the head of a bed. Why is that ? " " Oh," said the Empress, " we sleep that side of the room in the summer as then it is too hot to sleep in that built-in niche in the wall."

Can anyone imagine anything *more* uncomfortable than *one* bed surrounded with *screens* and on the opposite wall a gloomy meaningless canopy suspended from the ceiling. " The summer awning "—but left hanging there all the autumn and winter.

The Marmor Palace is rather nice but too small for the Crown Prince and Princess.

December 23, 1907. Fürstenstein.

Have not had a moment to write since I came back here ; Christmas trees every day ; I have given away such lovely warm clothes and delicious toys, and it almost made me want to be a child myself this morning when I went into the rooms where my lady-in-waiting keeps all the things ; one room full of toys, one room full of clothes for *men and women*, another filled with caps and shawls for big girls. . . .

December 30, 1907. In the train for Ostend, going to England for three weeks.

. . . Little L. is very much in love with A.B., a pale hairless young man who is delicate, can't sleep, and has to " rest " after tea ; he hasn't even any " fluff " on his head, and can't grow a moustache. It hurts his head to shoot, and his heart to smoke, so he does neither ; and to my mind he doesn't even *seem* to be in love—this might hurt him too. He has manners and a voice very like a shy curate's. Hans and I were laughing about him one night in my bedroom. The next day at lunch, he being present, we were talking about milk and he said : " At home I live on sour milk." I winked at Hans and very nearly exploded with laughter ; fortunately I choked over an orange pip, and though this was unpleasant it saved me from an embarrassing situation. And then, he wears an eye-glass stiffly stuck in one eye which makes him look even funnier. As long as L. remains quietly in the little corner where A.B.'s Schloss is, and never sees or knows anything more of the-world-the-flesh-and-the-devil than he will show her, then all may be well ; but if ever her eyes are opened—I pity her.

The sables that Hans gave me are a great success ; instead of taking the most expensive skins I took the half-price ones without telling him as I really couldn't spend a thousand and fifty pounds on a boa and muff. So now I have a lovely long cape with sleeves, a boa, and muff for one thousand two hundred and fifty pounds. I wanted to pay the odd two hundred and fifty myself but Hans insisted on paying the whole lot. It was a great responsibility choosing the cheaper fur, and if I had asked Hans he would have said *no*, so I was dreadfully afraid he would be furious ; but really the Leipsic merchant has given me such *beautiful* black skins that one can't help being pleased. The man is anxious for me to be a patron of his, and this spurred him to do his best for me. Hans gave me also a lovely little diamond brooch. The King of England sent me a bag with topaz and amethyst in it ; Queen Alexandra sent a lovely little Monte Carlo bag with inlaid opera glasses in it ; Lonsdale an umbrella handle ; Shelagh silver animals for my *Schwarzengraben* ; Poppets a lovely oil painting ; Patsy a delicious china inkstand ; Mathilde a picture of Vater ; Anna and Willusch a silver box ; Conny and Fritz a lovely pair of amethyst and diamond earrings.

CHAPTER TEN

1908

January 11, 1908. Eaton Hall, Cheshire.

LAST night we were to have had a happy evening at the Liverpool pantomime with Juliet and Robin Duff, but I wasn't well enough to travel so Shelagh went without me. The doctor doesn't want me to travel but I have *so* much to do and so many people to see on Monday in London, that I must leave to-day, though I shall not be well enough to dine with Consuelo Manchester to meet the King. I shall write to His Majesty to tell him how disappointed I am as I shall now probably not see him till August.

Count Metternich is at the Embassy, he arrived on the 10th ; I found a little present from him waiting for me when I got here ; two little diamond D's, and I wrote to ask him what the initials stood for, whether it was " dear Daisy," " Daisy darling," " Damn'd Daisy," or what ! . . .

I used rather to like being admired (as every woman does, I suppose), but somehow now, I do not bother to arouse admiration, nor do I often notice it when it is there. I feel much older and when my mind wanders away into dreamland it hears no echo of the hard world around me—not even of the songs I sing ; it carries no remembrance of the books I read, my travels, the people that pass to and fro before my very eyes : only the sun and flowers and my boys follow me there and make me feel happy. I love the sun and flowers above all things in this world ; so now to have to miss a dinner with the King does not disturb me, although he is *so* nice and I should have had lots to tell him, about Hans's succession, our new position, Germany, and heaps more : in the old days nothing would have kept me away !

February 23, 1908. Cap Martin, Villa Cynthia.

A whole month since I last wrote. I love walking here and talking to the funny old *cochers* and the fishermen. I have been twice to Mentone to buy flowers and fishing rods. I walked there alone and a carriage picked me up in the town and brought me back. I felt young and happy, perhaps my face showed it, as in the shops they called me " Mademoiselle."

. . . I went to Nice for the Carnival with Hans and the children, Fräulein Freyer and Smith ; I had promised the children, and felt I had to go. I had telephoned to the *Préfet des Alpes Maritimes* to ask his advice about taking a box, and he invited us to his, met us, and arranged for the motor to be near when we left. It was very comfortable for *us* and *he* looked upon it, poor man, as a great honour. I don't know *what* he thought we were as he kept on calling Hans " Monseigneur," introduced me to lots of the Nice officials and their wives, then gave me his arm and led me formally to the centre dais where all the processional cars and streams of people passed by.

. . . I look at Fürstenstein with a restless eye now, feeling that so many walls are to be pulled down and rebuilt, so much dust raised and disorder made. I shall know no peace there for years.

February 25, 1908. Villa Cynthia, Cap Martin.

Yesterday was a very full day ; people came to lunch : the *Préfet* and his wife, whom we asked because they were so nice to us at the Carnival ; he is so polite and anxious to please . . . At Nice his wife was dressed in bright green ; yesterday she wore bright salmon-coloured cloth, her lips matched her dress, and her face matched the blue tablecloth at luncheon ; she had rings on *all* her fingers. Paula Schaffgotsch and her husband [1] came ; and Frau von Hergermann and her daughter (her husband is Danish Minister in Berlin—she is a clever, rather interesting old lady) ; Prince Lynar and Prince and Princess (Charlotte) of Saxe-Meiningen (the sister of the Emperor).

February 27, 1908. Villa Cynthia, Cap Martin.

I called on Mrs. Hartmann (the tenant of White Lodge, Richmond) and her sister the Marquise de Jaucourt whose

---

[1] Count Karl Schaffgotsch, b. 1850, m. 1889, Baroness Paula Fürstenberg-Stammheim.

husband died a year ago ; the Marquise is the mother of Princess Biron.[1] They both talked at the same time and asked questions which they proceeded to answer themselves. Mrs. Hartmann said : " Oh yes, I know your father-in-law gave you Fürstenstein to live in only because he couldn't bear to use it himself, his wife having died there." I said : " As it happens Hans's mother died at Pless and three years later Vater married again ! "

March 10, 1908. Villa Cynthia, Cap Martin.

Have had a few delicious quiet days with the children ; we picnicked at Cap Ferrat on the rocks.

To-day I took Hansel to Cannes. . . . While there he went for a drive with the Torby children [2] and the two little girls [3] of the Grand Duchess George, Nina and Xénie. Sophy had made a muddle ; I was not expected to lunch, and I found no one at home except the children. I went upstairs to the schoolroom and we had a very cheerful improvised meal, Miss Frank and Mary both very pleased to see me ! During luncheon a footman came in to say that they had telephoned from the Villa Cynthia to say that the Prince (Hans) had arrived. So here he is. . . .

March 29, 1908. Villa Cynthia, Cap Martin.

Same sunshine, same blue sea, same delight at being here. I do not in the least feel inclined to rush off to Spain in a week. I feel very well now and I am therefore in wild spirits ; Shelagh and I can't stop laughing all day. Bend Or left on Friday viâ Paris for England. Lord Wodehouse, who is here now, had a fall playing polo and is rather shaken. Shelagh and I have been twice to the Opera : I love Opera. Hans never comes with us.

June 25, 1908. Fürstenstein.

We have been here just over a fortnight. The weather is glorious to-day and I am writing in my garden, a mass of

---

[1] Gustave Prince Biron von Curland, b. 1859, m. as his 2nd wife, Françoise, d. of Marquis de Jaucourt, b. in Paris 1874.

[2] Countess Zia Torby, now Lady Zia Wernher ; Countess Nada Torby, now the Marchioness of Milford Haven ; and Count Michael, b. 1898.

[3] Cousins of the above ; Princess Nina, now Princess Paul Tchavtchavadzé ; and Princess Xénie, until lately Mrs. William Leeds.

roses and Mrs. Simkins picotees, the dear little white pink which grows in the borders at Newlands. . . .

It will be *three* years before this place is finished; then it will be *beautiful*. It is nice to feel that Hans trusts me and likes me to buy things; I only hope he will not spend too much money. Coal is now a shilling more a ton which means about another twenty thousand pounds this year; also a new coal mine which Vater opened three years ago now brings in twenty-five thousand pounds a year. Hans assures me that the two Comptrollers [1] would tell him if his proposed expenditure was too great. . . .

Betka Potocka, looking so well and young, came here for two nights on her way back from her mother.[2] Dear Fanny Sternberg was coming to-morrow with her little boy but now wires that she cannot do so. I am sorry for this as I wanted a little homely party for my birthday on the 28th. Thirty-five —how terrible! I feel very old and as if all our dressing-up times, our dancing and paper-chases were over: I have no daughter for whom to arrange such things, but perhaps, when this mood passes, I shall feel young again: I hope so. Hans is very well, very busy, and works and writes a lot; he will, I am sure, carry out the duties of his station *well*!

The blessed boys are playing hide-and-seek and running and laughing; I *long* to run with them.

July 6, 1908. In the train to Berlin.

We left Fürstenstein about one o'clock and get to Berlin to-night at eight. We have a comfortable saloon which takes us on to-morrow to Wildungen, where I am going to " do a cure." . . .

Fräulein Freyer [3] just now began paying me compliments (at least that is what I feel they are meant to be, and I hate compliments), saying she felt happy when she could be with me for one hour, that to live with me made her better—and rubbish of that sort. I told her that as she scarcely ever saw me her feelings must be imaginary. Fräulein Suttes [4] wrote me to the same effect the other day, saying she felt a

---

[1] Herr Keindorff was Comptroller-General at Fürstenstein and Herr Nasse at Pless.

[2] Princess Antoine Radziwill (1840–1915), born a Countess of Castellane; resided at Schloss Kleinitz, Lower Silesia.

[3] The governess.

[4] A *Hofdame* or lady-in-waiting.

better girl after a spell of duty at Fürstenstein. When Violet
Mar left the Villa Cynthia she wrote : " Daisy darling, I have
loved my few days with you ; it does one good morally and
physically to be with you." Well, diary—what they mean
I can't tell you as I have a horrid temper and know I am like
a spoilt child sometimes—when, for instance, I can't find just
the special wallpaper and chintz I want. Indeed there are
tons of little things which I ought to take quietly—but don't.

July 7, 1908. In the train to Wildungen.

We left Berlin this morning at twelve, and are now very
comfy in the saloon carriage. I went to Professor " Jumble
Sale " or some such name, and his room looked what his name
sounded like. A thing like a confessional box in one corner
with a black hole in it, instruments lying about everywhere,
and cords and tassels. It nearly gave Marie my maid fits,
and she asked me if I wasn't frightened. The old Professor
who came to Fürstenstein was also there. I was fastened down
across the chest with an enormous machine while I lay on a
thin board with a cushion under my head. And then a great
light was placed on my stomach, the photographic plate being
under my back. It made me feel rather sick and it felt prickly.
They told me not to talk, so I made the old Professor hold
my hand—which pleased him enormously. Marie asked if
she shouldn't fetch brandy. Well, I suppose in a day or
two they will really be able to tell if I have a rock anywhere
or a curve in anything. It hurt me afterwards to lift up my
arms to put on my veil. To-night I see the doctor in Wildungen.

The boys are great fun running about and tumbling, as
the train shakes so, and of course they won't keep clean.
Smith has been reading them a children's book by Countess
von Arnim, an American, and the author of *Elizabeth and her
German Garden*. It was rumoured that this charming book
was written by me. I only wish I had the ability to do anything of the kind. Smith said : " I am not a bit surprised
at their thinking Your Highness wrote these books as there is
so much in them like you." And there really is ; all the
funny little things she notices. I always wanted to know
her and write to her. . . . One is generally disappointed in
authors and authoresses. But at any rate, when their books
are nice, there must be something nice in the heart or soul of
the writer which the outsider does not observe. I long to

write a book about Hansel and Baby and call it, *An English Mother's Two Little German Boys*. I should have to add *and* a German dog, as he is a very important member of our children's side of the house—a little Spitz called *Laddy* ; both boys quarrel over him and pull him in different directions ; he then bites the one he doesn't at that moment wish to be with, and stays with the other. But he must always do what they do, if they jump on a chair to look out of the window he must at once do the same ; if they run in the long grass to pick me bunches of the big daisies and wild flowers, he runs too and bites off the flower heads. He is a direct descendant of the little dog that Hans had when he was a little boy, at least that is what Fritz said when he gave the dog to Hansel.

I forgot to say that on my birthday I had a nice long letter from the Empress in answer to the one I had written her some weeks before about the poor lace makers in Hirschberg— whom I want to help by getting rid of two horrid old women there who take all the profit for themselves. I had asked the Empress to allow me to say that she took an interest in it all and would be glad to know what work we had done at the end of the year. . . .

July 16, 1908. Wildungen, in the Principality of Waldeck.

There is a Russian here (with a *Jäger*), and the maids say he is very nice. I imagine that he is a bit cracky. The other night we met on the stairs outside the baby's room ; he bowed and of course I said *Guten-abend*. He afterwards told Hedwig that I was so much prettier than the photograph they had shown him, that I ought to be a Queen, and that if I were, my subjects would carry me on their hands. At the time I thought this a delightful expression, but have wondered since how many subjects it would take to do so !

Fräulein Suttes leaves here next Monday ; it is impossible to say how much I shall miss her, as this is the first time she has been with me in the capacity of secretary and companion or *Hofdame*. She and Hedwig had arranged the rooms so nicely before we arrived. She had hired a motor, ordered dinner (which she always does). It is she who arranges the drives for us, carries things for me, makes me comfy wherever I sit, plays with the children, looks over the hotel bill, in fact thinks of every little thing to please me, and, with all this, she is an artiste at the piano and speaks French and English.

Now, alas, she is going to be married the first week in August ;
her young man (he is over forty and she twenty-seven) came
here for a night and a day to see her ; he is very short and fat
and has no hair, but a nice face. He is a large farmer, having
taken one of the Royal Farms with a nice house. He has an
income of about twelve hundred a year ; for her, quite well off.
I only hope she will be happy, but I am very sorry as she is
very fond of me and it will be, I imagine, *impossible* to find
an equally nice girl who will look after the poor people and
hospitals with me, besides being able to take care of my guests
when I am tired, write my letters, arrange the rooms and get
on well with the servants—and all this Fräulein Suttes did to
perfection.

Mrs. Laurence Drummond [1] is here with Lady Cowper,[2]
whom I do not know. The former is a very nice, good-looking
woman, very very tall with grey hair and a young face. I *know*
she is nice and everyone in England loves her, but somehow
just now I am not in the mood to see *anyone* : it interferes
with my visits to the woods with the children. When I go
out I take my bag with letters to answer or my book and I
like to be quiet, and not have to make conversation. I am
in rather a wild mood. I want the open spaces and flowers
and my beloved boys and no one else to come near me ; it is
so nice like that.

Now I must go and drink the waters. Yesterday we walked
miles all of us, followed by the motor coming down backwards,
as we had made a mistake about the road and found ourselves
in impassable places. We all got out twice and the motor
went on through boggy ground without us, but at last the road
got too narrow and we did not dare go on ! We all laughed
and thought it great fun. . . .

I have always refused to accept even playful admiration
from a married man ! And I think a woman who flirts in
earnest with a married man is a fiend !

August 7, 1908. West Cliff, Bembridge, Isle of Wight.

On the Monday we came here, such delicious hot weather
and now it has changed and is quite cold. I have been sailing

---

[1] D. of Hugh Antrobus, m. 1886, Major-General Laurence Drummond, who commanded the Scots Guards.

[2] D. of 4th Marquess of Northampton, m. 1870, last Earl Cowper
(d. 1905).

with Robin Duff every afternoon ; once we took part in the racing but did not win. The day before yesterday we all sailed on the dear old *Britannia* (except Christa Salm and her husband who were not invited but dined last night on the *Victoria and Albert* instead). I never saw the Queen in such good spirits, and the King was very cheerful and *content* (although Egypt House is empty this year, so *all* His Majesty's friends are not at Cowes). The Queen was not dressed in chiffon—like the German Empress at Kiel—nor were there any fussy old ladies-in-waiting on board. We ate shrimps and laughed and sat about and did what we liked. Shelagh and Patsy came too ; Shelagh is on her yacht the *Granaig* with Patsy and Alba.

August 16, 1908. Eaton Hall, Cheshire.

Here all the women call the men by their nick names, Captain de Crespigny is Creepy, Rocksavage is Jippy or Tippy, Captain Wilson is Bertie, the Duke of Roxburghe is Bumbles, and so on. It puts everyone on a very homely footing and there is no formality or stiffness. All the men are nice, young, mostly good-looking, and thorough sportsmen ; *where* in Germany is this class of man to be found in such numbers ?
. . . I should like to have nice unmarried men in my house to ride, dance, fish and talk to the women ; it has made me feel *young* this week, and now and then this sort of thing would be good for Hans too—and take him out of *himself* ; it isn't good for people to be by themselves and think only of themselves. They become stiff and dried up.

And now at the end of the month I leave for Pless. I shall hate passing Breslau and not going to Fürstenstein, and I dread Pless ; and I shall not see this green happy Island till next year, and I have had this year, only six weeks in England. Oh, diary, I want to do what is right, and you *know* I *do* think of other people, all the servants and agents, but it *is* only fair that I should be able to spend three or two months every year in this country.

August 30, 1908. The German Embassy, London.

Monday night we all—including Patsy and her maid—start for Germany viâ Flushing and go straight through, without stopping in Berlin for the night. It seems I am continually getting in or out of a train, and really I feel sad to go to Pless,

CASTLE PLESS.

Room used as a Sitting-room by the Emperor William II, 1915-17, when Pless was Great
Headquarters of the German Armies in the East.

passing Breslau so *near* Fürstenstein and not being able to get out there ! I cannot imagine myself ever caring for Pless.

This month in England has flown : I have been so happy, it has done me good too ; I have felt younger, and having nothing to think of but my own affairs for once has been a rest.

The Salms are still in England enjoying themselves. I got Lonsdale to ask them to Lowther as I knew it would interest them, and from there they went to the Guinnesses [1] for the Dublin Horse Show.

September 6, 1908. Pless.

All these days Patsy and I have been very busy trying to get Promnitz ready for the 10th ; there are about sixteen people working there, putting up chintz, and wallpaper, and laying carpets. I do hope Hans and Lulu will like it. I shall be *miserable* if they don't : I want to keep it as Vater meant, but I feel that it needs to be made brighter.

The last two nights we have had two Colonels and lots of officers quartered here, all very nice, unspoilt, easily-pleased men. Last night their regimental band played up in the gallery while we were at dinner and then this morning, as a surprise, they played under my windows before Church. It made me long to sing. To-night I *did* sing ; I rehearsed a little with the band and I sang after dinner : they were really all delighted—I can't help saying it. I sang some German songs and an English one. They all told Patsy they would never forget the evening, and then I accompanied the *Kapelle-meister* while he played his violin, and he was very proud ; it is *nice* to please people. Balka, the Master-of-the-horse, Bertlemann the secretary, and an old gentleman (who is in charge of all the farms and the forests) dined here too, and I *felt* they were pleased with me ; I am so anxious to do what is right, and I have to do it *alone*. Hans says " no " to every-thing as he is so afraid of my losing dignity, and yet when I sing like to-night, he is so pleased and proud of me after all.

To-morrow morning we all go to the Manœuvres on horse-back and have to be there by nine o'clock. I have a little

---

[1] Hon. Walter Guinness, s. of 1st Earl of Iveagh, m. 1903, Lady Evelyn, d. of 14th Earl of Buchan.

pain to-night which makes me sad as I long to start riding and hunting again, now that I have some beautiful horses.

The Larisches came over for the day : it is only one hour from here to Solza by motor ; I am glad it is such a short journey and I *was* pleased to see them again. We had all the officers from Pless to tea this afternoon and the band played on the terrace ; three of the officers brought their wives ; some of our head agents' wives came, and the Comptroller in Chief also brought his wife : some of these ladies have been here for *years* and I believe they have never before been *inside* the house !

In church this morning I prayed that I might do what is right here, and that by doing good I might succeed in making the people like me. I hope it will all go well with me but —I shall never love this place as I love Fürstenstein.

September 17, 1908. Promnitz.

We came here on the 10th from Pless, a heavenly summer's day ; and it was lovely on the lake in the evening after dinner, the full moon reflected in the water, and the lights of the house gleaming in the distance. Hans is quite pleased with the changes I have made in this dear little place. Bright wallpaper and chintzes, the big dining-room turned into a hall to sit in with comfortable arm-chairs and cushions, all the sofas and chairs covered in red or green linen ; cushions of old fifteenth-century work and curtains to match, everything according harmoniously with the style of the hall which is a sort of gothic Renaissance. Mathilde's old bedroom is now a dining-room ; though very small, it holds nine people comfortably, and we are never more. Lulu and Fritz Solms have been here, both quite pleased and happy.

I have had two days of bad headache : I suppose it is the riding, and I must therefore make up my mind not to ride at all this year : I *am* disappointed as at last I have got some good horses to ride and must not do so. Yesterday, on seeing Hans's new red coat, which was put out for him to try on, I *howled*. I couldn't help it. Men are never very sympathetic when a woman is ill : they look on it as a great nuisance. Hans says I ought not to give in, but that I ought to ride quietly twice a day and get used to it. I really am not strong enough to entertain people for shooting all October in Pless (Hans wants to shoot there every Wednesday and Thursday between his hunting days in Parduwitz), November in Fürsten-

stein, December in Pless again, and then to go to Berlin in
January.   It leaves me not one moment of peace.   I wrote to
Fräulein Suttes yesterday (she is now Frau Szckzo, or some
funny name like that) and I told her I felt a little better, but
I was like a ship always expected to be in full sail and smiling,
to go forward in every wind, mild or fierce, to sail in every
water, calm or wild, shallow or deep—to go for ever on without
a halt. . . .   I should prefer to find myself with less money,
fewer servants and horses, and clothes, obliged to economize
in every item of expenditure if only I could retire with my
boys in a sweet little clean cottage in England . . . my God,
how happy I should be !   To live " on the cheap " here or
in any other large house would of course be awful—but to live
modestly in England or anywhere else in the country would be
lovely.

Baby is as sweet as ever.   They all say he is like me and has
my smile.   If so I suppose my smile must be rather nice as
Baby's is delicious.   Hansel has now the green hunting uniform
like the one Hans and the *jägers* wear ; and, as a surprise, I
ordered a green tunic for the baby and a little felt hat.   He
will look a duck.

We are now alone for two days, thank God.   Sophy and
the Grand Duke Michael, Aunt Min Wyndham, the Sternbergs and Heine Larisch come on Sunday, the 20th.

September 24, 1908.   Promnitz.

How time flies !   The people in the little house change ;
but, thank God, weather changes too : after being horrible
it is now lovely.   Natalie and Prince Hatzfeldt have been here,
both very pleased—two nice old friends.   We are supposed to
be able to afford killing thirty stags here every year.   To
my mind that is too many.   Hans told me that each stag costs
over two hundred pounds.   Eighteen good stag to shoot a
year should be quite enough.

Last night the Grand Duke, Sophy, Min, Patsy and I went
over for the night to Solza to the Larisches and I was
pleased to see that nice cheery home again ; it reminded me
of old times and the fun Shelagh and I used to have there.
Everyone was well and seemed not a bit changed.

Their private band played after dinner most beautifully.
Count Heine offered to lend it to me when the King and Queen
of Spain come to Pless on the 14th of October, but I think I
will get our own band from Salzbrunn and rehearse with them

a little, as when we have the full orchestra they play extremely well. (Of course when we have little dances in Fürstenstein we have out only about five players.) There is still a lot to be done in Pless for the Spanish visit : all the rooms downstairs have to be got ready. In the " Imperial Suite " I am having the woodwork painted cream for the present ; it is not really in keeping with the ceilings and fireplace and the *awful* stoves which are " gothic," but it makes the rooms much brighter, and I will put in some pretty brocade curtains and comfortable sofas. The end room I have made into a bathroom and opened out another window which lets in much more light. I can't make out why Vater never did a thing ; I think he was too indolent, and so would Hans be when it came to choosing stuffs and paint and so on.

Patsy is going with me to the Royal Wedding [1] in Berlin ; she wrote to the Emperor asking if she might go and he wired to-day : " With pleasure for your sake I make this exception and invite you to the wedding." Reischach [2] says foreigners are never asked to a Royal wedding.

On Tuesday we leave this little house and go to dear old Fürstenstein for a few days to choose some furniture to send here. From there we motor to Castolowitz (close to Parduwitz) and stay for two nights with Fanny Sternberg while we are arranging the apartments in our Hunting Box at Parduwitz. They are busy at it now. I do hope it will be finished and that Hans will be pleased when he sees it. A representative from Waring and Gillow is doing it. On the 6th we come back to Pless to make final arrangements for the visit of the King and Queen of Spain.

October 2, 1908. Fürstenstein.

We arrived here on the 29th after a very successful motor drive of six and a half hours from Promnitz, through ugly country ; it was cold and windy and dark when we arrived. But the next morning, oh, the loveliness of it, the brightest sunshine and a thin haze over the valley, the house rising like a fairy castle from a sea of silver, the woods in all their autumn glory. It has been heavenly all the time, my garden even now a mass of roses and gladioli, pale pink and yellow.

---

[1] That of Prince August-Wilhelm, 4th s. of Wilhelm II., to Princess Alexandra-Victoria of Schleswig-Holstein-Glucksburg.

[2] Baron von Reischach, then Master of the Horse, and later Marshal of the Court, to the Emperor William II.

Guy Wyndham, Minnie's husband, arrived yesterday ; we went to meet him in Breslau, where Patsy, Minnie and I spent three hours trying to find some decent stuffs and furniture for Pless for the visit of the King and Queen of Spain. The furniture we saw was awful *jugend* style and the silk would have cost over four pounds a yard ; so, for the present, I shall take curtains from here for my boudoir, drawing-room and bedroom.

Just had a nice wire from the Crown Princess saying, " Very sorry we cannot come in October but would love to later, letter follows, love, Cecile."

I shall not consent to take any active interest in the Women's Congress in Breslau, until I have seen Countess Zedlitz, the *Oberpräsident's* wife, and got her advice.

October 11, 1908. Pless.

Still the most glorious weather. To-day I had a rest going with Patsy in a punt up the little river ; the servants brought out our cold lunch and hot vegetables ; then we went up a little further till the reeds stopped us and we got out and walked and sat in the sun ; the children had swords and shields with them, took off practically all their clothes and played wild Indians all day. I wonder why every child always pretends to be an Indian, never a Zulu, Arab, nor Chinese, nor even a cannibal but always an Indian. Min and Guy were away for the night at a place in Moravia belonging to Count and Countess Berchtold [1]—he is Austrian Ambassador in Petersburg. . . .

November 22, 1908. Wiesbaden.

Hans arrived this morning to see me but only for the day and has just left by night train for Berlin. He *would* have stayed longer if I had asked him, but I saw he would have been sorry to miss his hunting at Pardubitz where he will go to-morrow, Monday, in the hope of hunting Tuesday and Wednesday. He was charming and full of news, he is always full of ideas and knows well what he thinks, but he is a man who will never come forward as a personality ; he has not the tact or whatever is necessary, and he cannot flatter, or say what he does not feel. He has got far more sense than half the people round the

---

[1] Count Berchtold, b. 1860 ; Austrian Ambassador to Russia 1906–12 ; Foreign Minister 1912–15 ; following the Sarajevo murders he presented the fatal ultimatum to Belgrade in Aug. 1914.

Emperor ; so also has Prince Hatzfeldt, but because neither of them *cringe* before His Majesty they are not in high favour. . . . Philip Eulenburg is taken out of prison—in case he might die there. . . . It is said that Bülow [1] is sure to have to go, and that *Eulenburg* will nominate the next Prime Minister ! ! !

November 25, 1908. Wiesbaden.

Just back from the Opera House where Herr von Something, the Intendant, lends me his box when I care to go. *Valkürie*, which I like very much, is announced for to-morrow. How I love the theatre—the stage itself, the smell of the scenery and even the dust—and the paint, the somewhat faded clothes. I miss the acting this year at Chatsworth ; we used to grumble, but it was great fun.

I forgot to say the Crown Prince and Crown Princess are not coming to Pless to shoot in December, and they are not even going to any of their own country places ; she wrote me such a touching letter this morning saying : " Now that the Emperor and my mother-in-law have to go through such a dreadful time I feel we must give up our pleasure and think of the great things, and raise again our prestige." [2] Poor little lady, I think it is very touching of them both, but so childish ; besides it is playing too much into the hands of the Press, which has been *dreadful* lately—such illustrations ! As the German Press is " free " (I suppose this is as it ought to be) I daresay it is too much to expect that they should not be tempted to caricature other kings and statesmen, but to ridicule their own monarch, the Head of their country—it is disgraceful. I do not know that the Crown Prince and Princess will help matters by refraining from *visiting* ; nobody will even notice it. Well, now, *the Interview has* been printed, Bülow's speech *has* been

---

[1] Prince Bülow resigned the Imperial Chancellorship in 1909 : Philip 1st Prince Eulenburg must not be confused with Count Auguste zu Eulenburg, who was for many years Comptroller of the Imperial Household. It has been shown by Emile Ludwig and Professor Haller that Prince Philip, who was the chief scapegoat of the " Round Table " scandals, consistently gave his Imperial friend sound, frank and disinterested advice, although the Crown Prince, the authoress, and the many others who distrusted him, could not know this.

[2] The reference is to the indiscreet interview, now famous, given by the Emperor to the *Daily Telegraph* in October (1908). Bülow disclaimed responsibility, and the Emperor reluctantly swallowed a reprimand from his Chancellor.

made, the Emperor has undertaken, or is said to have undertaken, not to make in future any remarks on his own hook in connection with foreign affairs—surely it would be far better to let the whole thing be dead and buried as soon as possible rather than that the Court should make itself ridiculous by going into mourning.

November 28, 1908. *Sunday.* Wiesbaden.

The precious boys arrived yesterday. Baby too amusing; he sits on my knee and tells stories which he invents about giants. The one last night ended in : " He bought a lot of ladies and ate them, then they filled his tummy full of stones and then he had a hot bath and the water came over him and he got no air—and sunk under and died."

December 8, 1908. Wiesbaden.

My wedding day sixteen years ago to-day. I cried myself (but not to sleep) last night thinking of all the " might-have-beens " ; the little intimate things I prayed and tried and longed for years ago between Hans and myself—but what's the use now ? Even the *remembrance* of my desires ought to have died in me long ago, and it is just my restless nerves that won't *let* it die.

I have been a few times to the Opera which I love, but I found I slept worse after Wagner's Operas : they awaken in one every mood and passion of human nature ; and running through them is the perpetual longing which is as old as the world and which must have troubled the heart of Eve herself —and of every woman since.

I went one day (taking Fräulein Freyer and Smith) to see Princess " Mossy " of Hesse, the Emperor's sister ; the children played upstairs with her youngest twins who are delightful, such good-looking boys. She and I sat downstairs and talked of everything—Germany, the Emperor, England. She said, just as the Duchess of Sparta does : " England is the one place where I feel free and happy, where I can stretch out my arms and *breathe*, where people are kind ; of course I love Germany which is my own country, but it is all so small, so *klein* here ; everyone is suspicious of everyone else." The same old story ; and I do feel the truth of it—God knows I do. It is extraordinary that the Emperor's sisters are all alike in this ; and I believe in his secret heart the Emperor feels the same thing too though he fights against it ; in his heart he is English but, politically, he is against us. I think he simply plays up to what he thinks are the feelings of his people. " His people," with their horrible, vile, vulgar illustrated papers, ridiculing their Emperor, ought to make him, poor man, disgusted with the German race. After all, he has his country's best interests at heart, he works for her good ; he means well. It is he who has enlarged her navy and army and extended her commercial power. What has he done *against* his own people that they should dare to make comic pictures of him and ridicule him—their reigning Sovereign ? I have said, and have written here years ago, that he will die of men the most disappointed, broken in spirit and health—that is, if he doesn't lose his sanity and kill himself. . . .

I wrote a long letter to the Crown Princess and told her just what I thought, and sent her forty pounds from Hans and myself for the widows at Hamm.[1]

December 20, 1908. Fürstenstein.

Arrived here yesterday from Pless. The shoot there was very cheery and successful ; everyone seemed happy and in the evenings we danced and played cards. Betka and Roman Potocki came, Christa Salm and her husband, Pia Fürstenberg and her husband. She is getting a baby and looks so young and pretty. . . . The Lichnowskys came—she is a nice woman with individuality : I like her, she sees the fun in things, and she is extremely good-looking. X. is a bore and so is his wife ; she never opens her mouth and he somehow does not look a gentleman ; always *forcing* himself on one, trying to be nice, and when talking to Christa always says *Sie* although even Hans makes a point of saying " Imperial Highness " occasionally.

I could have shot a buffalo. We all sat in little built-up stands to which we climbed up by ladders, and which were hidden in Christmas-tree bushes. Three buffaloes came close and would have passed between me and Prince Lichnowsky if I hadn't sneezed and coughed and frightened them back on purpose as I did not feel I wanted to shoot one. But I did want brother George to get one and Potocki another, and they didn't ; but Count Tiele, Betka and Salm got one each. If I

---

[1] On Nov. 11, 1908, in the Radbod coalmine at Hamm, Westphalia, an explosion of firedamp caused loss of 360 lives.

had known that Betka was going to shoot I certainly wouldn't have frightened them back. Hans said he wouldn't have minded if I had shot one. Anyway, I shot three wild boar which I think are far more amusing to shoot with a rifle while they move. Then we had some pheasant shoots too, occasionally some quite nice high birds ; the weather was mild though deep snow was on the ground.

I arranged two big Christmas trees in the hotel at Pless, four hundred children at one and a lot of old men and women and more children at the other. The next evening I gave a Christmas tree for the indoor and outdoor servants at the Castle. One night the *Oberforstmeister* and another *Ober*-something man, called Lasch (both of whom wear a lovely green and gold coat) dined with us, and after dinner I gave each of them a reproduction of the little statuette of Vater in his shooting dress with dog and gun. In fact I thought of everyone and tried my best. . . .

Brother George and Jennie leave the day after to-morrow, I am sorry to say : they promised to spend Christmas at Blenheim, and they thought they must, as " Sonny " Marlborough is a bit low, Jennie says. Consuelo's relations, they say, are preventing them from going back to each other ; and now his mother and his sister go to Consuelo's London house and help her at her charity meetings and so on. Jennie says : " Of course they do as she has all the money," but this is nonsense. " Sonny's " father and Randolph, Jennie's first husband, were brothers.

CHAPTER ELEVEN

1909

February 20, 1909. Villa la Vigie, Monte Carlo.

I HAVE got this villa quite nice at last with some gay chintz (which I love), mauve and pink wistaria, and instead of the horrible glaring chandeliers in the middle of the ceiling I have hired some shaded lamps. I had to send for a kitchen-maid and an " odd boy " from Fürstenstein ; I could hire no decent help here. They both arrived this morning delighted ! This villa is right on the sea, built high up on a rock, a beautiful situation, one side grass and olive trees and in front cedar trees down to the sea. I hope Hans will like it, but I should have much preferred Cannes, as I don't like Monte Carlo.

Little Patsy comes to-morrow, I *am* so pleased, she is a marvel of comfort when one is lonely.

Dear Hans went over for the funeral of Shelagh's little son [1] to Chester ; I would have gone but there was only two hours' notice and the children arrived that evening, and I couldn't have left them alone in Berlin, as Hansel had not been at all well. Hans is in Berlin now to see his dentist ; he comes here soon I hope !

March 7, 1909. Villa la Vigie, Monte Carlo.

The weather has been awful, snowstorms, rain and thunder ; we tried to sail this afternoon on Shelagh's little seven-metre boat ; (I want to hire one to race against her) but there was so much wind we had to put back ; the sea was dreadful, enormous waves breaking on the shore and a swell on, just as if a great

---

[1] Earl Grosvenor, only son of the Duke of Westminster and Constance, Duchess of Westminster, d. suddenly, Feb. 13, 1909, aged four.

AUGUSTA CAROLINA GRAND DUCHESS OF MECKLENBURG
STRELITZ (PRINCESS OF GREAT BRITAIN AND IRELAND)
(AUNT OF H.M. QUEEN MARY).
Her Last Portrait.

tidal wave was running over us. We went up—and then right down.

We walked afterwards to the stone pier (not very high)—really a sort of breakwater—in Cannes. A lot of children were playing about and as we turned to go home they shouted that a child had fallen in and was drowned. We ran back, but there was nothing to be done—only a cap floating about. Shelagh turned and said : " Bend Or will go in, for God's sake stop him ; Dany, don't let him," and as I climbed down to the rocks to hold him I heard him groan. He would have gone in, in a moment, if there had been the slightest chance, but the waves were enormous and there was nothing to be seen. . . .

March 20, 1909. Villa la Vigie, Monte Carlo.

Shelagh and little Ursula stayed here during the three days Bend Or was in London. Ursula and Hansel had great fun together, bless them ; then Shelagh took Hansel back with her for three days to Cannes, and told him they would have great fun and ride donkeys up to the hills, on which Hansel burst into tears and said : " But Mummilie, if I go and ride a donkey with Ursula I shan't be able to hunt next winter in Pardubitz." He meant that he would miss two days' lessons with his tutor and perhaps not be able to pass his examination which, if he does, Hans has promised he may have one or two days in Pardubitz. I told him one day would make no difference, and that he was to go and take care of Aunty Shelagh and Ursula and be a man ; so he left with a very proud though sad little face, and came back happy and full of news :

" Oh, Mummilie, do you know what we did. We stole Kate's boots and hid them in the garden—and built an Indian house in the garden with some old sacks which a groom gave us—we had a booby-trap over each door with a wet sponge—and then Ursula had a lovely idea—she put a basin of water under the tea-table close to Esther's place so that she should put her foot into it—but she didn't—she felt it—and it upset—so she had her feet in an enormous puddle."

Bend Or has come back looking much better. His motor-boat arrives to-day and he starts racing : I wish he wouldn't.

May 4, 1909. In the train to Pless.

A saloon carriage with Nanny and Baby ; we left Monte Carlo yesterday in the morning and get to Pless to-morrow morning at ten o'clock.

Hans left with Hansel on the 21st to be at home for his birthday. I heard from him the other day, quite a serious letter, saying : " I had seventy people to lunch and a reception afterwards of two hundred ; the list of honours was small. Nasse and Kindorff (the Comptrollers) and Bertlemann got the *Jagd* uniform ; Freytag was given the title of *Geheim Sekretär*, and Fritz got the *Hubertus* buttons " ! ! ! ! I laugh when I think of it. Bertlemann, his old tutor, and Vater's secretary, the ugliest man I ever saw, in the green hunt uniform ! And Fritz (as an honour) having the Hunt Buttons ! ! ! And Hans doing it all quite seriously—this touch of grandiose snobbishness is the funniest trait in his character ; however, his heart is sometimes gold—so there is nothing to say—I only hope he will be pleased to see me to-morrow, and not be " all Prince," but natural, homely and bright, as he was most of the time on the Riviera ! I hear Pless is lovely in the spring, and am quite excited to get there, though I am sorry in a way not to be going to dear Fürstenstein and my gardens ; but I shall make " my own garden " in Pless too.

I went to Cannes for three days after Hans left and stayed with Sophy and the Grand Duke Michael. He and his brother George were furious because I talked and sat with their other brother, the Grand Duke Alexander,[1] whom I like much the best. He is clever and intelligent and has ideals. . . .

I have a lot of letters to write. I hope Frau von Pohl [2] will be a success, she and her husband come to Pless in a few days. I shall dictate letters to her and embroider at the same time, so shall kill two birds with one stone. I want to put the Egyptian tent on the terrace which gets the sun, so that I can sit out even if it is not very warm, but I am afraid Hans will say it is not " princely " to put a tent up so near the front door where the beautiful man stands with a cocked hat and a high silver stick !

It is nice, diary, to be liked, isn't it ? I only hope that little Shelagh will grasp at the little rays of sun in her life and be thankful for every bright day. Of course she must miss terribly the bright face of her little boy. . . .

---

[1] B. 1866, m. 1894, Grand Duchess Xenie, a sister of the late Czar.
[2] My new *Hofdame* or lady-in-waiting ; her husband was something —I have forgotten what—on the House Marshal's Staff.—D. OF P.

May 11, 1909. Pless.

Just in from a " shooting expedition " on which I went
alone. I know I ought to take it all very seriously but I can't.
Hans had business to do all the afternoon with the *Regierungsrat* [1] (it sounds like a new species of motor wheel) and little
Hansel is in bed to-day with a cold ; so that is why I started
alone at three *in a victoria* for a shoot ! Relitz—Hans's
Leibjäger—on the box with a gun and a rifle, a small seat for
me to sit on, and a long stick with cloth on the top to hold
on to while one shoots ; this is a help I do not laugh at it.
I sat with my feet in a footsack as it is very cold, and when I
got out of the park and on to the old road to Promnitz which
I know so well, I took out the *Daily Mail* and read it, and found
several things of interest ; the marriage of Fitch Colloredo
to an American ; I was talking about him to Hans only yesterday. Then it gave a list of the possible future Prime Ministers
if Bülow resigns, saying : " Prince Lichnowsky of Polish
extraction and sympathies, another dark horse." I laughed,
as he hates the Poles and works with the Government against
them !

Well, I finished my paper just as we got into the great
silent woods ; we drove on a bit and then Bäcker, a very nice
man and, like Relitz, beautiful in the green *Jagd* uniform (but
without the new gloves that Relitz wore), led us into a selected
spot and I got out. Bäcker walked first, I followed and Relitz
walked behind with the two guns over one shoulder, the folding
seat in his hand and, over the other arm, the *fur footsack*
and my coat. I kept wondering if I was supposed to shoot
trussed up in a fur footsack.

We got into a boggy but beautiful meadow and walked to a
little green house into which Bäcker shut me together with
Relitz, footsack, guns, seat and sticks ! He said " *Weidmann-
sheil !* " [2] and went. I tried to stand up, but couldn't, as the
roof of boughs and branches of fir was too low and, when I
moved, a shower of little brown prickles fell into my hat and
down my neck. By degrees we got settled and presently we
saw five blackcock. I missed the first shot aṣ I couldn't
really stand up comfortably ; I had to lean down to get
the gun into one of the " port-holes " and keep my legs so
far apart that I had no control. The happy cock and hen

---

[1] Lit. A Counsellor of the Government.
[2] Lit. Sportsman's health—or luck.

flew away ; in about a quarter of an hour four more appeared and I shot *one*.

We then decided to go home. Bäcker delighted because I promised him to get up at two o'clock one morning when the weather is warmer and go out shooting ; it is more amusing in the early morning as the cocks all fight each other.

We came in sight of the house in about half an hour and just in front of the doors Relitz put up his silver trumpet. I said : " Oh, don't blow, we haven't shot anything," but he answered : " *Ach, Durchlaucht, eins genug,*" and he *blew*. We passed through the porch in my victoria ; the beautiful man in the cocked hat and stick drew himself up and looked as if made of stone (I call him Guy Fawkes to Nanny), out rushed the servants—Hannussek and two footmen. Hannussek, as he helped me out, smiled—like me he saw the absurdity of the whole proceedings. Anyway it set me off, and I ran in laughing ; I have laughed ever since and I can't help it. So much fuss over the poor little blackcock lying forlornly under Relitz's feet on the box of a victoria !

To-night we are eleven to dinner, the *Regierungsrat*, our General Director, Balka, Bertlemann, Lasch, besides Herr and Frau von Pohl, who really are most agreeable and want to do their best. They only came two days ago.

July 18, 1909. Cassiobury, near Watford.

We came here yesterday for the three days from Saturday to Monday ; it is thirty-five minutes by motor from London ; and belongs to Adèle and her husband, Lord Essex. He was married before. . . . It is a lovely old Charles I. place with tapestry and nice old furniture. I have just come in from playing croquet with the King, Alice Keppel and Sir Charles Cust ; [1] he is a sailor-man and used to be, and is still, I believe, in-waiting on the Prince of Wales. The King is staying close by with Lord and Lady Clarendon.[2]

Oh, diary, how nice it is to feel well at *last*. I do not in all my life remember to have felt as well as I have done this last

---

[1] Third Bt., G.C.V.O., C.M.G., etc., Equerry to King George V. since 1892. Joined H.M.S. *Britannia* in 1877, retired from the Navy in 1918.

[2] The 5th Earl of Clarendon (1846–1914), Lord-in-Waiting to Queen Victoria 1895–1900 ; Lord Chamberlain 1900–5 ; m. as his 2nd wife in 1908, Emmie, widow of Major the Honble. Edward Bourke.

month—and in Pless, too, this spring I rode, and now my body is able to do what I want and work with my mind, which it has never done lately. Now I must dress for dinner. I lost again last night at poker ; and the other night at Claridge's with the Torbys, before the Portlands' Ball, I lost sixty-four pounds.

July 24, 1909. *Saturday*. Cliveden.

We came here to-day and will stay till Monday. I brought Poppets with me, as he so seldom sees people and they wired that they would be delighted to have him. " *They* " are Mr. and Mrs. Waldorf Astor.[1] He is old Astor's son who bought this heavenly place from the old Duke of Westminster—which makes Bend Or sad. The house is full of people, amongst these being Sophy Torby, and the Grand Duke Michael, and Winston Churchill, who sat next to me at dinner. I am awfully sorry for him, he is like a race horse wanting to start at once—even on the wrong race track ; he has so much impetuousness that he cannot hold himself back, and he is too clever and has too much personal magnetism. . . . At present his politics are all personal, the politics of an American advertiser ; his mother, George's wife, *is* American. He is not happy if he is not always before the public, and he may some day be Prime Minister—and why not, he has energy and brains. . . .

I forgot to say that during Ascot week the children came to Windsor [2] from London ; they spoke to the King and Queen and stood on the grass and saw the State procession leave, and afterwards had lunch, and a nice old butler showed them all over the Castle. Smith and the tutor were delighted.

August 8, 1909. Cowes.

We came here on Saturday, that is yesterday week. I left Newlands on Friday, where we had had a nice little cosy time and bathed every day.

On Friday night I joined the Angleseys' yacht at Southampton, slept on board and saw the Naval Review by the King

---

[1] Now Viscount and Viscountess Astor.

[2] The Prince and Princess of Pless were the guests of King Edward VII. and Queen Alexandra for Ascot Week, 1909. See *Daisy Princess of Pless*, pp. 186, 187.

on Saturday morning.   All the ships are in readiness to escort
the Czar [1] and Czarina here on Tuesday.

. . . Twice I went racing on the *Meteor*, the Emperor's
boat, but she didn't do much, and once on the *Hispania*, the
fifteen-metre boat of the King of Spain ; he lent her to me for
the week.   I wrote to him while I was on board, and this
morning he wires : " Want to answer but you give me no
address," so I wired it back to him.   He is so young and plucky,
in some ways such a child, and yet so clever and determined. . . .

Hans left yesterday with Evelyn FitzGerald for Badminton [2]
and took little Hansel with him.

I dined at Egypt House last night, Consuelo Manchester
has got it as usual.   I sat next to Jimmy Alba.   In the afternoon I sailed on the *Britannia* with the King.   Mrs. Keppel
and Emily Yznaga, Consuelo Manchester's sister, were on
board.   There was no wind so a *cruiser* towed us round the
Island ; it was delicious.   Nice Seymour Fortescue was also
aboard, Harry Stonor [3] and Sir Frederick Ponsonby,[4] all in-
Waiting.

I had wanted to leave Cowes that evening but on board
the *Britannia* the King said : " The Queen wants you to dine
to-morrow night."   I said : " Oh, Sir, all my clothes are
packed and I did so want to get to Newlands as I leave there
on Thursday."   He was very nice—he *is* so nice always—and
said : " Think it over and do just what you like."   I thought
only half a second.   I couldn't refuse to say good-bye to the
Queen after all their great kindness to us—and I living abroad
too—so a launch was sent off to stop my maid and just reached
her in time.

This morning Isabelle Metternich, Lady Evelyn Guinness
and her husband lunched with me ; afterwards I went to say
good-bye to the Empress Eugènie ; then I had a comfy chair
put in the launch, took a book, which I did not read, and
leant back in my chair and steamed alone round the coast
on a sea like a lake.   Then I came home and bathed ; as
I was about to go out I overheard " Daisy " and in the

---

[1] The Czar and Czarina paid a visit on their yacht to King Edward
VII. at Cowes, August 2–5.

[2] The Gloucestershire residence of the Duke of Beaufort.

[3] Honble Sir Harry Stonor, Groom-in-Waiting to King George V.
since 1882.

[4] Rt. Hon. Sir Frederick Ponsonby, Treasurer to H.M. since 1920 ;
m. 1899, Ria, d. of Colonel Hegan Kennard.

hall stood Blanchie Lennox [1] and her girl, Derek Keppel [2] (so happy with his nice wife) and Seymour Fortescue. I tried to hide but they saw me and said I looked very nice and ought always to dress like that! When they left I went into the water just across the road. While I was in the sea who should pass but the Queen and Princess Victoria, Soveral, and Lady Helen Stanley (in-Waiting). The motor stopped, as they had seen me, and Seymour Fortescue was sent back with the Queen's camera to photograph me ; then I walked in the water until I was opposite the car and Princess Victoria photographed me through the open window !

Now I must dress ; I hope to get away early to-night after dinner and arrive at Newlands about midnight with the help of Sir Thomas Lipton's launch and that of his motor which is to meet me on the other side. A dear, nice man, it is most kind of him. Jimmy Alba comes too.

September 2, 1909. Pless.

Yesterday in the train Patsy said to me : " Isn't it nice to feel that we needn't wonder whether Hans will be in a good temper ? He always is now." I said : " Yes, isn't it nice."

But—the darling was cross at everything, furious that I wanted to go now, or at the end of the month, to get Fürstenstein ready for the party, but I only smiled and was patient, and said later : " Wait, Patsy, and you'll see."

In the evening everything was happy again ; I was just kind and kissed him and told him I only wanted to do what was best, but that I would do what he liked and begged him to talk things over happily and quietly. And at last he did. But I must own in the old days when I felt seedy and ill and after a long journey and longing for a happy and kind look from my own husband—I should have walked off alone and felt miserable.

September 13, 1909. Promnitz.

Since I wrote Hans and I have been to Fürstenstein for four days. I had many things to arrange and have put right before my party in October ; it is a good thing I *did* go, as

---

[1] Grand-daughter of last Viscount Maynard, m. 1886, Lord Algernon Gordon-Lennox (1847–1921) (br. of 7th Duke of Richmond) ; their only child Ivy m. 1915, the Marquess of Titchfield.

[2] Sir Derek, brother of 8th Earl of Albemarle, m. 1898, Bridget, d. of 5th Lord Suffield.

otherwise we should have had no water in the house. Hans also had the pleasure of finding out that the little house in the *Fohlen Busch* which he did up and which was estimated to cost six thousand marks has cost twenty-five thousand, and also that the new tiles on the new stables are a hideous colour. . . . They are now building a Louis Quatorze Palace in Salzbrunn instead of a nice country hotel as in the Semmering or in Switzerland. The few days in Fürstenstein were divine. Herr von Pohl came from Pless to help, and little Patsy was with me. Strangely enough, I had horrible headaches all the time I was in Fürstenstein, much as I love the place ; but it is too high and the air too dry for me.[1] *Ma Fantaisie* was lovely, lots of flowers and so peaceful and looks so nice with the chintz curtains and all my china about. I tried to bathe but did not stay in the water one moment, I was almost paralysed with cold. I *never* felt anything like it.

October 15, 1909. Fürstenstein.

A long time has passed since I last wrote and now I am alone in my boudoir with my darling Poppets and we have had a cosy little dinner upstairs. . . .

Hans and Hansel, old Prince Christian of Schleswig-Holstein and Otto Salm,[2] were upset out of the motor-car in Promnitz before we left ; the spring broke, but no serious harm was done, thank God ; except that Salm got a cut in his throat and old Prince Christian got shaken and in consequence had to stay five days in Pless.

I arrived from Berlin yesterday where I went for two nights to show my English guests the capital. They were Lord and Lady Herbert,[3] her cousin Muriel Beckett, Evelyn FitzGerald [4] and Bertie Wilson. We motored there in a powerful Mercèdes car ; it was a glorious autumn day, a thin clear yellow light over everything ; one felt as if one were drinking pale sunshine. To be rested we went to bed soon after dinner and the next day I took them to the Emperor's Berlin Palace in the morning, and in the afternoon to Potsdam where we saw

---

[1] I have just had to give up my Munich home for a similar reason. Munich is 1,705 feet up, the second highest capital in Europe.— D. OF P.

[2] Otto, 3rd Prince of Salm-Horstmar, b. 1867, m. 1803, Countess Rose Solms-Baruth, my husband's niece.—D. OF P

[3] Now Earl and Countess of Pembroke.

[4] Captain the Honble Evelyn FitzGerald, C.B.

the Stadt Schloss and Sans Souci. I love that little palace and the autumn garden was looking really delicious with a mass of pink dahlias. We drove to Charlottenburg and saw the Royal Mausoleum by the light of a lantern, which made it very mysterious, white and peaceful ; but it is most beautiful seen by the pale yellow light from the stained-glass windows falling in the daytime on the white recumbent figures like a golden blessing. . . .

It was to have been a party for Shelagh (such as we used to have in the old days) to cheer her up and change her thoughts a little, poor darling. She writes to me from Eaton saying how she misses the little footsteps, and thinks she hears them all the time.

The party included the Duke and Duchess of Arenberg,[1] Prince and Princess Otto Windischgrätz (she is an Austrian Archduchess, daughter of the unfortunate Crown Prince Rudolph), the Sierstorpffs, Victoria Sackville-West [2] and her daughter,[3] one or two Silesians from here, Marquess de Gontaut-Biron, and a lot of Hungarians—Count Sigray, Count Esterhazy, Marquess Pallavicini, Count Thun and Hohenstein, and others. They brought a Hungarian band with them and we danced. Then I led them a follow-my-leader on horseback and hid from them in the woods ; we had a glorious ride but two days afterwards I was ill all day, and now I *know* it is the riding, and this makes me *so* sad and disappointed.

October 16, 1909. Fürstenstein.

A heavenly day ; I walked this morning with Poppets and showed him the new house of Aleck the head groom ; it is in the new stable yard which I have not seen till now. Of course S. has used all the most expensive materials, oak for the stairs and banisters, big marble tiles for the floor of kitchen and larder ; the last new sort of kitchen range, a bathroom with nickel plate instead of brass, and the nicest stoves and fireplaces that he could find. It is absurd the amount of money that old brute spends on a house for a head servant.

---

[1] Engelbert, 9th Duke of Arenberg, m. 1897, Princess Hedwig de Ligne of Hainault, whose mother was a Gontaut-Biron.

[2] M. 1890, her cousin Lionel Sackville-West (1867–1928) ; in 1908 he succeeded as 3rd Baron. The 2nd Lord Sackville was a son of the 5th Earl de la Warr.

[3] The distinguished author, V. Sackville-West (the Honble Mrs. Harold Nicolson).

The Crown Princess wrote and wired twice, saying she was sorry not to be able to see me at Potsdam, as she is not allowed to do too much—after her third baby. Her letters are always charming and her telegrams are like letters! I hope they will both come to Pless in December.

Hans came back from Parubitz, rather inclined to give himself airs, particularly so this evening when I asked him if they didn't expect him to make a speech to-morrow at the laying of the foundation-stone of the statue to be put up in memory of the Saxons and Austrians who fell at Hohenfriedberg.[1] He said the word " expect " could not be used to him! But I made him play the piano after dinner and forget the importance he attaches to being a Prince, and left him far happier and more natural; then came upstairs to write this stupid diary.

November 14, 1909. Fürstenstein.

I have had two surprises, diary, yesterday, one a happy one and one *not*. By order of Hans all letters are now sorted in the secretariat, placed in large yellow sealed envelopes and sent direct to his sitting-room and mine, and to the rooms of our guests. One therefore opens them without looking at the addresses. Amongst the others was one looking like a bill and marked " Urgent." I opened it without thinking and found that it was for Hans. . . .

Perhaps the day had been too full of sunshine and autumn tints and the boys' smiles. . . . *If* ever I were to find out he *really* wanted to *marry* someone else I would separate from him *at once* and never believe in anything again. Oh, well, I sigh, and the clocks tick in my boudoir, and the wind seems to sigh outside, little bits of wood are falling in the grate; soon all things fall—and a last sigh finishes this little life. . . .

My precious boys have had their supper as usual with me and I read to them that never-ending book, *The Swiss Family Robinson*. . . .

My happy surprise is—that little Shelagh writes she is almost certain she is getting a baby—and oh, I *am* so glad, please God it will be a boy; she adds: " Anyway, little Dany, I am coming to Fürstenstein for Christmas, it is the only thing I look forward to, in this year—or the next." And surely,

---

[1] Frederick the Great defeated the Austrians and Saxons here on June 4, 1745.

surely, she has much to look forward to now, and must lift
her eyes to Heaven and thank God that our prayer (that of the
boys' and mine) is to be granted. I hope everything will go
all right with her, and that she will take care.

The Emperor wired in answer to my letter saying that he
thanked me very much for my letter and was looking forward
so much to visiting Pless again, and that he was so sorry to
hear that dear old Monty Guest [1] had died suddenly at
Sandringham.

November 15, 1909. Fürstenstein.

A nasty day ; tried on some tea-gowns this morning and
saw Freytag, Frau von Pohl and Frau Keindorff, wife of the
(excitable) General Director, and so did a lot of business :
Keindorff asks me to see him to-morrow but I shall not receive
him. . . .

Hans wants to have Berkisch from Budapest, and the Hungarian band ; for *two* nights they calmly ask four thousand
marks. I wired Hans that it would be throwing money away,
so I hope he will not insist on it.

December 2, 1909. Pless.

They have all arrived ! After having finished dinner at
nine-thirty, I had to sit down again in the dining-room at
ten and watch several of them who had just arrived eating
supper. But I hurried them off to bed by half-past eleven ;
I really could not make conversation any longer, besides, I am
a bit irritable to-night and I want to laugh ; but if you could
only see some of them—for instance, if S. S. and H. P. stand
in front of each other and talk, their tummies touch ; they
came out like this ()(), in front and behind. W. arrived in
a *large* checked suit and his wife in a very short skirt and
enormous hat ; they looked like two people on the stage at the
Wintergarten. Frau von Pohl noticed this too and laughed.
Then Frau von B., whom I have never seen before, looks like
a little maid ; when she arrived with a bag in her hand
and stood by the Duchess of Holstein (as her husband
was fumbling for something in the motor), Frau von Pohl
and I both thought, good gracious, the Duchess has brought
another maid *with* her as well as the one who arrived before.
Count D. is very nice and looks like an opera tenor singer ;

---

[1] (1839–1909) Brother of 1st Lord Wimborne.

he is rather like Jean de Reszke with whom I once had singing lessons in Paris. Then M. S. told me how often the
Emperor had spoken with her, and how many Grand Dukes
she had seen lately. Countess P., whom I don't really know,
seems dowdy and nice. Altogether it's a funny party, but I
shall *not* see them to-morrow till at least twelve o'clock. Now
good-night.

December 14, 1909. Eaton Hall, Cheshire.

It seems a long time since I last wrote but in reality it isn't.
The party at Pless which I had to entertain alone, went off
well, at least everyone seemed most happy. We played bridge
in the evenings and although I never play, I pretended I could,
as it was impossible to talk for the whole evening. I sang
one evening.

In the early morning of the 5th I left for Vienna, arrived
there at three, had tea with Yetta Larisch and went to the new
operetta *Graf von Luxemburg* with May and Hansie Larisch and
Georg Pallavicini. The next morning I left for Paris ; I
stayed in bed at the hotel there and had a good rest until Hans
arrived at three from Berlin. We stayed three nights in Paris ;
twice we dined by ourselves and went to a theatre, and once
with Anthony Drexel, who had asked Madame Letelier and
Mrs. Gallet and the Duke of Sparta—who has just been expelled
from Greece. He is nice to meet. I have asked them to
Fürstenstein in January, as I think it would be a good thing
to cheer him up a little in Germany. I left Hans in Paris.

December 30, 1909. Fürstenstein.

Such a lot has passed and I have not had a moment to
write ; three nights at dear little Newlands, when the weather
was divine ; we shot duck on the 18th and on Sunday the 19th
went to Church and I took the Sacrament with my beloved
father. The duck would not fly very well and the pheasants
were disturbed by foxes, but we shot a few and were, anyway,
all quite happy until the Sunday when Sophy and the Grand
Duke Michael who, with Zia, were staying with us, got the
news of the death of his father, the old Grand Duke Michael
. . . so they all three left for Cannes where he died. Brother
George came for Sunday night and, with Lord Elcho,
Jimmy Alba and Prince Bibesco, made up the party. I had
a day's shopping in London and then we came here, Shelagh
and little Ursula and I. Hans joined us *somewhere*, in the

PRINCESS VICTORIA OF PRUSSIA, 1916.
Frau von Zoubkoff.

morning about nine, coming straight from Paris. The saloon met us at Flushing and brought us here direct ; we arrived on the 22nd ; on the 23rd we had three Christmas trees ; then on the 24th of course Christmas trees for ourselves and the servants, and on the 27th a big one in Waldenburg : the old people there were so pleased to see me. Pat and Grace FitzPatrick are here, Minnie and Guy and their children, and Jimmy Alba. Isabelle Metternich was supposed to be coming but now can't.

The weather has been just like spring, green grass and sunshine, it seemed as if the snow would never come, and now all of a sudden it is *here*—since last night, but not hard enough to toboggan. We played hare-and-hounds this afternoon, I and Hansel, Dick and Ursula were hares, and all the others hounds. We had no coloured paper so had to mark our route by making crosses on the snow ; this idea was Hans's and answered very well. Poor old boy, he has to go to Berlin to-morrow for the New Year to greet the Emperor. I shall always say it is too much to be expected—not to be with his family on New Year's eve.

The Crown Prince and Crown Princess come on the 7th till the 9th for one day's shooting ; they would not stay longer and I cannot have a big party with dancing, as she is in mourning for her grandfather, the father of the Grand Duke Michael.

CHAPTER TWELVE

1910

January 3, 1910. Fürstenstein.

A NEW year, diary, a new year. What will it bring and what shall I do, what ought I to do, what does God wish of me, I wonder. . . .

All England is busy now over the " socialist budget," but, to my mind, the deteriorating character of the nation, its laziness and inferior education, are far more serious questions. . . . Certainly the great gateway of world commerce, of which England once held the key, is now being stormed by other nations. . . . England will find soon that old systems and methods are useless. . . . It makes me sad. . . . Violet Mar gave me, as " the latest thing from England," a little watch with radium hands to put by my bed. It only cost thirty-five shillings, so I wanted to get several to give to the servants here for Christmas. I went to Vickery in London who said : " Very sorry, Madam, we are sold out, but hope to have some more in, in ten days' time," so I took with delight the last one they had.

Marie my maid happened to go to the jeweller here in Freiburg where she found half-a-dozen exactly the same at twenty-five shillings each, and in nice little red, stand-up leather cases ! Frau von Pohl says all the officers of the regiment in Schweidnitz have had them since two years. So much for English enterprise and " the latest thing from England." Germany is always ahead.

January 17, 1910. Fürstenstein.

I really have not felt inclined to write lately because, as soon as my parties left, I have wished only to sit down and do nothing. How I *wish* we had not so many pheasants !

The Crown Prince and Princess were delighted [1] . . . I
have had two telegrams from her—here is one :

" So amusing meeting your husband en grand gala after dear
unconventional Fürstenstein. Should be so pleased if you
both came dinner 21st to meet Missy Rumania ; love
" CECILE."

I forgot to say that Hans went to Berlin on the 15th for the
Ordens Fest and came back last night.

February 19, 1910.   Hotel Esplanade, Berlin.

In a very comfortable bed, having had a nice little dinner
with Hans ; oysters, sole au vin blanc and cold beef with
salad and hot potatoes, and then a macedoine de fruits. I
talked to him very seriously about money matters ; the enormous size of his *Verwaltung* (far too large a staff) and considering the *value* of his property, the ridiculously small income
we gain from it. . . . He was very nice ; we talked quite
quietly and he was not angry.

Yesterday and to-day Frau von Pohl and I have spent hours
with Count Pückler about the Silesian lace industry ; he is
Landrat. I want to start a central depôt in Hirschberg where
all lace will be brought in, and bought by me—or rather by a
committee, and then sold to the shops ; the workers, therefore,
making as much profit as possible ; and later, to put by money
to make a pension fund for the workers. I have had this lace
depôt in my head for some time, and I never give in—unless
a matter seems quite hopeless—I will therefore fight on and
gain the day.

Now I am here for a fortnight and, except when I *have* to
be *en evidence*, I shall rest as much as possible. I have been
entertaining so long—ever since September in Promnitz—
that my brain is tired and I long to be alone somewhere.

Later, at Antibes I shall have a delicious quiet time with
the children. Hans says he can't come at all as he would be
bored—it is too far from Monte—but I hope he will change
his mind. . . .

May 1, 1910.   In the train on my way back to Germany.

Fürstenstein first for two days, to see about the new Salzbrunn hotel, and then to Pless to join Hans and Hansel ; they

---

[1] See *Daisy Princess of Pless*, pp. 104–6.

both left about a fortnight ago to be in Pless for Hans's birthday. I heard from Freytag to-day who writes : " The weather is not so warm now as it was in March, and on His Highness's birthday it snowed all day." So thank goodness I was not there.

We stayed this year at an hotel at Cap Ferrat ; as I have started a little baby—which makes me so happy that I can think of nothing else—I thought an hotel with only a few servants and no extra bills to pay, but just to live " en pension " would be cheaper and more restful than a villa. But it cost a hundred pounds a week, and one had no comfort or homeliness ; so I tried Cimiez where Shelagh has a villa and there I felt quite different in two days. I found a charming little villa which had never been let before and for which I paid, from April 1st to May 5th, a hundred and twenty pounds ; I sent for Hannussek and the little German cook (Hedwig's husband), and the old woman from the Café Kirche and her daughter Louise helped in the house.

Patsy and Poppets stayed with me, the latter only ten days, simply marvellous for his seventy-six years. Patsy stayed most of the time with Shelagh and Bend Or. Shelagh gets her baby in July, and I mine the end of September. I had settled in my mind to have it in Potsdam, or near there to be close to the good Berlin doctor, but somehow I *feel* they are not so good as English doctors, or else the nurses are not ; as poor little Christa had her second boy a week ago and her husband wrote and said it was a *fine strong* baby, but died after the confinement, which I cannot understand. So I must find out the reason for this before settling anything.

Lexel is so well, and laughing in the next compartment ; we have the dog *Wolff* with us ; he killed one rabbit of Lexel's and eight belonging to the gardener's wife at the villa, and now we have another one which we show him and tell him he is not to touch ; this morning, he let the rabbit run all round him and on to his back—he and Baby and the rabbit were on the sofa together.

From a wordly point of view—which, since I have known it so long, I would not in the least mind never seeing again—everything is going well ; Hans has been made President of the Union Club, and of the big new Race Course in Berlin, which the Emperor wants made like Ascot !

. . . I have had such a nice letter from Henri Bernstein, the famous dramatist, whom I met at Monte Carlo. He is ugly to look at but so clever and amusing.[1] Here is a translation of his letter :

CAP D'AIL, *April* 30, 1910.

DEAR PRINCESS,—

It is necessary that I tell you again of my dazzling gratitude. Your presence brought splendour to our little improvised party. To look at you is a joy and a feast, but you are not content with being magnificent, you reveal yourself as so perfectly, so divinely, " charming," that one could not have dared to hope for so much charm united to so much beauty. And then, you sing to make beat more fiercely, if it were possible, hearts that are already much disturbed. You sing with a voice at once spontaneous, profound and generous, and the Season could not finish in a more moving way.

Madame, I thank you for having come. A deep memory is with me which shall not be extinguished.

At your feet, beautiful Princess, I lay my admiration and my charmed respect.

HENRI BERNSTEIN.

May 23, 1910. Hotel Bristol, Vienna.

I left Pless at four and arrived here at half-past nine ; Hans who got here from Berlin to-day met me at the station, which was very nice of him. All the motors have gone on strike so he came in a fiacre ; it was a lovely moonlight night.

I have come here for three days to see the Exhibition and must now go to sleep. I feel pretty well and the little baby moves ! Oh, how mysterious all things are, graves are open for the dead at the same moment little babies are born into the world. Life is *within* one, and yet perhaps I shall never know how that life will develop ; will it be for good or ill, happiness or sorrow. The years fly and oh, I feel so old, so old, thirty-seven next birthday and Hans will be fifty-six next April and tells me I must be back for his birthday as it will be a great feast day ! Fancy wishing to celebrate one's fifty-sixth birthday ! There are so few years before us both and he undertakes so much ; I wonder if this Fürstenstein building is *right* : I can't think so. It is too vast and costly.

Pless, I now find, can be delicious in the spring, so peaceful and green.

---

[1] See *Daisy Princess of Pless*, p. 104.

June 3, 1910. Fürstenstein.

Little Hansel was in great disgrace yesterday and was locked in his room all the afternoon as he ran away *again* without rhyme or reason, just to have some fun and feel a hero, I suppose ; but what made me furious was that he took Lexel as well as Allen with him ; they were out walking in the hot sun from half-past ten till half-past one when Herr von Selle and Count Heinrich Herberstein found them right far in the woods over the railway line hiding in a ditch, as they had seen the searchers coming. Baby was black and had started out without any stockings on, only sandals on his feet, and carrying a big spear. Hansel had a gun, and his Sunday clothes on as he was dressed for church.

They have taken up the spring flowers on the Schloss Platz, so the spring has passed—my spring too—I feel it, but I hate to believe it. I felt so young a little while ago, and now I feel that I am suffering from an incurable disease which is " middle age." I think it was the cuckoo that told me in the *Schwarzengraben*—I think that in future I shall always hate that bird, as its call, like its own life, is a lie ; it cannot even lay its eggs in its own nest, or hatch them or bring up and feed its own young.. I wonder why I ever chose such a bird as a friend for my soul, as, six years ago, I loved it. Even this spring on the Riviera—but then I had not heard the swan sing— before she died !

June 18, 1910. Fürstenstein.

It is eleven and we have all just come back from Salzbrunn where we dined in the new hotel, excellent dinner and Hans and everyone delighted with the furnishing and decorations, over which I must say I did take trouble. Afterwards we sat on the Promenade and listened to the band, but the crowd was awful and followed us about, so we came home. Hans is looking so well and cheery and young for his age ; I wrote to Laszlo about painting his portrait ; if I do not force him to have it done and get the painter here to do it nothing will ever happen.

The clergyman from Waldenburg came yesterday and we settled about a milk depôt there, where the poor women will be able to buy properly sterilized milk for their babies ; the milk will be prepared for children of all ages. I played all the afternoon alone with the children in the hay ; it was delightful.

July 2, 1910. Fürstenstein.

Count Vico Voss and Cousin Adelaide Taylour left on the
29th. On the 30th Gottfried Hohenlohe and the Archduchess
Henriette,[1] his wife, came, and Count Trautmannsdorff, the
one with whom I bought the race-horse ; he has lost a lot of
money, so I ask him no questions as out of the big race prize
two years ago of forty thousand kronen, I got four hundred
pounds—and never any more—and now the mare is sold and
I do not even know for how much.

To-day Deym and his Portuguese wife arrive ; it is years
since I have seen him, and years since his dear old father was
Ambassador in London.[2] The wife is said to be pretty.

A Major von Something and his wife come too ; it is dreadful how people think it is the right thing for them to propose
to pay us a visit, when I do not even know what they look like.
After lunch, though, I shall say " I always rest," and Hans
can show them about ; it is almost true, as anyway I cannot
stand about, it makes me too tired now.

Shelagh's little baby [3] was born on my birthday ; it is, alas,
a little girl ! Patsy writes she has only seen it once in the
dark, and Bend Or not at all. . . . God help them both.

August 22, 1910. Newlands, Newlands, Newlands !

 . . . where all the peace in the world that I ever knew is
gathered together. I came here from London just a month
and four days ago ; it has passed like ten days. . . .

I have taken a villa at Lichterfelde [4] which the Pohls found
for me, but unfurnished ; everything has to be brought in
vans from Fürstenstein. I hope it won't be too awful ;
anyway, it is new.

Cousin Adelaide comes here on the 24th for a day or two ;
she has just been to Paris with Shelagh. I wonder what
clothes Shelagh bought ; she was looking lovely after the birth
of her little girl ; it is rather a nice moment for the woman
after she is up, to feel she looks herself again and can be interested in the fashions, after nine months of old clothes being

---

[1] On June 3, 1908, Prince Gottfried Hohenlohe-Schillingsfürst
m. the d. of Archduke Frederick of Austria, younger sister of Princess
Emmanuel Salm.

[2] Count Franz de Paula von Deym (1838–1903), German Ambassador in London, 1888–1903.

[3] Lady Mary Grosvenor.

[4] A suburb of Berlin.

" let out." I am godmother to the little girl, God bless her ;
I hope she will have as happy a life as it is possible to have in
this world.

Shelagh was in very good spirits here, but of course they
felt very much the disappointment that it was not a boy. I
saw Bend Or only once ; he was always playing polo at Roe-
hampton and then later at Ostend and I was in London only
three days, just for the christening ; the other five or six days
I stayed with Sophy and the Grand Duke Michael ; they
have rented Kenwood, a really lovely Adam house, for a long
term ; the decorations and furniture are all in keeping and
it has Angelica Kauffmann ceilings. Zia is " out " now—a
charming girl.

I went to see Queen Alexandra at Buckingham Palace while
I was in London. I spoke to dear old Charlotte Knollys [1] for
one moment. The Queen looked lovely in her widow's weeds,[2]
but the interview was difficult. . . . She was very sad and
said : " My life is finished, there is nothing left for me in the
future, all my things to move, and no garden like there is here."
I said that a garden could be made at Marlborough House,
though not so big of course. . . . (So far as I remember,
Queen Alexandra never had a garden there, and the present
Queen and King have done a great deal to improve the whole
house ; it looks quite different from what it did in the old
days.) Then the darling—because she *is* a darling anyway—
said : . . . " George and Mary are on the *Osborne* now, and
she hates the sea, but George writes they are having excellent
weather." . . .

Hans says that in Russia the Dowager Empress takes precedence of the ruling Empress.

Before I left—it was very very dear of her—she gave me a little
silver match-box with the *Britannia* flag on it, that the King
always used at Cowes. I remember it well and can see it in
his hand now ! The Queen also gave me a little gold pencil
with a shamrock in emeralds that always lay on the King's
table and which I gave him for luck when he was racing five
years ago. I was also given a photograph of them both, hand-
in-hand, in their coronation robes—the last they ever had
taken together. Poor little Queen, she loved being on the
Throne ; and I understand her loneliness.

---

[1] Sister of 1st Viscount Knollys ; was a Bedchamber Woman to
Queen Alexandra 1870–1925.
[2] King Edward VII. died May 6, 1910.

Hans said when he was here : " I suppose next year we shall have to bring horses over for the Coronation in June." But I said no, I saw no necessity, that in fact it would *hurt* me to see another Coronation in England ; at least I feel this way now. It seems only the other day that King Edward was crowned—after his fearful operation ; how well he walked up the aisle, and how well he looked. I can scarcely believe it. I really *loved* him as a man, and friend ; he was an example of what sympathy can mean not only to individuals but to the whole world, God bless him. I hope his spirit is resting in peace and happiness, and that he has work of interest to do. How short life is, and how soon youth passes ; joys are dimmed with sorrow ; then clouds break to let in a gleam of sunshine, only to be darkened again by the clouds of the world's tears. . . . I felt lonely sitting here at my window looking over the lake across to the sea, watching some ships come home, and some ships go out. . . .

August 24, 1910. Newlands.

The Flower Show was very homely and amusing ; all the same old faces : Miles the butcher ; Hollywell, one of the old garden men from here, who always takes first prize for the " cottage exhibits " ; the little girls, grown into big girls, doing all sorts of things on bicycles ; the doctor, a practical man, the clergyman, a new one—and Poppets made a speech. Patsy, Lexel and I gave the prizes. . . . Now all the men and girls are dancing on the lawn. It is almost dark . . . the voices and laughter carry upwards to my open window, with just the light of a match now and then shining for a second, against a face in the darkness ; so do we sometimes, accidentally striking a match, get a gleam into someone's heart or soul—by look, or voice, a tiny act maybe, or a line in a letter—and then all is darkness and forgetfulness again.

. . . Why is it, when rich mad youth leaves one, that a day comes, somehow suddenly, when one notices the autumn leaves drop . . . one feels the summer passing, but one does not look forward to " next spring " as in the old days. . . . *One is afraid*. Well, I hope there are many happy spirits under my window to-night ; it is too dark to see them, but they seem to be playing games now, as I hear a shriek of laughter. Both my maids were out and came in smiling to give me by the open window my dinner, which I hurried over, so that they could smile again downstairs ; they are both so young. The band has come back and is playing French valses—if I felt in the mood I could laugh, they are so out of tune. . . .

. . . better than this, arrange your hair, look in the hand-glass at the best part of your face, and laugh ; be pleased *with* yourself, and thank God you are not lame. Even dance in front of your glass, while the band still plays, dance, dance, till you get tired and forget, far too tired to dream. This is only to dispel a mood which I hope comes rarely . . . look to your children, and at the sky and clouds, the waves of the sea, the flowers in the fields, and your spirit will be calmed, while your soul will cry : " God forgive me, do not forsake me for my many moments of weakness, give me strength to fight on, and help others, and forget myself and life's disappointments, imaginary or real ! "

August 27, 1910. Newlands.

Did I tell you that the other day on our way to the sea in my Bath-chair, alone with little Lexel, we passed Milford Church and as the doors were open he and I went in ; there was no service, but the new clergyman has what some people would call " advanced " ideas : I say, Thank God for this. We were alone and it was still and peaceful and we went to the old pew where I have sat before I married ; we prayed to God together ; my little boy in his blue suit and looking up at me with his bright blue eyes asked, " What shall I say, Mummilie ? " and I told him, and because he saw me praying quietly, he knelt and did the same. Afterwards I asked, " Did you tell God everything, darling ? " and he said, " Yes, Mummilie," and I shall always wonder how that little baby mind worded his prayer. I felt happy when I came out. Surely God heard us.

This afternoon we went over to Rhinefield, the Munroes' place in the Forest, and took Cousin Adelaide who arrived yesterday.

We had tea there, the house with its cut yew and box hedges look like an old place of the sixteenth century, but they built it themselves twenty years ago. Mr. Munroe[1] made the organ play, it is glorious ; it played Wagner, and I had to explain to little Lexel all the time who sat with me on the sofa, what it all meant. I had to tell him about Siegfried making his sword,

---

[1] Lieut.-Commander L. E. Walker Munro (d. 1920), m. 1887, Mabel Zoe, d. of late T. Walker, of Eastwood Hall, Notts.

VILLA PLESS, MUNICH.
Winter, 1927.

then the walk in the forest, the dawn and all the birds singing, and the leaves and flowers opening their petals ; and then the dragon coming out of his den and being killed by Siegfried ; of course that was the part which interested him the most, and he kept on asking, " Is the dragon dead yet, is there fire coming out of his mouth and nose ? " He understands, notices, and takes an interest in everything.

Hans is at Ostend, and comes here on Tuesday, and leaves soon for Germany.

I tried some new songs to-day ; the words of one I copy here ; they are so full of life and hope !

J'ai pleuré en rêve—j'ai rêvé que tu étais morte :
Je m'éveillai—et les larmes coulèrent de mes joues.
J'ai pleuré en rêve—j'ai rêvé que tu me quittais :
Je m'éveillai—et je pleurai amèrement longtemps après.

J'ai pleuré en rêve—j'ai rêvé—que tu m'aimais encore
Je m'éveillai—je m'éveillai—et le torrent de mes larmes coule
toujours—toujours.

September 9, 1910. Newlands : in bed : my last night here.

To-morrow we start viâ Plymouth to Hamburg and from there to my villa at Lichterfelde : Hans wires to say that the villa is charming—I am so glad. To-day I feel better but the last three days have been awful, and I dreaded the journey, had scarcely any sleep all these nights and felt so weak throughout the day-time. The little baby ought to come in about a fortnight ; I feel frightened this time I don't know why. I hope all will go well. I am longing to see little Hansel, but as he has not seen me for so long, I feel now (considering his age) it is wiser to wait and not let him see me till after the little baby is born. Hans left here a few days ago but meets me in Berlin, stays for two nights and then goes back to Promnitz.

I sang to Poppets to-night. I love the piano and the room here, so full of old remembrances. We are going to enlarge it by taking in the passage behind, which is now wasted ; we shall build four rooms for the children over the drawing-room ; this will greatly improve the house. Hans has taken it on lease for twenty-one years, which is very nice of him.

The last days have been lovely, the most lovely lights and shadows, and the sea blue and glistening in the distance. Jimmy Alba and Isabel Metternich motored over yesterday from Farnborough Hill where they are staying with the Empress Eugénie ; she is the sister of Jimmy's grandmother.

Well, little Newlands, God bless you, till next summer. May only happy days be passed beneath your roof and happy thoughts abide in your dear surroundings.

September 11, 1910. In the North Sea, on the *Kaiserin Augusta Victoria.*

Little Patsy is with me, and thank God the baby has not arrived yet, *umberufen*, but I had a horrid night. I had a bed in the train yesterday, and a special tender to take us on board this ship so that I had not to wait about in the crowd, which would have been too tiring. We brought tea and shrimps with us and had them on the tender, and Lexel ran about and was very happy.

Yesterday in one of the papers I saw a picture of the Brothers Wright flying machine at the German Manœuvres. I think they are Americans ; anyway, they offered the design and invention two years ago to the English War Office who refused, with the result that they went at once to Germany who accepted ! oh, the blind folly of England. She grumbles at every other country that keeps a look-out for means to advance, and hates Germany for its speed and thoroughness in everything. The English sit at home throwing pebbles in a sea which they say they rule, not realizing that tides turn, sandbanks move, and storms arise big enough to tear down rocks and cliffs.

The Emperor's last speech has aroused great criticism in the German Socialist press ; he spoke of his " Divine Right " and said that he would not be ruled by a class, but would always go his own way, and follow the path of duty. I know quite well what he meant. . . . Although he has taken no oath at a coronation, as our English kings do, pledging themselves to be constitutional monarchs, yet he *is* a constitutional monarch all the same, and the country is ruled not by him personally, but by the Government. Well, he has the worst luck of any man living in that he is always in the glare of the world's footlights. He is too much of an artist to come forward on the stage and merely recite the words he has been told to speak ; he must add the expression of his own personal views, must dramatize himself. And, therefore, in a country with a free press, he is always open to criticism. He is a religious man and all he really intends when he speaks of " Divine Right " is to impress on the public the thought that we are all by divine right bound, as the catechism says, to fulfil our duty in that state of life to which it has pleased God to call us.

October 14, 1910. Grosslichterfelde, Berlin.

How time flies and what a lot has happened ; as little Lexel says, he didn't see the stork but the Polish nursery maid did, the very day the baby was born ! A little boy, a third little son born on September 23rd, which delighted Hans. I was a little disappointed as I would have liked a girl, to dress prettily and let her hair grow long.

The specialist, for whose sake I came here, Professor B., was in Petersburg at the critical moment, and I had never even seen either the doctor in whose charge he left me, or the nurse ; so I felt very upset and lonely. Little Patsy was marvellous and gave me drops of chloroform, but the whole thing was awful and done in a way that *could* not be done in London ; a husband would not allow it. In fact, thank God Hans was not there, and no doctor should treat a woman like that—like a piece of suffering flesh, neither male, or female, and no help or care or thought shown. I suppose, at my age, this is the last baby I shall have ; but I would have another with pleasure, only—in England !

Hans arrived the next morning, it was a great delight to me ; he stayed a week and came here again the day before yesterday morning from Pardubitz, and left last night. He is hunting there, and little Hansel too ; he says the " going " is very deep. They both come here together on the eighteenth for the christening. The Crown Princess is to be a godmother.

I have been out driving the last two days, it was delicious to get air at last and see space but I did not put my feet down till the last day of the three weeks. The weather is lovely to-day ; the wind was fresh, but I was able to sit out and we had lunch as usual in the garden, which consists of pear and apple trees (with sour fruit), lots of wasps and not one flower.

The little baby I love of course, and think he is a darling and I cuddle him, but he isn't beautiful ; his eyes are small and he has a large nose (Patsy says he is going to have Granny's —a Headfort nose !). But he has dear little ears and lots of mousey-coloured hair, which doesn't seem as if it were coming off. This villa is quite comfortable inside, and my bedroom has a nice balcony on to which I am carried on a sofa.

CHAPTER THIRTEEN

1911-1914

1911

January 1, 1911. Villa La Pastourelle, Cimiez.

OH God, what will this New Year bring ? I am lying in the window of my bedroom having been very very ill . . . septic poisoning after the birth of my baby. All the time I said—and I knew it—that something had been left in my inside. German doctors are scientists, operators, but not doctors in the true sense of the word ; those that attended me took no care about the nurses they sent or about anything else. I was dying, and they dared not (at least Professor B. dare not) own up to the truth until G. from London was sent for, which cost my dear old Hans a thousand pounds. I never heard of such a fee and am furious. God so nearly called me and oh, I felt the tender spirits near me and a sense of pride at being called before I was old, and I loved the peace that surrounded me ; I longed to go. Then I felt little Patsy near me, close close to me, and I thought of my boys ; I wondered if it would be right to resist recovering. I prayed for what was best, and they dropped me down again from the great wide paths of peace and truth, dropped me back into this sad, struggling and cruel little world, always divided against itself ; and now I am again one of the strugglers.

Soon I hope to put my feet to the ground and try to walk ; if only I could move my body, then perhaps my spirit would not feel so chained.

I want to motor to a spot I know near Cap Ferrat that calls and calls me. From there I can see in the distance the flashes of the lighthouse when the sun goes down in the sea. It was there three years ago we used to take cushions and a tea-basket with us, and made nests in the rocks, and we laughed and sang in the sun.

268

Last night, New Year's eve, Hans would have stayed with me to see the New Year in, but I did not think I should be able to remain awake so long (I was in bed yesterday) so he went to Nice. . . . I watched the clock and just at twelve I called the nurse (she has been with me since the baby was born twelve weeks ago) and she opened the window and made the room dark, and the light from the lighthouse flashed towards me ; and I saw three stars ; then I sat up in bed and prayed, and I read a little in my prayer-book and wrote two letters !

Indeed I beg God to make this year brighter and happier for me than the old year. Oh, please God do. I have been so ill. Little Shelagh comes here this week for a few days ; she writes she has a bad cold, so it will do her good. I shall be here, I suppose, till the end of April ; what a long time it seems and oh, how old I feel, and Hans and they all say I look twenty ; it is absurd of course.

. . . The Emperor came to the nursing home at Lichter-felde (near Berlin) and stayed one and a half hours. (I made Lulu come to pour out tea, as I couldn't.) He brought me a bunch of dark red roses which he told me were his favourite flowers and said I looked like " a coloured supplement in an English Christmas journal."

Oh, how tired I am of it all, how I long for a small cottage, peace and quietness ; sometimes I *can't* think any more, I become desperate ; and now as long as I do continue to live, I shall always know that longing I had for the peace eternal ! The light at Cap Ferrat is lit, I will stop now, try and grow old— and live only for duty.

January 15, 1911. Villa La Pastourelle, Cimiez.

In bed till lunch as my feet and legs were very swollen yesterday. I try to walk with two sticks ; and I have begun to sing again ; at any rate the rest has helped my voice. Little Shelagh has been here for a week, and roused me up, so gentle and tender ; she did me a lot of good. . . .

My beloved boys ! Please God I shall be a help to them in their lives and they will love and trust their mother. I shall be old soon and their wives will probably find me a terrible bore. Hans says I look seventeen and Patsy says she never saw me look better, that I look twenty-five, so that is nice anyway, and it is true that when I look at myself in the glass

I do *not* look at all old. If I had had a daughter living I wonder what she would have been like. It would have been terrible to have to " take her out " in Berlin and other places. The idea, when one faces the *truth* of it, is rather horrible. To launch a young girl and dress her up for the sake of showing her to men, in the hope of finding a suitable husband ; she has first of all to be looked over and round, and inspected like a mannequin at the dressmakers ; and even then what does the poor little girl know of men : what did I know ? Nothing ; and what does a woman ever really know ?

The sea is rough and strong and blue and glorious to-day. I wish I were well enough to walk along the sea at Cap Martin, but it will be months I expect before I can do this. I wonder if I shall ever be really well ; as I write now, all my body aches inside ; it is the after-effects of the inflammation I suppose. Well, God's will be done in all things.

January 31, 1911. La Pastourelle, Cimiez.

Hans came back yesterday, very full of Berlin and all the Emperor had said and done, including much about the Polish Question ; they reported him to the Emperor for talking Polish in Pless, but the Emperor was very nice about it, although Hans had to see two Ministers on the subject. . . .

Fritz comes on the 3rd which will be very nice ; he may wear funny clothes and look funny in a way and different from other men, but his soul is also different ; he feels so much for others, believes so truly in God and another world that he may now help me ; for I feel lonely to a degree unmentionable. . . . I have to learn to come to life again ; and the learning is pain, pain to me. The same road, the same road of life, but somehow . . . the lighthouse with its light which helped me so greatly, is fading from me ; I shall be left alone. I may wreck myself upon one of the miserable rocks of life, of which up to now I have been able to keep clear, because the lighthouse took care of me.

I think perhaps in the future I shall take very seriously to singing, but it is difficult, as in the winter in Berlin where there is a very good master, I always get irritation of the throat ; I even have it here after driving, and I get hoarse. But, as on the stage when acting, I always forget myself when I sing ; then I can be myself absolutely and alone ; and no one ever guesses what the words and the music bring to me !

February 3, 1911. La Pastourelle, Cimiez.

Yesterday was Hansel's birthday and the day before was little Lexel's, so we had tea and cake and candles and fireworks in the evening in my room ; the smell was not very nice afterwards. . . . I sang. . . .

Hans is very well and cheery, very busy with his racing business and talks of breeding horses and racing himself " some day." Good Heavens ; " some day "—and life is so short and " some day " the lid is closed over us. I feel as if I had lived a century and the world could teach me no more ! The baby is a little darling, poor little thing.

In watching the Cap Ferrat lighthouse the other day I thought of these lines which I copy here :

> There is a port beyond the farthest sea
> Whose placid harbour evermore invites ;
> Across its waters gleam no signal lights
> And solemn silence reigns unceasingly :
> And for that distant port the great, the small,
> Aye—all of us alike shall steer in vain
> When, tossed upon life's ever restless main,
> We drink from memory's bitter cup of gall ;
> But—ever faring on—and on—and on—
> By day and night, in futile quest, we see
> Before us—where the other ships have gone—
> The trackless vastness of eternity.
> Where is the port ? Ah, we can only guess—
> The silent city of—Forgetfulness.

And that city can never be in this world ; for people may talk of forgetting, but one forgets nothing that has been in our short little lives, unless, perhaps, in old age when our memories grow dim. . . .

February 5, 1911. La Pastourelle, Cimiez.

Just in from a lovely drive to Monte Boron with Hans, all in the sun ; from the old fortress there is a most gorgeous view. On our way we met Hansel and Lexel and Joseph (the valet) and Braga (my maid) all going after poor dear old *Wolff* who never comes home now (except when he is hungry), because he has found the dearest little brown lady friend. When he was tied up because he had killed a cat she used to come and sit and stare at him. But now he is free and has run away with her into the mountains—" the call of the wild " (the title of that book which I love). It is a call we all have felt at times but may not answer. To be free, quite quite free, to run wild for a bit ! What a lot of good it would do us all. Anyway I stopped them going after *Wolff* with bamboo poles to try and catch him, and looked myself with longing eyes up to the sunny side of the hill and longed to be following in *Wolff's* footsteps.

. . . Hans also talked about what a terrible mistake it is that everyone in Berlin now should be allowed to drive with a *Leibjäger* ; it ought to be only the privilege of the Princes. If Fritz Solms does not tell the Emperor, Hans will do so. How serious, how serious this all is, isn't it ? A big crown has been put on the back of our car, as the other chauffeur says it is a help to them to know who we are ; also the police are more polite ! Do you think I am mad, diary, grumbling against all the " good " things I have, which would perfectly content most women ? But then I *feel* things too much, I hear little sounds in life, and echoing voices—in a way I cannot explain—call to me from another world. . . .

February 8, 1911.   Villa La Pastourelle, Cimiez.

Little Shelagh and Ursula arrived this morning, it *was* a glad surprise, both looking lovely, Shelagh with her glorious eyes and lovely figure and little Ursula with her pale red hair full of different colours, her large questioning blue eyes and the dearest little mouth and face ; she is nine—ten in May, I think.

March 11, 1911.

I am at little Shelagh's bungalow near Roquebrunne ; it belongs to Sir William Ingram [1] from whom she has hired it.

She has just left for Genoa and Milan ; I was to have gone too, but they all thought it would be too much for me and I agreed.

Last night we went to *Ivan the Terrible* at Monte Carlo in the Prince of Monaco's box. Between the acts they all went to the Rooms, but I did not feel inclined to go near a gambling table ; indeed it seems to make me miserable. So I sat in a corner of the box on a sofa and closed my eyes. One learns in quietness to feel the power of music. Music can express

---

[1] (1847-1924) 1st Bt. ; proprietor of *Illustrated London News*.

for us the whole of life. In Wagner's operas, when the first motif occurs again and again, it carries one back—and then gloriously forward. But one should live for, and always come back to, one's moments of vision . . . love, goodness, truth, generosity, kindness, a lofty pride in thought and deed. . . . If only I could find someone to *share* such thoughts with me. . . .

I am here in this little garden ; a cock is crowing and there is a little bird that chirps all the time, and there are carts on the lower road with bells round the horses' necks.

Hansel and Lexel are coming to lunch and to play with Ursula. I shall stay quietly here all day.

Robin and Juliet Duff and Cyril Foley will amuse themselves I hope. Lord Falconer [1] comes to-day, to make up a four for golf.

April 14, 1911. Little Newlands, little Newlands.

I motored down here to-day from London. It is Good Friday. Jennie and I left Nice together on Tuesday and travelled straight through to London.

Last night we went to the play with Maitland Kersey, Lord Falconer and Sir Thomas Shaughnessy,[2] a rich and very interesting man from Canada. . . . I did not write all these weeks ; there was not anything particular to say.

June 23, 1911. Grosvenor House, London.

For many months I have not written, but everything seemed to weigh so heavily on my spirits that I could not bother to take paper and pen and write. I had a very happy spring in England ; I went to dear old Ruthin which was looking lovely, and Patsy and I went to Llanarmon which was looking more wildly beautiful than ever, and fished for trout in a lovely river.

I got back to Pless the first days of May and celebrated Hans's birthday on the 23rd—a month late. Then we went to Fürstenstein ; little Patsy came to us there for ten days and we cut down trees at the *Daisysee* which was a great success in showing up some fine old beech and birch. Count Vico Voss came for a day or two and we fished there together.

Then we were suddenly asked to London for the Coronation ;

---

[1] Now Earl of Kintore ; s. 1930.
[2] 1st Lord Shaughnessy (1853–1923) of Montreal ; for many years President of the Canadian Pacific Railway.

it was very nice of the King [1] as, except a heap of Royalties,
foreigners are never invited. . . .

1912

February 12, 1912. On the Nile.

We are on our way down from Khartoum. . . . I haven't
written since last year. . . .

I ought to tell what happened after the Coronation in
London in June. I spent only ten days there, but it made
my phlebitis so bad that I simply could not dance, or stand,
so Shelagh and I went in her yacht to Holland, which was
lovely and so interesting. Cousin Adelaide Taylour came with
us, and Jimmy Alba, Lord Falconer and Lord Alexander
Thynne,[2] all very nice but not " stupidly amusing." We had
motors to meet us whenever we stopped with the yacht. I
loved Bruges, the old houses and the canal, and all the beautiful
Memling pictures ; of course the Franz Hals and the Rem-
brandts in Holland surpass those to be seen anywhere. I
hope I shall go to Holland again.

After that I went to Newlands to the precious boys ; Baby
was not well enough to travel, he has a weak heart which
I hope and pray he may grow out of. I stayed at Newlands and bathed, and went to Cowes on Shelagh's yacht.
Hans went to Marienbad and has looked years younger ever
since.

After Cowes I went to Bagnolles in Normandy to do a cure
for phlebitis ; it did me a lot of good and I suppose I shall
have to go there again this year ; it is a nuisance.

After Bagnolles I went to Promnitz and then we all went to
Fürstenstein. In October Shelagh came out to us as did lots of
friends from England.

The second week in November the Emperor came to Pless ;
we acted, and he was delighted, and so was Hans, as it really
went off beautifully.

. . . After the Emperor left we had another party which
was of course much more free ; we all acted again and Gottfried
Hohenlohe acted, while the Archduchess his wife prompted out

---

[1] Of Their Majesties King George V. and Queen Mary.
[2] S. of 4th Marquess of Bath.

loud ; he is just the same as ever, nicer if anything. I love him, and she is a dear little thing, quite as nice as Christa her sister, though I know her less.

After Christmas I went to Shelagh to Eaton ; Poppets was there, poor little Patsy was ill with influenza in London ; Granny, who is eighty-five, was there, so picturesque with her mittens and her white tulle ruffle round her neck. Grace and Pat FitzPatrick, Brother George and Jennie, and one or two others, who were not relations, were there ; I acted in a very good piece with George.

But all the winter, and when the Emperor was at Pless, I felt my legs growing weaker and weaker and thought I was getting creeping paralysis ; I saw three doctors in London, with the result that I had to go to bed for a month and have electricity and Swedish massage.

Hans came on the dahabeeah as far as Luxor ; he joined us half-way by train and stayed two days with us ; but temples and desert sand do not appeal to him so he is going back to Berlin for a little and then to the Riviera ; the two big boys are at St. Moritz, the baby is at Fürstenstein.

This is my second visit to Egypt ; Fritz has been here often ; Shelagh never. And she is disappointed and expected to find more foliage and " oases in the desert " ! Yet I knew what to expect and I love to feel the silent mystery of it all and the spirit of its magnificent buried history—buried, but to which the Temples, with their little traces of colouring still surviving, have not yet ceased, however faintly, to hint. I love the placid dignity, or call it laziness, of the camels' movements, the patient donkey's cheerful trot, the little children with their naughty eyes enlivening serious brown faces with mischief. And then the grown-up Arabs—I love to search in the faces of some of them for the look of hidden evil, though possibly I might discover a twinkle of amusement at my expense if they could guess my intention ! The women (owing perhaps to their Mohammedan religion) are the only things that " leave me cold " in Egypt, but they lead a life of total insignificance. Some day this will change I expect, though slowly. Cairo has changed quickly and is no longer a town of old palace gardens, with homely one-horse carriages ; those old palace gardens are hotels now, and everywhere there are motors. It is simply horrid—a second-rate Paris. I will not describe the different places we go to ; little Hansel and Lexel will some day see them all for themselves, and Baby too

I hope, grown by then to be a strong man. As for myself, I shall never forget them even if I do not read of them again in this poor scribbly diary.

I have got tired painting, but I dash on too much colour (one has to be quick as the colouring of the scene changes so rapidly), so my paintings look like those that one is shown and is told are done by a spiritualistic medium, almost alarming ! But the warmth, the sun and the rest—all this is doing me good.

Lord Kitchener, and one of his staff, Lord Colum Crichton-Stuart,[1] were more than kind to us at Cairo. Lord Kitchener wired Sir Francis Wingate [2] about our stay in Khartoum and, when we got there, Slatin Pasha [3] was charming to us and Shelagh and I both fell in love with him. Although so high up in the British Army he is really an Austrian. . . .

September 15, 1912. La Napoule.

My spring was a disappointment ; I had been so much looking forward to peace and green grass with the boys, but Pless was always full of officers, or people who came to look at the river as an excuse ; we had enormous luncheons which began at two and lasted till half-past three and then one had to talk for an hour afterwards. In Fürstenstein it was the same, *Oberpräsidents* or *Unterpräsidents*, and *Excellencies* without end ; in both places they said they had business to do (knowing that one would not like to refuse them) ; and even Pohl at last said it was going too far ; they all naturally like to eat good dinners and shoot roebuck. . . .

At the end of June I went to England to help Jennie with her Shakespeare Tournament at Earl's Court. . . .

In London I went to a Court Ball and danced the quadrille with the King ; somehow it did not seem like the old Court functions ; it seemed only lately that I had danced with King Edward and I could hardly realize that his son has succeeded him. King George, as always, was most kind and courteous

---

[1] S. of 3rd Marquess of Bute, b. 1886, Diplomatic Service 1910–20.

[2] General Sir Reginald Wingate, b. 1861, Sirdar Egyptian Army and Governor-General of Sudan 1899–1916, High Commissioner for Egypt 1917–19.

[3] Baron Rudolf Slatin Pasha, b. 1857, m. 1914, Baroness Alice von Ramberg (d. 1921) ; served under General Gordon ; British Inspector-General of the Sudan 1900–14.

MY MOTHER
Mrs. Cornwallis-West.

and came right across the room to the Diplomat's Bench, to wait till I came down to him. . . .

It is strange how the feelings of nations are changing ; a socialist feeling is growing in us all without our knowing it or wishing it—even in China, the last country in the world where one would have expected it.

1913

July 31, 1913.

The other day at dinner at the Ritz—my last night in London —suddenly up came Prince Eitel Fritz and Prince August Wilhelm, and treated me like a sort of relation ; they were travelling incognito, and their wives were with them. I expect all the people, or a good many, would have turned to look, if they had known they were the Emperor's sons.

At the races in Berlin I was in the Royal Box with the King and Queen of England.[1] Late in the afternoon they and the Crown Princess left to go and have tea with the Emperor's sisters. The Crown Princess had been much annoyed because her husband was away from us most of the time. When the Royal Visitors had gone I said to him :

" I think, Sir, you ought to have remained in the Pavilion all the afternoon and talked to the King and Queen of England ! "

" Perhaps ; but I was bored, and wanted to be somewhere else playing golf."

" But, Sir, it was a great mistake. One must keep to etiquette on formal occasions. You, especially, should set a good example and not forget that one day you will be in the highest position of all. Then you will have to be correct."

" If I ever am, I will do away with all this bother and etiquette."

I was very angry because I felt that he had slighted the British Sovereigns and the Crown Princess, so I retorted :

" The day you do away with all ceremony and etiquette you will lose your Crown."

He saw how angry I was and tried to mollify me by saying laughingly :

---

[1] State visit by their Majesties King George V. and Queen Mary.

" Well, then, we will put the Crown on you, and make you look after us all."

" I should be too old then to wear a Crown. But, anyhow, I should always try to do what is tactful and right. *Noblesse oblige.* Besides, Sir, I should make you wash your face ! " One side of his face was dirty—I can't think why !

. . . *I* did not ask anyone to come and stay with me, but they heard I was very ill and so all asked to come, one all the way from Budapest, one from Marienbad, and one from Venice. It is nice to have friends, and they know somehow that I wish well to them ; it is extraordinary how people love me ; I truly cannot understand. I do not tell you this in conceit, you old diary, but simply because it is one of the puzzles of my life. I wonder if they will all drop me and forget when I get old and ugly.

November 19, 1913. Fürstenstein.

Touching this book is like raising the blind of a closed window and looking out again on an old landscape.[1]

In London I bought clothes and went to see Shelagh's new house in Warwickshire in a good hunting country. Minnie and Guy were there and Pat and Grace ; just the same, and all four happy. . . .

Shelagh and I went to the King and Queen's party at St. James's Palace for Prince Arthur of Connaught's marriage with the young Duchess of Fife.

The boys are well and Herr von Selle (who has now been appointed their Governor) has been given the Order of the Knights of Malta and put on the uniform this morning at half-past seven when Prince August Wilhelm arrived ; it is red with a black hat and white feather ! Well, he and von Pohl now rule the whole place and I feel rather like " the wife of the Prince who has to be endured " !

Zanda Münster, the Salms, Maurice Esterhazy and Alphy Clary have been here for one night. At this moment we have eight men in the house. Seebach, who does the Opera in Dresden, very nice ; Prince Eitel Friedrich, the Emperor's second son, and several generals ; they stay three more days. They are all quite nice and homely, and to-day we had a picnic and cooked bacon and eggs in the sand.

---

[1] From August to November the authoress had been in South America with her brother ; the visit is described in her former book.

December 13, 1913. Pless.

What terrible dates to write—two thirteens. To-day, driving home from the Miners' Hospital, I felt a longing to pass quietly away (if possible without too much pain) into another world ; for this life of clothes and gold and jewels and servants makes me ill and tired ; it is all so useless and does good to no one.

The Emperor and Empress have been to Primkenau ; the Empress stayed on after the Emperor left ; I sang and told her stories about old women and babies which delighted her, and to Hans's pleasure, she kissed me when she left. . . .

Well, diary, good-night ; perhaps 1914 will be better and happier ; any good spirits that are near me as I write please save and help me.

1914

February 8, 1914. Villa Liberia, Mandelieu, France.

I arrived here two days ago from England. Brazil did me so much good, the warmth of it (I adore the heat) and the freedom ; the loneliness in a strange country was even a rest to me as I fear nothing.

I left Berlin for England on the 3rd of January, spending the New Year with Hans, as he said it was his duty to be with the Emperor. We saw the New Year in with Baron and Baroness Reischach, very old friends ; with the Emperor he is now—Master of Everything . . . instead of merely Master of the Horse ; I could not bear to be at Fürstenstein and wait alone for the bell in the great tower to ring in 1914. . . . While I was at Newlands Shelagh and I acted for charity in Lymington and Bournemouth. Shelagh, and Grace FitzPatrick, are here now, also Muriel Beckett and her husband, and the Ingestres [1] (she is Bee Pembroke's sister) ; Jimmy Alba arrives on Wednesday. The two darling boys are at the little villa at La Napoule which they had last year ; they have had whooping-cough and we may not go near them. I was terrified when I heard of it in London, and took the villa quickly by tele-

---

[1] (1882–1915) He was heir to his father, 20th Earl of Shrewsbury ; m. 1904, Lady Winifred, d. of late Lord Alexander Paget ; their son is now 21st Earl of Shrewsbury. Lady Winifred m. 1917, R. E. Pennoyer of the U.S. Diplomatic Service.

gram, realizing that the danger to Baby would be past all helping, as his heart and lungs could not have stood it. Thank God, now, he is very well, and looks so bright and happy; and the two darling boys look well too. I went at once to the doctor and, as they are quite fit in themselves, asked if they could ride, and he said of course; so the two days I have been here they have done so, cantering past my windows on the grass; to-morrow we shall all ride out together as I have three ponies which were given me in Buenos Aires, and have hired two grooms from Cannes. Now I just feel inclined to sit in the sun and rest and talk and think of no one for once.

Hans is very busy with the Emperor; I hope he will come here soon. Fritz came for Christmas to Fürstenstein which pleased me enormously. He is the one great help I have.

June 15, 1914. Fürstenstein.

I see the last date was February 8th and now we have June 15th. It is not laziness that kept me from writing, it was the peace and quiet in France after being so ill again. I simply rested there, I mean I walked very little as my legs are still so weak; saw lots of friends and rode ponies in the hills, and the darling boys used to ride with me. They were not allowed into the villa because Baby might have caught the whooping-cough. We went fishing too, once at night, with a flare on the boat and we speared the fish as they do around there. Shelagh and Poppets came, the Salms, Aggie Barclay, Cousin Adelaide Taylour, Isabelle Metternich, Oscar Herren and lots of others.

I am now building my little house in the woods; I did not start before as I did not think that Hans would perhaps care about spending the money, although he gave it to me over two and a half years ago. I want to go and live there while this house is being altered. We went yesterday and had tea in my garden in the *Schwarzengraben*, but that name is too sad indeed for such a charming place, so I call it " the Garden of Kama," which means in Hindustani—remembrance, love, hope, strength, peace, in fact all that a heart could desire. Hansel likes it too, and the garden is full of flowers and Baby simply loves it, and so do all their boy friends as they catch craw-fish there. Baby is such a darling with such pink cheeks and so full of life and impertinence. I will not, and cannot, believe all the doctors when they say a child like that cannot live. That he has a weakness of the heart I know ; but I quite believe he will grow strong, and lead a useful, peaceful life. He need not find happiness only in riding races and climbing Mont Blanc. At any rate we have many happy times together.

When I am looking at dear old Fürstenstein now, I try not to remember the past and all the nice times, days of sunshine and days of rain, which have passed there, beginning with a very young girl's life up to the present moment. But it has always been a battle, won sometimes in a garden, and sometimes on very rough ground. . . .

Now I am going for a ride with Count Maurice Esterhazy to the *Daisysee*, and Baby and Lexel are going to meet us there with the tutor. Hansel has gone out to shoot a roebuck. It is a lovely day. . . .

I leave here on the 25th and go to England.[1] I arrive there on Friday and stay from Saturday till Monday with Gordon Leith's [2] mother on the river Thames ; she is a dear old lady ; then I shall see Shelagh and others. I have not been in London in the summer now for two years, and it will really make me feel quite shy to go into a ballroom. There is a Court Ball on the 29th of this month ; I shall go to it and probably be bored. I have not the faintest idea what people wear, as the fashions change all the time and the pictures in the papers look very extraordinary.

---

[1] A full account of the life of the authoress between June 1914 and November 1918 is to be found in her previous book, *Daisy Princess of Pless*. (John Murray.)

[2] Colonel Gordon Leith, C.B., late Northumberland Hussars.

CHAPTER FOURTEEN

SOON after the war I ceased to keep a regular diary although, from time to time, I make notes of anything that specially interested me ; however, so many people seem sincerely to wish to know what has happened to me since, that I must say something about my post-war experiences.

The last weeks of 1918 were spent at my villa at Garmisch-Partenkirchen in the Bavarian Alps, or at Munich in the rather ugly furnished house I had taken in the suburbs. It was a little out of the way, but had the great advantage of being near Princess Pilar and her father and mother, Prince and Princess Ludwig Ferdinand, who were then in residence at Nymphenburg : the change from one place to the other emphasized the dramatic happenings of the moment. When visiting Nymphenburg I was a guest in an old Royal Palace ; at Partenkirchen the local Soldiers' and Sailors' Council had its headquarters in my house !

When the Emperor was forced to flee to Holland during the first week in November I was terribly sorry, and wished so much that he had abdicated voluntarily, thus proving his foresight and disinterestedness, and, in all probability, saving the Crown for the dynasty.

I had first met the Emperor at Pless shortly after my marriage and even then, as a mere girl, although I immediately liked him and thought him clever, I felt that he was vain and always " acting." Of course all public personages have to act a part, because democracy demands it of them ; but the Emperor, I fear, posed to his intimates and friends, perhaps even to himself, and this is wrong because it inevitably breeds insincerity. I saw him for the last time in Pless in July, 1917 [1] when he seemed well, and not unhappy. In the intervening years we had met often, exchanged ideas frankly and, each in their degree, rendered services of friendship to the other. I have no personal regrets because, whatever the risks, I was amongst the few, pitifully few, who were always honest and outspoken to their Sovereign. He, in his turn, was unfailingly kind, indulgent and loyal to me, and gave practical and valuable proofs of his friendship again and again.

Even during his reign there was whispered gossip about the Emperor's morals, and, since his fall, it has of course become loud and sometimes virulent. I don't believe there was one iota of truth in the charge. I am vain enough to think that the Emperor liked me better and treated me with more sincerity and frankness than almost any other woman he knew. There were many reasons for this. I was English ; I was different ; I was never afraid of him. Apart altogether from what a man may say or do, a woman, in time, gets to know what he thinks about such fundamental matters as sex. The Emperor was very German in some ways and, in those days, and even now, the typical German is a good family man who, when he can afford it, marries early, begets lots of children, never beats his wife and—forgets all about her. The Germans are not " romantic " in the English sense, and the Emperor, I feel sure, harboured no dark secrets, concealed no hidden episodes of any kind. His attitude to me was always protective and fatherly.

[1] Pless was Great Headquarters of the German Armies in the East from 1915 to 1917.

True, he liked to be with me and look at me because my beauty was of the pink, white and gold " English " type that appealed to him. Did he not once, by way of a great compliment, compare me to one of those rather dreadful tinted pictures of beautiful women that were so popular as Christmas supplements to the English periodicals and magazines of the late " nineties " of the last century ! He often kissed my hand, and once said that he preferred to do so with the glove off : but what sensible person likes kissing a kid glove —they always smell so horrid !

All the writings about the Emperor's suffering under a morbid sense of his incapacity to use his left arm and his feeling crippled is so much nonsense. Of course, like anyone else he would have preferred to have the full use of his limbs ; from birth he had no useful left arm, was brought up to do without one and, I feel certain, never seriously missed it. In public, and when posing for his pictures, naturally he did not stick out his ungrown arm and hand for people to wonder at ; nevertheless, in private he never bothered about it. I have sat next to him hundreds of times, watched him use the special combined knife and fork he always carried, or I have cut up his food for him and he never once showed the slightest sign of any foolish sensitiveness or embarrassment. Ludwig's book about the Emperor is brilliant in many ways, but the author insists on being " dramatic " at all costs ; he, therefore, talks a great deal about morbidity ; he is, moreover, often more than a little unfair to both the Empress Frederick and her eldest son. It is for historians to judge the Emperor in his public capacity ; nevertheless, his personal friends have the right, indeed the duty, to make it perfectly clear that there was nothing either morbid or neurotic in his personality.

What was the Emperor really like to look at ?   Oddly enough, although he was the most painted and be-photographed man in the world, none of his pictures, to my mind, do him justice.   The state portrait painted by Laszló to hang with those of his ancestors in the gallery adjoining the throne room in the Royal Palace in Berlin is not a success.   The Emperor wears the white Cuirassier Guards' uniform with silver breast-plate and silver eagle-crowned helmet of which he was so fond, and which was certainly very " paintable." He stands beside what is, I think, supposed to be a horse ; the colour scheme is pink and white and chocolate-boxy, and the whole thing is deplorable. The Emperor quite liked it, because he had no more knowledge of pictures (in spite of his delusions to the contrary) than the average Royalty has.   In how few Palaces are there any good modern pictures !

I had often to beg the Emperor to " shake hands nicely " ; his right hand was very big and, without realizing it, he had the grasp of a tiger.   Of course his horses were all perfectly broken to suit him ; neverthe-less, he hated a " dead " horse, had a perfect seat and could manage a horse very skilfully with his one hand. He had, perhaps not plenty, but enough, nice brown hair, beautiful penetrating brown eyes and good teeth. I read the other day in one of the fashionable new, stupid war books that he had false teeth, but that was not so : he was tall and had a brown complexion inclined to ruddiness.   I write down these things because, when reading about a person, I like to know exactly what they looked like, and because someone told me the other day that nobody knows what Napo-leon's appearance really was !

The Emperor appreciated and respected the Empress, but I don't think, after the first year or so, that he had a devouring passion for her.   How could he ?

He had great intellectual quickness and ability and she, poor darling person, remained intellectually where she was in 1880 when they became engaged—secretly engaged, because she was not considered in German Court circles a good enough match. My feeling is that the Emperor was never madly in love with anyone.

How difficult it is to educate any high-spirited sensitive boy, who has a ready brain and a quick, but not profound, intelligence ! How enormously these difficulties are intensified when the boy is heir to one of the greatest positions in the world and, from his earliest years, the object of flattery and intrigue ! The Emperor *always* thought he *knew*. And, after the retirement of his mother, the Empress Frederick, from public affairs, and the death of his grandmother, Queen Victoria, no one except, occasionally, his uncle King Edward ever dared to tell him he was sometimes wrong. That, to my mind, as I have elsewhere said, and always shall say, was *the* great betrayal. Of course he hated to be told, and seldom, perhaps never, forgave those who insisted on brutally telling him the truth. In his vanity and dislike of the unpalatable and unflattering he was not very different from the rest of us ; but what is comparatively harmless in the circumscribed circles of private life can become disastrous in great affairs. Bismarck was truthful with the Emperor only when it suited his purposes. His motto was : Deceive—and rule. Herbert Bismarck never counted. General Caprivi, who succeeded Bismarck as Imperial Chancellor, was honest and had ability, but he was a soldier and, to him, " the King could do no wrong." Chlodwig von Hohenlohe, the next Chancellor, in spite of some fine qualities, never stood up to the Emperor. The two Imperial Chancellors whom I knew personally—Bülow and Bethmann-Hollweg—were, in different degrees, afraid of the

PRINCESS HANSEL OF PLESS.
My Daughter-in-law.

Emperor. Dr. Georg Michaelis was merely a war-time stop-gap ; Count Georg von Hertling, who was Chancellor from October, 1917, to September, 1918, was a devoted and patriotic Bavarian noble. He had been Prime Minister of Bavaria, where he was highly respected and greatly liked, but when he became Imperial Chancellor he was over seventy, and totally unable to cope with the power of the General Staff. The last one of all, dear, noble Prince Max of Baden, dared to tell the Emperor the fatal truth in October and November, 1918. But it was too late. He was not listened to ; the Empire fell ; Germany was dismembered : the Emperor fled. One cannot, I suppose, consistently refuse to hear the truth for years, and then, suddenly, instinctively recognize it and accept it with alacrity.

I know that many Germans thought, and perhaps still think, that Prince Max behaved badly to the Emperor. He failed to save the Empire only because the Emperor never trusted him. The Emperor, instead of being in Berlin, insisted on remaining with the Army and listening to the advice of soldiers who, however admirable in their own sphere, never have been, and never can be, in touch with the minds of the people. The Duke of Wellington, one of the greatest soldiers in history, was a political failure ; while poor Lord Kitchener met disaster, and eventually death, through his natural inability to understand or cope with the machinations of politics.

At the end of January, 1919, my dear sister-in-law Lulu (Hans's sister) wrote me as follows. Her letter expresses the view to which I have referred :

20. 1. 19.

DEAREST DAISY,—

Thank you so much for your dear letter. *I* voted yesterday ! I suppose you would think I voted for the wrong

man, but I am old-fashioned and a Tory ; I can't help
it. . . .

I don't know why the kind friend [1] left us, and I think it was
the worst thing he could do. His daughter's brother-in-law [2]
made all the mischief, and, I believe, forced him to go at last.
I won't call anathema on his head, because it is unchristian,
but I think he served Germany in the worst manner. . . .

If Vater had lived and been young, or if my Fritz had been
ten or twenty years younger, the kind friend would have
stayed here, *and not gone away*, and I think it would have
been much better for everything. But it was God's will :
and I don't think he had any energetic adviser.

I have just heard that they are both well. I sometimes
hear from my nephew's wife, Isabelle. She has friends and
relations with them, as you know.

Dear Daisy, I hope you have good news from your mother
. . . Best love dear, three grandchildren are poking their
nose into this letter, whilst I am writing.

Yours,
LOUISE.

If only his grandfather William I. had died reasonably young, or his father Frederick III. reasonably
old, then William II. might have been on the German
Imperial Throne to-day. The Emperor never had a
real chance. He served no apprenticeship. Look at
the long, tedious and, as it proved, invaluable apprenticeship served by his uncle, Edward VII. of England.
Even so, I am not quite sure that any apprenticeship,
any friend or adviser, however faithful and disinterested, could have saved the Emperor from himself.
Certainly no woman could have done so. In his
secret heart he thought little of us women : he almost
despised us. Had all the circumstances been different,
there was one woman who might, possibly, have helped
the Emperor's fine native qualities to develop along

---

[1] The Emperor William II.
[2] Prince Max of Baden (1867–1929), m. in 1900 Princess Marie-
Louise of Brunswick. Her brother was the Emperor's son-in-law

different lines, and that was his mother, the Empress Frederick. She had vision, brains, disinterestedness. But, with her sons, she was incredibly tactless. Like myself, she so acted that, quite legitimately, the German people could always accuse her of appearing to be ultra English. Moreover, she had what seems to us an almost incredible ignorance of the psychology of manhood. I loved and admired her; but she was as stupid with her sons as my own beloved parents were with me—and as I, perhaps, am with my own children. The Emperor has himself said that in Germany the Empress Frederick was impossibly English, and in England hopelessly German.[1] The charge is pointed and, I think, true; it is one that might easily be made against myself. But is it a very serious charge? Surely it is the spontaneous instinct of any warm-hearted person to stand up for the absent.

Well, when all is said, the Emperor knew how to be a friend, and that may well be the finest thing of all. I don't know why one writes of him as if he were dead; he is very much alive. When he married again in 1922 I was delighted, and sent him a letter saying so. As these are probably the last words I shall ever write about him, perhaps I may anticipate a little and transcribe here the nice letter (the last of many) which he wrote me with his own hand. I trust that all the hopes he expresses in it have been amply fulfilled:

DOORN, 13. X. 22.

MY DEAR PRINCESS DAISY,—

Very sincere thanks for your kind lines of congratulations for my engagement and wedding with Princess Schönaich-

---

[1] See article in *Quarterly Review* by Brig.-General Waters, April, 1929. (John Murray.)

Carolath.[1] I have found peace and happiness again after such terrible years of loss and trials, through the affection of this winning lady, who has consented to become my wife and bring sunlight into this house of darkness, sorrow and mourning. I am so deeply affected by what you communicate to me about your husband's newest decisions and plans ; I cannot understand what happened, and what his ultimate ideas are. Accept my warmest sympathy in your troubles and sorrows and believe me, Ever yours respectfully,

WILLIAM, I.R.

" I have found peace and happiness again after such terrible years. . . ." These are comforting words and, for our old friendship's sake, I am indeed glad. Now, after twelve years, I am ashamed of the silly outcry against the Emperor and the German people that, largely inspired by inept newspaper-writers and politicians, swept over England between 1917 and 1920. Surely all rulers, peoples and persons make mistakes, nurse false hatreds, temporarily embrace false creeds. Yet men can quarrel handsomely like gentlemen. Silly, hysterical hatred was never a British characteristic. When the Black Prince acted himself as personal servant to the French King he had just conquered, that was truly English. Nor do I believe the Hymn of Hate was characteristic of the German people. Like much else of the evil of war, it was probably invented by those who stayed at home. I want Germany and England—all nations everywhere—to work together and be friends. Quarrels, rivalries and jealousies belong to the childhood of the world and surely, by now, it is time our silly, yet lovely old world had grown up.

[1] My husband's uncle, Bolko, married a Princess of Schönaich-Carolath, while his aunt, Anna, married a Prince Reuss : the Hochbergs are, therefore, connected with the family into which the Empress Hermine first married, as well as that into which she was born.— D. OF P.

II

Before I take leave of the German Imperial Family I would like to say something of Princess Victoria of Prussia, my friend for many years. She was four years younger than the Emperor, being born after Prince Henry and before Queen Sophie of Greece and, like her mother the Empress Frederick, had the pet name " Vicky." Before she was twenty she had the misfortune quite unwittingly to cross the plans of Bismarck, and all women, and most men, who did that were broken. I will name only three of my personal friends whose lives he shattered. The Empress Frederick, the Empress Eugénie and Princess Vicky. Princess Victoria fell violently in love with the handsome and fascinating Prince Alexander of Battenberg, who became Prince of Bulgaria, and whose equally handsome brother Henry later married Princess Beatrice of Great Britain. Queen Victoria and the Empress Frederick were warmly in favour of Vicky's marriage and it was the dying wish of the Emperor Frederick that it should take place, but, for political reasons, Bismarck and her brother the Emperor were against it, and poor Vicky was sacrificed. At the time the engagement was broken off [1] Bismarck brutally remarked that any other man would do for the Princess as well. Bismarck was a great man, but he knew nothing about women. My own feeling is that this disappointment—because the young people were deeply and romantically in love—spoiled the Princess's whole life.[2] In 1890 she married the Prince of Schaumburg-

[1] Princess Victoria of Prussia was engaged to Alexander, Prince of Bulgaria, from 1885 to 1888. Bismarck favoured a marriage between the Princess and King Carlos I. of Portugal, who married Princess Amelie of France in 1886 and became the father of King Manoel.

[2] In his will the Emperor Frederick said to his son and successor : " I charge you as a filial duty with the accomplishment of this my

Lippe, a nice, kind man who died in 1916. There were no children and the Prince was succeeded by his nephew.

Now the only way for a woman to cure a romantic love is to marry the man who inspires it. Otherwise she will go through life longing for and seeking that lost romance, and, if circumstances are favourable, sooner or later, she will do something very foolish in trying to find it. I saw a great deal of Vicky soon after her husband's death ; she was depressed, unsettled, terribly lonely. Then her brother lost his Throne, her whole family their high position and a great deal of their money. Her favourite sister Princess Mossy had a wounded husband and was grieving for two sons killed in the war ; her other sister, Queen Sophy of Greece, throneless and in exile, was immersed in troubles. Many, indeed most, of those who in the old days were only too proud to claim friendship with the sisters of the Emperor now stood aloof. Vicky had no sensible friends near her to lessen her loneliness or give her sound advice. Then Zoubkoff came along with his handsome face and insinuating tongue. All the echoes of buried romance awoke. Dear Vicky imagined, as many another woman has done before, and will again, that the gauzy glamour of youth can be recaptured and, of course, she was mistaken. Zoubkoff, they told her, was an adventurer ; well, had not "Sandro," the love of her youth, also been an adventurer who gambled with the Czar and Bismarck for a throne and a bride—and lost ? They told her a Princess of Prussia could not so demean herself, and she retorted naturally enough by saying : "One moment they tell me I am only a

desire, which your sister Victoria for so many years has cherished in her heart."—Ponsonby, Sir Frederick : *Letters of the Empress Frederick.*

private person with no rank or claims to financial help ; the next, when I want the freedom of that position, they say that I am Royal and must never please myself. Well, I have pleased others all my life ; now I shall do what I want." Of course it was a miserable failure. She gambled, and lost—but she might have won. At the worst, before death came, she had her hour of illusion.

Immediately the marriage was announced I wrote and invited them both to visit me in Munich. Here is her reply. The visit, I regret to say, never took place.

BONN, 12. 1. 29.

DARLING DAISY,—

Ever so many thanks for your very kind letter and good wishes which we are most grateful for—*sweet* of you really. We are intensely happy ; we have been through hard times as we have been subjected to the scandalous rumours of harsh and narrow-minded persons, and the Press was a disgrace ; it's sad to think there are *such* people in the world. My husband is a splendid man in every respect and has been through terrible experiences in his life, knows the world and mankind and one can only respect and admire him for having worked so hard—having lost his big fortune through the Revolution, home, palaces, etc.

How kind of you to invite us to your home ! Perhaps some day there might be an opportunity for us to meet again ; such an age since last we were together. I have so often thought of you dearest Daisy and wondered where you might be ? !

We are still quite snowed under with business and correspondence ; over five thousand letters have reached us from all parts of the world, and we are longing for a rest and the " honeymoon " to come off—travelling alas, an expensive affair.

It would interest me very much to get an edition of your book.

With much love and renewed thanks, Yours affectionately,

VICTORIA (Vicky).

You say—but how could she, in her position, fall in love with a waiter ? Zoubkoff's origin and social status is very obscure, and darling Vicky hardly mended matters by " creating " him a Russian Baron on her own account. But, even if he were a waiter, it proved nothing as, since the war, more than one Austrian Archduke has been glad to adopt that profession. And there is another deeper reason why it would make no real difference. Princes have always sought romance in cottages, and peasants in palaces—and always will.

I think the couple lived together only a few months and any chance of happiness they had was ruined by money troubles. He went away and she was lonelier than ever because, now, her last forlorn, impossible romantic dream had finally vanished. Illusions or delusions—(perhaps it does not greatly matter which), so long as we can cling to one or two, we can keep going. Alone, poor, without friends or hopes, having made herself ridiculous in her old age Vicky, in desperation, one day visited the Kinema to try to find an hour of oblivion. More depressed than ever, she left the hot theatre and went alone for a walk in the public park at Bonn, caught a chill, and died. Her favourite sister, Princess Mossy, was with her to the end, and that sister's husband, kind, grave, courteous Prince Frederick Karl of Hesse, ever helpful and considerate, was near. The Emperor, who had naturally been estranged by the marriage, sent brotherly messages ; and Vicky went off, perhaps to find Sandro, who had gone years before.

I do not know how men feel about such tragedies, but I am sure no real woman could fail to understand Vicky, or seriously blame her. She was entitled to her dream, entitled, after all she had been through, to take a big risk on the chance of its fulfilment. It is

inhuman to dismiss such cases with a shrug and say
" a foolish woman." Perhaps. Many women are
foolish ; and all men are not wise. I loved Vicky ;
like the rest of us she had her faults and failings.
Life, in appearance, gave her everything, and denied
her the only two things that matter—love and children.
I wish that in those last months I could have been
near her and helped her. But we seldom are near
when our friends are most forlorn and alone. Cal-
vary is always companionless. Remembering this, let
us not begrudge any human being the understanding,
the forgiving, tear.

III

At the time of the Armistice, and for long after,
the political situation on the eastern border of Germany was so unsettled that any idea of trying to stay
at Fürstenstein or Pless was quite out of the question.
Hans came to see me at Partenkirchen and Munich,
and I had our two youngest boys with me ; Hansel
was, of course, still in the Army.

All this being so, and little Patsy being very ill,
I did my utmost to get to England. It was quite
useless. I then heard that Evelyn Blücher [1] and
Muriel Münster,[2] both Englishwomen, were going at
once to Switzerland. Eventually I also got leave to
go there and was met by kind Nancy Leeds [3] at Lau-
sanne. She had been the most faithful of friends ;
taking care of my house in Savile Row when I fled
hurriedly from London in August, 1914, storing my
personal effects and linen, paying pressing bills for
me and generally acting the good Samaritan. A

[1] Miss Evelyn Stapleton-Bretherton, granddaughter of 12th Lord
Petre, m. 1907, 4th Prince Blücher von Wahlstatt.
[2] See p. 148.
[3] Mrs. William Leeds (1883–1923), m. 1920, Prince Christopher of
Greece.

warm-hearted, dear American woman—I shall never forget her. I have heard it said that her divorce from her first husband to marry Mr. Leeds was not a pretty one. But how few divorces are as artless as an angel's song ! And, anyway, if a woman is real, I am utterly indifferent to such complaints.

Post-war red tape was even more formidable than war red tape, and for the English-born wife of a German to reach England seemed impossible. I had often thought, and said, that I considered Lord Balfour, although a great man, lazy, slow, and dawdling. Young, inexperienced, ignorant of the many formidable difficulties he had to confront, and by nature foolishly impulsive, I was always overquick to criticize inaction. Looking back now I see that Lord Balfour was nearly always right. He was right in Ireland ; right when he told Mr. Chamberlain that Great Britain would not accept food taxes ; [1] right when he said the United States would decide the issue of the Great War ; right when he said of the policy of the allied statesmen at Versailles that wars might be won, but peace must be wooed. No woman in a difficulty would ever hesitate to apply for help to him—a great gentleman, with a courtesy that was imperturbable and perfect. I wrote, begging him to help me to get to England. Here is what he replied :

BRITISH DELEGATION, PARIS, *February* 25, 1919.
MY DEAR PRINCESS OF PLESS,—
Since receiving your letter I have been made very unhappy by reflecting how little I can do to give you any assistance in all your troubles and difficulties.

Often have I thought of you during these four and a half years of war and of the expedition we took together five years

---

[1] Mr. A. J. (afterwards 1st Earl of) Balfour (1848–1930) was Prime Minister 1902–5, when Mr. Chamberlain, to some extent without his concurrence, was strenuously advocating Tariff Reform.

ago to look at the land which you bought near Napoule. It seems a thousand ages since then. The sufferings which the world has gone through in that period are beyond computation, but perhaps those are most to be pitied who, by the accident of marriage, have become citizens of a State at war with the country of their birth. The worst of it is that there is no alleviation possible for their position till peace is declared. Before that happy day arrives they must in law be counted as belonging to an enemy State and it is not possible, with the best will in the world, to treat them as still belonging to the land of their fathers. Believe me I know how much you must have gone through and I would most willingly help you by every method at my disposal. But Rumbold [1] will have told you how matters stand and how impossible it is to do more than give you my very sincere expressions of sympathy.

Yours sincerely,

ARTHUR JAMES BALFOUR.

In spite of shamelessly badgering Queen Alexandra and everyone I knew, I did not succeed in getting from Switzerland to London until September. Some " kind friends," I believe, said loudly that I ought to have been ashamed to show my face in England so soon. I arrived at Southampton and never shall I forget my tears of joy when a dear old railway porter, a friend of bygone days, greeted me as " Miss Daisy." The tact, the beautiful, instinctive tact of this simple English gentleman ! By mischance there was no one to meet me at Waterloo and, feeling lonely and forlorn, I drove to Kenwood, which Nancy Leeds had taken from Sophy and the Grand Duke Michael when they lost nearly all their money as a result of the Russian Revolution in 1917.

From Kenwood I went to Clouds in Wiltshire to stay with Guy and Auntie Min. They met me at Salisbury, and oh, the delight of that motor run of

[1] Rt. Hon. Sir Horace Rumbold, 9th Bt. (b. 1869, s. 1913), was Chargé d'Affaires at Berlin, July 1–27, 1914 ; British Minister, Switzerland, 1916–19 ; British Ambassador at Berlin since 1928.

twenty miles through the lovely Wiltshire Downs and valleys, drenched in September beauty.

Patsy was still ill and staying at Clouds. Just before the war I had taken Arnwood, in the New Forest, on lease. Newlands was let, so we started trying to get Arnwood habitable in order that Patsy and I could go there. While this was being done I paid a visit to the Empress Eugénie at Farnborough Hill. Apart from those of my own family, the first homes where I was invited to stay after my long, miserable, enforced exile were those of an American and a Frenchwoman!

Yet there was one faithful friend who did not forget. Higher in station by far than any of them, her heart was one of the sweetest and greatest I have ever known and, in their success or their adversity, she was always the same to her friends. However chilly my reception by some in England who had once eagerly claimed my friendship, I was not without a " Royal welcome." Queen Alexandra, God bless her, did not wait for me to ask for an audience (after first formally announcing my arrival in the land of my birth), nor did she wait to see how the wind blew socially or politically, before venturing to renew the ties of old affection. She, alas, can never know now what a moral help her spontaneous letter was to me at the time, nor how much it did to heal spiritual wounds. Here is what she wrote in her own characteristic handwriting :

SANDRINGHAM, NORFOLK, *September* 18, 1919.
MY POOR DEAR DAISY,—

I see by the papers that at last you have actually been *allowed* to come back to your beloved home and poor suffering little Mother dear ! I really am *so* delighted to hear it as I know *what* you have gone through and suffered during all those five years of awful horrible war and when you were banned from England. I was so sorry I was unable to help last Spring when you wrote to me from Switzerland. I do hope you found

MYSELF.

1927.

[Foulsham & Banfield, Ltd.

your poor Mother better and that you still found her in your old home ! which I hear your brother wants to sell—too bad and horrid ! Please write and tell me all about *yourself* and all you have and are going through even now, and where your children and husband are, and about your poor mother and sister, who seems also deserted now. Oh, *what* terrible sorrows and trials the world is full of now everywhere—and believe me,
Yours affectionately,

ALEXANDRA.

If I had thought I would find peace in England I was mistaken. Early in October darling Aunt Min died at Clouds, and was buried there. It made us all more nervous than ever about little Patsy, who was still ill, and during the last week of October Shelagh and I, overcoming all difficulties and formalities, got her off to the South of France. Breaking the journey in Paris, she spent what proved to be her last birthday, October the twenty-sixth, in Marjorie Anglesey's [1] flat, which she most kindly lent us.

Patsy stood the journey rather badly and implored me to join her. But the difficulties of getting into England were as nothing compared with those one had to face in getting out. I went to London and saw everyone of importance that I knew ; but it was wasted energy. All the British officials were quite charming and only too willing to do everything possible to facilitate my movements. But I could not get a French visa. What ! Allow a ' Hun ' woman to tread the sacred soil of France ? Never ! I was defeated.

Then one night I was at the Opera in Maud Cunard's [2] box (another American), when Major Chapman-Huston came in to see me. He is a sort of relative as his uncle married a FitzPatrick. I asked him to come

---

[1] The Marchioness of Anglesey, b. 1883, d. of 8th Duke of Rutland.
[2] Maud Alice Burke of New York m. in 1895 Sir Bache Cunard (1851-1925), 3rd Bt.

and have tea with me next day at Brown's Hotel, when
I poured out my story. I thought that he, a soldier
in khaki, was sure to be able to do something. He
explained that, the war being over, soldiers were now
by far the least important members of the community
—and counselled guile. I was to go to bed at once,
send for the French doctor who was appointed officially
to the French Embassy, and get him to say I would
die if I did not proceed immediately to the South of
France. Major Chapman-Huston obtained the doctor's name and address ; my maid telephoned to him
in perfect French ; I had no difficulty whatever in
being ill, as I was worn to a shadow. The doctor,
bless him, got me my French visa. I have often
wondered if he suspected anything. If so, his professional calm was perfect, and he never allowed his
kind heart to show in his face. By the end of November I was with Patsy in Cannes.

IV

1920 was a dreadful year. In January I moved Patsy
into a tiny villa overhanging the sea at La Napoule.
It was quiet and far from everything, and is being
absorbed in the precincts of the Chateau de la Napoule
in the extensive building operations now being carried out by my friends and neighbours, Mr. and Mrs.
Henry Clews ; Shelagh and Mary joined us, and lived
in a neighbouring villa.

One day I went to Maryland to lunch with Muriel
Wilson (Mrs. Dick Warde) to meet the Duke of
Connaught. He was the first British Royalty I had
spoken to after the war and, needless to say, he was the
friendly, charming, gallant gentleman he has ever
been. We had much to talk over, so he invited me
to lunch with him at his villa at Beaulieu a day or two
later. This I did, and was glad to be able to tell

him how the news of the death of the Duchess of
Connaught was received in Germany.[1]

I made a point of telling the Duke how wonderful
and unfailing a friend his eldest daughter the Crown
Princess of Sweden,[2] " the other Daisy," had been
to me throughout the war. I also told him all about
Queen Mary's aunt, my beloved Granny-Grand Duchess of Mecklenburg-Strelitz, and as much as I felt
I could tell him about the tragic death of my friend,
her grandson.[3]

There were few English people on the Riviera that
spring, and I can only remember seeing Adèle Essex,
Violet de Trafford [4] and dear Rosie Headfort.[5]

In March I went to Fürstenstein, my first visit
after the war ; but in June, was again summoned to
the Riviera to Patsy. She knew that she was dying,
and clamoured to be allowed to end her days in
England. Removing her was very difficult as railway
facilities were still far from normal. However, Lord
Rothschild, hearing of our difficulties, lent us his
saloon coach, the French authorities were helpful,
and early in June we got her away. We were a
queer party, and little Patsy laughed and loved the
excitement. I can see us now as we set off : Shelagh,
Fitz,[6] Lexel, Dollie,[7] several servants—and two canaries.
We took Patsy to a nursing home in Eaton Square,
while I stayed with Guy Wyndham in Lowndes Street,

[1] The late Duchess of Connaught (1860–1917) was the d. of Prince
Frederick Charles of Prussia, " the Red Prince." Her brother married
a sister of the German Empress.   [2] Died May 1, 1920.

[3] Adolphus Friedrich VI., Grand Duke of Mecklenburg-Strelitz,
died by his own hand in February, 1918 : see *Daisy Princess of Pless*,
pp. 458–60.

[4] Miss Violet Franklin m. in 1886 Sir Humphrey de Trafford,
3rd Bt. ; she d. 1925.

[5] Miss Rose Boote m. in 1901 4th Marquess of Headfort.

[6] In January, 1920, the authoress's sister married Captain J.
FitzPatrick Lewes, R.A.F.

[7] Miss D. Crowther, friend and companion of Mrs. Cornwallis-
West and, since her death, of the authoress.

near by. An operation was advised and Patsy was duly prepared. I went in to see her early on the morning on which it was to take place. She was full of spirit, bubbling over with laughter, and greeted me with :

" What do you think they wanted me to do last night, Daisy ? "

" I have no notion, darling ; do tell me ? "

" Take out my teeth ! "

She was delighted. Her teeth were so white and perfect that the nurses, thinking they must be artificial, wanted them removed before she went to sleep.

To complicate matters I was now ordered to go into a nursing home immediately, and like many another, took up my abode in a famous one in Park Lane. A few days later a nurse came into my room and said the Duke of something or other was downstairs and wished to see me. I replied that I did not wish to see anyone, more particularly a foreign Duke whom I did not know. The nurse explained that " the Duke " spoke English, seemed certain of what he wanted, and, apparently, accustomed to getting it. I was quite firm, the nurse equally so, and while we were arguing the door of my sitting-room was pushed open and in walked the King of Spain and Jimmy Alba. I suppose the King did not wish to cause trouble by announcing himself, and therefore used his incognito, which he, very foolishly, thought I would recognize—I, who never can remember anyone's name or title !

One knows how crammed up King Alfonso's days are when he pays one of his hurried visits to London, and it was dear and characteristic of him to come without fuss and see an old friend who was ill. The visit did me heaps of good, because the King is one of the most magnetic and inspiring persons I know

It was now fatefully clear to us all that nothing human beings could do would save Patsy. The only thing, therefore, was to indulge her little whims to the utmost. She wanted to die " at home," either at Ruthin or Newlands. Ruthin, a post-war convalescent home, was quite impossible and Newlands was let. So we took her to Arnwood in the Forest. It was a place she and I always loved and, being the Newlands dower house, was at any rate a part of home. There she left us one summer day,[1] her gaiety, indomitable courage, love-laden heart, and zest for life, unconquerable to the end. Shelagh and I were with her ; George and his dear, brilliant, artist wife,[2] and her grandson Lexel whom she adored, were near her when she went to join Poppets, who for forty-six years had been her true lover and unfailingly loyal friend in sunshine and in shadow.

I must pay her tribute here, because we shall see no one like her any more. Had she faults and failings ? Masses of them, but such endearing, human ones. How she was produced by the early Victorian environment from which she emerged, and which she alternately shocked and delighted, I shall never understand. She was quick in everything : in thought, speech, repartee, temper, sympathy, likes and dislikes ; she seldom let judgment wait on reflection, and such was the fineness of her intelligence that she was not very often wrong. A woman who could capture and keep as faithful romantic friends such different men as Mr. Gladstone and King Edward VII. was no ordinary person. The poor are by far the best and truest judges of character, and the villagers in and around Ruthin, who knew her in and out, just adored her. They understood her impulsiveness, her wild,

[1] July 21, 1920.
[2] Major Cornwallis-West married Mrs. Patrick Campbell in 1914.

at times almost foolish, disregard of conventions, because they saw at close quarters and appreciated her affectionate heart. To them, she was such a great lady, so innately an aristocrat, that she could defy all laws and customs, not only with impunity, but with applause. Only the poorer country people can understand this because, in their own degree, they themselves demand and exercise a similar freedom. Unlike the middle classes, they put life before mere living. Patsy could, and did, make friends everywhere. If her motor broke down (and in the early days it always did) she sat smiling by the wayside until the good samaritan of her choice came along, and then calmly asked to be driven to Eaton or Newlands or Ruthin or wherever she was going. Neither Shelagh nor I are by any means the helpless type of woman—we are far too much Patsy's daughters for that—but we have both often sat by amazed at the decision, soundness and success of Patsy's staff work in an emergency. She could make friends instantly with the oddest people, and if ever a boat or train journey of hers was dull it was not because of her having failed to find a travelling companion to talk to. Like all real aristocrats she had no " class feeling," and would be as intimate and fascinating with a washerwoman, a carpenter or a commercial traveller as with King Edward or the German Emperor : no one with Irish blood in them can ever really be a snob.

Of course she was spoiled ; but it never made her conceited or vain. She could be as completely indifferent to her personal appearance as she was to all other appearances ; and would demand help from anyone as readily as she was prepared to render it to anyone.

I think one of the great secrets of her enduring charm was her exhaustless vitality. Death himself could scarcely succeed in drawing her into his arms.

That she was a good wife and mother in the Victorian sense one could perhaps hardly claim : but she was something rarer, better : the world is filled with good, humdrum wives, and they are priceless. But Patsy was unique. It is difficult to explain. She had a love for birds amounting almost to adoration —or mania—which is perhaps the same thing. I always think of Patsy as a bird. One admires the homely dove, sparrow, robin, even the indispensable farmyard chicken, but one's rapturous love is reserved for the irridescent beauty of the flamingo, kingfisher, or peacock, or for the ravishing loveliness of the thrush and the lark. Yes, I think of Patsy as a bird —of the rapturous kind.

With such a quick brain Patsy was bound at times to say sharp things, but she never said a mean or spiteful thing, never bore malice, and went from us full of love for the world and all—even its most unlovely—inhabitants.

If they gave her a high dull place in Paradise she would laughingly swear she did not deserve it, flit off and find a corner where those saved by the skin of their teeth chuckle gleefully amongst themselves at those others who foolishly sacrificed all the innocent joys of life for the dull safety of a seat in the reserved enclosure near the Eternal Throne.

Some months ago I received from an unknown friend in New Zealand a letter about Patsy : it gives, from an outsider's point of view, such a true and vivid glimpse of her during the war that I will quote it here. I feel the writer will not mind my doing so.

NAPIER, NEW ZEALAND, *December* 15, 1929.
YOUR HIGHNESS,—
Having recently read your very interesting book I am taking the liberty of asking a favour. I wish very much to possess a photograph of Mrs. Cornwallis-West. There is a portrait

in your book, but as I only knew her in 1918 it means nothing to me.

Perhaps I should explain why I make this request.

I was a private soldier in the New Zealand army and in May, 1918, was invalided from France to Brockenhurst. One day a friend and I hired a governess cart and drove to Milford. Returning, with the " cheek " I fear we colonials became famous for, we went into the grounds of Newlands to explore. Mrs. West saw us and invited us to tea. Thus began a series of visits that are one of my most precious memories, for, though I fear she was far from strong, she laid herself out to please two obscure men from the other end of the world. Indeed she went so far as to organize a dance for us in the Music Room at which the Duchess of Westminster was present and sang for us. Your sister also gave us tea at Boldre Grange one day. I have now a pair of sleeve-links given to me as a keep-sake which belonged to Colonel West.

Mrs. West also gave me a water-colour of Newlands as a wedding present.

I do hope I have established a claim to that photograph if one is available and that you will not mind my presumption.

So, even in far-off New Zealand there are those to whom little Patsy's memory is green and fragrant. I think Patsy would have loved that spontaneous tribute from a private soldier in the New Zealand Army far better than any Royal token of remembrance.

V

My visit to Bagnolles in 1911 had done me so much good that, in August, 1920, it was thought worth while trying it again. Shelagh and I went there together, but of course it was too late. Had I been able to return there in the autumn of 1914 as I had intended, I might have been cured. Four years and a quarter of the wear and tear of war, and many months on my hind legs in hospitals and in hospital trains, made, I am afraid, any real hope of recovery almost impossible.

I spent Christmas, 1920, at Fürstenstein with Hans and the boys, and in March went again to that loveliest of lovely spots, Garmisch-Partenkirchen in the Bavarian Alps. I had with me a queer Spanish lady-in-waiting, Countess de Alcoy, and found several friends there, including Prince Eitel Fritz, who had with him the only son of his brother Prince Joachim, who died so tragically in July, 1920. I believe Prince Eitel Fritz, who has no children of his own, told me that he wanted to adopt the boy, but I don't think this was ever arranged.

In June I was again at Fürstenstein, where I was formally received by Hans with considerable pomp. I think this was meant to convey to the world of Silesia that I was really a quite harmless person. The night of my arrival there were great festivities and, for a time, both Hans and I hoped and believed that we could settle down together happily after the war. But it was not to be ;[1] too much, perhaps, had happened in our personal, our domestic, and our national life to make such a hope realizable. Moreover, I knew only too well that I could never again feel at home in Prussia ; Bavaria and South Germany was different, never having shown me signs of bitter enmity—but Silesia . . .

In the late autumn of 1924 I paid my last visit to Fürstenstein, but did not stay in the Castle. I occupied the cottage which I had christened *Ma Fantaisie* or the *Garden of Kama*.[2] Hans had caused the little house, where I had spent so many happy hours in the old days—and which had of course been empty during the war—to be comfortably fitted up with furniture

---

[1] The Princess divorced her husband in December, 1923.

[2] Title of a well-known volume of verses ; the authoress, Laurence Hope, was the only white woman who ever committed *suttee* on her husband's grave.

from the Castle, and all our food was cooked there and sent down to us.

I went for the marriage of my eldest son [1] and, when that was over, felt that I had no longer any ties in Silesia. The young things spent their honeymoon at Pless and from there my dear daughter-in-law wrote to me :

THE CASTLE, PLESS, 22. xii. 24.

DEAREST MUMMIE DAISY,—

Ever so many thanks for your dear long letter. We arrived on the fourteenth and I am delighted with everything I see here. Pless is really a *charming* place. We are living on the second floor, and I love the big window in the little salon. What would you like for Christmas ? But you must wait till January as one cannot get anything nice here. We went to a theatrical performance this evening acted by children from the German school ; it was very well played.

Best love from both of us and hearty wishes for Christmas. Ever your devoted

SISSY.

VI

It has been said that happy is the nation without a history : for the past few years I have been a private person, to whom nothing remarkable has happened, of whom there is nothing interesting to tell.

[1] In December, 1924, Prince Hansel of Pless m. Marie (Sissy), d of Clement Count Schönborn-Wiesentheid.

INDEX

F.M.P.D.